T0326273

VOICE OF HEZBOLLAH

Nicholas Noe is founder and editor-in-chief of the Beirut-based news translation service mideastwire.com. He was previously a news editor on the *Lebanon Daily Star/Herald Tribune*, and has written for numerous regional and international publications. **Nicholas Blanford** is Beirut correspondent for *The Times*, the *Christian Science Monitor* and the *Lebanon Daily Star*. He is the author of *Killing Mr Lebanon: The Assassination of Rafik Hariri and its impact on the Middle East*. **Ellen Khouri** is a consultant on human rights and democracy, and managing director of the Lebanese publisher Al Kutba. She has worked as a translator and editor for over 25 years.

VOICE OF HEZBOLLAH

The Statements of Sayyed Hassan Nasrallah

Edited by
NICHOLAS NOE

Introduced by
NICHOLAS BLANFORD

Translated by
ELLEN KHOURI

VERSO

London • New York

First published by Verso 2007
Introduction © Nicholas Blanford 2007
Translation © Ellen Khouri 2006
All rights reserved

3 5 7 9 10 8 6 4 2

Verso
UK: 6 Meard Street, London W1F 0EG
USA: 20 Jay Street, Suite 1010, Brooklyn, NY 11201
www.versobooks.com

Verso is the imprint of New Left Books

ISBN-13: 978-1-84467-153-3

British Library Cataloguing in Publication Data
A catalogue record for this book is available from the British Library

Library of Congress Cataloging-in-Publication Data
A catalog record for this book is available from the Library of Congress

Typeset in Bembo by Hewer Text UK Ltd, Edinburgh
Printed in the USA

CONTENTS

CONTENTS

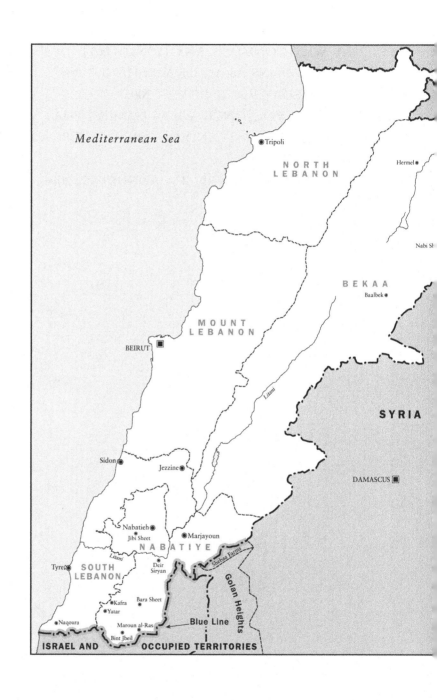

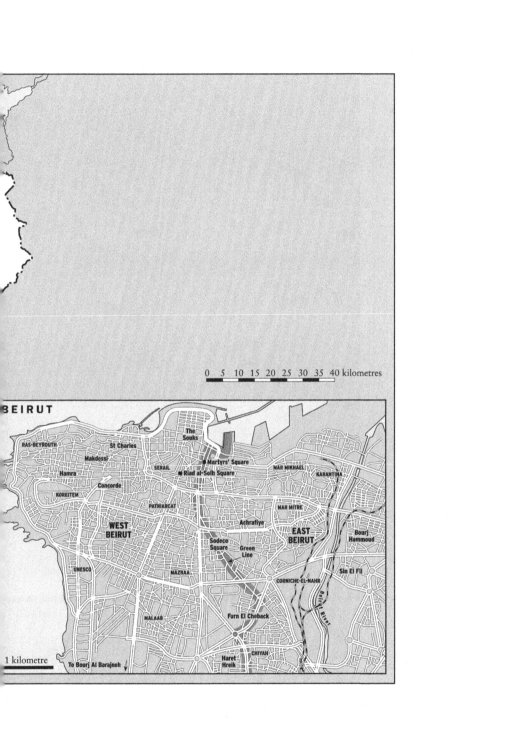

0 5 10 15 20 25 30 35 40 kilometres

BEIRUT

RAS-BEYROUTH

St Charles

The Souks

Makdessi

Martyrs' Square

Hamra

SERAIL

Riad al-Solh Square

MAR MIKHAEL

KARANTINA

Concorde

KOREITEM

PATRIARCAT

MAR MITRE

WEST BEIRUT

Achrafiye

EAST BEIRUT

Bourj Hammoud

Sodeco Square

Green Line

UNESCO

MAZRAA

CORNICHE-EL-NAHR

Sin El Fil

Beirut River

MALAAB

Furn El Cheback

1 kilometre

To Bourj Al Barajneh

CHIYAH

Haret Hreik

INTRODUCTION

Nicholas Blanford

At the end of the month-long *Harb Tammuz* (July War) in 2006 between Hezbollah and Israel, a woman contacted the party and begged to be given the *abaya* worn by Sayyed Hassan Nasrallah during his wartime televised addresses to the nation. After the woman's request was granted, she traveled around Lebanon displaying the simple brown woolen cloak to crowds of adoring Hezbollah supporters, treating the garment with a reverence usually afforded to an ancient holy relic.

The incident illustrates the veneration this 46-year-old cleric can evoke not just among his fellow Shiites but throughout the Islamic and Arab worlds. That Nasrallah is a Shiite—belonging to a minority in the Muslim world that is considered a heretical sect by some Sunnis—merely underlines the extent of his charisma and appeal to Muslims. Even at a time of heightened tensions between Sunnis and Shiites, a poll in Egypt conducted after the war asked respondents to name their two favorite political leaders. The first choice was Nasrallah, the second Mahmoud Ahmadinejad, the president of Iran.

Under Nasrallah's 14-year leadership, Hezbollah has evolved from an uncompromising band of zealots into a political and military powerhouse. It is the most influential political player in Lebanon, and its military wing, the Islamic Resistance, is probably the most proficient guerrilla organization in the world, the only Arab army to have compelled Israel to unconditionally abandon occupied territory through force of arms.

And yet relatively little is known about the architect of Hezbollah's accomplishments. Nasrallah remains something of an enigma, whose core motivations continue to perplex and confound. Is he the pragmatist who has learned

1

to tailor his obedience to the *wilayat al-faqih* with the realities of Lebanon's political and social milieu? Or is it the other way around, in which the "Lebanonization" process Nasrallah helmed from the early 1990s is little more than a disguise—a *taqiyya*—to protect the party as it pursues an open-ended pan-Islamic struggle against the West and Israel, according to the dictates of the *wali al-faqih* in Tehran? And what path will Hezbollah ultimately choose if, or when, its obligations to the *wali al-faqih* and the struggle against Israel can no longer be reconciled with its role as the political champion of Lebanon's Shiite community? The answer to those questions will determine to a large extent the future of Lebanon, which once more has reprised its unenviable role as a battleground for competing local and regional powers in a struggle for control of the Middle East.

Hassan Nasrallah was born on August 31, 1960, the eldest of nine children to Abdel-Karim Nasrallah, an impoverished fruit and vegetable salesman. Although the family was originally from Bazouriyeh, a small Shiite village three miles east of the coastal town of Tyre in south Lebanon, the young Nasrallah was raised in the slum quarter of Karantina in East Beirut. He showed an early proclivity for studying and religion, preferring to walk to the city center to purchase second-hand books rather than playing with his contemporaries. Those books he was too young to understand he set aside for reading when he grew older. While his brothers helped their father with his fruit and vegetable stall, Nasrallah chose to read or pray at mosques in the nearby districts of Sin al-Fil, Nabaa and Bourj Hammoud. After his father secured enough money to open a small store, Nasrallah recalls spending much time in the shop gazing at a picture on the wall of Imam Musa Sadr, an activist Iranian cleric who had moved to Lebanon in the 1960s and began mobilizing the marginalized Shiites, and challenging the sect's domination by a handful of feudal families.

The outbreak of the civil war in 1975 forced the Nasrallah family to relocate to Bazouriyeh in south Lebanon. While Nasrallah finished his education in a state school in Tyre, he found himself drawn into politics, becoming a member, along with his brother Hussein, of the *Harakat al-Muhrumin* (Movement of the Deprived) which had been established by Musa Sadr a year earlier, and later became better known as Amal, the name of its military wing.

Despite being only 15 years old, Nasrallah was appointed the head of Amal for Bazouriyeh in apparent recognition of his maturity. Amal had gained little traction in the village, with most politically active young men joining secular leftist groups, like the Syrian Social Nationalist Party and the Communist Party. But Nasrallah gathered together several friends who shared his religious ardor and helped organize meetings in the village's Islamic center.

"There was a very decent, good and respected Sheikh in our town, by the name of Ali Shamseddin, who has died since," Nasrallah recalled in a 1993 interview; "so we worked together to found a library at the town's Islamic Center where the youth could come, read and receive lessons. It attracted a considerable number of young men and women, and I was the one who gave the lessons."[1]

Although he was politically active, his ambition was to travel to Najaf in Iraq to begin his religious studies in earnest. He spent much of his spare time hanging around the main mosque in Tyre, and it was here that he was befriended by Sayyed Mohammed Gharawi, a religious teacher who was impressed by the young man's obvious intelligence and enthusiasm. Agreeing to help, Gharawi wrote a letter of introduction to Sayyed Mohammed Baqr al-Sadr, one of the foremost Shiite scholars and theoreticians, asking him to accept Nasrallah into his *hawza*, or religious seminary.

With some money given him by his father and friends, Nasrallah left Lebanon for Iraq in 1976 with the letter for Baqr al-Sadr in his pocket. By the time he arrived in Najaf, he was penniless and had nowhere to stay. While pondering what to do next, he was introduced to Sayyed Abbas Mussawi, a 25-year-old disciple of Baqr al-Sadr. Nasrallah recalls that on first meeting Mussawi he took him to be an Iraqi, because of the dark color of his skin, and spoke to him in Iraqi-accented Arabic. But Mussawi responded in colloquial Lebanese Arabic, telling Nasrallah that he was from the village of Nabi Sheet in the Bekaa Valley. Nasrallah later described his first encounter with Mussawi as the "sweet start" of a relationship with someone he would come to consider as a "friend, brother, mentor and companion."[2]

Nasrallah was accepted into Baqr al-Sadr's *hawza* and began his studies under the tutelage of Mussawi, who had already passed through the first phase of religious instruction. It was an ascetic existence for the teenage Nasrallah. He shared a room with other students, sleeping on a foam mattress

---

1. "Who is Sayyed Hassan Nasrallah?" August 31, 1993. See Statement 8.
2. "Hezbollah leader Nasrallah details life history, political career," *Ya Li Tharat al-Hoseyn*, August 2, 2006.

and given a few dinars each month by Baqr al-Sadr to pay his way. But Nasrallah had little spare time, as Mussawi proved a diligent and strict teacher. His class of fellow Lebanese students worked through holidays and weekends, completing preliminary instruction in just two years, instead of the more usual five.

Through Mussawi, Nasrallah was introduced to the radical teachings of Baqr al-Sadr, and of influential Iranian cleric Ruhollah Khomeini. The latter had formulated the theory of *wilayat al-faqih*, or the Jurisdiction of the Jurist–Theologian, which advocated the creation of an Islamic state governed by sharia law and administered by an expert in Islamic jurisprudence—a *faqih*. Khomeini's revolutionary theory stood in marked contrast to the more traditional "quietist" school of Shiite religious practice, in which jurists restricted their activities to settling disputes, implementing statutory penalties, and collecting religious donations. Although the opinions of senior *marja*—such as Ayatollah Ali Sistani in Najaf or Lebanon's Sayyed Mohammad Hussein Fadlallah—can carry significant political influence, they eschew any direct role in day-to-day governance. Nasrallah was profoundly influenced by the teachings of Khomeini, whom he later described as "the greatest, most dignified, and undisputed personality of the [twentieth] century."[3]

In 1977, Iraq's Baathist regime launched a crackdown on Shiite Islamists, arresting and subsequently executing Baqr al-Sadr and expelling dozens of Lebanese students on the pretext that they were spies for Syria. Nasrallah avoided arrest and returned to Lebanon in 1978, where he enrolled in a new theological school established by Mussawi in Baalbek. Nasrallah's return came at a pivotal moment for Lebanese Shiites. In March 1978, Israel invaded south Lebanon to drive out the Palestine Liberation Organization, which used the area as a launch-pad for attacks into the Jewish state. It marked the beginning of Israel's 22-year occupation of south Lebanon.

Then in August, Imam Musa Sadr disappeared while on a trip to Libya. The Libyan authorities insisted that Sadr and his two companions had departed the country on a flight to Rome, but the cleric has never been seen since. Sadr's mysterious disappearance was steeped in religious significance, echoing the Shiite dogma of the "hidden Imam," who went into occultation in the eighth century and whose eventual return, Shiites believe, will herald the

3. Ibid.

4

advent of Islamic rule on earth. The vanishing imam was a potent symbol for Shiites, and paradoxically helped to revive Amal's then flagging fortunes. The third critical factor was the Iranian Revolution of February 1979, in which the ousting of the Shah and the establishment of Khomeini's Islamic Republic served as a powerful exemplar and inspiration for Lebanese Shiites.

In addition to his religious studies, Nasrallah had resumed his political activities with Amal, and by 1982 was in charge of the Bekaa region and a member of the movement's politburo. Following Israel's invasion of Lebanon in June 1982, the leadership of Amal, which was headed by Nabih Berri, decided to cease resisting the Israeli advance and join a "national salvation" government grouping representatives of most political parties and sects. The decision aggravated a growing schism within Amal's ranks between the secular-oriented leadership, under Berri, and those, such as co-founder Hussein Mussawi, who sought to Islamicize the movement. Nasrallah was among the latter, and he left Amal to join up with a new movement taking shape in the Bekaa that would become known as Hezbollah.

Hezbollah was established with the assistance of Iran, which dispatched a contingent of Iranian Revolutionary Guards to the Bekaa to begin a process of recruitment, religious indoctrination and military training. Nasrallah played an important role in galvanizing young Shiites to join the new resistance group, and by 1985 was Hezbollah's chief for the Bekaa. That same year he was sent to Beirut to serve as deputy to Sayyed Ibrahim al-Amine al-Sayyed, assuming the same organizational role that he had held in the Bekaa.

In February 1985, Hezbollah formally announced its existence in an "Open Letter"—a political manifesto that outlined the party's aims and ideology. Among the party's stated goals were to continue resisting the Israeli occupation, a rejection of Lebanon's "rotten" sectarian political system, and support for the establishment of an Islamic state in Lebanon.

Nasrallah's public profile began to grow from 1987, when he was appointed to Hezbollah's leading Shura Council and began delivering speeches and giving his first interviews. A year later, he narrowly survived an assassination attempt when a car bomb exploded beside a vehicle carrying him, Mussawi, and Sheikh Subhi Tufeili, a senior Hezbollah figure who was elected the party's first secretary-general in 1989. Hezbollah's influence gradually spread further south, particularly after Israel withdrew its forces in 1985 to a border strip in south Lebanon. But the southward move brought it into conflict with Amal, which had been waging a resistance campaign in the villages east and south of Tyre since 1983, and resented the encroachment of this Iran-backed interloper.

Although it was born during the civil war, Hezbollah has publicly prided itself on not having participated in the sectarian clashes that marked the conflict in the 1980s, despite its deep antipathy to Christian groups that were at one time backed by Israel, such as the Phalange. Hezbollah did fight against non-Shiite Lebanese allied to the Israelis in south Lebanon, and was sucked into brief factional fighting with the Communists in early 1986, but otherwise it remained focused on resisting Israeli occupation. "We are still careful not to be dragged into the quagmire of civil war from which God Almighty has protected us in years past," Nasrallah said in comments about the Hezbollah–Communist fighting; "we are always very careful to avoid fighting with anyone and, most of all, with those with whom we have ideological differences, like the communists ... Our strategy is to build a future for ourselves through confrontation with the Zionist enemy."[4]

Tensions between Hezbollah and Amal erupted in 1988, however, when the two groups fought the first of two brutal intra-Shiite wars in southern Beirut and in the south. Although Hezbollah crushed Amal's forces in southern Beirut, its fighters were chased out of much of south Lebanon. Nasrallah, who never played an active military role, found himself inadvertently caught up in the conflict while on a visit to the mountainous Iqlim al-Touffah province east of Sidon at the end of 1988. Amal fighters surrounded Hezbollah's stronghold in the villages of Jbaa and Ain Boussoir, trapping Nasrallah along with several hundred fighters for three weeks. The intra-Shiite war ended in January 1989 with the adoption of the Damascus Agreement, which allowed a gradual return of Hezbollah fighters to the south in exchange for the deployment of Syrian troops into the party's bastion in southern Beirut. Renewed fighting between Hezbollah and Amal flared up again in 1990, and relations would remain frayed between the two groups in the years to come.

With the Arab League-brokered Taif Accord in 1989 signaling the end of the civil war, Hezbollah's leaders engaged in a heated debate over whether to participate more fully within Lebanon's political system. Toufeili opposed

---

4. Civil War & Resistance, March 11, 1986. See Statement 1.

any participation within a confessional-based system, in accordance with the party's Open Letter manifesto. But Mussawi and Nasrallah disagreed, believing that a parliamentary presence was not inimical to its ideology and would strengthen Hezbollah's resistance priority in the post-war era. "Regardless of the resistance … there are internal issues that are important to the people in the political and economic spheres, and in their daily lives," Nasrallah explained soon after the 1992 parliamentary elections. "In Islam, the act of serving the people and God's families, rescuing the oppressed, saving the distressed and stretching one's hand to the weak and the dispossessed, are major to the faith. These are mentioned in the Quran, and we care to encourage them anew."[5] The "pragmatist" line of Mussawi and Nasrallah prevailed over that of the hard-liners, although the debate caused a lasting division within the party. Tufeili was replaced by Mussawi in May 1991, and was gradually marginalized until he broke from the party in 1997.

The disagreement between Toufeili and Nasrallah over the future direction of the party was not only ideological but reflected a personal antipathy between the two clerics. In 1989, Nasrallah decided he could no longer work under Tufeili and left Lebanon to continue his religious studies in the Iranian city of Qom. Although he planned to spend five years in Qom to complete his religious education, Nasrallah was persuaded to return to Beirut after a few months and take up his responsibilities once more within the party.

He was not yet 30 years old, but it was clear that Nasrallah's star was in the ascendant. His charisma and organizational skills had won him many admirers within the party. One veteran Hezbollah official recalls that, even after the popular Mussawi had been elected secretary-general, it was his protégé who drew the eyes of the party's rank and file.

The end of the war and the advent of Syrian dominion over Lebanese affairs allowed Hezbollah to concentrate its resources on battling Israel in south Lebanon. After Nasrallah was elected secretary-general in February 1992, following Mussawi's death in an Israeli helicopter attack on his car, the Islamic resistance underwent a tactical revolution. Gone were the suicidal "human wave" assaults against well-defended Israeli positions that marked many resistance operations during the 1980s. Under Nasrallah's leadership,

---

5. See Statement 6.

the resistance became more compartmentalized, with units specializing in different weapons and tactics. Intelligence-gathering measures were improved, and greater autonomy given to field commanders.

The improvements to the Islamic resistance were evident in the escalating rate of attacks in the early 1990s, from 19 in 1990 to 187 in 1994. In the final months of the occupation, in 1999–2000, the resistance was recording as many as 300 attacks a month. More significantly, the fatality ratio shifted in Hezbollah's favor, dropping from an average of five-to-one in 1990 to an average of three-to-two in the late 1990s.[6]

Other than air-tight secrecy, intense planning and the ability to learn from mistakes, Nasrallah explained that a central factor was the determination and morale of the individual combatant.

> This group of fighters does not go to war in order to flex their military muscles, score a publicity coup or to achieve material advantages; they fight and do jihad with serious intent and a deep conviction that the only way to regain their usurped territory is by waging war on the enemy.[7]

Israel launched air and artillery blitzes against Lebanon in July 1993, April 1996, June 1999 and February 2000, targeting infrastructure such as bridges and power stations, and, in the first two campaigns, forcing hundreds of thousands of southern Lebanese to flee their homes. The offensives were miserable failures—they only strengthened domestic support for Hezbollah, and highlighted the inability of the Israeli military to curb the Islamic Resistance.

Nasrallah's reputation soared immeasurably in September 1997, when his 18-year-old son Hadi was killed in a clash with Israeli commandos inside the occupation zone. In May 2000, Israel's occupation collapsed almost overnight, and the last few hundred soldiers dashed for the border as Hezbollah's fighters streamed into the newly liberated area. It was the crowning moment of the 18-year resistance campaign, and confirmed Nasrallah as one of the most respected, effective and popular leaders in the Arab world.

By then, Hezbollah was also an important actor on the domestic political

6. Major Christopher E. Whitting, "When David Became Goliath," MA dissertation, US army Command and General Staff College, Fort Leavenworth, Kansas, 2001.
7. Towards Liberation, June 21, 1999. See Statement 13.

stage, having secured 12 parliamentary seats in the 1992 elections and nine in the 1996 elections. Hezbollah's parliamentary bloc served as a counter-weight to the economic and social policies of Prime Minister Rafik Hariri during the reconstruction boom of the mid-1990s, which emphasized Beirut and Mount Lebanon over the poorer Shiite areas of the south and Bekaa. The parliamentary presence helped entrench Hezbollah within Lebanon's political framework, giving it a relevance beyond the finite role of the resist-ance against Israeli occupation and bolstering its position as an alternative Shiite voice to Amal, which had steadily ossified under Berri's autocratic leadership. Nonetheless, with its resistance priority guaranteed and protected by Damascus, the party's leadership shunned a deeper political engagement—such as pressing for a share of the cabinet—to avoid the "bazaar" of compro-mises and quid pro quos that are an unavoidable element of Lebanese politics.

Following the Israeli troop withdrawal from south Lebanon in May 2000, Hezbollah deployed into the former occupation zone and began installing a comprehensive and largely secret military infrastructure consisting of weapons stores, bunkers, tunnels, and firing positions. In October 2000, Hezbollah launched a campaign to liberate the Shebaa Farms, a 25-square-kilometer pocket of Israeli-occupied mountainside running along Lebanon's south-east border with the Golan Heights. The campaign developed into a sporadic but finely calibrated series of harassing attacks in the Shebaa Farms and else-where along the Blue Line—the UN's name for the Lebanon–Israel border. Hezbollah's intention was to needle the Israelis without goading them into a massive response which could backfire on the party's domestic popularity. Israel had to take into account that if it reacted disproportionately to Hezbollah's attacks, the party could unleash its arsenal of thousands of rockets—some of them long-range—into northern Israel. The "balance of terror" along the Blue Line helped ensure a period of tense stability for nearly six years.

Hezbollah also provided assistance to the Palestinian *intifada* raging in the West Bank and Gaza from September 2000. Hezbollah's Al-Manar satellite channel beamed a steady stream of anti-Israeli propaganda into Palestinian homes, making it one of the most widely watched television stations. Clan-destine assistance included training specialist fighters, providing funds to Palestinian cells, attempting to smuggle weapons into the West Bank and Gaza, and passing on bomb-making skills. Hezbollah strengthened its political ties with the Hamas movement and Palestinian Islamic Jihad, as well as several smaller pro-Damascus secular Palestinian groups, such as the Popular Front for the Liberation of Palestine–General Command.

The support for the Palestinian *intifada* was rooted in Hezbollah's anti-Israel credo, as well as a desire to offer its successful resistance to Israeli occupation in Lebanon as a model for other oppressed people to emulate and adapt to their own circumstances. "We offer this lofty Lebanese example to our people in Palestine," Nasrallah said in his victory speech in May 2000.

> You do not need tanks, strategic balance, rockets or cannons to liberate your land, all you need are the martyrs who shook and scared this angry Zionist entity. You can regain your land, you oppressed, helpless and besieged people of Palestine; you can force the invading Zionists to return from whence they came … the choice is yours and the example is clear before your eyes.[8]

By late 2004, Damascus was under stiff international pressure to withdraw its troops from Lebanon, and Hezbollah was facing growing demands to dismantle the Islamic Resistance. Hariri's assassination in February 2005, and the subsequent "independence *intifada*" protests in Beirut, compelled the Syrian regime to disengage from Lebanon in April, ending a military presence of nearly three decades.

The collapse of the Pax Syriana had profound implications for Hezbollah. With Syria's protective umbrella gone, Hezbollah was required to play a more assertive political role to defend its interests. It struck a strategic alliance with Amal, effectively subsuming its long-standing rival, and in July 2005 joined the Western-friendly government of Prime Minister Fouad Siniora, giving it tacit control of the five Shiite ministerial seats. In January 2006, Hezbollah forged an unlikely alliance with General Michel Aoun, a prominent Christian leader who, as an exile in France before 2005, had been a fierce critic of Syria's involvement in Lebanon.

Hezbollah's deft political juggling was in marked contrast to its more aloof attitude towards parochial politics during the 1990s, illustrating the party's declining options and narrowing margins of maneuver as it struggles to reconcile its often conflicting domestic and regional obligations.

---

8. Victory, May 26, 2000. See Statement 15.

The Islamic Resistance is Hezbollah's beating heart, giving it regional prominence and ideological fulfillment. But the cruel paradox for Hezbollah is that, as the Islamic Resistance has steadily evolved over the years into one of the most formidable guerrilla movements in the world, its *raison d'être* as a resistance force has been gradually eroded. When it began to coalesce in the summer of 1982, Israeli troops were in Beirut and occupying the entire southern half of the country, and no one questioned the efficacy of a resistance force. The same held true during the 1990s when the Pax Syriana and continued Israeli occupation allowed Hezbollah to pursue its resistance campaign unhindered and with at least the tacit support of all Lebanon's communities. Hezbollah's quandary began inevitably with the Israeli troop withdrawal in May 2000, which highlighted the stark fact that, for a party determined to retain its arms, victory over Israel was always going to possess a certain Pyrrhic quality. How can Hezbollah continue to justify resistance where there is nothing left to justifiably resist?

The collapse of Syrian–Israeli peace talks in March 2000, and the Shebaa Farms pretext, bought Hezbollah an extra five years. But Syria's disengagement from Lebanon, international pressure, and rising unhappiness from non-Shiite Lebanese at Hezbollah's continued armed status presented new challenges. Then came the month-long war between Hezbollah and Israel in the summer of 2006. The conflict demonstrated just how remarkable a military force the Islamic Resistance had become. Israel suffered a serious military and political reversal in the hills and wadis of south Lebanon, its vaunted deterrence capabilities publicly smashed by a few hundred devoted resistance fighters.

Yet even though Hezbollah's reputation in the Arab and Islamic worlds had never been higher, this was a war that the party would have preferred to avoid. The argument that Hezbollah deliberately triggered the conflict by kidnapping two IDF soldiers on July 12 does not hold. There were no guarantees at the onset of the conflict that Hezbollah would emerge militarily triumphant—particularly as Israel had the full backing of the US. Indeed, part of Hezbollah's ultimate battlefield success must be attributed to Israel's poor planning, woeful intelligence failings, unrealistic political expectations, and hubris on the part of the IDF general staff.

Furthermore, Hezbollah may have emerged from the war with its resistance credentials freshly burnished, but it came at a steep price: it lost its military autonomy over the south Lebanon border district, and was forced to yield to an expanded UN peacekeeping force of some 10,000 troops, the bulk of them drawn from NATO countries, as well as 15,000 Lebanese soldiers.

Lebanese critics of Hezbollah bit their lips during the war, to present a unified front against the Israeli onslaught; but a post-conflict day of reckoning was inevitable. Crucially, the people who suffered most from the war were Hezbollah's Shiite constituents who, for all their public praise for the resistance, were not pleased to have their homes and livelihoods destroyed. That perhaps explains Nasrallah's *mea culpa* in a televised interview two weeks after the August 14 ceasefire, in which he stated that if the party's leadership had predicted by "1 per cent" the Israeli response to the kidnapping of the IDF soldiers, the operation would not have proceeded.[9] The party's sense of post-war vulnerability also partly explains why Hezbollah subsequently launched its bold political gambit of cabinet resignations and street action to topple the Western-backed Siniora government—offense being the best form of defense. Hezbollah sought to increase the opposition's share in the government, allowing it to block any potential legislation that threatened the party's interests or those of its allies in Damascus and Tehran.

Regional dynamics have a deep influence on the unfolding political struggle in Lebanon, and thus shape Hezbollah's courses of action. Hezbollah is a vital component in a strengthening anti-Western alliance uniting Iran, Syria, Hezbollah, Hamas and some smaller pro-Damascus factions. This alliance challenges the US, Israel, and Washington's Arab allies for control of the Middle East. The alliance is attempting to draw Lebanon firmly back into its orbit, thus denying the US its Levantine toehold, and reversing the Bush administration's self-declared policy "success" in having helped Lebanon gain independence from Syria in 2005.

But Hezbollah's regional commitments can conflict with its domestic interests. The timing of Hezbollah's campaign to unseat the Siniora government coincided with a key moment in the process of forming an international tribunal to try those eventually indicted by a UN commission investigating Hariri's murder. Syria is widely blamed for the Hariri assassination, and Hezbollah's critics in Lebanon accused the party of deliberately attempting to block the formation of the international tribunal to protect its allies in Damascus. Hezbollah denied the charge; but if the Syrian regime is seriously

---

9. Interview with New TV, August 27, 2006. See Statement 32.

weakened, or even falls, as a result of the Hariri judicial process, it would have significant ramifications for the durability of the anti-Western alliance. The perception that Shiite Hezbollah is protecting the killers of the Sunni Hariri has fostered a growing intra-Muslim schism in Lebanon, itself a reflection of the broader Sunni–Shiite tensions generated by the regional confrontation between an expansionist Shiite Iran and a nervous Sunni Arab Middle East.

Nasrallah has long championed intra-Muslim unity, believing that disagreements between Sunnis and Shiites only benefit the enemies of Islam, and detract from the goal of confronting Israel. So it can have been of little comfort to note, at the beginning of 2007, that some of those Sunni Islamists around the region who had been cheering on Hezbollah's resistance fighters during the war with Israel six months earlier, were now criticizing the party for being a duplicitous agent of the Persian "Magian" state.

Hezbollah is scheduled to hold internal elections in the summer of 2007, although Nasrallah's mandate as secretary-general is likely to be extended, granting him a sixth three-year term in office. To an extent, Nasrallah long ago transcended the prosaic role of party functionary to become, for many members of Hezbollah, the very embodiment of the organization. Hezbollah is often regarded as a rigid, tightly controlled monolithic entity, but in fact it is more a coalition of shifting views and constantly evolving debate. Arguably, Nasrallah's greatest feat as Hezbollah's leader is to have prevented the party from fracturing or becoming fatally mired in internecine squabbles. In a moment of candor, a party official admitted that if Nasrallah were to retire or become incapacitated, it would represent a "catastrophe" for Hezbollah. Sayyed Hashem Safieddine, the head of Hezbollah's executive council, has been tipped as a replacement secretary-general in the event of a calamity, but it is unlikely that he or anyone else can replace Nasrallah in substance.

Nasrallah's leadership is the glue that binds the party together even as Hezbollah's often contrary regional and domestic agendas threaten to pull it apart. Hezbollah's Achilles heel is that one day it will have to make an existential choice: Is it to be a Lebanese party serving Lebanese interests, or Iran's spearhead in the pan-Islamic struggle against Israel? Nasrallah has so far deftly sidestepped that critical decision, but for how much longer?

Nicholas Blanford
Beirut, January 2007

EDITOR'S INTRODUCTION

Nicholas Noe

Even before the July War between Hezbollah and Israel, there was a clear need for a comprehensive English-language volume of speeches and interviews given by Hezbollah secretary-general Sayyed Hassan Nasrallah. Indeed, for almost fifteen years Nasrallah's prominence and power in the Arab and Islamic worlds had been steadily growing, a function both of Hezbollah's various accomplishments (whether viewed positively or negatively) and of Nasrallah's own compelling oratory. At the same time, concern among some Western policymakers and analysts, especially in the United States, increasingly focused on both Hezbollah and Nasrallah as key impediments to resolving—ostensibly in the West's favor—a number of burning issues, including the Arab-Israeli conflict, the "War on Terror," and the Iranian nuclear program.

However, even as recent public interest has grown beyond the boundaries of the policy and media elites, there are still relatively few reliable, full-length texts readily accessible to English-language readers who want to consider, compare and/or criticize the ideas expressed directly by a leader routinely mentioned alongside some of the modern Middle East's most significant figures.

To this end, the present volume is devoted.

It should be noted at the outset, though, that the task of pulling together relevant material was hampered by a number of factors which necessarily shape, and to a certain degree limit, what is offered below. Although post-war confusion in Lebanon certainly provided a number of obstacles, perhaps the primary impediment was the destruction of the Hezbollah-affiliated Consultative Center for Studies and Documentation in the southern suburbs of Beirut.

15

Although we will probably never truly know whether there was some kind of military target lying beneath the Center, or whether it was purely dedicated to shaping historical discourse—much like the Khiam Detention Center museum in south Lebanon, also destroyed by Israel (Khiam's former jailers) in the first days of the war—the fact remains that researchers lost a wealth of original documents concerning the party and Nasrallah himself. According to Dr. Ali Fayyad, the Center's long-serving director, 55,000 books, countless speeches and lectures, a special library of maps and recordings, and his own personal papers reflecting over twenty years of work on Islamic movements were all lost. With the destruction of the nearby offices of the Hezbollah-affiliated TV station Al-Manar, an equally significant archive—including recordings of many of Nasrallah's speeches and interviews throughout the years—was also destroyed.

In order to gather, in a timely fashion, the original Arabic materials translated below, we therefore had to rely on the excellent archives provided by the Lebanese daily newspaper *As Safir*, in addition to the several Arabic volumes of published Nasrallah speeches available on the market in Beirut. In this way, my research assistant Aya Eldika and I were able to locate a good number of complete—or almost complete—texts, as well as interviews in a variety of Lebanese and pan-Arab publications. Towards the end of the process, we came to rely on transcriptions of original recordings provided by Lebanese media outlets and official transcripts provided by the Lebanese National News Agency, as well as an invaluable resource that only became accessible to us in November 2006—bound volumes of Hezbollah's weekly magazine *Al Intiqad*, going back to its founding in the mid-1990s.

One difficulty in relying on newspaper, agency or book reproductions of speeches, however, is that one cannot be certain of the accuracy of the Arabic transcription itself. Moreover, all three sources tend to excerpt speeches, either in the interest of space or for some other unknown reasons (missing text therefore is represented in this volume by parenthesized ellipses, while our own periodic omissions of text, either in the interest of length or relevancy, are represented by square-bracketed ellipses).

Another downside to our focus on published material is that many significant interviews given by Nasrallah on radio and television are not included in the present volume—a gap largely attributable to the relative inaccessibility of the material after the destruction of some of the major in-country archives.

The reader will note, however, that one such presentation is indeed included: a 2003 *60 Minutes* piece on Hezbollah that, while not necessarily representative of the limited number of English-language interviews granted by Nasrallah, is nevertheless unique in standing as his most high-profile (and, to date, last) televised interview before an American audience.

Perhaps as a consequence of this focus on published material, the reader will find that the statements we have included in the present volume overwhelmingly center on the long-running conflict with Israel and/or the United States. This is partly because we found that many of the clippings of interviews and speeches available at the *As Safir* archive and elsewhere focused on this (admittedly expansive) topic, rather than on, for example, Hezbollah's social programs, its domestic political efforts unrelated to the conflict, or strictly religious and cultural issues. The gap may, however, be the result of Nasrallah's status as the primary communicator and advocate for resistance against Israel—with other issues left to Hezbollah's Parliamentary bloc or *Shura* Council representatives. Either way, it underscores the absolutely critical point that *Voice of Hezbollah* is intended as an introduction to Nasrallah's thinking, and not as any kind of a comprehensive, final word.

As far as the organization of this volume is concerned, the statements that follow below are divided into three periods, which I believe follow the three major periods in Hezbollah's relatively recent history: Radicalism and Resistance, 1986–99; Repositioning after the Israeli withdrawal in May 2000; and, finally, the period following the assassination of ex-Premier Rafik Hariri on February 14, 2005. Because Nasrallah's speeches and interviews during the July War were almost all reliably translated into English, we have chosen not to include these statements, save for the New TV interview (Statement 32), which is not readily accessible in English. (Readers who wish to view accurate translations of most of Nasrallah's speeches and interviews during and after the war are advised to visit Nasrallah's Wikipedia page, as well as Hezbollah's website at www.moqawama.org/english.)

It is also important to say that Hezbollah was informed at various points about the materials we were interested in obtaining and translating. Hezbollah's media unit received a rough listing of materials we intended to include, as well as examples of Ellen Khouri's translations. A final set of proof pages was provided to a third party, approved by Hezbollah, for comment on issues related to the accuracy of the translation, as well as the accuracy of the original text.

I would like especially to thank my research assistants, Aya Eldika, Nick Greenough and Maya Ammar, without whom this project would not have been possible, especially given my own still limited grasp of the Arabic language. I would also single out Ellen Khouri, as well as Tom Penn at Verso, who were more than tolerant of my delays and occasional indecision as the amount of relevant material only grew ever larger.

Leila and Majdoline Hatoum, my partners at Mideastwire.com, provided invaluable assistance throughout, especially in facilitating permissions, as did my thesis supervisor, Professor George Joffe, who guided my approach to the party at the earliest stage while I was working on my M. Phil. thesis at Cambridge University through 2005–6. Mirella Dagher and Ali BouMelhem, who headed up the Mideastwire.com translation effort for this book (statements 7, 11, 12 and 32 were translated by Mideastwire.com), deserve particular praise for going beyond their duties at our small company.

Several individuals should be thanked for providing initial advice on how to approach the project and, in some cases, which statements to include. Among them were Amal Saad-Ghorayeb, Timur Goksel, Nicholas Blanford, Daniel Sobelman, Judith Palmer Harik, Alastair Crooke, Mark Penn and Michael Young.

I also owe special thanks to Ibrahim Mussawi at Al-Manar, who provided assistance, advice and—perhaps most importantly—encouragement throughout.

Nicholas Noe
Beirut, March 2007

TRANSLATOR'S NOTE

A translation as good as the original is especially challenging in the case of a consummate public speaker whose words are carefully chosen and skillfully crafted to transmit as clear and determined a message as possible. Sayyed Hassan Nasrallah's mastery of the Arabic language cannot be divorced from his devotion to Shia Islam, the strength of his political convictions, his personality, and his public appeal as a political and religious leader. My main challenge was therefore to allow the personality of the man and the integrity of his ideas to filter through every word and sentence, while also capturing the breadth of the rich Arabic language he employs, without sounding trite in the more utilitarian English language. To this end, I constantly had to strike a balance in his easy shifts from poetry to hard facts, from affection to condescension, from the religious to the profane, from pride to humility, and from steely determination to consummate pragmatism, without losing any of the style, tempo or tenor of the language that makes him who he is.

Even for a translator who does what she does because she enjoys word-crafting and the subtleties of language, not all translations are equally interesting. Sayyed Hassan Nasrallah' speeches and interviews—vehicles through which he shares his ideology and opinions with the Lebanese, Arabs and Muslims in general—are among the most thought-provoking and challenging documents I have ever worked on. I could not forget for a single moment that I was duty bound to transmit diligently to a worldwide audience the words and intentions of a controversial leader whose impact on Lebanon, on the Middle East region, and beyond, has increased significantly in recent years, and will undoubtedly continue to do so.

Ellen Kettaneh Khouri
Beirut, March 2007

I

RADICALISM AND RESISTANCE
1986–1999

1

CIVIL WAR AND RESISTANCE

March 11, 1986

While this interview, carried by the Emirati newspaper Al-Khaleej, *was not his first, it posi-*
tioned Nasrallah as a key figure in Hezbollah for a wider regional audience eager to learn
more about the party that had just played such a critical role the previous year in prompting
Israel's first major withdrawal under fire from Lebanese territory. Fluent in both the military
and political aspects of the rapidly deteriorating internal situation in Lebanon, Nasrallah
demonstrates what would serve as the hallmarks of his later speeches and interviews—especially
after he assumed the post of secretary-general in 1992: a clear delineation of Hezbollah's
position on the multitude of problems facing the country, combined with enough nuance to
leave rivals and enemies alike questioning the party's next move.

On one key issue, however—that of Israel—there is little ambiguity. "Our strategy," he
says, "is to build a future for ourselves through confrontation with the Zionist enemy." Seeking
to avoid internal competition and enmity that might drain Hezbollah's resources from this central
concern, Nasrallah makes it clear that the party would exercise pragmatism in the domestic scene,
no matter its "unconditional" doctrinal allegiance to Iran's Ayatollah Khomeini, but that resistance
activities would constitute Hezbollah's non-negotiable priority, potentially in perpetuity.

AL-KHALEEJ: *The situation in the south, especially after the Israeli enemy expanded*
beyond the security zone under the pretext of searching for the two prisoners which

---

1. By this point, Israeli forces had withdrawn from Beirut, as well as from the major southern
port cities of Sidon and Tyre, to a self-declared "security zone" near the Israeli-Lebanese provisional
border (as demarcated by the UN's Blue Line, see below n.15 p.30), and in parts of the south-
eastern Bekaa Valley, covering approximately 1,100km², or 11 per cent of Lebanese land. After
Hezbollah captured two Israeli military personnel on February 16, 1986, in the southern village
of Kounin, the IDF reoccupied seventeen villages outside the security zone, and undertook an
expanded campaign against both the party and locales seen as supportive of Hezbollah operations.
It was not until July 21, 1996 that the bodies of the two Israelis were traded for forty-five men
and women held by Israel in south Lebanon, as well as the remains of 123 fighters.

you had abducted, is still the focus of much attention. How do you view what has happened, and is happening, in this domain, and what are the details of the events that took place during and after the recent invasion?[1]

HN: Israel does not lack pretexts when it decides to attack; on the battlefield, it seems that the recent military operation had two objectives:

First: To search for their detainees; in this attack, Israel followed a new military procedure which is to drop its fighters down beyond the occupied zone on roads used by the *mujahidin*.[2] The enemy launched this operation less than 45 minutes after we abducted the two Israeli officers, which indicates that the intention of expanding their attack was already in the offing.

Second: They wanted to teach us a lesson, namely, that anybody who even considers launching an operation against Israel would invite a violent response. This places many obstacles in the resistance's path, since any plans for such daring operations in the future would require a great deal of equipment, and appropriate and large-scale measures to be put into place.

In fact, Israel gave up expecting to achieve results in the areas under its occupation; added to that [there were] the hard battles it fought with the *mujahidin* in frontline villages where there were high concentrations of Muslim fighters. Moreover, Israel incurred heavy human and material losses as a result of its ferocious reaction; they suffered a number of killed and wounded and much of their equipment, tanks and military vehicles were burned. Our losses on the other hand were much more modest, which compelled Israel to use even more violence. It destroyed people's homes, burned a number of them, killed or arrested a large number of citizens, and looted their belongings. After a few days of this, it realized that it would not be able to find the prisoners and that to continue in such a manner would be very costly at all levels. It therefore thought of withdrawing, since staying in the villages it had occupied would only give the resistance more opportunities to target the occupying troops.

Prior to the latest Israeli military expansion, the *mujahidin* had to walk for dozens of hours inside the frontier zone to be able to hit an Israeli post or

2. The term *mujahidin*—literally "strugglers"—is generally employed by Nasrallah to name those individuals fighting against an occupying enemy.

set an ambush; now, after this latest invasion, the enemy has moved much closer to the resistance's guns. Indeed, the invading Israeli troops were clearly terrified by the situation, and this left them no choice but to retreat in the direction of the occupied territories.[3]

AL-KHALEEJ: *Do you have precise numbers for your losses?*

HN: We do not differentiate between martyred *mujahidin*; the political context is not important when the issue of martyrdom is concerned. Five men fell from among our brethren in the Amal Movement[4] and Hezbollah, and two were executed by the enemy after their arrest; according to some information, they were buried alive after they were accused of being part of the group that had planned the operation. Four civilians were also martyred, and there were a number of wounded. There was also widespread looting and destruction; a large number of citizens were displaced, and many others detained in public squares for hours, and beaten, tortured and abused. At the beginning, Israel tried to play an obvious game: it differentiated between homes that belonged to the Amal Movement and those that belonged to Hezbollah. But this game was soon thwarted, and the enemy was forced to go back to treating everyone with the same severity.[5]

3. Nasrallah uses the term "occupied territories" not only to refer to the "security zone" in south Lebanon, but also to the whole of Israel.

4. The acronym Amal, forming the Arabic word for "hope," stands for "The Brigades of the Lebanese Resistance." The Amal Movement was, at the time, the main political and military party representing the Lebanese Shia. Although founded in 1974 by the popular Iranian-born cleric Imam Mousa Sadr, the secular lawyer Nabih Berri (1938–) took control of the movement after Sadr disappeared while on an official visit to Libya in 1978. Berri's stewardship of Amal subsequently came under harsh criticism from the Islamists in the movement, eventually precipitating the exit, in the summer of 1982, of leading figures, who soon formed the nucleus of Hezbollah.

5. Especially after the second Israeli invasion of Lebanon in June 1982, Amal worked behind the scenes with the Israeli Defence Force (IDF) and military intelligence in their efforts to uproot Palestinian Liberation Organization (PLO) guerrillas. Indeed, for Amal, and arguably for the Lebanese of the south generally, the PLO had come to be seen as a mostly menacing presence. But as the occupation wore on, and as Israel began to fight a nascent, Hezbollah-dominated insurgency in late 1983, the Israeli response of overwhelming force and brutality only served to further alienate the Shia community, Amal, and many Lebanese across the confessional spectrum. By 1986, Israeli efforts to treat Amal or Amal areas of control differently from Hezbollah had mostly ceased—or, at best, were pursued only half-heartedly. For the most illuminating account of these events, see Augustus Richard Norton, *Amal and the Shia*, (Austin: University of Texas Press, 1987).

AL-KHALEEJ: *Since we are on the topic of Hezbollah and the Amal Movement, we would like to know if rumors regarding a potentially widespread conflict between you two in the south and elsewhere are true, especially given that [these rumors] come on the heels of a wave of statements and innuendos in this direction.*

HN: I would like to be brief on this particular subject. Many political currents are active on the scene in Lebanon, and the Amal Movement is one of them, as are other Islamic movements. The Movement had considerable political appeal—for example, I and many of my colleagues in Hezbollah were members of Amal before the Israeli invasion. The political issue surfaced after the disappearance of Sayyed Mousa al-Sadr,[6] due to a difference in vision, work, and other elements; but the problem remained confined to Amal and the Muslim scene until the [Israeli] invasion of 1982.[7] This changed everything, and all the political movements became simple zeroes in the face of the very challenging Israeli number. Iranian revolutionary guards arrived in the Bekaa upon the orders of Imam al-Khomeini,[8] and the faithful were of the opinion that a revolutionary and Islamist current should be established to adequately confront the new challenge facing Lebanon. This current was to have a clear Islamist political vision, and operate through a consistent ideology based on the principles and political line of Imam al-Khomeini, and according to the principle of *wilayat al-faqih* in which we believe.[9] This is how Hezbollah came to be.

The party started developing and growing by virtue of the Islamic Resistance's

---

6. In addition to founding Amal and serving as the spiritual leader for many Shiites in Lebanon, Imam Mousa al-Sadr (1928–78) was also a noted philosopher–theologian and a fierce public advocate for the rights of all the economically and politically disadvantaged in the country.

7. For details of Israel's 1982 invasion of Lebanon, see Introduction.

8. The Iranian Revolutionary Guards Corps (IRGC) were composed of members highly loyal to the radical Islamist project of Grand Ayatollah Ruhollah al-Musavi al-Khomeini (1900–89), who was, by the summer of 1982, still attempting to consolidate his control over post-Revolution Iran. Estimates vary, but it is generally thought that as many as 1,000 IRGC personnel were stationed by Iran in Lebanon after the Israeli invasion.

9. Literally, "the Jurisdiction of the Jurist–Theologian." As expounded by Khomeini in his Najaf juridical lectures of 1969–70, *wilayat al-faqih* practically meant a dramatic expansion of the governing role and power of clerics, and of one supreme, learned cleric in particular—thus providing for a major reinterpretation of traditional Shia theory, which had generally separated the political realm from the religious one. For Hezbollah, allegiance to the principle of *wilayat al-faqih* opened the party to charges that it followed non-nationalist—and in particular Iranian—dictates, since it apparently had to comply with any final decision issued by the *faqih*.

confrontation with Israel, and it was therefore only natural to see developing on the Islamic scene in general—and in particular the Shia scene—an entity called the Amal Movement and a current called Hezbollah. Our disagreement with Amal revolves around the vision, methodology and the fundamental, serious need to unconditionally follow al-Khomeini's leadership. We believe, however, that our relationship with the Amal Movement should be based on a dialogue that aims at crystallizing a common vision and at finding a way of dealing with one another as brothers; we reject the notion of a potential conflict between us, regardless of whether it is political or non-political. At the same time, this does not mean that there is no rivalry between us, for both of us claim to work in order to further the interests of Islam and the Muslims. Therefore, let there be competition between us, in both the political and military spheres, for the sake of the wretched in Lebanon.

On the domestic front, and concerning the rumored potential armed conflict between us, we say that we have already overcome this [situation] and will undoubtedly be able to overcome it again in the future. In the past, the psychological and military situation lent itself to a potential armed clash, but the people in charge and the Iranian government managed to contain the situation.[10] Any talk now about a future clash is nothing but a fanciful dream on the part of the enemy [Israel].

AL-KHALEEJ: *However, from time to time abductions do take place and threats are exchanged between you; there is also the fact that the Amal Movement is preventing Hezbollah from deploying in the south, especially in the liberated areas.*[11]

HN: Arrests and bans on weapons[12] do occur from time to time, but our brothers are dealing with this issue with patience and in a spirit of brotherhood. These problems are being solved immediately as and where they occur, to prevent them from spreading further afield.

10. Though occasionally strained by competing interests, the relationship between the Iranian and Syrian governments had already been employed on several occasions by 1986 to contain conflict between Amal and Hezbollah.

11. Amal long resisted allowing Hezbollah to operate—politically or militarily—in any territory vacated by Israel and/or its indigenous proxy, the South Lebanon army. In the following years, however, Amal's ability to physically control Hezbollah's influence in south Lebanon would decline precipitously.

12. Presumably by Amal members.

AL-KHALEEJ: *Your conflict with the Communist Party has recently come to light in a bloody and violent manner; does anything in particular stand behind it, or was the page turned after the latest meeting between you?*[13]

HN: Hezbollah is seen as the main player on the Muslim scene in Lebanon, and the rise of the Islamic Resistance could possibly have provoked a number of patriots (…) Such opposition manifested itself in the shape of a campaign against the Islamic case before it became known as such, and spread the word that the Resistance now belongs to one sect in particular [the Shia sect]. Those who closely follow these statements and articles would be aware of the mobilization aspect of this campaign. Furthermore, the Communist Party is blaming us for something we did not do: they are trying to blame the killing of a number of their officials on the Islamists and involve the Iranian embassy in the matter, using various media outlets to do so. They tried on several occasions to use the Noous incident; they first blamed the Amal Movement, then blamed Hezbollah again, and on a third occasion blamed the Islamic al-Tawhid movement.[14] What is significant, however, is that judging by the various recent incidents, efforts are underway to mobilize the people against the Islamists.

There is no doubt that the climate created by the Communist Party was responsible for the armed clashes in West Beirut. It is clear that the incident which led to the martyrdom of one of the *mujahidin* had been planned, as evidenced by the military deployment of the Communists in the area where the clash took place. When shots and rockets were later fired at the Iranian embassy from the Communist Center, the equation totally changed and our response became severe, although we tried to contain the incident and prevent it from spreading to other areas. We are still careful not to be dragged into the quagmire of civil war from which God Almighty has protected us in years past.

13. Relations between the Lebanese Communist Party (LCP) and Hezbollah had steadily worsened as inter-party conflict mounted across the country. In the middle of that same year, the killing of several Communist Party leaders—"The Noous incident"—was attributed to Hezbollah by the LCP. Hezbollah strongly denied that it had had any hand in the incident, but violence between the two nevertheless broke out on several occasions, prompting the intervention of Syria in an effort to calm matters.

14. A reference to the Tripoli-based Islamic Unification Movement, which operated primarily in northern Lebanon.

Finally, a meeting took place under the auspices of the Iranian embassy, and the incident was resolved. However, we still have one remark to make regarding this incident: we are always very careful to avoid fighting with anyone, and most of all with those with whom we have ideological differences, like the Communists. The methodology according to which we operate does not involve building ourselves our own canton or competing with anyone for positions in the Lebanese state system. Our strategy is to build a future for ourselves through confrontation with the Zionist enemy. Let them therefore leave us be to fight Israel, for we have no ambitions in the liberated areas of the south; the [75km] occupied border zone [with Israel] is a different matter, and should be left to us. We would like to warn, however, that any attack on our *mujahidin* would be unacceptable and costly, as the incidents that have taken place recently have clearly shown; we also still intend to contain any incident that might occur.

AL-KHALEEJ: *The situation in West Beirut is still worrying on account of what has happened and is happening on a daily basis, including clashes, assassinations, explosions, thefts, and violations. How long can this situation continue, how do you explain it, and what do you expect to happen in the future?*

HN: The scene in West Beirut has been internationally, regionally, and locally infiltrated; various political, military, and intelligence parties are operating on the scene, and it is the theatre on which the current political game is being played out. This means that we cannot view what is taking place there as being separate from what is happening in Lebanon and the region as a whole. The situation in West Beirut is in a state of total collapse, and is a reflection of the entire political game; all parties on the scene, therefore, should bear the responsibility for this collapse. All previous security plans have failed, and all future plans are doomed to fail because those in charge of maintaining security are also the ones responsible for this collapse.

We believe that the scene in West Beirut is on the verge of a dangerous political and security explosion, which has so far been lurking like embers under the ash. There are also other possibilities of which I will not speak now, because they are not entirely clear yet.

AL-KHALEEJ: *In light of this situation, what is the current state of the refugee camps, and did any of the solutions so far succeed in bridging the gap and ending the bloodshed?*[15]

HN: The wound of the camps is still open, but joint efforts are underway by the Amal Movements and the Palestinians to heal it. They themselves admit, through self-criticism, that what took place was not right from the start, and should therefore be brought to an end. I do not know if the [players in the] political game in the region would want the matter to be reopened or remain closed, but it will probably come to an end. The future will witness a large-scale return by Arafat to West Beirut; it might not involve Arafat in person, but rather a heavy presence of individuals from the second and third tiers.[16] This issue, however, should be solved within the context of an agreement between Lebanese, Syrian, and Palestinian leaders.

AL-KHALEEJ: *The situation in Lebanon is passing through a stifling state of stagnation in the wake of the failure of the Tripartite Agreement;[17] how do you see the situation on the ground, and what are the possibilities, especially since some are considering a military solution?*

HN: For the past ten years, a play produced, directed, and written by America

15. Nasrallah is referring to the so-called War of the Camps that raged from 1985 to 1988, mainly between the Shiite Amal party and various Palestinian groups based in refugee camps across Lebanon, but especially in the South Beirut camps of Bourj al Burajneh, Sabra and Chatila. By some accounts, Amal had been recruited by Syria's president and ruler, Hafez al-Assad, to break the control that Palestinian leader Yassir Arafat's Fatah movement, as well as other PLO-affiliated parties, still exercised over the Lebanese scene, despite Arafat's exiting of the country following the Israeli invasion of 1982. The effort was designed to further assert Syria's control over the country, and to reduce the possibility that such relatively independent actors might provoke another Israeli invasion of Lebanon. The War of the Camps was officially estimated to have claimed 3,781 lives.

16. As head of the PLO, and its largest party, Fatah, Arafat (1929–2004) had coordinated operations against Israel from Lebanon since his effective expulsion from Jordan in 1971. Following Israel's June 1982 invasion of Lebanon, and a subsequent agreement brokered by Washington, Arafat left Beirut on August 30 for Tunisia, accompanied by thousands of his fighters. He remained based in Tunisia until his return to the occupied Palestinian territories in 1994.

17. The Syrian-brokered Tripartite Agreement of December 28, 1985 was meant to bring an end to the decade-old Lebanese Civil War. Signed by Nabih Berri of Amal, the Druze and Progressive Socialist Party leader Walid Jumblatt (1949–), and the Christian Lebanese Forces (LF) leader Elie Hobeika (1956–2002)—who had led a breakaway group from the main Christian party, the Phalange—the agreement effectively collapsed when Hobeika was ousted, in January 1986, by Lebanese Forces commander Samir Geagea (1952–).

and other concerned regional and international powers, has been acted out in Lebanon. After every battle, even in the absence of a military balance, political leaders insist that a military victory should be a red line. The scenario starts with a battle, then moves on to dialogue, then to a solution being proposed once more and, finally, to a truce. A short time later, the situation explodes again, the game resumes, and the play is played out all over again.

In our estimation, the current situation in Lebanon is not moving in the direction of a military solution; even those who promote such a scenario are not very serious about it. What is actually taking place is an attempt at wasting time until a new round of negotiations can take place, either through independent Maronite parliamentarians or others.[18] This would usher in a new game, possibly accompanied by a limited military campaign, or maybe not. We noticed, however, that the tone of voice that followed the abolition of the Tripartite Agreement has abated, which indicates that the climate is now ready for entering once again into the labyrinth of wasted and useless dialogue, to allow the game to continue.

We support a military solution because we do not see a better alternative. Here, it is important to differentiate between the Christians, the Lebanese Forces, and the *Kataeb*.[19] We are ready to start a dialogue with the weak Christians who have been taken for granted, and who desire coexistence and who did not commit crimes against the people. However, dialoguing with Israel's agents is like dialoguing with Israel itself; it is as absolute a condition as it is regarding Israel.[20]

The establishment of peace in Lebanon, therefore, can only take place once we extract the black, cancerous gland from Lebanon. We call upon

18. The largest Christian sect in Lebanon, the Eastern Catholic Maronites, also held title to significant political power, both through their patriarch (currently Cardinal Mar Nasrallah Boutros Sfeir) and through the country's decades-old National Pact, whereby the president, the army commander, and the head of the central bank were required to be from the Maronite sect.

19. During the mid-1980s, the Lebanese Forces and Phalange, or *Kataeb*, were the two main right-wing parties vying for power and influence among Lebanon's Christian communities— although the Lebanese Forces had originally been conceived as the military arm of the Phalange. Both the LF and Phalange militias were subsequently disbanded in the wake of the 1989 Taif Accord, which effectively ended the Lebanese Civil War.

20. Nasrallah is probably suggesting that any form of contact with Israel's allies in Lebanon would be shunned, almost as surely as would contact with Israel itself. As the years wore on, however, Hezbollah and Nasrallah would steadily step back from this position, eventually engaging even some figures who had previously publicly allied themselves with Israel—foremost of which were those individuals leading both the right-wing Christian parties, the LF and the Phalange.

all national and Islamic, political and military forces in Lebanon to opt for a military solution and urge them not to be afraid of the red lines. Experience has shown us that red blood is capable of obliterating red lines, and if the nation chooses to follow this path, Israel and America will find that they are incapable of changing anything in the equation. We hope that all the talk about a military solution on the part of various political leaders is not simply a political card to play with. We would like this scenario to become an established plan, and an option in which future generations will be brought up to believe. These past few years have provided ample proof of that.

AL-KHALEEJ: *Assuming, for the sake of argument, that a military solution does take place, what sort of system would you envisage for Lebanon, and can the Islam you propose govern a place so full of contradictions?*

HN: From the point of view of ideology and sharia,[21] we are required to establish God's rule over any part of this earth, regardless of particularities and details; this can only happen, however, if the nation adopts this ideology and safeguards it. We would like to allay the fears of those who think that Hezbollah intends to impose Islamic rule by force, and to tell them that we shall not impose Islam; for us, this is a matter of general principle. We are now intent on removing colonialism from this region, doing away with colonial means of information and culture, and making the people understand Islam as it should be understood; a lot of Muslim political terminology has been distorted by colonial interpretations.

We do not believe in multiple Islamic republics; we do believe, however, in a single Islamic world governed by a central government, because we consider all borders throughout the Muslim world as fake and colonialist, and therefore doomed to disappear.

We do not believe in a nation whose borders are 10,452 square kilometers in Lebanon; our project foresees Lebanon as part of the political map of an Islamic world in which specificities would cease to exist, but in which the rights, freedom, and dignity of minorities within it are guaranteed.

Therefore, in order for this project to be realized, priority should be given

21. The code of Islamic law derived from the Quran, and from the teachings and examples of the Prophet Muhammad (c.570–632).

to removing Israel from the scene, because it was established for the express purpose of dividing and partitioning the Muslim world. We are not only against the partition of Lebanon, but also against the partition of the Muslim world; this explains why we see no alternative to fighting Israel, with all means at our disposal, until it ceases to exist. Then we will attend to following [certain] steps (...)

2

SHIITE RECONCILIATION

February 3, 1989

For at least two years, Hezbollah and Amal had been engaged in intermittent conflict across south Lebanon and the suburbs of Beirut. Nasrallah, as a military commander, was involved in a number of early battles, but soon left to pursue further religious study in Qom, Iran.[1] By the end of 1988, however, the fighting between the two Shiite parties had intensified, and he returned home to Beirut to reassume his field command. The interview below, published in the pan-Arab newspaper Al-Wahda Al-Islamiya *was conducted shortly after Syria and Iran had brokered a four-way ceasefire, known as the Tehran–Damascus Agreement, which, at its second attempt in November 1990, would largely bring intra-Shiite party violence to an end in Lebanon. The development was particularly welcomed by Iran, where a weakened Ayatollah Khomeini (who would die in June 1989) and his more pragmatic potential successor, Hashemi Rafsanjani, were said to have been increasingly disturbed by the Shiite-on-Shiite killing in Lebanon. But it was Damascus that was ultimately most pleased by the Agreement: Syria's chief ally in Lebanon, Amal, would no longer be directly challenged by Hezbollah's guns, while Hafez al-Assad's supremacy over the situation on the ground in Beirut and in the south was recognized and effectively expanded.[2]*

For Hezbollah, which had fought the Syrian army as well as Amal at certain points during the civil war, the agreement brought official recognition from both. This meant, more importantly, that the ultimate conflict with Israel could now be the focus of its growing capacities.

1. See Introduction.
2. Hafez al-Assad (1930–2000) was head of the Syrian Baath Party, president and absolute ruler of Syria for almost thirty years, after assuming power in a 1970 coup. In June 1976, he sent Syrian troops into Lebanon, ostensibly in response to a request for Syrian assistance in bringing the Lebanese Civil War to an end from the then Lebanese president, Suleiman Frangieh. Syrian troops were finally withdrawn from Lebanon in May 2005, following the assassination of ex-Premier Rafik Hariri. Unlike his son and successor Bashar, Hafez al-Assad was said never to have met with Nasrallah.

"Allow us to pursue the path of resistance," Nasrallah tells his interviewer, "and we will not compete with you over anything."

AL-WAHDA: *Can you describe for us the atmosphere of the Damascus negotiations that preceded the conclusion of the recent final Agreement?*

HN: The final Agreement concluded by our brethren in Damascus is the result of a two-stage negotiating process. The first stage ended with the trip of Dr. Wilayati to Tehran[3] and the announcement of a preliminary agreement on a ceasefire, on putting an end to adverse publicity campaigns, and on pursuing negotiations towards reaching a comprehensive political agreement. The second phase started in the wake of Dr. Wilayati's return, and lasted until a solution was reached. Bilateral and trilateral meetings were held during this phase, as well as a final quadripartite meeting during which an agreement was signed. After each side presented its own vision of an eventual solution, and each of these visions was discussed at tripartite meetings, continuous and diligent efforts led to an agreement between the two parties, and a Draft Agreement was penned, approved, and then signed by both sides.

AL-WAHDA: *Who prepared this Draft?*

HN: The referees, Iran and Syria, wrote the provisions of the Agreement.

AL-WAHDA: *How?*

HN: Based upon the points discussed at the meetings.

AL-WAHDA: *Now that this final Agreement has been signed, can we consider this war to be over?*

HN: We hope so; from the very beginning, we were of the opinion that only a comprehensive political solution could bring this war to an end, and saw the limited security agreements as nothing but anesthetics to dull the pain. During our meetings with various parties, we were careful to push

---

3. Dr. Ali Akbar Wilayati was foreign minister of Iran from 1981 to 1997.

matters in the direction of a comprehensive solution, and this is what happened with God Almighty's help. With this Agreement, we can now say that steps towards the putting in place of real solutions have started, and that everything now depends on how seriously they will be implemented. Based on the climate that prevailed at the talks, we believe that intentions are indeed serious, and that the Iranian–Syrian sponsorship of the Agreement is intent on seeing that all the Agreement's provisions are implemented on the ground, and all obstacles in its path are removed.

AL-WAHDA: *What will ensure that this happens?*

HN: The next phase of this Agreement provides for the formation of a committee named the Central Coordination Committee, which will comprise two representatives from Hezbollah and two from the Amal Movement. The Committee, which should start its work within 24 hours, is charged with discussing the details and implementing the Agreement within a specific framework.

AL-WAHDA: *Is this Committee similar to the Joint Security Committee formed by Hezbollah, Amal, and the Syrians, or is it different?*

HN: No, the Committee is at the leadership level, and representatives from both parties who will sit on it have already been designated. If things go as seriously as they are supposed to, we should have entered a phase in which the wound can be healed and everyone can return to the right path. In any case, the mere fact that the bloodshed shall cease is a great achievement for Islam and Shiism in Lebanon; we can now be very optimistic about the future.

AL-WAHDA: *You said that the Agreement was concluded under the auspices of the Islamic Republic and Syria; some, however, say that other such agreements were concluded in the past, but failed because they were never implemented. Will this Agreement's fate be similar to those that preceded it?*

HN: A comprehensive political agreement was never concluded between Iran and Syria in the past regarding the Shia situation.

AL-WAHDA: *The agreement concluded under the auspices of Mohtashemi after the [1982 Israeli] invasion…*[4]

Nasrallah [interrupting]: The agreement that was concluded in Syria in the presence of Mohtashemi was under Iranian, not Iranian–Syrian, auspices, and left some unresolved issues; had they been resolved, a solution to the problem would have been guaranteed. What we have now is the first political agreement ever concluded under the auspices of the Islamic Republic, and what took place after the incident in the southern suburbs was simply a security arrangement meant to deal with a number of security-related matters. This Agreement is not only about security.

AL-WAHDA: *Could we consider this Agreement as a continuation of the one that was concluded earlier in Damascus?*

HN: Some of this Agreement's provisions are different, because the previous agreement did not include guarantees; this one is an Iranian–Syrian Agreement.

AL-WAHDA: *Some say that Syria had participated in a number of agreements that ended in failure in the past, and are betting on the failure of this one too (…)*

HN: During the negotiations, the intentions of the Iranians and Syrians suggested that they both had a debt of blood to pay;[5] this serious intent is reason enough for optimism. In any case, there is a lot of hope that this Agreement will be implemented, and the guarantees that were given are ones that we respect and appreciate.

AL-WAHDA: *The Preliminary Agreement quickly failed,[6] and today the people are*

4. At the time of the second Israeli invasion of Lebanon, in the summer of 1982, Hojatolislam Ali Akbar Mohtashemi was the Iranian ambassador in Damascus. Widely viewed as having helped foster the emergence and subsequent rise of Hezbollah, he also tried to broker several agreements between Amal and Hezbollah.

5. Nasrallah may be referring to Syria's backing of Amal in its attempt to crush certain Palestinian groups in Lebanon during the War of the Camps (for which, see above, p. 30 n. 15), as well as Iran's moral obligation to prevent intra-Shiite violence.

6. Presumably the ceasefire arrangement called for in advance of the negotiations that led to the Tehran–Damascus Agreement.

afraid that this Agreement might meet with the same fate. What guarantees are there to ensure that it will be implemented, and are you at ease with them?

HN: As we said before, the Preliminary Agreement was not implemented in full because it was a security agreement and not part of a comprehensive political agreement; this made it vulnerable to failure. The Preliminary Agreement also did not have a sponsor or a guarantor for the implementation of its provisions. Now, if a problem arises during implementation, the concerned committee will intervene to repair the damage; and if one party or the other drags its feet or causes intentional harm to the Agreement, the committee would ensure that it is being properly implemented. These matters were specified both at the moment of signature and after it.

AL-WAHDA: *On the ground?*[7]

HN: Yes. This means that there is a reference authority which the parties can resort to, and this authority will attend to the problem. This is a good omen and a factor that could speed up the implementation process.

AL-WAHDA: *Who is this reference authority?*

HN: The Quadripartite Committee of leaders, and the body responsible for solving any problem that might arise.

AL-WAHDA: *Is it under the leadership of Hezbollah and the Amal Movement?*

HN: It is under Iranian–Syrian sponsorship. Representatives from Amal, Hezbollah, Iran, and Syria have formed a Quadripartite Committee; there are also Subsidiary Committees for Beirut, a Coordination Committee, and another Coordination Committee for the south.

AL-WAHDA: *What is the role of the Central Committee, then?*

7. The exchange that follows is perhaps illustrative of precisely the ambiguities that ultimately contributed to making the first Tehran–Damascus Agreement unworkable. It also stands as a reminder of how opaque Nasrallah can be when he chooses not to reveal certain operational details.

38

HN: It is in charge of discussing the details.

AL-WAHDA: *And it has subsidiary committees in various regions?*

A: Yes. The Coordination Committee meets and decides on the modes of implementation; it could also form subsidiary committees.

AL-WAHDA: *And if a problem arises?*

HN: They resort to the Quadripartite Committee.

AL-WAHDA: *There is one question we would like you to answer frankly: Do you in Hezbollah see this Agreement as something you wanted and aspired to?*

HN [laughing]: Based upon a general evaluation of the Agreement, we estimate that it is a genuine political achievement because it safeguards, first and foremost, the Islamic Resistance. In all our previous statements we have said, and reconfirm [here], that we do not seek power and do not wish to compete with anyone over state positions; our political movement is based on the premise of fighting Israel. Our only concern and interest is to safeguard the core—that is to say, the Islamic Resistance— and we have given many martyrs for this purpose. We suffered many wounded, went through a lot of pain, endured all these difficult situations, and found that there is no harm in agreeing to a number of security measures in order to safeguard what is most important to us, namely the Islamic Resistance and its freedom of operation. That is why the most important provision in the Agreement is the one that regulates the moves of the resistance from a joint operations room. For us, safeguarding the Islamic Resistance is what really matters.

AL-WAHDA: *This is, of course, if it is implemented?*

HN: Of course. We are currently evaluating the Agreement, and believe that the provisions that cover security matters will help keep the situation on the ground under control. We said: "Allow us to pursue the path of resistance and we will not compete with you over anything." The first positive aspect of this Agreement is the preservation of the Islamic Resistance and the escalation of the fight against Israel, whether jointly or separately. The implementation of this Agreement also means that bloodshed will cease—and this, in itself, is an objective very dear to our and our society's heart. We estimated that what was taking place was going to weaken the resistance and destroy Shia society; this Agreement will safeguard the resistance and, by extension, Shia society. If we achieve nothing but these two positive aspects, we will consider ourselves as having achieved a great deal.

AL-WAHDA: *Are there winners and losers in this Agreement?*

HN: I think the Agreement was very fair to both sides.

AL-WAHDA: *Some say that the Agreement is a political and military endorsement of Hezbollah at the expense of Amal, and Sayyed Mohammad Hussein[8] said that the winner in this battle is actually a loser (…)*

HN: It would be wrong to say that the Agreement endorsed the political and military survival of Hezbollah at the expense of Amal. It actually endorsed the political and military survival of both sides, and placed controls to bolster the situation on the ground from the political and security points of view. The main winner is the resistance against Israel; and by "resistance" I mean both sides, which makes it a victory for us all. Such controls are mentioned in both the addenda and the details regarding the relationship between Amal and Hezbollah on the ground in the south. This is designed to keep responsibility for security as meaning for security's sake only, and not for transforming security into an authority.

---

8. Most likely a reference to Lebanon's Sayyed Mohammad Hussein Fadlallah (1935–), an Iraqi-born scholar and clerical figure often identified in the Western and Arab media as Hezbollah's spiritual leader. A supporter of Iran's Islamic Revolution, his Islamic Sharia Institute in Beirut produced several prominent religious scholars, including Sheikh Ragheb Harb (see below, p. 53, n. 8). While he has been a major political and religious reference for Hezbollah cadres, and one of Shiism's pre-eminent jurists, both Fadlallah and Hezbollah have long denied any official relationship. Despite this, however, Fadlallah clearly has had an enormous impact on the religious, military and political ideology of Hezbollah—an impact that arguably moderated the party as it sought to embed itself ever deeper into the Lebanese body politic.

AL-WAHDA: *We need a definitive answer from you to one specific question: Are Hezbollah's mujahidin and weapons returning to the south, and will the situation really revert back to what it was prior to April 5?*[9]

HN: Based on the Agreement's provisions, given the guarantees given to us, and the seriousness with which implementation is proceeding, this is what should take place. But to say that this is definite, only God knows that for sure.

AL-WAHDA: *If Hezbollah does indeed return to the south, do you, in light of Lubrani's threats, expect Israel to interfere in order to confound the new-found situation?*[10]

HN: Many [enemies] have been harmed by this Agreement: America, Israel, Israel's friends in East Beirut, the Iraqi Baath Party, and many others could interfere,[11] using all means at their disposal, to thwart the Agreement and impede its implementation. They will use all their power to infiltrate the Islamic and Shia scenes in order to foil the Accord. These parties could rest easy as long as the [civil] war continued, because they knew that it was bound to weaken the resistance and, by extension, the majority of Lebanon's Muslims. The latter would have scattered and made it easier for others to implement their own plans without any deterrence or opposition. These people were [therefore] very upset by the Accord, because it puts the gun back where it belongs, and will protect this steadfast society; this Agreement could also lead to them actually carrying out some of their threats. In fact, if the south was really strengthened and kept far from a seditious atmosphere, it would be strong enough to confront Israel's threats. It would also be an honor for the south and the Shia there

---

9. Presumably a reference to the beginning of the War of the Camps, in April 1985.

10. Uri Lubrani (1926–) was Israel's long-time coordinator of policy in Lebanon. He previously served Israeli Premier David Ben-Gurion (1886–1973) as his advisor on Arab affairs and was, before the 1979 Revolution, ambassador to Iran.

11. A reference, in particular to the Phalange and the LF. The Iraqi Baath Party, for its part, had long been seeking to undermine Syria's interests in both Lebanon and Syria, and had regarded the rise of Shiite power anywhere as a potential danger vis-à-vis its own majority Shiite population. Iraq's president and Baath Party leader, Saddam Hussein (1937–2006), skirmished with Assad and the Syrian Baath Party for much of the 1980s.

to see their sons martyred in a confrontation with Israel, rather than with Amal.

AL-WAHDA: *You mean that an Israeli intervention is bound to have positive results?*

HN: In fact, any intervention on Israel's part would lead to an escalation in the confrontation and to the forging of even closer ranks.[12] We believe that a genuine resistance will incapacitate Israel in the face of its unity, loyalty, and spirit of sacrifice in defense of its land, and the integrity and dignity of its people. This in itself would produce positive results. Over the past few months, Israel has sat there watching and feeling safe in its positions; now, however, it is issuing threats because it wants young Shia men to be killed in Lebanon. All Shiites should wake up to these threats and be ready to confront the original enemy, Israel, as well as overcome all obstacles and grudges, on account of the threat facing the south and the Muslims.

AL-WAHDA: *Do you foresee, on your part, an escalation in the number of operations?*

HN: If the Agreement is implemented, the *mujahidin*'s main task in Lebanon would be to bring the resistance back to its original focus, its central issues and sophisticated operations. I also believe that the fight against Israel is the real arena, and the gateway through which everybody can express their pent-up hatred and pain as a result of the [civil] war that was taking place.

AL-WAHDA: *People wonder why the Agreement took so long in coming—was it not possible to avoid all these deaths? And how has the Shia community been affected by all [that] has happened?*

HN: From the outset, we insisted on reconciliation [between the Shia groups], and our political program called for reconciliation; it was never among our plans to negate the other, but rather to reach an understanding with him.

---

12. Especially, Nasrallah seems to suggest, among the Shia.

We were and still are ready for any kind of coordination, if not complementarity, and have tried hard, and continuously, to arrive at a comprehensive political agreement. As to why this did not happen earlier, this question should be put to the other side.

AL-WAHDA: *But who takes responsibility for all that has happened? Is Hezbollah totally innocent of everything that has taken place?*

HN: This war was imposed on us; we ran away from it to the south, it moved to Beirut's southern suburbs;[13] we tried to solve it politically, and were left with only the option of self-defense; so we kept this option open and sought reconciliation. We tried our very best to achieve reconciliation, and God was generous to the Shia Muslims by granting them this Accord, even if it has taken some time.

AL-WAHDA: *There were previously some stumbling blocks that prevented a solution, and during the celebration in Bourj al-Barajneh Refugee Camp you said that there were three such stumbling blocks: handing over the accused, the security of southern Lebanon, and the resistance. What was it that did away with them?*

HN: Continuous negotiations and the insistence on reaching an agreement have contributed a great deal to removing these stumbling blocks; the fact that we were all able to remove them completely is a positive sign and reason for optimism.

AL-WAHDA: *It was noticed that the issue of handing over the accused does not figure in the Agreement, although it was the main stumbling block on the path towards a solution. How was this issue resolved?*

13. Many Shiite residents of Beirut fled the intra-sect and general civil war violence, which became especially bloody after 1985, for the relative safety of home villages in the south and the Bekaa. Indeed, Beirut's Southern Suburb, a loose grouping of several mainly Shiite neighborhoods just south of the capital, were major flashpoints during the Amal–Hezbollah conflict—all the more so because the suburbs included the Palestinian refugee camp of Bourj al-Barajneh. In subsequent years, the Southern Suburb, also referred to as *Dahiyeh* (the suburb), would come to be identified as a staunchly pro-Hezbollah area, where many official party activities were centered and where Hezbollah maintained a "security zone" of several blocks.

HN: Within the context of the tripartite meetings that dealt with these issues and proposals. We agreed that the three individuals accused of killing Amal officials and assassinating the martyr Sheikh Ali Kareem should be handed over to the Syrian Arab army; and this is what actually happened.

AL-WAHDA: *But isn't this tantamount to an admission of responsibility by Hezbollah for the killing of the three Amal leaders?*

HN: We agreed to hand them over based on the accusations against them, and accepted to hold an investigation. We did not act based on a predetermination that these individuals were "killers"; we refused to hand them over in the past for precisely this reason.

AL-WAHDA: *What do you mean by there are names...?*

HN: Names [of the killers] were put forward, yes.

AL-WAHDA: *By whom? Amal?*

HN: We also put names forward, and the issue will be pursued in detail.

AL-WAHDA: *And how will the outcome be presented?*

HN: The file will be given to those concerned.

AL-WAHDA: *What is the outcome of the investigation into the accused?*

HN: We accepted that the handover take place, based on the accusations, in order to help the Shia out of the crisis, as part and parcel of the Agreement to end problems among the Shiites. We have no problem with this, and I wish to confirm that we agreed to do so based only on the accusations. The matter is therefore now subject to an investigation.

AL-WAHDA: *One of the Agreement's provisions is not entirely clear: namely the security of the south and the joint operations room. Does it concern only Hezbollah, or others as well?*

HN: As a matter of principle, everything that concerns the security of the south applies to everyone.

AL-WAHDA: *And security?*

HN: Security is Amal's responsibility. As to the movements of political parties, this matter is left up to Amal and is governed by a different set of principles; Amal is bound by this.

AL-WAHDA: *Bound by it? Why isn't Hezbollah also bound by it, for example?*

HN: This provision is binding on both sides; Amal does not have the right to conclude agreements that would take the situation back to what it was prior to 1982.[14]

AL-WAHDA: *Does this refer to the last agreement concluded between Amal and the Palestinians?*[15]

HN: Every agreement should be considered separately. This provision is based on the consideration that security is the responsibility of Amal, but this does not mean that the situation can go back to what it was prior to 1982.

AL-WAHDA: *What applies to Hezbollah applies to all the others?*

HN: This Agreement is between Amal and Hezbollah, and the issue of other parties is not included because it concerns only Amal and Hezbollah. Other agreements may or may not involve other parties.

AL-WAHDA: *What is meant by a "joint operations room"? Will it be under the leadership of Amal, Hezbollah or someone else?*

HN: Nothing in the text of the Agreement specifies whether the operations

14. In other words, back to a time when Amal exercised near-unchallenged control over the political and military activities of the Shia, especially in regard to operations in the south.
15. Perhaps a reference to the April 1987 agreement, which ended the Amal siege of several Palestinian refugee camps.

room will be under Amal's or Hezbollah's leadership; representatives from both sides are working together.

AL-WAHDA: *Should individual operations be dependent upon decisions from the joint operations room?*

HN: According to the text, each side has the right to carry out individual operations.

AL-WAHDA: *Does provision number 4 regarding the security of the south have anything to do with military activities?*

HN: The military activities that are mentioned in the Agreement have to do with the resistance, and issues such as these will be discussed within the context of the Coordination Committee. What is required is an area of operations, and the means by which the *mujahidin* can access it; all these details will be specified by the Committee.

AL-WAHDA: *It will specify the zones [of military operation]?*

HN: The military front is open all along the borderline.

AL-WAHDA: *For everyone?*

HN: This Agreement concerns Hezbollah and Amal, and calls for total freedom of movement for the *mujahidin* along the line adjacent to the border zone [with Israel]; it is all an area of operations.

AL-WAHDA: *The zone specified is all along the borderline?*

HN: No—it is not specified, but includes the entire occupied zone stretching from Lwaiza to Naqoura.[16]

16. The town of Naqoura, which headquarters the United Nations Interim Force in Lebanon (UNIFIL), created by the Security Council in 1978 to confirm the Israeli withdrawal from Lebanon, restore international peace and security, and assist the Lebanese Government in restoring its effective authority in the area, lies south of the main port city of Tyre on the Mediterranean. Lwaiza lies to the south-east of Tyre.

AL-WAHDA: *Provision number 5 calls for the return of the situation to what it was prior to April 5. What does prior to April 5 mean?*

HN: The return of the scholars, the exiles, and the *mujahidin* (…) the return of cultural activities and prayer halls; all these are considered cultural, political, and media activities. Everything that is incompatible with the security of the south will be delineated by the Coordination Committee.

AL-WAHDA: *Would the freedom of political and cultural activities depend on the approval of the Central Committee?*

HN: No—and the provision relevant to political and cultural activities is clear on that.

AL-WAHDA: *Is there a guarantee against returning once again to a situation where demonstrations are fired upon, for example?*

HN: This is part of the Agreement. Upholding these guarantees, coupled with serious follow-up [on any issues that should arise], is among the responsibilities of the Quadripartite Committee; this Committee is also responsible for repairing any damage[17] that could lead to a lack of serious implementation.

AL-WAHDA: *There is talk about the Lebanese army deploying in the South?*

HN: This does not contradict the provisions of the Agreement; we have no problem with an army ready to fight Israel.

AL-WAHDA: *How true are rumors circulated by the Lebanese News Agency, to the effect that the southern suburbs are to be considered a part of Beirut, regardless of whether the Syrians assume control over the city's boundaries or relinquish their posts?*[18]

17. Presumably in relations between the various parties to the Agreement.
18. After the civil war, the southern suburbs continued to remain outside the administrative control of the Beirut municipality, thus underlining the de facto independence that the area had already gained, partially as a result of Hezbollah's ascendancy.

HN: A security agreement relevant to the status of the southern suburbs, and signed within the context of the Quadripartite Committee, will be implemented once again.

AL-WAHDA: *What is this agreement?*

HN: It specifies the number of offices and divides the southern suburbs into two security zones. One security zone would be under the control of the Syrians and the Lebanese internal security forces, with each side allowed a specific number of non-military offices; the second security zone would run along the line of contact where both sides are present,[19] and will also be subject to a specific set of rules.

AL-WAHDA: *How?*

HN: Before the situation deteriorated, the Quadripartite Committee had already started to meet, and at the last such meeting it looked into ways of delineating which zones should fall under Amal's control, and which should fall under Hezbollah's. This exercise did not achieve its objectives at the time, and should now be restarted.

AL-WAHDA: *[...] How do you categorize the martyrs who fell in that battle?*

HN: Had it not been for these martyrs, our presence would not have been safeguarded and this Agreement, which protects the resistance, would not have been possible. We named these martyrs "martyrs for the defense of the Islamic Resistance," because without them we would not have concluded a comprehensive agreement such as this one.

19. Nasrallah is referring to the complicated and contentious issue of dividing the spheres of control in the Shiite areas around Beirut between Hezbollah and Amal. Since many such areas were home to supporters of both parties, the issue proved to be one of the most difficult hurdles to jump in order to end the violence. For Hezbollah, too, the issue of the precise locations and numbers of Syrian and Lebanese army personnel was particularly sensitive. The Syrians had strongly backed Amal throughout the conflict, and its forces had been responsible for the deaths of Hezbollah cadres and supporters. Indeed, in 1987, Syrian forces had executed 24 Hezbollah fighters who had resisted Syrian attempts at controlling mostly Muslim West Beirut—an event that prompted some 50,000 party supporters to march through the streets of the southern suburbs chanting "death to Ghazi Kanaan," then head of Syrian military intelligence in Lebanon.

AL-WAHDA: *If regional circumstances change, could this Accord be violated or annulled even by Syria and Iran?*

HN: What is now required is for this Accord to be implemented; if circumstances change, they should be dealt with in a manner that safeguards the Shia community and the resistance.

AL-WAHDA: *And if, God forbid, this Accord is not implemented?*

HN: If it is not implemented we might go back to the climate of [civil] war that prevailed in the past, and chances for a solution would become minimal. I believe that the Muslims and the Shia have here a historic opportunity that should not be wasted. The Shia, the Shia constituency, their leaders and institutions should view this as a historic opportunity capable of extricating the Shia Muslims from the most dangerous predicament in their history.

AL-WAHDA: *How does Hezbollah view the next phase that will follow the Agreement?*

HN: We are optimistic. In the future, the return of the Islamist scene, and in particular the Shia scene, will undoubtedly create a very positive atmosphere throughout Lebanon, and foil numerous attempts at preserving privileges and executing schemes at the Muslims' expense.[20] There is talk in political circles about explosions, but so far it is only talk; it is also true that there are signs it could happen again, but this is not the first time that people have talked about explosions. The future is one of war [against Israel], not settlement; the line that Arafat is pursuing will only lead him to a closed door,[21] and the day will come when warfare and the elimination of Israel will be the only options.

Based on these facts, the region is not proceeding towards a settlement,

---

20. As before, Nasrallah is asserting that the intra-Shia conflict had prevented a unified Muslim front in fighting both Israel and what Hezbollah regarded as a grossly inequitable system of political power, especially with regard to the Maronites.

21. In Geneva one year earlier, Yassir Arafat had moved to meet US preconditions for direct talks and negotiations by effectively stating that the PLO recognized Israel's right to exist within its pre-1967 borders.

due to the fact that the problem is not in toppling leaderships [opposed to Israel's existence]; rather, it is Israel's hegemony, obstinacy, and historic unlimited cupidity. This is where Imam al-Khomeini's words ring most true, namely that "Jerusalem and Palestine will not be regained with political games but with guns." We believe that gambling on a settlement with Israel would never bring integrity and dignity to the Muslims; the only option open to everyone is that of resistance.

3

ELEGY FOR SAYYED ABBAS MUSSAWI

February 18, 1992

Nasrallah delivered this elegy in the eastern Bekaa village of Nabi Sheet, following an Israeli helicopter assault in Jibi Sheet, south Lebanon, which had killed Hezbollah secretary-general Abbas Mussawi,[1] his wife and baby son. Elected only one year before his death, Mussawi was seen as a relatively pragmatic voice in the party, compared to both the former Hezbollah leader Subhi Tufeili[2] and, according to some accounts, Nasrallah himself. Shortly after the assassination, however, Nasrallah assumed the leadership and promptly renewed Mussawi's earlier commitment to participate in Lebanon's upcoming summer parliamentary elections— the first since the beginning of the civil war in 1975. He also continued Hezbollah's strategy of carefully considered operations against Israel and its allies in south Lebanon, demonstrated in his displeasure—made clear in Statement 4—over an apparently uncoordinated Hezbollah rocket attack in the south following Mussawi's death.

Not surprisingly, the elegy itself rings with an uncompromising enmity towards Israel's existence, which would characterize Nasrallah's public rhetoric at least until early 2000, when peace between Syria and Israel [and therefore Lebanon and Israel] seemed almost at hand. Viewing Mussawi's death at the hands of his enemies as a modern-day version of the martyrdom of Ali, the first Shia Imam, Nasrallah says: "You Jews, leave our land, you have no home among us, go back from where you came ... You are leaving and we are staying."

1. Sayyed Abbas Mussawi (c. 1952–92).
2. Sheikh Subhi Tufeili was one of the founding members of Hezbollah, and became the first elected secretary-general of the party in November 1989. After Mussawi replaced him in May 1991, however, he was increasingly sidelined by both the party and by Iran. Staunchly opposed to Hezbollah's participation in the 1992 parliamentary elections, by the late 1990s he would lead a revolt among some of Bekaa's Shiites centered on the alleged lack of resources devoted to certain Shia areas by the party and the Lebanese state (especially in the eastern Bekaa), as well as the pernicious influence of Iran.

In the name of God the Merciful, the Compassionate. I had to write this down to be able to summarize the feelings and attitude on the day of your journey to heaven where God Almighty is awaiting, a journey that started as you wished and chose with enthusiasm; a death that epitomized the events at Karbala.[3] You were just like al-Hussein, a body without a head; just like al-Abbas, with your hands severed; and just like the greatest Ali, with your torn flesh. It is as if your infant son Hussein is the suckling child of Karbala, who did not die from a severed vein, but whose body parts mingled with your own. It is as if your spouse and life's companion Um Yasser, as if Zeinab[4] is screaming in revolution not through words or tears, but with her blood that speaks even louder at a time when words have lost their value. As if your bombed and destroyed cortège were Hussein's tents burning in the desert, as if you were that same Hussein, the commander on the battlefield, Hussein the rebel in the face of oppression and despotism, and Hussein who rejected humiliation and shame. Just like the committed and faithful Abbas, loyal to the revolution and to the leader, You, My Master, epitomize all that Karbala represented, from resistance to enthusiasm, to the path, to the tragedy.[5]

You always raised your voice with courage to address the nation about the Israeli enemy, about the great Satan,[6] about cupidity and danger, barbarism and savagery, racism and enmity towards humanity. Today, your voice, your wounds and your blood will ring in our ears and beat in our hearts as

3. Nasrallah is referring to the Battle of Karbala, which took place on 10 Muharram, 61 AH (October 10 680CE) in Karbala, Iraq. Although the events and their subsequent interpretation are highly contentious, the battle and the ensuing martyrdom of Hussein (626–680), the son of the first Imam Ali (599–691; also martyred), and himself the third Shia Imam, at the hands of Yazid, the Umayyad caliph, stands as a founding narrative of resistance and suffering for the Shia. It also marks a culmination of the major split in the Islamic nation after the death of the Prophet Muhammad, and is annually marked by the Ashoura commemoration. Ali, in particular, is seen by the mainline Twelver Shiites as the true guardian of the Islamic nation after the death of the Prophet.

4. Zeinab bint Ali (c.628–682), the sister of Hussein and granddaughter of the Prophet, was forced to march unveiled back to Damascus by Yazid's army after the Battle of Karbala, along with other prisoners also taken as spoils of war.

5. Abbas (648–683), the half-brother of Hussein, was also eventually martyred at the Battle of Karbala, having had both his arms cut off early in the conflict.

6. A term for the United States. Israel is customarily referred to by both Hezbollah and some Iranian leaders and media as the Little Satan. Nasrallah is also using the word nation (*ummah*) here as he usually does—that is, with a certain degree of ambiguity as to whether he is referring to the Lebanese nation, the Arab nation, or the Islamic nation, or all three as one.

witnesses to what you have always told us. We promise to carry your rebellious voice to all the dispossessed people of this world, and to sprinkle your blood in every corner of the earth so that jihad[7] and resistance can germinate and grow.

You looked forward to meeting your God and He looked forward to meeting you, and you speeded your departure and realized your long-time wish; so rejoice at God's side, rejoice in the company of His Messenger [the Prophet Muhammad]. It is as if up in the Kingdom of Heaven everyone is busier than usual, busy welcoming him, while he, Sayyed Abbas, moves from the Messenger's lap to the Messenger's lap once again, and from Ali to his grandmother al-Zahra, then to al-Hassan, al-Hussein, the Imams, al-Khomeini, the martyr al-Sadr, and Sheikh Ragheb (...).[8] As if the entire cortège of the Islamic Resistance and Hezbollah martyrs are standing at attention in readiness to greet the mighty man. Rejoice O Abu Bajiji, Rida al-Sha'er, Ahmad Shu'eib, Hajj Jawad, Ahmad Kassir, Asaad Berro, and all you martyrs, and make haste, for the beloved one has arrived, carrying with him messages from all those who love you, those who are still awaiting their turn and have not changed nor will ever change at all.

Dear brothers, this savage crime is another testament to the Israeli enemy's racism and barbarism, which should be added to the series of their ugly attacks on our families, villages, cities, and holy sites. It is another testament to the conspiratorial arrogance of the mighty of this world, and to their responsibility for these crimes. For His Eminence, al-Sayyed, symbolizes all the martyred men, Um Yasser all the martyred women, and little Hussein all the martyred children, and all of them together symbolize every family that suffers from oppression and prejudice in our Islamic world. We blame Israel for this blood-soaked carnage, and blame its protector, the United States of America, which is responsible for all Israel's massacres and all the destruction, murder, and displacement it wreaks. Everybody knows that Israel would not have been able to stand on its own in the region had it not been for Western and American support.

7. Literally, striving in the way of God. Although a multifaceted term, most contemporary references to jihad are associated with an armed struggle fought in the name of Islam.

8. For al-Sadr, see above, p. 26 n. 6. Sheikh Ragheb Harb (1953–84), from the south Lebanon village of Jibi Sheet, was an influential Shiite cleric and founding Hezbollah member assassinated by Israeli agents on February 16, 1984.

By murdering His Eminence al-Sayyed, our secretary-general, they wanted to kill our spirit of resistance and destroy our will for jihad, but his blood will keep simmering in our veins and will only increase our determination to forge ahead and heighten our enthusiasm to pursue the path. The martyrdom of Hezbollah's secretary-general is proof of the maturity and grandeur attained by Hezbollah in Lebanon; it is also proof of its loyalty to God's objectives, the extent of harmony between the leadership and the base, of giving without restraint, of its considerable presence in the battle, and of its deep commitment to the entire project and nation. It is also proof of the beginning of a far-reaching spiritual, moral, and jihadist transformation that no one had expected, not even those who murdered him.

As we bid farewell to our great martyr and to his wife and child, we pledge ourselves to his pure soul and to our oppressed people, that we shall continue to walk in his footsteps. We pledge to persevere on the path he had chosen, the path of Khomeini and Khameini,[9] and that we shall remain steadfast to everything we believe in and shall not relinquish any of [our beliefs] even should they cut us to pieces, tear us apart, or commit the worst atrocities against us.

America will remain the nation's chief enemy and the greatest Satan of all. Israel will always be for us a cancerous growth that needs to be eradicated, and an artificial entity that should be removed, even if all the rulers [of the world] recognize it. The Supreme Guide Ayatollah Khameini will remain our leader, imam, master, and inspiration in jihad, patience, and willpower. Islam, the true original religion of Muhammad, will remain our way of thinking, our religion, and the guide in which we take pride, which we pray for, and in whose name we fight. The Islamic Resistance will remain our only option, our constant response, the path that we shall not relinquish, and the battle we will pursue even if the entire world surrenders. Our oppressed people in Lebanon, whom our great martyr loved so dearly, will remain our living conscience and soul, for whose freedom, self-esteem, and dignity we work and sacrifice. We shall also struggle to achieve this people's will, to remove the conditions of oppression, injustice, and deprivation under

9. Sayyed Ali Husseini Khameini (1939–) was elected *wilayat al-faqih* of Iran in June 1989, after the death of Khomeini, and subsequently acknowledged as such by Hezbollah—although his religious credentials were to be greatly challenged by both indigenous Iranian figures and notable figures in Lebanon, such as Sayyed Fadlallah. See p. 40 n. 8 above for Fadlallah.

which they live; and realize the real peace and security they crave. Jerusalem will remain present in our memory as a compelling objective, an ambition without limits, and the source of our burning desire to regain the place where the Prophet ascended to heaven and our First Qibla.[10] Palestine, all of Palestine, will remain part of this nation, and we shall not relinquish a single grain of its sand. The jihadist movement and the resistance—who stretch out their hands to all Lebanese, Arab, and Islamic forces that are aware of the danger that this enemy poses, and are ready to defend this nation—shall remain steadfast.

Finally, as we stand in front of your torn body and pure soul, we pledge ourselves always to echo your words:

> You Jews, leave our land, you have no home among us, go back from where you came, for there will never be peace or reconciliation between us, only war, resistance, and the language of war and bullets. You are leaving and we are staying; dawn is upon us, the sun will shine and the entire nation will rise to greet its God. This era will witness the victory of the dispossessed over the oppressor; it is the era of our beloved Islam and of the Great Khomeini, in spite of the hatred that the Godless and tyrants harbor towards us.

May God's peace be with you.

10. Qibla is the direction that Muslims must face while praying to God. The Al-Aqsa mosque in Jerusalem was the First Qibla until that position was accorded to the Holy Kaaba in Mecca.

4

AFTER THE ASSASSINATION

February 27, 1992

This interview, conducted by the prominent Lebanese journalist Ibrahim al-Amine and published in the Lebanese leftist daily newspaper As-Safir, came just eleven days after Mussawi was killed, and shortly after Nasrallah was elected secretary-general of Hezbollah. Significantly, he goes to some length to present himself as far less extremist and far more rational in his calculations than some—in particular Hezbollah's traditional domestic opponents, the Christians—had suggested. Apparently, however, his efforts were unconvincing—at least as far as the US was concerned: according to one secret 1992 CIA assessment,[1] US analysts viewed Nasrallah's ascendancy as a boost for the radicals in Hezbollah, potentially increasing the threat of global Hezbollah operations directly targeting US interests. For the domestic Lebanese audience, however, his words provided an important degree of clarity as to the immediate ambitions of what was, largely as a result of a joint Syrian–Iranian modus vivendi, the only remaining armed political party after the end of the civil war.

AS-SAFIR: *We noticed, before the martyrdom of Sayyed Abbas Mussawi,[2] that Hezbollah had adopted a new policy regarding various issues in Lebanon, such as avoiding bloody internal conflicts, giving priority to resistance activities in the south, and opening up to non-Muslim groups. Today you confirm that you will be following Sayyed Mussawi's path. Could you tell us about the policy that you plan to pursue at this particular point in time, especially regarding other groups in the country?*

HN: The path pursued by the martyred Sayyed was not his own personal

---

1. The US Central Intelligence Agency, "Lebanon's Hizballah: Testing Political Waters, Keeping Militant" (The US Central Intelligence Agency: 1992), released under the US Freedom of Information Law, November 13, 2001.
2. For Mussawi, see Statement 3.

policy, but that of Hezbollah's leadership. This path does not shift or change, neither before nor after one secretary-general goes and the new one comes. Over the past few years, we were in the process of establishing ourselves— because, as is well known, Hezbollah is a jihadi[3] movement created in the wake of the Israeli invasion of 1982. The main basis upon which the movement was established was that of resistance against occupation.

During the first few years of our existence, we were in the process of establishing our movement, and sought first to complete the building of our infrastructure. It was therefore very natural for an entity still involved in its own construction, forming its own identity, and affirming its presence, not to be sufficiently able to take steps towards others. I mean by this, building relations with other groups, opening up to them, forming coalitions, and other such initiatives. People first have to affirm their own existence before starting to build relationships, coalitions, and policies that depend on it. Also during that period, a seditious atmosphere prevailed between us and our brethren in the Amal Movement, and this kept us all rather occupied.[4] Hezbollah's entire leadership was determined to get out of this predicament, and reach an agreement that would put an end to this conflict one way or another. The first such agreement between the two groups was signed by His Eminence the martyred Sayyed, may God rest his soul, and the second [in 1990] was signed by the former secretary-general, Sheikh Subhi Tufeili, which underlines the fact that the issue does not depend on differences of opinion between individuals in the party. They all pursue the same path, which depends on the circumstances prevailing at the time.

After the conflict between us and our brethren in Amal ended, the attention of Hezbollah's leadership once again turned towards escalating the resistance [against Israel], and taking steps towards other groups in the country; it was also time to start attending to the people's problems. Sayyed Abbas's personal belief in this path, coupled with a similar conviction by Hezbollah's leadership and the coinciding accession of the martyred Sayyed to the general secretariat of the party, placed him at the forefront of this policy. Undoubtedly the martyred Sayyed's distinguished personality and his character attributes helped ensure a good performance. I am sure that observers noticed the shift that had taken place, as well as secretary-general Sayyed Abbas Mussawi's laudable

3. See p. 53, n. 7.
4. For the Amal–Hezbollah conflict, see Statement 1

activities. I can tell you in all confidence that, after his martyrdom, nothing changed at all—neither in the direction we are taking, the path we are pursuing, our spirituality, nor on the level of our performance. All that has changed is that one person, who occupied an essential position within the Islamic community, was martyred, and it is now incumbent upon us to continue the journey. We will follow the same methods, pursue the same path, and strive to maintain the same high level of performance—whether at the level of the resistance, in taking steps towards other forces and sects in Lebanon, or in attending to the state of deprivation from which the people are suffering. As I said before, we are determined to stay the course and pursue the same path.

AS-SAFIR: *In its first comment on the assassination of Sayyed Abbas Mussawi, Israel predicted that the incident would have long-term repercussions.*

HN: The Israeli enemy has not thus far been able, in spite of its advanced intelligence capabilities, to understand Hezbollah's identity and make-up, or fathom the nature of the challenge facing it. The enemy is perhaps trying to draw lessons from its experience in previous wars and engagements with some Palestinian factions, and gauge the situation accordingly. It is also clear, based on published statements by the enemy's leaders, analyses in the Israeli press, and [statements by] Western commentators, that their main objective was to deal Hezbollah a fatal blow. They assumed that by killing the secretary-general in this manner, they would lower morale among the leaders and members of Hezbollah, and create a state of confusion and bewilderment, which in turn would incapacitate the party. Added to that is the failed military operation that they launched against Kafra and Yater,[5] the obvious objective of which was to go into the two villages, take control of a number of hilltops, destroy the homes of the *mujahidin*, and kill as many of them as possible. The idea was that, if this military operation succeeded and they managed to enter the two villages, a state of panic would ensue in the south and in all areas in which the resistance is present. In other words, taken

5. These two villages, located directly to the east and north of Naqoura (see above, p. 46 n. 16), but just outside Israel's security zone, were briefly advanced upon by Israeli forces three days after Mussawi's assassination.

together, these actions would [they thought] accelerate the collapse of Hezbollah, the backbone of the resistance.

It seems that the Israelis were relying on a certain piece of press or intelligence information to the effect that there are different factions within Hezbollah, and that Sayyed Abbas Mussawi had become secretary-general a year ago as a result of a compromise deal between them. They thought that if they hit Sayyed Abbas, they would deal a blow to the person at the heart of this compromise, and as a result the conflict between the various factions, themselves still in shock at the incident, would increase, further weaken Hezbollah, and cause it to unravel. We, of course, believe that the Israeli enemy has not achieved any of its objectives through this assassination except for one—namely, the removal from the scene of a personality of the caliber of Sayyed Abbas Mussawi. What they have done, in fact, is awaken that very scene, put it on the alert, sharpened its awareness, increased its determination, unified it even further, caused it to rally round the resistance, and increased its enmity towards Israel in a manner that Abbas Mussawi himself could not have done during his lifetime.

AS-SAFIR: *Don't you think that what happened could have been avoided if the right measures had been put into place? Did something go wrong in this respect?*

HN: Our brother Abbas, may God be pleased with him, and our brethren in general, were very determined not to allow any security measures to constitute a barrier between them and the people. They considered their presence in certain areas, their appearance at a number of occasions, and opportunities to address the nation, as necessary steps even if they involve a certain amount of risk and sacrifice. The martyrdom of Sayyed Abbas will undoubtedly teach the present leadership a lesson and highlight the importance of taking additional security precautions.

When we were just a small jihadi group fighting the Israeli enemy, we were able to hide underground whenever we read in the papers that there was reason for us to disappear; that was only possible when we were just a small jihadi group. But we soon became a movement as large as this, and started viewing our project as non-partisan and non-factional, and as one that operates at the level of the entire Lebanese nation and people. We had also urged the Lebanese people to resist Israel and harbor enmity towards it, as the main present and genuine danger to all; and this made it impossible for us to do our job from the underground, as other military and security services are able to do. Appearing among our people, families, and supporters is essential, especially at an occasion such as the martyrdom of the Sheikh of all martyrs, Sheikh Ragheb Harb, in Jibi Sheet,[6] which Sayyed wanted very much to attend personally. In any case, we are trying our best to strike a balance between being able to be present among the people as often as possible and taking the necessary security measures, which with God's help will eliminate such threats towards our leaders.

AS-SAFIR: *This question has additional aspects. The arrest was announced in Egypt of a spy network working for Israel that has branches in a number of Arab countries, including Lebanon. To your knowledge, is there a network that could have provided information about Sayyed Abbas Mussawi's movements? And did he receive any warnings in the past regarding the possibility of his being the target of an assassination attempt?*

HN: You all know that Israel has succeeded in infiltrating Lebanon to a considerable extent, and that it is active in the south and in other Lebanese areas. Its spy network in Lebanon has undoubtedly helped carry out this operation. Regarding warnings in the past, there was general information that Muslim leaders—especially Hezbollah's—were on an assassination list. This is still the case, which means that this situation is nothing new for us; every single day, and as far back as the beginning of our activities in 1982, we [have been conscious of being] the target of assassination attempts. People in Lebanon who declare their enmity towards America and Israel, and insist on persevering on the path of jihad under this banner, will become a target. This is the nature of the battle we are engaged in, and any analysis of the situation presupposes and confirms that fact. In spite of this, we insisted on balancing between taking security measures and being present in public. For example, some people believe, as a result of the state of shock produced by the painful assassination of the secretary-general, that the new secretary-general should not attend the funeral for security reasons, and that for that same reason he should not appear on this or that occasion. We cannot

6. For Sheikh Ragheb Harb, see above, p. 53, n. 8.

perform our duties under such strict conditions, [which means] that we cannot put our secretary-general and our entire leadership in hiding and ask them to address the people through television screens. This does not suit the nature of our movement. As I said before, we have to balance between the stringency of the security measures we adopt and the need for us to maintain a public presence.

AS-SAFIR: *According to your information, who launched the Katyusha rockets?*[7]

HN: We have no information in this regard, and cannot point a finger at anyone. The south is an open area, and any group could bring a small number of rockets close to the frontier zone, and launch them from there.

AS-SAFIR: *This kind of behavior will produce a reaction that could affect the people (...)*

HN (interrupting): ... as a resistance activity, it is very elementary, but a very frank one (...) by God; a quiet front without any fighting or shelling (...) or "just a little." A group of resistance fighters erected a rocket launcher and shelled the occupied territories [Israel] (...) we do not condone this kind of behavior or work in this manner. However, if on the battlefield the enemy attacks, shells, and advances, it is only natural and right for us, and for resistance fighters and defenders, to use all means at our disposal to defend our families, our citizens, and our villages. The situation is always presented as the reverse of what it is: Israeli aggression becomes a reaction while, in reality, the situation is the opposite. The Israelis were the ones to start the shelling, and the Israelis were the ones to attack first, and what took place was a reaction to the Israeli attack. Here, we have a request to the Lebanese

7. Supplementing Nasrallah's clarification here on this issue, the deputy secretary-general of Hezbollah, Naim Qassem (1953–), would later write: "For the first time, the Resistance launched Katyusha rockets at the settlements in northern occupied Palestine in response to the assassination [of Mussawi], thereby introducing the rockets as a new factor in the confrontation. Afterwards, Hezbollah clearly tied such action to reciprocity of the same suffered by Lebanese civilians at the hands of Israeli aggression, the latter not sparing an opportunity to target civilians of any town or village alongside civilian infrastructure." Naim Qassem, *Hezbollah: The Story From Within* (London: Saqi, 2005), p. 109. The Katyusha rocket, originally built and employed by the Soviet Union during World War II, has a maximum range of 20 kilometers and can be launched from either fixed or mobile positions. It carries a 30 kilogram warhead.

government that negotiates, makes contacts, and undertakes political and diplomatic activities; it is illogical for the enemy to tell us "We will not attack only if you stop the Katyushas"—this puts us in a position where we are subject to the enemy's conditions. We have to work instead towards creating a situation in which the enemy is subject to our conditions. We should tell him: "If you attack us, we will use our Katyushas; if you do not attack us, we will not use our Katyushas. We will, however, keep fighting you as an occupier, using all our tactical options." We have to turn the situation around; it is not acceptable that the resistance, or anyone fighting for his land, should be defined as the aggressor, while the enemy applies pressure to prevent a counterattack. This is not fair.

AS-SAFIR: *Your Eminence's words have a tone of [self-] justification. Who are they aimed at?*

HN: They are aimed at all the politicians who, under pressure, believe the enemy's claims, accept them, or agree with them, and deal with the situation accordingly. From the practical point of view, experience has proved that we care about the people through our performance in the resistance; and as soon as the Israeli enemy was repelled, and the operation failed, contacts were established between us and the Amal Movement. We know very well what the uncontrolled proliferation of weapons would mean, and the negative effect it could have on the people and the resistance itself. We took the initiative, made the necessary contacts and said: "Come, let us agree on the cancellation of all armed manifestations; there is no need for them and the move will help control the situation on the ground. We achieved a great victory together, so let's preserve it; we can agree, coordinate our efforts, and help one another mount a resistance." From the political point of view— and this is what I want to comment on—it is not correct to say that this is not our right; it is. We believe that this is our right. I said, "Come, let us see where the interest of the resistance lies, and where the interest of the people lies." This is the main difference as far as we are concerned.

AS-SAFIR: *This is part of the resistance's strategy: Will the Islamic Resistance's activities be confined to liberating the frontier zone, or is the frontier zone an open battlefield through which operations against Israel can be launched?*

HN: The long-term strategy of the Islamic Resistance is clear and does not require additional explanation. It involves fighting against Israel and liberating Jerusalem, as well as Imam Khomeini's proposal—namely, ending Israel as a state. The fact that we are engaged in an existentialist battle with Israel is an honor for us, as is the fact that the Israeli enemy deals with Hezbollah on that basis. We view the Israeli enemy with a different eye—namely, that its very existence in the region poses a constant threat to Lebanon as a whole, even if it withdraws from the frontier zone.

We are not unrealistic. We do not pretend that our military capabilities and the numbers of our *mujahidin* would be enough to regain Jerusalem; none of us have ever made that claim. We do, however, believe that the resistance has to finish the job it started. It is impossible for us to fight the Israeli enemy through traditional and classical methods, but rather [we must fight] through a war of attrition, whereby we drain its energy, weaken it, then one day force it to withdraw. Some claim that the withdrawal that took place in 1985 came as a result of political pressure and negotiations; this is obviously a misguided notion.[8] The amount of losses the enemy incurred, and the fear it lived through, created enormous pressure on the Jews in the occupied territories; they, in turn, put a lot of pressure on their own government and forced it to withdraw. The enemy considered the price it paid on the ground as exceedingly high, and [former Israeli Premier Yitzak] Rabin admitted earlier on that their 1982 invasion was a very big mistake, because it introduced another group onto the battlefield, and created new enemies for Israel.[9]

AS-SAFIR: *We noticed that in the salute you addressed to the fighters, you said that there would not be an internal agreement as long as there are Christians who count on Israel's support, and as long as there is an outstretched arm towards the enemy; who were you referring to?*

HN: There is a priority issue that the Lebanese have to agree on, namely whether the Israeli is an enemy or not. They went to Taif,[10] and before

8. See Statement 1.

9. Rabin was widely quoted as saying, in regard to the subsequent Israeli occupation of parts of Lebanon, "We let the Shia genie out of the bottle."

10. The Taif Accord, signed on October 22, 1989, by Lebanese parliamentarians in the Saudi Arabian city of the same name, marked the beginning of the end of the Lebanese Civil War. Under Taif, part of the 1943 National Pact, Lebanon's tacit outline of a multi-confessional *(cont'd over)*

that to Lausanne and Geneva, and discussed several issues at length—while the serious and important issue that they should discuss is their position regarding Israel, and in particular whether or not Israel is the enemy of Lebanon and its people.

If we want to find a common denominator between all the Lebanese factions today, we will undoubtedly not find any intellectual, ideological or religious denominators, because there are many such currents in this country. On the domestic front, we might find certain common denominators that bunch a number of groups together, and another bunch of other denominators that bring still other groups together. However, if we really want to find a genuine and realistic common denominator that goes right to the heart of the interests of Lebanon and the Lebanese, and that would really help them face up to future challenges, it would be enmity towards Israel. Is Israel an enemy or not? It is time now to address this issue and decide whether Israel is Lebanon's enemy, and whether we want to be involved in defending Lebanon against Israel. In the past—and we are speaking here about historical facts, not about security information—certain Lebanese groups from East Beirut dealt with the Israeli enemy, stretched their arms out to it and counted on its support to win the presidency of the republic and build Lebanon according to its measurements.[11] These groups' options were Israeli options in every sense of the word; and instead of standing on the side of their own people's resistance against the enemy, they collaborated with that enemy against the people. But we do not wish to dwell too long on the past here.

I did not say that there would be no agreement, but that any internal agreement will always be flimsy and weak if the issue of enmity towards Israel is not resolved; and so far, it has not been. In our opinion, the most important common denominator around which the Lebanese could coalesce is that of enmity towards Israel. If the efforts to forge a solid and unified Lebanese position are genuine, this is where we could start. Judging by the

---

(cont'd from previous page) political system, was restructured via amendments to the Lebanese Constitution. Parliament's composition was equally divided between Christians and Muslims, and greater power was given to the Sunni Muslim prime minister. Notably, however, the Shia, a plurality among the 18 official confessions in Lebanon were still restricted to disproportionately fewer seats for their confession, while their leaders remained barred from anything higher than the Speakership.

11. See p. 31, n. 20.

people's stand on the martyrdom of Sayyed Abbas Mussawi and his wife and child—the outpouring of genuine emotion, and condemnations by Lebanese personalities, forces, and parties from all sects—this could be the starting point of this long road ahead. This is where our invitation to the Lebanese people to agree on a common denominator and start on the road ahead comes from.

AS-SAFIR: *Have you already taken the initiative to contact some Christian parties in order to arrive at the common denominator for which you are calling?*

HN: Previously, when Sheikh Subhi Tufeili and then Sayyed Abbas Mussawi were secretaries-general, contacts were made with Christian spiritual and political personalities who did not have any meaningful relationship with Israel. When we launched this call, we addressed it to all the Christians; we are ready to maintain contacts with all Christian personalities and groups that have at least no current dealings with the Israeli enemy. This is what we did before, and will be doing in the next few days, God willing.

AS-SAFIR: *Who with, and how?*

HN: Meetings were held with Christian clergymen under the auspices of our brother, the martyred Sayyed. I remember among them Bishop Khalil Abi Nader from Baalbek, and the Bishop of Tyre, may God rest his soul, who passed away at Christmas. A delegation from Hezbollah also paid a visit to the Bishop of Baalbek, and another delegation from the party's Political Bureau visited a number of Christian families in the Southern Suburb and West Beirut, to wish them Merry Christmas. The same happened in some areas of the south.

AS-SAFIR: *Regarding other parties and forces, such as the Lebanese Forces and the Kataeb...*[12]

HN: I was clear when I said that we have not sought contact with those groups and personalities regarding which there is, so far, no proof that they have ended their dealings with Israel; and we shall not do so in the future.

12. For the Lebanese Forces and *Kataeb*, or Phalange, see above, p. 31 n. 19.

AS-SAFIR: *Does that mean you believe that the Lebanese Forces still have dealings with Israel? Do you still have doubts regarding that matter?*

HN: We are convinced of that (...)

AS-SAFIR: And the Kataeb Party?

HN [continuing]: ... the proof is that there was a number of abductees in the hands of the Lebanese Forces, whose families had visited them several times before they were taken to the occupied territories, and took them clothes and food, and used to receive letters from them.[13] A while later they lost contact with them, only to discover that they were in the occupied territories; their parents received letters from them, written in their own hand, through the Red Cross. Reports by Amnesty International also confirm that fact. Does handing their detainees over to the Israelis mean that they still have dealings with Israel, or that they have ended them?

AS-SAFIR: *Your Eminence; allow us to delve into what you said concerning the Christians. You wondered about the possibility of reaching an internal agreement as long as some parties still have dealings with Israel. There are also some Christians who wonder about the possibility of reaching an agreement as long as the party calls for an Islamic Republic, for the cancellation of political pluralism, and for forcing the others to coexist with extremist Islamic ideologies like the Ahlul Thimma[14] and others.*

---

13. One 1997 report by Amnesty International said, "Amnesty International knows of 21 Lebanese nationals who have been captured in Lebanon and transferred to Israeli prisons either without ever having been sentenced or held beyond the expiry of their sentences. These are just some of the detainees whom Amnesty International believes Israel to be holding as hostages. Most of them were captured by the Israeli Defence Force (IDF) or by one of the pro-Israeli Christian militias in Lebanon, the Lebanese Forces or the South Lebanon army [SLA]. Many of them were held in detention centers in Lebanon under Lebanese Forces' or SLA control before being transferred, usually secretly, to Israel. For many years they were scattered among different prisons and they were frequently moved from one prison to another." Amnesty International, "Israel's Forgotten Hostages: Lebanese Detainees in Israel and Khiam Detention Center," July 10, 1997, accessed online. The mainly Christian-led South Lebanon army was commanded by Major General Antoine Lahd (see below, p. 97 n. 23), and operated inside, and in some areas beyond, the Israeli-declared "security zone" in South Lebanon after 1985.

14. The term refers to non-Muslims who live in the Islamic state, and who must therefore pay sums of money to the government in order to bring them into line with Muslims who already pay part of their income to charity and/or as a contribution to the state.

We have seen an example of this in the southern suburbs, where there was still a limited presence of the Lebanese Forces; but then after 1984 a mass exodus of Christians took place, and the character of the suburbs, which had been a center for Christian–Shia coexistence, totally changed. What can you tell the Christians today? And what guarantees do you offer in return? Categorizing the Christians as agents [of Israel] and nationalists takes us back to an era, prior to 1982, when each side accused the other of treason; and we have seen where this has led us.

HN: When we speak about Christians, we naturally are not talking about all of them, but about those who had dealings with the Israeli enemy. We sometimes also speak about certain Muslims in the south and the western Bekaa,[15] who were even more significant Israeli agents and more treacherous and corrupt; and history is witness to that. I will use the question you asked me to elucidate Hezbollah's vision. In our political statement regarding our vision for the future, we never said that we want to build an Islamic identity through oppression and compulsion at any level. We do not believe in such behavior, because the nature of the issue does not accept it, meaning that we should not build an Islamic government on oppression and compulsion. Any Islamic government anywhere in the world that does not, as a necessary precondition, have a very wide popular base that adopts, defends, and remains loyal to it, cannot succeed. The Islamic government is different from any other government in the world; it is different from a regime that comes to power through a military coup, from a dictatorship, a monarchy, or a tribal regime propped up by the country's army and intelligence service. Historically, and by virtue of its nature, an Islamic government cannot survive or last if it does not have a wide popular base, or if the nation as a whole does not support it. Based on that, I believe that we are entitled—as is every Lebanese citizen—to aspire to the best project or notion that, in our opinion, would lead to the most just, prosperous, secure, and peaceful society. For proof, you can go to Iran and see for yourselves what is happening there.

AS-SAFIR: *But the scope of the country's plurality and its distribution are different in Iran (...)*

15. Here, Nasrallah is probably referring to the presence of Muslim Druze and Shia in the ranks of the SLA.

HN: There are churches being built and (...)

AS-SAFIR: (...) *in also the size of this plurality. By* thimmiya *they might mean a moral and psychological* thimmiya, *not necessarily a materialistic one?*

HN: Let me help you a little here. For example, there are churches and schools (...) during the war,[16] the Christians in Iran fought without there being a general conscription. The Iranian people that volunteered included Christians from all denominations, including Armenians; they all took part in the fighting and gave many martyrs. Before I talk to you about what the Lebanon of tomorrow should look like or anything else, we have to ask, "Will Lebanon remain for the Lebanese or will it escape from their hands?" This essential issue should be our point of departure. Starting a dialogue between Lebanese to plan and agree on the future of this country is very possible, and we are not at all against it. However, there is a saying in our vernacular that says "First the throne, then the etching on the throne"; which means that we have to build the throne first. We see Israel as a danger to us, and do not overestimate the extent of this danger; we see it as it really is and, on the other hand, believe that others are underestimating it. We are saying to the Lebanese, "Come, let us give Lebanon a minimum degree of protection so that the Israeli enemy will not gobble it up; come, let us liberate Lebanon and eliminate the Israeli danger to it and, based on that, we can then solve all impending issues through dialogue." Experience has shown both Christians and Muslims that civil war leads nowhere.

AS-SAFIR: *If Israel implements Resolution 425,[17] pulls back to the internationally recognized borders, and the situation returns to what it was prior to 1982, would*

---

16. A reference to the 1980–88 Iran–Iraq War.

17. See Statement 11 for Nasrallah's discussion of United Nations Security Resolution 425 of 1978—a resolution that, key among four provisions, called upon Israel "immediately to cease its military action against Lebanese territorial integrity and withdraw forthwith its forces from all Lebanese territory." In June 2000, twenty-two years after UNSCR 425 was passed, the United Nations determined that Israel had complied with the Resolution—a contentious claim especially for Hezbollah, who argued that parts of Lebanon remained occupied by Israel. Moreover, despite the ruling, the United Nations Interim Force in Lebanon remained at numerous points along the provisional Lebanon–Israel border, ostensibly as a buffer force between two states still officially in a state of war.

Hezbollah abide by the Resolution or continue to launch operations against Israel across the Lebanese borders?

HN: Let Israel first withdraw and implement Resolution 425; this is a theoretical issue.

AS-SAFIR: *You said before that the battle with Israel is a strategic one. Does this mean that the party will continue launching operations across the borders even if Israel implements Resolution 425?*

HN: The responsibility of liberating Palestine is not only the responsibility of the Palestinian people, but also that of the entire Arab and Islamic nation.

AS-SAFIR: *The perfect harmony between Hezbollah and Iran's policies makes it seem like an Iranian community within Lebanon. What are the particularities that make this party acceptable to all Lebanese?*

HN: When Hezbollah was established in the wake of the invasion and started its resistance against the occupation, it did not fight and give martyrs for Iran's sake, in the strict regional sense. It fought for Lebanese territory, defended Lebanese citizens, and confronted an enemy behaving aggressively against the Lebanese people. I would like to ask, if we want to judge whether or not a given party is genuinely Lebanese: Is there a greater or more important yardstick than one's defense of the land and its people?

We in Lebanon sought to benefit from the experience of the Islamic Revolution in Iran, because it is a pioneering movement, on a global scale, that succeeded in defying the old world order. It also succeeded in building a state, a regime, and an entity outside the framework of compulsory loyalty to either East or West. It gave us many examples from which the Arab and Muslim world could learn.

As to our decision-making process and its links to Iran, we in Hezbollah have a *Shura* [Council] elected rather than appointed by the General Conference;[18] this is proof enough that Hezbollah is an entity unto itself. From the religious point of view, we have a tenet that says that a legitimate leader is

---

18. See Statement 8 for more details on the structure of Hezbollah.

a hard-working and religious scholar who enjoys many relevant attributes. These are, among other things, ability, knowledge, a sense of justice, experience, historical awareness, good management skills, and faith (...) when this man assumes the leadership of the Muslims, and is accepted by the majority, he becomes their leader and legal guardian (...). It is from this perspective that we viewed the legitimacy of Imam al-Khomeini's leadership and guardianship, and now view Sayyed Khameini's leadership and guardianship and deal with him accordingly.[19]

AS-SAFIR: *Let me go back to the latest Israeli military operation. It is clear that you came under pressure to rein in your resistance movement's activities as part of a "small deal" to calm the situation down. Are you worried about what is being planned against you? I am speaking of an Israeli withdrawal in return for the head of the Islamic Resistance movement and Hezbollah.*

HN: I followed up on this issue personally, and we were never under pressure. We fought alongside other brethren within the limits of our abilities, and in the context of a defensive strategy, and when the enemy failed to achieve its objectives we saw the wisdom of containing the situation and returning to our usual resistance methods. It might be true that this move coincided with attempts to put pressure on the Lebanese Government and others, but I can say in all confidence that our decision to cease all armed manifestations and contain the situation[20] was purely based on our own conviction, and not due to any kind of pressure. We made contact with our brothers in Amal, and agreed to call a meeting of the military Quadripartite Committee in the Sidon area—not to formulate an agreement as such, but to implement a number of measures on which we had agreed earlier.

AS-SAFIR: *What about the next phase?*

HN: Previously, we were concerned that Hezbollah's head would be the

---

19. For Khameini, see above, (p. 54 n. 9), and *wilayat al-faqih* (p. 26 n. 9)

20. Nasrallah is referring to Hezbollah's recent prohibition on the display of arms other than in direct operations against Israeli or Israeli-backed forces—a prohibition which would mostly be upheld, save for periodic military parades, and in some areas of the country where Hezbollah operations were centered.

price to pay for Israel's withdrawal; we had some information in this regard and some nationalistic ministers confirmed it to us. I, however, believe that the Lebanese Government is incapable of taking a decision of this kind; there are regional and international factors that prevent this from happening.

AS-SAFIR: What are these regional factors—Iran's position?

HN: Not only Iran; Syria would also not accept that the resistance be targeted. When the [Lebanese] state says that resistance is a legitimate right, it cannot then turn around and target this resistance in return for such a small deal.

AS-SAFIR: *How about the Higher Defense Council's decisions?*

HN: If the objective is to ban armed manifestations, then we are committed to prevent such manifestations in areas where the Lebanese army is deployed, and everywhere else. But if the objective is to ban the resistance, even from areas where the army is deployed, then we would disagree on this.

The way we see it, the reverse is true: it is in areas where the army is deployed that there should be resistance. The army is supposed to be an army of resistance, and should therefore reinforce the resistance and allow it to operate from any area, without parading itself, and [with the resistance operating] in full compliance with security-related conditions.

AS-SAFIR: *Let us move to the issue of the hostages. Some people said that one of the reasons behind the assassination of Sayyed Mussawi was the fact that the release of the two Israelis, detained by the resistance, was not part of the deal.[21] We would like you to elaborate on that and on the issue of the two German hostages.[22]*

---

21. See above, p. 24 n. 1.
22. The systematic kidnapping of Western civilians in Lebanon first came to the fore with the abduction of American University of Beirut President David Dodge in 1981, although he was freed the following year. In just one year, 1984/85, seven US citizens were kidnapped, among them the CIA's station chief in Beirut, William Buckley (March 16, 1984; died in captivity June 1985); the US journalist Terry Anderson (March 16, 1985; released December 4, 1991); and the US Navy diver Robert Dean Stethem, a passenger on board the hijacked TWA Flight 847 (shot and killed June 15, 1985). In January 1987, two citizens of West Germany were abducted by an organization calling itself the "Struggle for Freedom," shortly after the West German government had arrested Muhammad Ali Hamadeh, a Lebanese Shiite who had allegedly masterminded the *(cont'd over)*

HN: Journalists and politicians still insist that Hezbollah has something to do with this hostage issue (...). Let me tell you frankly, the hostages are in the hands of certain groups which have detainees of their own in jails around the world, and are using the only means available to them to get them released. This is also the case with the Germans; Hezbollah has nothing to do with their detention.

AS-SAFIR: *Why was the file of the American hostages so hurriedly closed? What was the quid pro quo?*

HN: What really helped solve the issue of the American hostages was the release of the fifteen prisoners held in Kuwaiti jails, after the events that took place in Kuwait in the wake of the Iraqi invasion.[23] In fact, the group that was holding the American hostages was applying pressure to get prisoners in Kuwait released. Now that this has been accomplished, the group that abducted them has turned its attention to securing the release of prisoners in Israeli jails and bringing back the agents.[24] The main objective, however, has now been accomplished.

AS-SAFIR: *Regarding the issue of the German hostages, Bonn is urging the Europeans to halt their assistance to Lebanon until the release of the hostages. Do you believe that the issue of assistance really depends on the hostages' release?*

HN: The Americans used to say that they would grant assistance to Lebanon after the release of the American hostages, but look what happened. All the

---

(cont'd from previous page) 1985 TWA hijacking (Hamadeh was imprisoned, and eventually granted parole by the German government in 2005). In 1988, the hostage-taking began to subside: indeed, that year, the last French hostages were freed. In 1991, the last American and British hostages were released (among them Anderson and the Archbishop of Canterbury's envoy Terry Waite), while the remaining two Germans were released in 1992. In addition to denying any involvement, Hezbollah officials would routinely note that the Western hostages taken during the Lebanese Civil War were small in number, in light of the fact that, by September 1987, an estimated 6,000 Lebanese had been kidnapped and/or had disappeared since the outbreak of the civil war in 1975.

23. Nasrallah is referring to the Shiite Islamic Dawa party's prisoners, held by Kuwait for an earlier attempted assassination of the Emir of Kuwait. The prisoners, some of whom had direct familial connections with Lebanese Shiites, escaped (although Nasrallah uses the word "release") from jail following the chaos of the Iraqi occupation of Kuwait in 1990.

24. Presumably, those collaborators who had assisted Israel in Lebanon.

Western hostages were released—the Americans, French and English—and where is this assistance? The issue is linked to the political situation, not the hostage situation; it is also linked to the issue of submission to the American fiat.

AS-SAFIR: *What is the latest information you have?*

HN: In the past, contacts revolved around dislodging some of the legal obstacles to get the Hamadeh brothers released from prison in Germany.

AS-SAFIR: *There is talk about contacts regarding the Israeli prisoners. Do you think that the martyrdom of Sayyed Mussawi has further complicated matters?*

HN: We considered the martyrdom of Sayyed Mussawi, his wife and child, as a natural part of our jihadist activities; the incident was expected. We do not function in reaction to given events; we believe in and work for a number of issues, and will continue to believe in and work for them. One of these issues is the release of detainees in enemy hands; this is also Sayyed Mussawi's testament.

AS-SAFIR: *How is Hezbollah's relationship with Syria?*

HN: Those who follow our party's political line and its leaders' statements know full well our position regarding Syria and President Hafez al-Assad; all I can do is reconfirm this position. We see Syria as a genuine support for both Lebanon and the resistance, and we say this not to compliment them—we view Syria as the country most able to lend its support to Lebanon and its people. As far as regional and major issues are concerned, we have asserted that we will stand at Syria's side as it confronts the dangers that threaten Lebanon, Syria, and the entire region.

AS-SAFIR: *In the context of the relationship between Hezbollah and the state, we find that members of Hezbollah refrain from assuming positions in the state's administration, such as the army, security services, and other departments. You took no part in the allotment of positions, and refused to be part of the 30-member government and the national assembly. Now there is talk of municipal and parliamentary elections. What is your position in this regard?*

HN: We have a basic problem with the current regime, for we do not approve of its present formation. We rejected the Taif Agreement, and in a statement released by our Political Bureau we said why this is the case.

We want a formula for governing Lebanon that reflects the will of the Lebanese people, and like any self-respecting country we do not want a formula imposed on the people. The people are well able to elect their own representatives, who will then meet and work on a formula for a new state structure.

The Taif Agreement was transformed into the country's constitution, and this we cannot accept, especially because it enshrines sectarianism; sectarianism was merely a custom in the past, but after Taif it became enshrined in the constitution.[25] The Lebanese have gone backwards instead of forwards. This is precisely why we refuse to take part in a government that has for [its] objective the implementation of the Taif Agreement, which we rejected. We are unimpressed by the status that a ministerial position, a parliamentary seat, or a presidency confers; those who chose the path of martyrdom are naturally not familiar with such phenomena.[26]

AS-SAFIR: *Why not be an opposition from within the government?*

HN: Opposition from within the government in its current formation would not be a real opposition, and would produce nothing; it would just exhaust people's energies.

25. Although Taif identified the abolition of political sectarianism as a national priority, neither Taif nor the amended constitution provided a timeframe for doing so. In a similar vein, and to the further consternation of Hezbollah, since Taif and a subsequent constitutional amendment mandated an equal number of parliamentarians between Christians and Muslims, the one-man, one-vote system of universal suffrage was therefore, once again, precluded. Thus, both a (presumed) Muslim majority within the borders of Lebanon and the full electoral weight of the Shia were also deferred.

26. Nasrallah would, however, soon lead Hezbollah into Lebanon's first post-civil war parliamentary elections, during the summer of 1992. The turnaround had required the approval of Iran's Ayatollah Khameini, as well as a special Hezbollah delegation, which after much debate voted 10:2 in favor of participation. The electoral platform announced by Nasrallah in July 1992 elaborated on a number of themes originally propounded by Hezbollah's Open Letter of 1985: it stressed the essential need for thoroughgoing resistance to Israel; building a fairer political system ultimately freed from the confines of confessionalism; and the stimulation of wider socio-economic development. Overall, though, it was a frank declaration that in order to fight Israel's continuing occupation of Lebanese land (and quite possibly in order to fight Israel in perpetuity), Hezbollah would have to embed itself deeply within the fabric of the Lebanese, not just the Shia, body-politic.

AS-SAFIR: *Where do you want things to go—towards more hiding behind religion? When you refuse sectarianism, and refuse secularism, you are simply reinforcing the fears of others. You seem to want the country to go towards "Islamization", instead of it taking you towards "Lebanonization."*

HN: Would the Christians put up with what some of them did in Lebanon? Would the Muslims put up with what some of them did? We are calling on everybody to come to the negotiating table to agree on a formula for governing Lebanon, and we are ready to cooperate and interact with any formula on which there will be agreement. We will agree to be part of this formula if it further assists this population's interests.

No, sectarianism is not the alternative to a secularism that removes religion from the scene—as if Lebanon's problem right now simply has to do with religious marriage courts, and replacing them by civil courts will further the development of the country. Even in the religious sense, we have many beliefs (…) when Imam Ali was sent to Egypt as governor, he was given Malek al-Ashtari's covenant.[27] This covenant elucidates the notion of non-sectarian political Islam and says, among other things, "Do not rule over them like a savage tiger that sets upon their food, for there are two kinds of people: either a brother to you in religion, or an equal to you in nature." Islamic non-sectarian ideology believes in a common denominator among people, either religion or humanity.

AS-SAFIR: *A Christian, however, does not really want any of that, and it is his right; he has always been here historically, and wants a real partnership in governance. There is pluralism here, and it ought to be respected. The Christian does not want a covenant; he tried that under the Fatimids, and we saw what happened.*

HN: One should not judge Islam based on the Fatimids and Mamelukes … look at what the Mamelukes did to the Shia of Jbeil and Keserouan![28] No, one should not judge Islam on that basis.

27. See p. 52, n. 3.
28. The Fatimids were a Shiite dynasty that ruled over parts of North Africa, Egypt and the Levant from 910 to 1171 CE. The Mamelukes were a Turkic military caste who converted to Islam, and who ruled from 1250 to 1517 CE. From the eleventh to the thirteenth centuries, Shiites migrated in large numbers from Syria, Iraq, and the Arabian Peninsula to the areas of Keserouan, north-east of Beirut and Jbeil, directly north of Beirut. In 1308 the Mamelukes crushed a Shia rebellion in these regions.

It seems, from the way the conversation is going, that the Christians want the Muslims to recognize their right to participate in power. The problem was in fact not like that; the Muslims were the ones who demanded the right to participate in power, and while some Christian leaders responded positively, others argued for privileges over each period and comma. At this point, the fact remains that Lebanon is home to all the Lebanese people, and they choose to coexist. Let us, therefore, find out who really represents this people, and then allow them to embark on a dialogue to arrive at the best formula to govern this country.

5

VICTORY AT THE POLLS

August 25, 1992

Two days after winning eight seats in the rolling parliamentary elections held in the areas in and around the Bekaa Valley, Nasrallah spoke with An-Nahar *newspaper, a decidedly secular daily whose columnists and editorials were generally critical of the party. His approach appears to be one of both confidence and caution—perhaps not surprising, given that the party's domination of the Baalbek-al-Hermel[1] district, as well as locations beyond, had come as a rude awakening for some of the traditional purveyors of sectarian political power in Lebanon.*

Indeed, Hezbollah's unexpectedly strong showing, a mere 50 days after Nasrallah had announced that the party would indeed participate in Lebanon's first post-civil war elections, was of particular concern, not so much for the Christians as for Shiite stalwarts like Speaker of the Parliament Hussein al-Husseini, who would soon resign his post, and to a lesser extent for Amal. Buoyed by the success of several of the party's Maronite, Catholic, and Sunni candidates in Bekaa, Nasrallah makes clear that Hezbollah would henceforth vie for democratic political power in Lebanon—and, more than this, could mobilize a constituency that might just "[pull] the carpet from under the others' feet."

AN-NAHAR: *How do you evaluate the electoral process so far, and how do you view your victory?*

HN: We can say that they went reasonably well from the procedural point of view; problems arise, in one ballot box or the other, in elections anywhere in the world. The fact remains that, in general, the electoral process that just took place was very important, and the number of problems was very

1. The towns of Baalbek and Hermel—in the eastern Bekaa region and north-eastern Lebanon, respectively—were both staunchly supportive of Hezbollah (and remain so), with the former having served as the original rallying place for the party's founding members.

small and far less than what we expected for a country holding elections on the heels of a 17-year war.

Of course, in the beginning we had a problem with the Election Law and submitted a complaint in this regard; but on the day of the elections, our delegates did not register any fundamental or important remarks on the ballot boxes. Delegates for various candidates made a strong showing, and displayed a high degree of awareness regarding the significance of the electoral process—especially since most of them were new to the scene. They were especially concerned about ballot boxes being empty before voting started, and checked the identity of each voter; delegates, especially our own, were given ample opportunity to control the scene. In the end, we believe that the process went well, and as it should have; and the few incidents that happened in certain areas could have happened in the best of elections in any country. I would like to say here that I am speaking only about the elections that have so far taken place; I cannot judge, as of now, elections that will take place later.

In response to the second part of your question, I would say that our victory in the electoral district of Baalbek-al-Hermel did not come as a surprise to us; it was natural and expected. Before the elections I met with a number of officials who asked me, "Do you expect your list to win?" I answered, "For sure." They then asked, "Would you be guaranteed of victory if you fill the two remaining Shiite seats on your list?" I said, "I am absolutely certain that our entire list would win."[2] Our victory and success in the Baalbek-al-Hermel district are both natural and expected; what was surprising, however, was the failure of one of the candidates on our list.

This [our victory] certainty comes from our experience in the region, the services we offer, and the nature of the relationship between our brethren there and people from various sects and groups. I would like to say, in this context, that we kept two Shiite seats on our list vacant because we wanted to avoid a conflict with President Hussein al-Husseini.[3] We entered into a

2. Hezbollah nominated only four party members out of six candidates allocated to the Shia in the district of Baalbek-al-Hermel, choosing instead to leave two seats empty for the purposes of bargaining with other tribal leaders – although some observers argued that the purpose of the maneuver was in fact designed to avoid completely humiliating al-Husseini.

3. Hussein al-Husseini (1937–) was secretary-general of Amal from 1978 until his resignation in 1980. He was elected speaker (a post referred to as president by Lebanese in order to draw equivalency with the Premiership and the Presidency) of the Lebanese parliament in 1984, and presided over the 1989 Taif Accords (for which see above, p. 64 n. 4).

competition between electoral lists only, and considered that leaving two seats vacant would keep the door open for President al-Husseini to return to the National Assembly. I tell you frankly, the numbers support what I am saying: if we had presented a closed and complete list to the public, it would have won in its entirety, and pulled the carpet from under the others' feet.

As for the districts of Zahle[4] and the Western Bekaa, we nominated two candidates there in response to popular demand on the part of our supporters and backers, and of the martyrs' families. These two regions have given a large number of martyrs for the liberation of the country, and we were bound to respond positively to their demands. We ran independently in these two districts against strong lists, and still were serious rivals, and those who follow the numbers closely can attest to this fact. I tell you frankly, our candidates' victory in these two districts was neither a forgone conclusion nor expected; we took part in order to give expression to the people's endorsement of our policies and path. The fact that our two candidates received such a high number of votes is an expression of the wide popular will behind this path. We would not be surprised if the final results reveal that our friends—especially those against whom we ran for the two Shiite seats—have won in these two districts, because this could very well happen given the nature of the elections in these two districts.

AN-NAHAR: *Were there efforts, before the elections, to form a coalition between yourselves and President al-Husseini?*

HN: Of course. There were attempts through intermediaries to form a coalition of sorts, but President al-Husseini has particular issues with that idea, and when these issues prevented the formation of a coalition, he chose to run on one of the lists and we chose to run on another. But we decided to keep our list open out of respect for President al-Husseini's role and status.

AN-NAHAR: *Some say that the elections were rigged in the Bekaa, especially in Baalbek-al-Hermel. What do you say to that?*

---

4. Zahle is the capital of the Bekaa governate, and a majority Christian city.

HN: There were many rumors concerning the presence of armed men and a military siege of the Baalbek brigade. I believe that the high voter turnout in Baalbek-al-Hermel—which, according to the numbers, is the highest ever—means that our people have gone to vote in strength because there is a general tendency in this particular area to take part in electoral processes.

I think that the delegates of those who talk about election-rigging were present on the ground alongside the army, the security forces, and the media, and I do not believe that delegates of other lists running against our own saw any armed presence, except for delegates of Mr. al-Husseini's list. Neither the people, the army, nor journalists saw any of that. Why? We issued a simple statement today, in response to claims regarding the electoral process, in which we said: "[W]e will not say anything ourselves, but leave it to the Lebanese people who took part in the elections, to the citizens of Baalbek-al-Hermel, and to the relevant loyal authorities to say their word on the matter."

As is well known, Hezbollah is not part of the establishment of power, and has therefore nothing to do with the army, the security forces, or editors-in-chief. We were there only as voters, and the ballot boxes were opened and closed in front of all the other candidates' delegates, and the same goes for the vote count. How and where did the rigging take place, then? Why did they contest the elections six hours after the vote-counting process had begun? If the elections were indeed rigged, something would have surfaced at the ballot box. The reasons behind this challenge are clear and known to all; we will say no more about this.

AN-NAHAR: *Some called for the cancellation of the elections in the Bekaa; what is your opinion about that?*

HN: We do not think that the elections will be cancelled. We do expect, however, as well as presume, the spirit of sacrifice and loyalty to the greater good, and to those who stand behind it, to be far larger than what we have witnessed so far. Sacrificing the entire electoral process for personal gain, and to raise one's own morale, only make us hold on to the electoral process even more. Any challenge to the elections should be made legally; and since we have our own delegates as well, we will be able to discuss these incidents wherever they occurred. It is not normal for one person to stand there, claim that there was rigging and cheating, and demand the cancellation of the entire electoral process. As I said before, we do not think that the government would cancel the elections.

AN-NAHAR: *What if this actually happens?*

HN: Then we would decide what our position should be in light of the circumstances.

AN-NAHAR: *Does this mean you do not have a position ready for such an eventuality?*

HN: We might have, but there is no need to announce it now. We are following every word as it is spoken, and every action as it is done.

AN-NAHAR: *Are you not afraid that the Algerian experience would be repeated here?*[5]

HN: There is a big difference between Lebanon and Algeria. The problem with the regime in Algeria is that the Islamists took over parliament and occupied more than two-thirds of its seats; this would have allowed them to change the shape of the country. In Lebanon, the country's make-up, its pluralistic nature, and the distribution of parliamentary seats, are not conducive to something along the lines of what happened in Algeria. I therefore believe that our party's participation in the National Assembly, regardless of the number of seats we eventually obtain, should not scare the people here like it did the Algerian regime. The reaction to our victory should therefore not be similar to what happened there. Our participation in the National Assembly would happen through true and loyal young people who have good experience, are ready for sacrifice, and therefore could not be bought or sold.

---

5. The interviewer is referring to the extremely bloody, decade-long Algerian Civil War, triggered in December 1991 when the government canceled elections after first round results showed an impending victory for the Islamic Salvation Front. The resultant conflict between Islamist guerrillas and government forces, as well as intra-Islamist fighting, is estimated to have resulted in the deaths of up to 200,000 people.

They would not bend under pressures or seek their own personal interests at the expense of the people and the country.

Our participation in the National Assembly will give us the added strength to assume our important and essential position in Lebanon's political life. One should therefore not view Hezbollah's victory the same way as the Islamist victory in Algeria.

AN-NAHAR: *What would your position be if the authorities cancel the election process?*

HN: This is also part of the whole issue. I do not expect the authorities to cancel the elections. Did anything new happen to justify the cancellation of the electoral process, of the entire project of elections, and waste all the important reasons behind [the elections] and all the relevant evaluations and analyses that went into it? Is it because a number of personalities on Mr. al-Husseini's list did not win? Does this new development justify wasting an entire process for which so much effort has been exerted? Would all those boycotts and declarations go with the wind just because a group of people were not lucky enough to win in one of the districts? If this happens, it would be one of the most bizarre aspects of Lebanese politics!

AN-NAHAR: *What would your next political move be if you do not win seats in the National Assembly? And would this mean that you would transform yourselves from a military into a political party?*

HN: We submitted an electoral program earlier based on action, not electoral propaganda. Our parliamentarians will take it to the National Assembly and try as hard as possible to see it implemented. They will do their best even if their courage and steadfastness put them under a lot of pressure and expose them to danger. Our brethren and our leaders are well known for their constancy and for caring about the people's problems, even if this leads to their martyrdom, as happened with His Eminence the secretary-general and master of all the Islamic Resistance's martyrs, Sayyed Abbas al-Mussawi.[6]

We were never a military party or militia; we put ourselves forward as a

6. For Mussawi, see Statement 3.

82

jihadi movement to confront the ongoing occupation and the aggression on our people and land. Our participation in the National Assembly does not detract whatsoever from our being a resistance movement, because the call to duty and the reasons that compel some individuals, or an entire people, to resist against continued occupation, are still valid.

AN-NAHAR: *What are your expectations regarding your candidates in the southern suburbs of Beirut? And what do you say regarding the electoral battle in the south?*

HN: As far as the southern suburbs of Beirut are concerned, we attach a lot of hope to our chances for victory, and I think that the picture there will become clearer this week. As for the south, we agreed with our brother, Nabih Berri,[7] and with our brethren in the Amal Movement, to participate in the elections in the south on a joint list, which would include candidates from the party, the Movement, and other forces and personalities.[8]

AN-NAHAR: *The issue of the elections in the Bekaa had many ramifications. How do you view the situation, especially in light of President al-Husseini's resignation?*

HN: In the course of our conversation, I expressed my astonishment at what has happened. We expected the will and choice of the people to be met with a degree of reason, with a democratic spirit, and with a readiness to sacrifice one's moral satisfaction, and personal interests, for the sake of the nation as a whole. However, now that this has happened, we hope and count on our ability to deal with it using the same psychological methods that led us to the situation we are in at present. I believe that all efforts will now go in that direction, and hope that, with God's help, things will continue to proceed normally, which is what we are noticing from the general atmosphere and statements made by a number of officials.

---

7. Nabih Berri (1938–) is head of the Shia Amal Party, and currently speaker of the Lebanese parliament. Berri became leader of Amal in April 1980, and led the movement through the Lebanese Civil War.

8. Despite Nasrallah's agreeable tone here, participating on joint lists with Amal would serve as a particular point of contention for Hezbollah in the future—especially as far as Syria was concerned. Indeed, Damascus would at times force Hezbollah to scale back its parliamentary demands in favor of its preferred Shiite ally, Amal.

6

"HEZBOLLAH IS NOT AN IRANIAN COMMUNITY IN LEBANON"

September 11, 1992

This interview with the Lebanese, pan-Arab magazine Al-Watan Al-Arabi *came as the party was well on its way towards winning an impressive presence in the soon-to-be constituted national parliament, with twelve seats out of 128 in all. Although Nasrallah stresses that resistance operations and an overall culture of resistance would still be Hezbollah's primary concerns in the future, he also makes clear that both can only survive on the basis of broad public support. However, he qualifies, while competing for democratic political power may be a necessity, Lebanon's current political system can only be engaged to a limited extent, given the persistence of formal and informal sectarianism.*

Of course, to a certain degree his argument is self-serving: Shiites were believed to hold a plurality in Lebanon's sectarian score-sheet. A deconfessionalized system closer to one-person, one-vote would most likely extend Shiite power and influence, perhaps even as far as the presidency or the premiership, reserved by tradition for a Maronite and a Sunni, respectively. Nasrallah attempts to defuse this issue by saying, "The aim is to establish a balance between rights and responsibilities, make ability the yardstick for promotion, and lay down the foundations of a suitable infrastructure headed by competent people." Why, he continues, "insist on appointing only a Maronite at the head of the Central Bank? What is the logic behind it? The most competent person for the job, and for establishing civil and economic peace in the country, could be a Greek Orthodox, a Druze, an Alawite, or someone from any other minority."

Elsewhere, Nasrallah goes to some length in stressing Hezbollah's focus on national concerns, downplaying the question of Iranian influence that is explicit, though still somewhat ambiguous, in the party's adherence to wilayat al-faqih.[1] *But stressing the specificity of any Islamic*

---

1. For *wilayat al-faqih,* see above, p. 26 n. 9.

84

project—and therefore the limitations of such a project in Lebanon—proves somewhat uncon-
vincing for Nasrallah's interlocutor, just as it would for later interviewers who, along with
some Lebanese, would continue to express concern over Hezbollah's ultimate direction.

AL-WATAN AL-ARABI: *Did the results recently achieved by Hezbollah in several*
electoral districts surprise you? Were they up to your expectations? And why did you
doubt your results, as Deputy Albert Mansour, who spoke about an armed occupation
of the Baalbek barracks, mentioned?[2]

HN: One of the reasons we took part in the parliamentary elections was our
confidence in the size of our public support, our popular base, and our credibility with the people.[3] Let me give you a brief summary of what happened
in the Bekaa. The area is divided into three electoral districts: Baalbek-al-
Hermel, Zahle, and the Western Bekaa-Rachaya.[4] The results of the Baalbek-
al-Hermel elections came as no surprise to us; they were natural and expected.
We would have been surprised had the opposite happened because, as you
all know, Hezbollah has a very strong popular base in the area.[5] No one

2. Albert Mansour (1939–) had been nominated for the Catholic seat on Speaker Hussein al-
Husseini's list. He called for the cancellation of the election results in the Baalbek-al-Hermel
district—due, he alleged, to forgery committed by Hezbollah delegates at the polling stations.
Professor Ahmad Nizar Hamzeh, formerly of the American University of Beirut, would later write
that "Hezbollah security forces immediately seized all centers threatening to use arms against anyone
who would call for cancellation," although the use or appearance of force is vigorously disputed
by Nasrallah in the interview that follows. Ahmad Nizar Hamzeh, "Lebanon's Hezbollah: from
Islamic revolution to parliamentary accommodation," (*Third World Quarterly*, Vol. 14, No. 2, 1993;
accessed online).
3. By the end of the rolling elections, Hezbollah had secured an impressive political bloc from a
number of districts, which included the following MPs: Ibrahim Amin al-Sayyid (Shia), Baalbek
Hermel; Ali Taha (Shia), Baalbek-al-Hermel; Muhammad Hasan Yaghi (Shia), Baalbek-al-Hermel;
Khodr Tlays (Shia), Baalbek-al-Hermel; Ibrahim Bayan (Sunni), Baalbek-al-Hermel; Munir al-Hujayri
(Sunni), Baalbek-al-Hermel; Rabiha Kayrouz (Maronite), Baalbek-al-Hermel; Saoud Rufayil (Greek
Orthodox), Baalbek-Hermel; Muhammad Finaysh (Shia), the south; Muhammad Raad (Shia), the
south; Muhammad Ahmad Berjawi (Shia), Beirut; Ali Fadl Ammar (Shia) Baabda.
4. For Zahle, and Baalbek, see above, p. 79, n. 3 and p. 77, n. 1, respectively.
5. According to one study by American University of Beirut professor Farid El Khazen, the
1992 parliamentary elections "were greatly blemished by irregularities and defects in preparation,
the most important case of which being the administrative chaos prior to the elections, and on Election
Day, especially in the north and the Bekaa. This is not to speak of the overt, armed presence by
some militias, specifically, Hezbollah and Amal in the Bekaa and the south, which had a direct
impact on the election campaigns, and of course, on the election results." Khazen further points
out that the rolling elections saw the lowest level of voter turnout since independence—30.34 per
cent, compared to a post-1960 percentages that had fluctuated between 50 and (cont'd over)

can deny that, especially in view of Hezbollah's long history of resistance, services, and cultural activities; granting the citizens what the authorities have failed to deliver; and the long tenure of the area's deputies in parliament. The people expressed their appreciation through popular rallies before the elections, and through the festival in Ras al-Ain Square, held under the slogan "Loyalty and acclamation for the list of the resistance."[6] The popular enthusiasm displayed in Baalbek al-Hermel towards Hezbollah can be mustered by no other political party or personality. These masses assured us of victory even before the ballot boxes were open, which explains our confidence that our electoral list would win. As for the incidents that are supposed to have happened, we did not hear about any challenges, problems, or remarks of this nature before vote-counting began. We can go into the details and say that the challenges and accusations started six hours after vote-counting began, and it became obvious, based on the preliminary results, that our party had won.

This is when the tumult started and rumors surfaced about an armed presence during the daytime. If these incidents really took place, why did no one mention anything about them on the day? The people of Baalbek-al-Hermel participated en masse in the elections because of their conviction; and the army, internal security services and journalists, who do not follow our orders, were present everywhere. The journalists were there, as were delegates from other lists, and no one except for President al-Husseini's delegate[7] noticed any armed presence. All these claims and pretences were therefore just an attempt to cover up failure; we will leave it to the people of Baalbek, and other concerned parties who witnessed the election process, to judge for themselves. Furthermore, official sources, such as the Ministry of the Interior and others, have confirmed what I am telling you.

(cont'd from previous page) 53 per cent—which was greatly exacerbated by a concerted Christian boycott in some areas of the country, especially in Mount Lebanon. Nevertheless, Khazen notes, "we can say that Hezbollah's crushing victory in winning eight seats ... was an obvious sign of the Party's influence and high level of organization in the region, and that this result did not surprise some observers." Farid El-Khazen, "The First Post-War Parliamentary Elections in Lebanon: Bulwarks of the New Democracy," in Farid el-Khazen and Paul Salem, eds, *Lebanon's First Postwar Elections: Facts, Figures, and Analysis* (Lebanese Center for Policy Studies: Beirut, 1993; accessed online).

6. Hezbollah's parliamentary representatives would later take their seats as the "Loyalty to the Resistance Bloc." Ras al-Ain Square is in Baalbek.

7. See p. 85, n. 2 and Statement 5.

There remains the issue of election-rigging. Here I should say that delegates from other currents and lists were present, and saw the ballot boxes being opened and closed, and made sure that they were empty. Voting then started, followed by a vote count undertaken by the same people who had supervised the elections; results were registered, and then signed by the delegates. Where and how did the rigging occur? On the other hand, we have proof that people from other lists did attempt to rig the elections, but we chose not to raise the issue. Challenging the election results six hours after vote-counting had started is no more than an attempt by President al-Husseini and his list to extricate themselves from the results. Not only have we won, but our list is way ahead of the others; the difference in the number of votes, between the lowest number on our list and the highest number polled by the head of the rival list, is in the thousands.

AL-WATAN AL-ARABI: *Why did Hezbollah not achieve the same results in the western Bekaa and Rachaya, against the list of the Interior Minister General Sami al-Khateeb,[8] in spite of your strong mobilization power and [social] services in the area?*

HN: There is a large sectarian variety in the districts of Zahle and the western Bekaa, and we ran independently for the Shia seat in both these districts. We faced a very tough list in Zahle, and two very tough ones in the western Bekaa, and still our candidates received a relatively high number of votes given that they were running independently. We did not expect them to receive a large number of votes, since they were running against candidates who usually benefit from the votes of various local groups; still, the difference between them was not so great. The results in both Zahle and the western Bekaa, as far as I am concerned, were very natural and logical considering that we did not participate based on the assumption that we were definitely going to win. We ran in response to our popular base, which put its trust in our candidates in spite of running independently.

---

8. Sami al-Khateeb, a Sunni from the western Bekaa, was a brigadier-general in the Lebanese army before being appointed interior minister under Prime Minister Rashid Al Solh in 1992. Khateeb eventually settled the running dispute over the election results in the Baalbek-al-Hermel elections by declaring them accurate and legitimate.

AL-WATAN AL-ARABI: *Do you expect a similar scenario to the one in Baalbek to take place in the south? And will your electoral rivalry with the leader of the Amal Movement, Nabih Berri, be a fight to the finish?*[9]

HN: The situation is different in the south. I cannot say that the south shelters the resistance, because the Bekaa shelters the resistance and remains its main source of energy. The south, however, is the battleground of the resistance, its area of confrontation, the place where various political differences are resolved, and an area laden with past tragedies. Hezbollah and Amal are therefore compelled to run there side by side, and as a unified force, due to various considerations relevant to Islam and national aspirations, and to liberation and unity. The two parties should therefore approach the elections while bearing in mind the importance of unity and the need to avoid falling into the trap of apportioning power, as well as the number of seats each can win. We agreed with Mr. Nabih Berri to run on a unified list in the south.

AL-WATAN AL-ARABI: *Why did you decide suddenly to play the local political game and be part of the deal-making, the bazaar-like atmosphere, and the buying and selling deals that take place there? Are you getting used to the system, which you at first refused to recognize, based on instructions you received from outside?*

HN: In reality, we were, and will always be, the party of the resistance that [operates] from Lebanon in reaction to occupation and daily aggression. Any party, movement or faction that abandons resistance under any pretext, and for any reason, is giving up on a sacred duty. Our participation in the elections and entry into the National Assembly do not alter the fact that we are a resistance party; we shall, in fact, work to turn the whole of Lebanon into a country of resistance, and the state into a state of resistance. In the past, a number of state officials promised that if negotiations did not lead to the liberation of the land, the entire population, and the state itself, would be transformed into a resistance force. We said before, and are saying again

9 Amal and Hezbollah had formed an electoral alliance that would soon take 22 of 23 seats in the south. But the strong showing was generally viewed as a boost for Hezbollah at the expense of Amal, not least because two of the party's candidates garnered more votes than did the southern stalwart Berri himself.

now, that negotiations will not succeed, and that it is now time to act on that promise.

This is as far as the resistance is concerned. As for the domestic situation, we feel that paying attention to it is a responsibility that we cannot abandon. There is a dialectical link, here, between the resistance and the internal situation in Lebanon, because for the resistance to survive there should be a community that adopts it and adopts the resistance fighter. This means that, in order to remain steadfast, that fighter needs to secure all the support he needs politically, security-wise, culturally, and economically—and [he needs to] be provided with the means of livelihood. The battle therefore also takes place on the domestic front. Regardless of the resistance, however, there are internal issues that are important to the people in the political and economic spheres, and in their daily lives. In Islam, the act of serving the people and God's families, rescuing the oppressed, saving the distressed, and stretching out one's hand to the weak and the dispossessed, are a huge part of the faith. These [actions] are mentioned in the Quran, and we want to encourage them anew.

As for the [current Lebanese] regime, we believe that its main problem is its sectarian nature; this compels us all to find ways of eliminating this flaw, by which I mean political sectarianism itself and the resulting apportioning of positions in the state administration, in development, and in various [social] services. This has led to major dysfunction, to tragedies, and even to the wars that this country has witnessed. The system is also beset by a mentality of distinction and superiority, which has led in the past to civil war, and might again be the spark that reignites it at any moment.

AL-WATAN AL-ARABI: *How can we convince the people that Hezbollah is actually non-sectarian and not trying to enshrine sectarianism; have you not called for an "Islamic State" in Lebanon?*

HN: We want to eliminate political sectarianism and lay down the foundations for a system of governance that reflects the people's aspirations for justice and equality in the [social] services and development sectors. The aim is to establish a balance between rights and responsibilities, to make ability the yardstick for promotion, and to lay down the foundations of a suitable infrastructure headed by competent people. For example, the most competent president of the Central Bank could be someone who is not a Maronite, but rather someone who—thanks to his financial and business acumen—is able to take the country out of the impasse. Why insist on appointing only a Maronite at the head of the Central Bank? What is the logic behind it? The most competent person for the job, and for establishing civil and economic peace in the country, could be a Greek Orthodox, a Druze, an Alawite, or someone from any other minority. The same question could be posed about the Maronite identity of the president of the republic.[10] This is why the elimination of political sectarianism, which we are focusing on, is one of our priorities, and we are very serious about it.

Regarding the project of the Islamic Republic, I can assure you that we will never propose this option per se in Lebanon, neither through statements, slogans or speeches. We also said that this sectarian system is unjust and corrupt, and should therefore be replaced by another that reflects the will of the Lebanese people and establishes justice, security, peace and equality. As far as a new system of governance is concerned, a communist could say that Marxism is the best system for the new state; any other ideologue could put forth another philosophy of governance, which he believes would be guaranteed to solve the country's problems. We are in effect saying to the Lebanese people that if they choose an Islamic system, we would hasten to support it. We believe, based on our Muslim faith, that a system that rests on Islamic principles will be able to solve all Lebanon's problems, be they legislative, legal, intellectual, spiritual or moral.

We have never proposed the idea of imposing an Islamic Republic on Lebanon by force, and will not do that in the future, because the nature of the Islamic Republic does not lend itself to forceful action. This government would not be able to govern according to Islamic principles, or indeed survive, in the absence of overwhelming popular support. An Islamic government is an ideological entity committed, by virtue of its religious teachings—as well as legislatively and legally—to follow divinely inspired rules; it is moreover not a government of intelligence services, or of political parties, that can impose itself on the people by the force of arms. To be able to exist, an Islamic government presupposes the existence of popular support and strong conviction behind it. We do not deny the fact that it is

10 The National Pact (see above, p. 31 n. 18) stipulated that the office of president always be held by a Maronite.

our wish and desire to see the emergence of an Islamic system, because we are first of all Muslims, and not about to give up on our religious identity.

What others object to, we will not propose in the first place; in other words, we do not want to establish an Islamic government by force. However, we are calling upon the people to join Islam, and saying that Lebanon should be an open space for all. We fully understand that a communist would want a communist state, and a Muslim or Christian would want a state that reflects his own faith or ideology. What we do not understand, however, is someone who wants to impose on others by force, or through violent means, his own beliefs and a governance system of his choice. This we will never do.

AL-WATAN AL-ARABI: *Why are you an extension of Iran in Lebanon and a tool in Tehran's hands? Most experts and specialists believe that Hezbollah is an Iranian tool whose duty is to Islamize Lebanon by force, as has happened in Tunisia and Algeria.[11] Even your theoretical infrastructure is a page out of the Iranian Revolution's textbook, and does not reflect your local credentials.*

HN: There are several points to attend to here. Ever since the Prophet, may God's blessing be upon Him, launched his message, Islam has been around not only as a religion and ritual of faith, but also to organize people's lives until judgment day. It has the ability to adapt and respond to changes in time and space, as well as to life's many reversals; it has been the dream of the Muslim people for hundreds of years, and its theory still exists and is still valid. Before the Islamic Revolution in Iran happened, many Muslim scholars and movements adopted this project and worked hard to implement it. In the meantime, the Western and Islamic worlds were awash in foreign-inspired ideologies pouring in from East and West. The most distinct achievement of the Iranian Revolution was its success in shaking up the world, giving a spiritual and moral boost to the already existing ideology, crystallizing it, and awakening the Muslims. It compelled them to re-examine various tenets and theories, and produced an awakening in the Islamic world.

Be assured that every Islamic entity is part of the particular milieu in which it exists; and each milieu, in turn, has its own specificities. Hezbollah is not

11 For Algeria, see above, p. 81 n. 5.

an Iranian community in Lebanon, and its fighters and *mujahidin* are not Iranian citizens. What is funny is that, a week ago, the American ambassador in Beirut went about gathering information regarding the resistance fighters in the south, in order to be able to answer the question, "Are they Lebanese or not?" In the meantime, as a Lebanese movement, when we lose a martyr, we are proud of him—we announce his name to the public and hold celebrations and weddings in his honor. These martyrs are the sons of southern towns and villages.

AL-WATAN AL-ARABI: *Where are Iranian financial aid, training, and armaments going?*[12] *Your party's submission to Iran's policies, calculations, and interests is almost total.*

HN: Even at the level of international law and internationally recognized norms, a people whose land is occupied has the right to resist occupation. It also has the right, whenever it needs assistance, to reach out to friends who are ready to lend it the support and assistance it needs to liberate its land.

AL-WATAN AL-ARABI: Why not appeal to Arab parties who are active, have the [necessary] means, are more concerned, and provoke less fear and suspicion in others? What does Iran have to do with Lebanon's fate?

HN: Iranian assistance is in any case available for Lebanon's *mujahidin*, regardless of whether Arab parties are willing to assist them or not. For humanitarian and faith-based reasons, our brothers in Iran consider themselves responsible and are eager to assist any oppressed and dispossessed people in the world; this policy, which the Islamic Republic is now putting into practice, was devised by Imam al-Khomeini. But whenever it was unable to assist an oppressed, defeated or dispossessed people, it was only because it did not have the means or the proper avenues to channel this aid to the intended recipient. I am certain that the Islamic Republic is equally generous to the oppressed Muslim population of Bosnia-Herzegovina, slaughtered on a daily

12 The US State Department, in its annual reports on global terrorism, repeatedly charged through the late 1990s that Hezbollah received approximately $100 million annually in financial support from Iran.

basis as the world watches.[13] If this assistance proves insufficient, the reasons would undoubtedly be beyond its control.

AL-WATAN AL-ARABI: *Do you think that, because of the existing imbalance of power, your resistance against Israel has converted the south into a scorched earth, and has not succeeded in liberating a single inch of it, especially given that there is no Lebanese consensus over this method of resistance? Why do you insist on burdening Lebanon with more than it can handle? Why resist now while direct negotiations are taking place in Washington?*[14]

HN: From the resistance's perspective, both the resistance in Lebanon and the future of the region follow the same logic, for since 1982 there have been two competing theories in Lebanon. One theory, which has been around since the day Israel invaded Lebanon in 1982, and which still persists, says that the Lebanese people have to tone down and limit their activities to the political and diplomatic spheres, both regionally and internationally. This theory focuses on international efforts underway to pressure Israel to withdraw from Lebanon. Others say, on the other hand, that they would support the resistance option provided it operates within the context of a unified Arab strategy—which is in fact an impossible proposition. Even if we adopt this theory, could this unified Arab strategy, in the aftermath of the 1982 invasion, go to Nabatieh[15] without having to pass through Israeli

13. Iran supplied humanitarian aid, including fuel, to Bosnian Muslims throughout the brutal Bosnian War that was fought between March 1992 and November 1995 in the former Yugoslavia. Iran was believed to have also funded various political parties and armed groups, however. Indeed, in one well-publicized incident, UN officials found weapons in an Iranian aircraft that was supposed to be delivering relief supplies—a violation of the UN arms embargo then in place.

14. Ever since the Madrid peace conference of 1991, which had brought together Israel and its neighbors in multilateral talks, US and Lebanese officials had been engaged in negotiations to end the Israeli occupation of south Lebanon. But the insistence of Syria's Hafez al-Assad that any deal between Lebanon and Israel conclude only after a deal with Syria (his famous "Syria First" dictate) greatly obstructed any separate progress on the Lebanese track. Still, as one former Lebanese ambassador would later note, the various terms that Israel insisted on also served as powerful impediments in their own right. Lebanese officials involved in the discussions, the former ambassador said, "had [their own] problems with conceding anything beyond the armistice framework. [And] Israel wanted to keep monitoring stations on Lebanese territory, for example, which was unacceptable to us." Nicholas Noe, "The Relationship Between Hezbollah and the United States in Light of the Current Situation in the Middle East," MPhil Dissertation, Cambridge University Center for International Studies, p. 58.

15 Nabatieh, one of the largest cities in south Lebanon, and only 25km from the provisional Israel-Lebanon border, stood just outside the "security zone" that Israel occupied until its withdrawal in 2000.

checkpoints? Of course not—for if the Israelis remain in the south, in the Southern Suburb and in the mountains, they would not have withdrawn a single inch.[16] If the political–diplomatic route had been any good, we would have regained the Golan Heights, the West Bank, the Gaza Strip, and the 1948 territories by now.[17]

AL-WATAN AL-ARABI: *Then why negotiate in Washington at all? Why are we Lebanese more royalist than the king? Why do you impose mirage-like liberation theories on a badly broken Lebanon, when the Palestinians are thirsting for self-rule, asking for municipal authority, making concessions, and all Arab fronts have quietened down?*

HN: Ours is another theory, one that contradicts that of diplomatic chivalry and international forums: it advocates going to war against the enemy. They said that those who advocate this are insane; we said in response, let us try—the sane can talk politics and the insane can fight. Be certain that the theory of the sane will not bear fruit, but that of the insane—the *mujahidin*, the martyrs and suicide bombers—has already caused the enemy to bleed, and has doubled the number of its dead and wounded. The bleeding within the Zionist entity has added public pressure on the enemy's government, and put in front of it two clear options: either it remains in the south and suffers additional human losses, or withdraws. This is why it has already withdrawn back to the frontier zone.

Experience and common sense have shown that the theory of resistance is still valid, and that the other logic has failed and should therefore not be counted on anymore. Some might then say, "Why is your front the only one open?"; and I would tell them that the front should remain open as

16. Although the Arabic text is unclear at this point, Nasrallah is most likely suggesting, as he had previously, that Israel would not have withdrawn from the environs of Beirut or elsewhere unless pressured to do so by resistance operations.
17. Syria's Golan Heights, as well as the West Bank, the Gaza Strip, and Egypt's Sinai Peninsula, were all lost to Israel during the Six-Day War of June 5–10, 1967. The term "1948 territories" refers to the land upon which the state of Israel was declared in May 1948 by future Israeli Prime Minister David Ben-Gurion, as well as the additional land included in the 1949 Armistices signed between Israel and her Arab neighbors after the hostilities of the previous year had ceased. The borders of the state of Israel before the Six-Day War thus comprised approximately 78 per cent of British Mandatory Palestine, compared to the pre-1948 54.5 per cent allotted by the UN Partition Plan of November 1947.

long as the land is still occupied. We have to continue to make the enemy bleed. The resistance has another aim—namely, to awaken the region's masses. This means that the resistance has two interim objectives: the first is to keep the enemy bleeding through guerrilla warfare against its military patrols and positions, and to cover its entire body with wounds; the other is to awaken the masses.

In 1983 the resistance started with 200 *mujahidin*, and now, in 1992, there are thousands of them. Do you think the miraculous *intifada* within the occupied territories[18] would have been possible if not for the resistance in Lebanon? The leaders of the *intifada* themselves say that they found revolutionary inspiration and were able to overcome the obstacle of fear, thanks to suicide operations in Lebanon. This is why we believe that it would be wrong to close down our front until another one opens up, so that we can then become a part of it; the right thing to say is that our front should remain open so that other fronts can also open. We are counting on the day when the will of the people is manifest to all.

In my estimation, a war of attrition rather than a classical war is liable to destroy the Zionist entity; this war might be ongoing even while negotiations are underway, or reconciliation is in the offing. I believe, based on our insight into the enemy's mentality—whether it is Shamir- or Rabin-inspired,[19] and given its revolutionary dreams and plans[20]—that [Israel] will give the Arabs too little in comparison with what the negotiators hope to achieve. I do not think anyone in the world can impose reconciliation and normal-

18. The first *intifada* (or "shaking off," alternatively "rebelling"), which effectively lasted from 1987 until the signing of the Oslo Agreement in 1993, came to define the seemingly untenable Israeli occupation of Palestinian territories—all the more so as Palestinian expressions of discontent, directed both at Israel and to a certain extent the Tunis-based PLO, became overshadowed by street violence, bloody crackdowns, and, increasingly, Palestinian-on-Palestinian violence. Some 1,500 Palestinians and 400 Israelis were killed during the uprising (see http://www.btselem. org/English/Statistics/First_Intifada_Tables.asp).

19. A Member of the Knesset (Israeli Parliament) for the right-wing Likud Party, Yitzhak Shamir (1915-) served as Israeli prime minister from 1983 to 1984, and again from 1986 to 1992. Labour's Yitzhak Rabin (1922–95) was prime minister from 1974 until 1977, and again from 1992 until his assassination at the hands of a radical Orthodox Israeli, Yigal Amir, in Tel Aviv in 1995.

20. Nasrallah is presumably referring to the "Greater Israel" vision promulgated by Israel's founding father, David Ben-Gurion, which imagined a Jewish state encompassing territory beyond British Mandate Palestine, including south Lebanon, the western parts of Jordan, and southern Syria around the Golan Heights. During and preceding the second Israeli invasion of Lebanon, in 1982, various political figures in Israel made it clear that Ben-Gurion's vision was not only achievable, insofar as Lebanon was concerned, but was also fast approaching realization

ization on the people of the region; America could impose certain regimes on the area—even reconciliation with Israel—but not normalization.

AL-WATAN AL-ARABI: *Could we say that, given its activities in Lebanon, Hezbollah is one of the outcomes of a political and strategic understanding between Iran and Syria?*

HN: Hezbollah is in fact the outcome of a self-propelled movement launched in the wake of the Israeli invasion of 1982. This means that it is the outcome of the will and decision of a group of Lebanese people who were inspired by Khomeini's ideology, and who took advantage of the climate created by the Islamic Revolution, and Syrian support, to launch a resistance movement against occupation.

AL-WATAN AL-ARABI: *A Western information source speaks about indirect negotiations taking place, at a hotel in Paris, between your party and Israel regarding the prisoner, Ron Arad,[21] and the possibility of exchanging him for some of your own prisoners and hostages in Israeli prison camps.*

HN: There is no link whatsoever between the issue of the hostages and that of the prisoners. Hezbollah has absolutely nothing to do with the foreign hostages who were in Lebanon, whether the West believes it or not.[22] The party has announced more than once that it did not detain them; nor did it have anything to do with the ensuing negotiations, no matter whether the West wishes to believe it or not. This is therefore not my problem, although for us this is clearly an important issue. As far as the Israeli prisoners are concerned, we are indeed holding a number of them, and indirect negotiations have actually taken place, because we believe that it is our legitimate, brotherly, and moral responsibility to secure the release of prisoners held in Israeli jails, without any sectarian, partisan or factional prejudice. There have also been some positive developments, since a number of prisoners were released. But the process stopped at the issue

21. Lt.-Col. Ron Arad's F-4 Phantom was shot down over Lebanon in 1986. The Amal leader Nabih Berri (see above, p. 25 n. 4) announced that Arad (1958–?) was being held by Amal, and proposed exchanging him for Shiite and Lebanese prisoners held in Israel. Hezbollah has constantly denied having any knowledge about Arad; in 2006 Nasrallah publicly stated that he believed Arad was dead, although some accounts have said that Arad was sold by Amal to the Iranian government, where he is currently being held.
22. See p. 72, n. 22.

of pilot Ron Arad, about whom we have no information whatsoever, since he is not in our custody, and we therefore know nothing about his fate.

We have nothing to do with the negotiations surrounding the fate of the pilot, but we do have two Israeli prisoners in custody, as well as a group of soldiers from Lahd's army,[23] and are trying to arrange an exchange through a third party. The same principles according to which the foreign hostages held in Lebanon were released should be applied to our own hostages in Khiam[24] and other prisons inside Israel.

AL-WATAN AL-ARABI: *Why have you evacuated the Sheikh Abdullah barracks in Baalbek at this particular point in time, and handed it over to the Lebanese army? Does it have anything to do with Secretary Baker's visit to the city of Zahle?*[25]

HN: Handing over the barracks is part of Hezbollah policy. When we took over the Sheikh Abdullah barracks we did so in a peaceful manner, through a popular demonstration at the head of which were women, children, and senior citizens, while the young men remained at the very back. This happened at a time when [President] Amine Gemayel was preparing to use the Lebanese army against large numbers of Lebanese citizens, both in the mountains and in Beirut's Southern Suburb.[26] When we advanced and marched to the

23 Major General Antoine Lahd (1927–) led the Israeli-backed SLA in the "security zone" in south Lebanon, following the death of the SLA's founder Saad Haddad in 1984. Seriously hurt in an assassination attempt in 1988, Lahd later moved to Israel following the May 2000 Israeli withdrawal, and the SLA's subsequent collapse.

24 Khiam Detention Center, probably the most notorious among the Israeli-controlled prisons on either side of the provisional Israel-Lebanon border, was located in the town of Khiam, south Lebanon, near Nabatieh. Controlled by Israel's proxy militia, the SLA, it was routinely cited by human rights groups as a center for torture and abuse. Its liberation in May 2000 brought incredible scenes, broadcast live around the Arab world, of stunned prisoners, some of whom had been in solitary confinement for over a decade, stumbling out of the prison into the embrace of cheering crowds of Lebanese. Although Khiam was later turned into a Hezbollah-affiliated museum, Israeli jets destroyed the site in the first days of the July War.

25 On July 23, 1992, US Secretary of State James Baker traveled from Syria to Lebanon's Bekaa Valley to meet Lebanese President Elias Hrawi, Prime Minister Rashid Solh, and Foreign Minister Fares Bouiez.

26 Amine Gemayel (1942–), son of the founder of the Kataeb or Phalange Party Pierre Gemayel, was elected president of Lebanon by the National Assembly on September 21, 1982, shortly after the assassination of his brother, President Bashir Gemayel. He served as president until 1988. The Sheikh Abdullah barracks became the locus point for joint Hezbollah-Iranian activities throughout the decade and was rumored to have been the holding site for numerous Western hostages.

barracks, the army left and Hezbollah elements went in. As the civil war was still raging, we found it necessary to deploy in military positions and barracks, along supply routes, and in areas of contact.

When the Taif Agreement was signed,[27] we opposed its political provisions but acquiesced to the ones relevant to security. We said that we were in favor of peace and of turning over a new leaf on the civil war. Many were expecting a bloody conflict to ensue between the Lebanese army and Hezbollah in the southern suburb, Iqlim al-Tuffah,[28] and Baalbek; these people obviously do not know our policies well enough. We said repeatedly that civil war in Lebanon would not produce any results, and seventeen years of it have if anything complicated the sectarian situation in the country. Dialogue, coexistence, agreement, and understanding are the only options open to the Lebanese people; war does not serve Lebanon's interests in any way, and has repercussions that go well beyond the country and its people. Based on that, we have always responded positively, and without pressure, to all calls and initiatives designed to reinforce civil peace in the country. We were surprised when the governmental delegation proposed the cancellation of all contacts, and I am sure that we are the ones who have the most difficulty with this premise. The moment the state decided to reclaim its property, in the name of reinforcing civil peace, we therefore handed the Sheikh Abdullah barracks over to them without any pressure.

AL-WATAN AL-ARABI: *What do you think about the establishment of the Shia protectorate in the south of Iraq?*[29] *Will it be enough to bring Saddam down or not?*

HN: The establishment of the American protectorate in southern Iraq is a form of sedition; it is a kind of sedition difficult to categorize. Part of the problem is that the Shia in the south—especially in the al-Ahwar region—are being bombed and murdered in the midst of total international silence. On one side, there are people trying to intervene to save the population of

---

27 For the Taif Accord, see above, p. 64 n. 10.

28 An area of south Lebanon north of Nabatieh and east of Sidon.

29 The interviewer is referring to the so-called "No-Fly Zones" instituted by the US and its coalition allies after the Gulf War of 1990–91. The prohibition on Iraqi air movements below the thirty-third parallel (a similar prohibition was put in place in Northern Iraq to protect Iraqi Kurdish areas) came as a belated effort to protect the Shia in southern Iraq from the increasingly brutal campaign waged against them by Saddam Hussein immediately following the end of hostilities.

these regions from a real social catastrophe; and on the other, there is this silence and this indifference. This went on until the Americans, who know how to seize opportunities to further their own interests, started talking about an American protectorate in the south—but they would not be able to hide the real long-term objectives of their game. Why did their conscience suddenly awaken? I do not think that it is a matter of conscience; the Iraqi air force has been shelling Kurdish villages with chemical weapons for years, without a single word out of Washington.[30] What is happening now has nothing to do with moral principles, conscience or human values; Bush simply needs to achieve an election coup, and the Shia protectorate would tighten the noose around the Iraqi regime's neck. And though this will not bring down the regime, it will lead to the division and dismemberment of Iraq. I am one of those who oppose American intervention in Iraq's internal affairs; I would like to see an Arab or Islamic protectorate in southern Iraq, not an American enclave.

30 Perhaps the most notorious attack by Iraqi forces in the Kurdish-dominated northern region of Iraq occurred in the town of Halabja in 1988, when chemical agents were allegedly used to kill thousands of mostly Kurdish civilians. At least 5,000 people died, and another 7,000 were injured. That incident was part of the especially brutal 1986–88 Anfal Campaign, which led to the deaths of as many as 100,000 Kurds and the displacement of hundreds of thousands more.

7

THE FIRST UNDERSTANDING
WITH ISRAEL

August 27, 1993

The summer of 1993 saw a dramatic series of regional developments that would deeply affect Hezbollah in the coming years. Most notably, and just days before Nasrallah gave this interview to As-Safir's Ibrahim al-Amine and George Bakassini, the PLO and Israel finalized the groundbreaking Declaration of Principles at Oslo[1]—prompting renewed speculation that a Lebanese–Israeli peace treaty of some kind might be closer at hand than previously thought.

Of great significance, too, was the first so-called "Understanding" which had emerged from the carnage of a concerted Israeli military assault between July 25 and July 31, mainly in south Lebanon, codenamed "Operation Accountability." That offensive had come after a Hezbollah attack, which killed several IDF soldiers within the "security zone" in the south, prompting an Israeli retaliation against the villages out of which Hezbollah guerrillas were operating. The party promptly launched Katyusha rockets into northern Israel, mainly at civilian areas, with Nasrallah declaring that Hezbollah "consider[s] [itself] to be in a state of open warfare with this enemy."

After seven days of combined land, air, and sea attacks, Israel had wreaked havoc across a substantial stretch of territory, but had not been able to stop the rocket fire, as its military had earlier predicted it would do. In all, 80 villages lay in ruin, approximately 6,000 homes had been destroyed, and more than 140 Lebanese civilians were dead. Nearly 250,000 refugees from the south, mainly Shiites, streamed towards Beirut, in a replay of earlier mass exoduses after the Israeli invasions of 1978 and 1982. In Israel, two civilians had been killed and 24 injured by Hezbollah rockets.

The unwritten 1993 "Understanding" that ended the fighting was, perhaps not surprisingly,

1 The 1993 Oslo Accords, the result of secret Israeli–PLO face-to-face negotiations, called for the withdrawal of Israeli forces from parts of the Gaza Strip and the West Bank (what became known as "Gaza and Jericho First"), while affirming the Palestinian right to self-government within those areas through the creation of a Palestinian Authority. Permanent issues, such as Jerusalem, the return of refugees, Israeli settlements, security, and borders were deliberately excluded from the Accords, and left for future negotiation.

vigorously disputed almost from its inception—as had been a similarly unwritten 1992 agreement brokered after a smaller flare-up of hostilities in the south. But the stage had been set for what would, in 1996, finally become a written agreement, with Lebanon, Syria, Israel, and the United States as signatories. Hezbollah, the Understandings effectively said, would refrain from rocket attacks into Israel if Israel refrained from attacks on Lebanese cities, towns, and villages. Fighting amongst combatants could therefore continue, but within boundaries—within the "rules of the game." "The Katyusha [rocket] bombardment," Nasrallah says pointedly, "has led to a new formula based on mutual forced displacement, mutual destruction, and equal terror. This formula was imposed by the Katyusha."

AS-SAFIR: *Let's start with the negotiations. Whenever the date of the next round nears, a new wave of optimism permeates the atmosphere. Maybe this time around, the optimism is stronger than ever. Do you believe that there is anything new in the negotiations, and do you expect new developments in the next round? And how do you interpret the latest Israeli aggression in this context?*[2]

HN: Regardless of all the forms of optimism spread in the previous periods, there were no advances in the ninth and tenth rounds, especially on the Lebanese and Syrian tracks, while the Palestinian track is mired in political complications. One of the most important reasons behind the latest Israeli aggression on Lebanon in the Seven-Day War may be that the Israelis arrived at a dead end in the negotiations, and were unable to solve certain issues through political negotiations. So they used the military operation to weaken the Lebanese situation and the Arab attitudes by overturning some of the strong cards in the hand of the Arab negotiator.

America will try to employ the latest aggression in the eleventh round, and the Israeli operation will leave its marks on the next round, but this remains dependent on the perseverance and fortitude of the Arab attitude. Will the Arab negotiator offer rewards and gains to Israel for the recent aggression? So far we have seen nothing new. Even the statements we heard yesterday from the enemy Prime Minister Rabin aren't new.[3] They were

2 For US–Lebanese negotiations, see above, p. 94 n. 14.

3 Nasrallah is referring to Yitzhak Rabin's "Jezzine First" proposal, so named after a Lebanese town north of the "security zone," but controlled by Lahd's SLA. The proposal, like so many later iterations, called for a phased pullback of Israeli forces from south Lebanon as long as a range of conditions—including a sustained ceasefire, the disarming of the party and the guaranteed presence of Israeli monitoring stations on Lebanese territory—were met by Hezbollah, the Lebanese government, and various other actors.

just an announcement of an old suggestion that had already been put before the Lebanese officials—whether they admitted their knowledge of it or not. The suggestion has been on the table for a while, and was discussed through mediators, and rejected as far as I know.

Rabin rephrased an old proposal and did not come up with anything new. According to our assessment of the overall situation, we do not believe that any important advances will take place in the eleventh round, especially as the Israelis are still intransigent. The problems facing the negotiators will remain the same in the coming rounds, because of the Israeli unwillingness to present compromises, while the Arab negotiators have come to the end of the [list of proposed] compromises that they could present. The American pressure is not new, and will continue.

AS-SAFIR: *Was what Rabin said yesterday discussed [immediately] after the recent war, [or] during the contacts made by the United States before arriving at what was called the ceasefire agreement?*

HN: As I remember, this suggestion was around during and after the aggression. But it is on the table, and it concerns the security [zone] as it aims to disarm the resistance and implement the necessary procedures with the security belt as an experiment. If it succeeded, then the discussion would start about security arrangements at the level of the borders. We announced back then that this offer contains a trap, because if the [Lebanese] government agrees to stop the operations of the resistance in this form with the occupation still there, then it is handing Israel a huge victory on the one hand, and another gain on the other, as this would plunge Lebanon into civil war, because we would never accept this. Israel knows our attitude, and knows that this suggestion will cause divisions among the Lebanese, because some of the Lebanese will not agree to stop the resistance while there is occupation. The hidden purpose of the Israeli suggestion is to cause strife inside the south between the government and the resistance. But ultimately, Israel will not implement the terms that it is talking about, because it won't abandon the card represented by its occupation in Lebanon. It will not withdraw without imposing a peace agreement on Lebanon.

AS-SAFIR: *After the aggression, you spoke about reports that point to a political scandal that borders on treason. Did you mean this matter?*

HN: I believe that this issue was discussed as part of the analyses, but what are important in this issue are the documents and data. There is an important question: Did the officials in Lebanon have prior knowledge of the Israeli operation? The evidence shows that some of those in authority knew, but we haven't raised this issue so far and we don't want to do so right now. But there are efforts to clarify this matter.

I believe that in any country, if rulers knew of an [impending] aggression but didn't warn the people or the resistance, which they say is a legitimate right, and thus left the resistance and the people prey to a surprise attack from the enemy that, had we not been naturally cautious, caused greater losses—if this is so, then the legal and correct classification of this enters the realm of treason; much more so if the matter goes beyond the extent of prior knowledge to what is being reported as agreements and coordination.

AS-SAFIR: *When the aggression ended, much talk was expended on a solution to reach a ceasefire, and about a signed written agreement dealing with the issue of the missiles and the status of the resistance. What is Hezbollah's story about what happened?*

HN: During the aggression we established political contacts with the official religious and political leaderships, and we ignored all the sensitivities and personal problems. We also contacted our brothers in Damascus, because the index of the strength in the political attitude pointed to Syria. We were anxious during the Seven-Day War to give them an image of the field, political, and popular situation, because this has major effects on attitudes. Here, the differences emerged between us and some of the "others" because there is a major difference between reporting the situation by saying that people are complaining, the country is under threat of dividing, and chaos will rule Beirut, and saying that there is incomparable fortitude in the south, high morale, popular cooperation between the Christians and the Muslims, and people largely understanding and helping each other. There wasn't a single slap [i.e. disruptive event] in the Southern Suburb or Beirut, and there was an unprecedented state of internal cohesion. But some politicians with certain political backgrounds can present the image in a way that serves their interests.

We went to Damascus at the time when Israel was starting to reduce its goals from the elimination of Hezbollah and the Islamic Resistance to the disarmament of Hezbollah, then to freezing the operations of the resistance—which implies a recognition of the resistance's right to keep its arms, but in return for freezing its operations. Then, finally, came [the proposal] preventing the Katyusha rockets from targeting Israeli civilians in the settlements in northern Israel. From here I enter into the issue of the communications that took place. After the Israelis downgraded their goals to this extent, they [still] weren't able to achieve them militarily. The air force and the artillery were bombarding all the valleys and points from which the Katyushas were being fired; but despite our lack of fortifications and bunkers, the missile barrage never stopped until the seventh day of the operation. This means that the Israelis, who possess the strongest military force in the region, were not able to stop the Katyusha bombardment of the settlements militarily. This is not so much a military defeat as a military scandal, given Israel's military capabilities.

Here the communications started, with the center point being Damascus. The Americans were the mediators, and on the other side were the Israelis. The discussion with us went as follows: the Israeli operation was a result of the perseverance of the resistance, the political situation in the country, Syria's attitude, and Iran's help. There are many elements that the Israelis want to be rid of. There were some discussions about an exit from the situation, and about whether there can be any solution for the issue of the missiles. This was the question directed at us. No one told us that there was a deal or an agreement, or that we should discuss it; the question (about the missiles) was the only thing told to us.

Of course, I was party to this issue, and the question was directed at me. I answered that if there was nothing that could affect the operations of the resistance or its movements, and if the issue only concerned the missiles, then it was easy to solve. There is nothing new in this [situation], as we have been announcing for the past two years that our purpose is not to bombard the settlements but to carry out operations inside the occupied [Lebanese] territory. But when our people, towns, cities, and villages are being bombarded, then it is our right to use all the weapons available to us to stop the aggression. This is our policy, and we have never started firing Katyusha missiles at the settlements. Even Rabin himself always used to say that Hezbollah doesn't start bombarding the settlements, but it only does so in response to [Israel's] military actions.[4] This is known, and the formula is simple: let the aggression on Lebanon stop, along with the bombing of the civilians, and we will stop firing missiles.[5] Thus, the reason for bombarding the settlements is removed. We have no problem in this regard. We were told that this was fine, so let us start specifying dates for the ceasefire. We replied that we weren't the ones that started the war. He who started the war must end it; for our part, as soon as we hear that the aggression will stop at a specific hour, then this means that at that time the firing of the Katyusha missiles will stop. If the aggression continues, then the Katyusha bombardment will continue. Then we returned to Lebanon. On Saturday,

4 As Judith Palmer Harik notes in her book, *Hezbollah: The Changing Face of Terrorism*, in a November 1992 press conference Rabin "conceded that Hezbollah had not fired on [settlements in Israel] without provocation from the Israeli army." Harik quotes Israeli General Shlomo Gazit as later acknowledging, "Hezbollah did observe the 'rules of the game' for a long period. They refrained from shelling Israeli territory and from infiltration. They limited their operations to the 'Security Zone.' It was our retaliation for their skilful strikes at our soldiers inside the zone that made them escalate the fighting. We bombed and shelled many targets in Lebanon, including some far to the north. Only then did Hezbollah retaliate by shelling some Israeli localities—with no casualties." Judith Palmer Harik, *Hezbollah: The Changing Face of Terrorism* (London: IB Tauris, 2004), p. 177.

5 Nasrallah at this point provides an interpretation of the 1993 Understanding that would presumably permit a Hezbollah rocket assault on civilian areas within Israel even if Hezbollah combatants were targeted directly (as was the case after the 1992 assassination of Mussawi and his family, although see Qassem on the subject p. 61 n. 7). Space is also potentially left open – at least in this passage – for attacks on any Israeli targets outside the theatre of conflict, given certain Israeli actions. This ambiguity would at least in part buffer charges by both the US and Israel, in particular, that Hezbollah had played a role, possibly under Iranian direction, in the March 1992 bombing of the Israeli embassy in Argentina as well as the July 1994 bombing of the Jewish cultural center, attacks which killed 114 people and injured hundreds more. Although both bombings came shortly after major incidents in Lebanon (the assassination of Mussawi and his family in the first instance, and, reportedly, a devastating Israeli raid on a Hezbollah training camp in the Bekaa in the second), Hezbollah vehemently denied any linkage, arguing that the party had long committed to only launching or supporting operations in the immediate theater of conflict between Lebanon and Israel. Subsequent to the 1994 bombing, Hezbollah would not again be accused of direct involvement in overseas acts of terrorism, save for a 2001 US indictment of one unnamed Hezbollah member accused of assisting in the bombing of the Khobar Towers in Saudi Arabia in June 1996, an attack which killed 20, including 19 US military personnel. Moreover, after the April Understanding of 1996, the scale and scope of Hezbollah's military operations became ever more rigidly tied to the narrower terms of the new "rules of the game" – rules which greatly mitigated the effects of violence against civilians on all sides.

we heard that the Israelis had announced that the ceasefire would take effect at six [p.m.], and the aggression stopped along with the bombardment.

AS-SAFIR: *Did you evaluate the results of the Katyusha policy that you had followed?*

HN: Before the end of the aggression, some of the officials started to evaluate the Katyusha policy to determine whether it was wrong and hurried, or correct, and tried to discover its achievements. I believe that this issue is one of the controversial points on the [political] scene.

After what happened, our belief in the correctness of this policy increased, despite what some are trying to suggest. Of course, we are talking about the policy which states that the purpose is not to fire Katyusha rockets, but that if our villages and towns are bombarded then the settlements of northern Israel will not be safe from the same treatment. We still believe that this policy produced something very important, which we all felt after the Shihine operation.[6] In the past, whenever the resistance used to carry out an operation against the Lahd army[7] and killed one of its members, the bombardments started against Nabatieh, Bara Sheet,[8] and the other towns, and the same happened whenever a bomb went off. The knee-jerk reaction to retaliate against any operation by the resistance was for the Israelis and the Lahd army to bombard the villages [of south Lebanon] and kill civilians. But we notice that after the Shihine operation, which led to results of this magnitude, not a single shell was fired at any southern village, and the Israeli enemy seemed confused. It responded by holding a meeting for the war cabinet, then attacked Jenta[9] and an anti-aircraft site in the Bekaa valley. But they didn't attack civilians—rather, they only tried to attack military sites that they thought belonged to Hezbollah.

Why didn't the Israelis bombard the southern villages following these losses and this operation, which was applauded by all? In case you ever visit the three presidents or any of the officials,[10] I want an answer to this question.

6 The Shihine operation—a strike against an IDF patrol in south Lebanon on August 19, 1993—resulted in the deaths of seven Israeli soldiers.

7 The South Lebanon army (see above, p. 66 n. 13).

8 The South Lebanese village of Bara Sheet lies just north of the "security zone."

9 The village of Jenta is located in the eastern Bekaa, near to the Lebanese–Syrian border.

10 The "three presidents" refers to the three highest political offices—the republic's president, premier, and speaker of parliament.

Our answer is clear: because the Israelis know that bombarding civilians will bring a resumption of the bombardment of the settlements in northern Palestine. As the bombardment of civilians is tiresome for our people, it is tiresome for others as well, and they can't handle it as well as we can.

The Katyusha bombardment has led to a new formula based on mutual forced displacement, mutual destruction, and equal terror. This formula was imposed by the Katyusha, and not the operations of the resistance in the border belt. There is a very sensitive topic for the Israelis right now—namely the security of their settlements in northern Palestine. If the settlements are bombarded again, then Rabin will be forced to stand in front of all his people and all [Israel's] political forces to answer the question: What did the seven-day operation achieve? This is why Rabin understands that there is a new formula. This formula was not imposed by the Israelis, but for the first time by the resistance because, in the past, the settlements were not bombarded, while since 1985 the villages of the south and western Bekaa have been under bombardment. The rule of the game used to be that we got bombarded while the settlements remained safe. The enemy destroys Maydun, Yatir, and Kafra while we are only allowed to move in the security zone.[11] But the resistance imposed a new formula through the Katyusha. Thus we say that we are committed to a new rule, one which was founded by us. I therefore believe that the experience of the war proved that this policy is wise and correct, and should reap benefits since it is not right for us to protect the enemy's weak points. We must fortify our strengths and apply pressure on the Israelis at their weak points to alleviate the suffering of our people. This is what we recently achieved.

We stopped the bombardment with the missiles. That is all that happened on our side. But regarding what took place among the others, according to our information it is certain that in the first day after the ceasefire, communications took place with Syrian officials, who assured us that there were no deals or agreements, and that the whole issue was within the boundary of stopping the [Israeli] aggression in return for stopping the Katyushas. I had issued a statement two days before the end of the operation in which I spoke these same words, because the only way to halt the Katyushas was to stop the aggression against our people.

11 Maydun, Yatir, and Kafra are small villages in south Lebanon.

Regarding the other leaderships in the country, and the deals that they made or the communications and promises that they issued, this is an issue we weren't a party to, and we are completely innocent of it, if anything happened. We do not possess accurate information in this regard. We heard the reports, but we do not possess information that confirms that there were written pledges offered by Lebanese officials.

AS-SAFIR: *In your opinion, what are the effects of the so-called ceasefire agreement on the eleventh round of negotiations? In other words, did the recent Shihine operation aim [to undermine] the next round?*

HN: This question suggests a wider one: is the resistance aimed at liberation or damaging the negotiations? We consider that the Americans and Israelis have dodged the issue of the existence of occupied lands, and that the resistance against the occupation is a legal right for any people. They [the Americans and the Israelis] treat the resistance as if it aims to sabotage the peace process, and that is why they call for taking stances against the Resistance. I read in the newspaper commentaries that the purpose behind the [Shihine] operation was to send local and regional messages. This is inaccurate, because the resistance existed before the negotiations, and will continue if they fail, because the resistance is linked to the occupation. As long as there is occupation, there is resistance. There were no [peace] negotiations when we started the resistance for it to be said that we started the resistance to sabotage the peace process in the region. No, we resist the occupation, which started in 1982. In 1985, a great victory was achieved when the Israelis were forced to withdraw. From 1985 until today, the Islamic Resistance has not stopped. Its actions are continuous, and are not subject to any temporal or political constraints. A day before the start of the seventh round of negotiations, or during the round, the Ahmadiyeh operation took place, and resulted in the deaths of five Israelis and the wounding of five others. This caused a stormy round of negotiations with the Lebanese delegation, and all the discussion turned to the issue of the resistance. At that time, many commented that the purpose behind the operation was to sabotage the round, so I confirmed back then that, even though we are in these certain positions, a small group of resistance fighters could be inside the security belt setting up an ambush for the enemy, or planting a roadside bomb, and I would know nothing of this, as it is a routine day's work for us. The operations of the resistance are not seasonal or political. This is the daily work of our brothers, and the top official in the resistance might not be aware of it.

The Ahmadiyeh bomb could have gone off while a patrol from the Lahd army was passing, but it so happened that it struck an Israeli patrol that day. The bomb might explode and kill only one Israeli, as we don't control the target. We possess the initiative to decide whether or not to attack this target, but we can't force the Israelis to pass at a specific time in a specific place instead of the Lahd army, as this is linked to their tactics. Even the Shihine operation came in the context of the resistance confirming that its operations would continue as usual. Before the Shihine operation, we had carried out ten operations since the end of the aggression, which contradicts the analyses that pointed out that the purpose behind the Shihine operation was to refute talk about the existence of a certain deal restraining the resistance's operations. But the uniqueness of the Shihine operation concerns its size, and the enormous scale of the Israeli losses. In reality, there is no relationship between the operations of the resistance and the rounds [of negotiation]; the operations are only linked to the issue of the occupation.

AS-SAFIR: *Washington and Israel are saying that [the Shihine operation] shows that the dimensions of the resistance in Lebanon are not local but regional, with links to Iran. This has once again caused confusion about the nature of Iran's view of the situation in Lebanon, through its relationship with Syria. So what is the truth of Iran's relationship with Syria regarding Lebanon, or with Lebanon through Syria?*

HN: There are two parts to this question. The first concerns Iran's relationship with the resistance, and the second concerns how to deal with this situation. It has always been said that the resistance in Lebanon has a certain regional dimension, with some meaning Iran, others meaning Syria and Iran, and yet others meaning Syria, each according to his political background. As far as the Iranian issue is concerned, before there came to be an Islamic Republic in Iran, Imam Khomeini was still a revolutionary against the Shah's regime, and he demanded that the Shah's regime end its relationship with Israel and cut off all its oil supplies and economic relations. He also used to call upon the Iranian people to support the Palestinian organizations that were fighting

Israel. Thus he expressed some very great opinions on this issue. But the issue of endorsing the resistance is a matter that pertains to Muslims in general, and Shiites specifically, and it bears no relation to Iran being an Islamic republic. It pertains to our ideology, and to religious clerics and references.

For example, when the British occupied Iraq in 1920, the religious clerics in Najaf declared a revolution against the English, which developed into the 1920 revolution. Some of the clerics who participated in it later became great religious references—such as Muhsin Al-Hakim, Ayatollah Kashani and others[12]—who spent a long time in British jails. Thus the issue of fighting the occupation, whether British or Israeli, is linked to our thinking, ideological background, and particular structure, as well as to our references and clerics, whether they are in Najaf, Qom, Karbala, or Jabal Amil.[13]

Regarding the regional issue and interests, after the regime in Iran became Islamic, it started dealing with the issue of the resistance not on the basis of the regional interests of the state of Iran, but on the basis of the mentality, ideology, and special structure of our clerics and references, which pre-dated the founding of the Islamic regime in Iran, as it had already been in existence in Najaf and elsewhere. This is true even for the great religious cleric, the late Sayyed al-Khoei, as I remember from 1978 when I was in Najaf, when the Israeli attack on Lebanon started. We went as a group of students to Sayyed al-Khoei, and we asked him about his directives to fight this aggression. His answer was that "aggression necessitates defense. If I had had armies and weapons, then I would have sent them to southern Lebanon."[14]

The conclusion is that the issue of the resistance and the rejection of the occupation is not related to any regional issue, and is not subject to any political bargaining. This is why the Islamic Republic stands behind the resistance, as everyone knows that the extent of pressure that Iran is under

12 Grand Ayatollah Muhsin al-Hakim (1889–1970) and Ayatollah Sayyed Abol-Qassem Mostafavi Kashani (1884–1961) were both leading Shiite clerics in Iran. Kashani was also an ardent nationalist, who played an influential role in the 1951 nationalization of the Iranian oil industry.

13 Respectively, the four major sites of Shia jurisprudence and scholarship. Najaf and Karbala lie in central Iraq, south of the capital Baghdad; Qom is located in central Iran, south-east of the capital Tehran; Jabal Amil customarily refers to the entire area of south Lebanon, although a more narrow definition excludes such major cities as Sidon and Jezzine.

14 Grand Ayatollah Abul-Qassem al-Khoei (1899–1992) lived and taught in Najaf, Iraq, and became the most prominent Shia Grand Ayatollah after the death of Muhsin al-Hakim

to end its support for the resistance is very great. I have knowledge of significant incentives that were offered to the Islamic Republic to give up this support, but Iran doesn't do so because the issue is linked to the ideology and mentality of Islam.

Iran has its serious stances on the Lebanese issue. It supports civil peace, the resistance, and internal stability, and it has taken the initiative on more than one unhappy occasion to stop internal crises from escalating. It is true that Iran is against negotiations with Israel, but this doesn't eliminate Iran's concern to preserve the strength of the Syrian and Lebanese stances. It thinks about how to support the Arab stances, to prevent Israel from imposing its terms on the Arabs. This is confirmed by Iran's behavior during the recent Israeli aggression, which is an additional sign that Iran's goal is to support the Arab stance and not to sabotage the situation. Everyone knows here that if the resistance had regional sponsors that wanted to use it to further political projects, then it could have used the Seven-Day War to draw everyone into a comprehensive war—but this wasn't done, neither by the resistance nor by Iran, which is accused of benefiting from this resistance to achieve a whole host of regional gains.

AS-SAFIR: *Do you believe that the Seven-Day War was a rehearsal for a greater war that is anticipated by the resistance, or was it aimed at reviving the bottlenecked negotiations?*

HN: Israel has a set of principles. It wants to dominate the whole region. When the Israeli was weak and dispersed throughout the world, he didn't give up this dream—so what about today, when he is in a strong position facing a divided and torn Arab and Islamic world, and also when he is supported by the New World Order? Negotiating is an Israeli necessity, and serves their interests because they hope through negotiations to control the whole region for the lowest number of casualties possible. The enemy wants bilateral peace, and is working with the United States to increase the pressure applied on the opposing powers, spearheaded by Syria, to achieve it.

I therefore believe that Israel doesn't need a comprehensive war, as it is getting what it wants for the lowest number of casualties—even without any casualties at all—and as it is working to offer booby-trapped initiatives to the Arab side, such as Rabin's offer to Lebanon yesterday, or the offer presented to the Palestinians known as 'Gaza First', which will be catastrophic if it comes to pass, because the Palestinian cause will be threatened with extinction.[15]

Thus, we see that the Seven-Day War was an operation that aimed to apply more pressure and to scare us by targeting principally the resistance card, but this goal has not been achieved. Anyway, the United States has threatened everyone, and especially the Arabs, that the war that took place will be repeated if the negotiations fail.

AS-SAFIR: *The Shihine operation has caused an unprecedented quake in the Israeli military apparatus. How do you see the enemy responding to it, especially as there are those who focus on the intelligence–security side more than the direct field situation?*

HN: You must read the statements issued by the leaders of the enemy accurately, as they say that they are incapable of repeating the recent aggression every week. They are issuing statements that do not suggest a widespread reaction, but this doesn't eliminate the possibility of large operations. We are paying attention to all the possibilities.

AS-SAFIR: *Talk of harmony between the resistance and the state has resurfaced. Some explain [this] as being linked to the issue of the negotiations. How do you see this issue?*

HN: The official who seems most concerned with this issue is [Foreign Minister] Fares Boueiz. We have not ignored this talk, but we tried to acquire explanations as to what is meant by it.

If what is meant is that the resistance should be used for political ends, then we reject it completely, because the resistance would then become a seasonal resistance. Then there are those who say: Now is the time for negotiations, so please ease up with the operations; or, We have heard positive talk from the Americans, so let us stop the resistance for a while, and sit down. We do not agree to this talk at all. I will not discuss the ability of this or that Arab faction to make use of the resistance.

15. See p. 100; n. 1.

If 'harmony' signifies a call for coordination in the performance of the resistance, then we have no problem in discussing this, but only with those concerned—that is to say, those who resist like us, not with those who refuse to resist. But we confirm that we are ready to cooperate and help all the forces that want to resume or intensify their participation in acts of resistance.

AS-SAFIR: *Moving to the issue under discussion of the aid to support the fortitude of the south Lebanese, and to compensate [them] for some of their losses. There is a reliance on Hezbollah to acquire lots of aid from Iran for this purpose. You have just returned from a long visit to the Iranian capital, so what were the communications like on this subject?*

HN: First, I would like to clarify something—not to detract from the performance of the government and the visits by Prime Minister Rafik Hariri to a number of Arab countries to acquire more aid,[16] but to clarify that the figures presented by the governing institutions to the media about the losses are hugely bloated. This might be to acquire more aid, or to terrorize the people through all this mass destruction that came as a reply to the operations of the resistance.

We will think well of them due to our concern over the unity of the internal political front, but the reality of the destruction doesn't need such bloated figures to erase the effects of the [Israeli] aggression. If there is correct, accurate, and clean management, then the Lebanese state can erase the effects of the aggression with a limited amount of aid from some of the friends and brothers. Concerning Iran, we can say that it is ready to offer aid.

There is a matter that should be noted in this context, which is the way the politicians here deal with issues of this magnitude. I can say with full certainty that most of the political leaderships in Lebanon still behave with an alleyway mentality. We also believe that, if the government is seriously

16 The Sunni business mogul Rafik Hariri (1944–2005) served as prime minister of Lebanon from 1992 to 1998, and again from 2000 until his resignation in October 2004. Although his relations with Hezbollah were strained over the years—not least because of his close ties to the West, as well as his sometimes controversial redevelopment initiatives—Hariri would later develop a close working relationship with Nasrallah in the years prior to his February 2005 assassination in Beirut.

convinced of the necessity of the resistance and of protecting it, then it should delegate the issue of the distribution of the aid to the men of the resistance in the south. It should have depended on the men of the resistance in each town to distribute aid—first because they are trustworthy, as they didn't ransack the houses during the aggression, since they are self-supplied; and secondly because it would have cemented and deepened the relationship between the men of the resistance and the people in the south—because Israel is trying to sow division between them. But the state didn't follow this method, and the issue of aid distribution became a means to achieve political and popular gains for this or that party or leader. The Islamic Republic decided to deliver aid to the Lebanese government, as did all the other countries that are sending food, medical, and physical assistance. We completely agreed to this and went along with it, despite the fact that we consider that the Lebanese government should hand over all the assistance to the men of the resistance. The Islamic Republic is continuing to send aid; I believe that a number of planes carrying aid will land soon in Beirut airport, and I hope that it will be distributed justly and without problems.

AS-SAFIR: *Is this the whole of the aid?*

HN: This is one part of the issue. The other part concerns the initiative we announced, which entails repairing all the houses that were damaged and not completely destroyed. When we announced this initiative we were embarking upon an adventure, because it was difficult to establish the full extent of this venture and its financial cost. I said that if we had to, then we would go to all the countries and contact all the Arab and Islamic communities and clerics to acquire assistance; I was serious about this, because it wasn't clear to us whether the Islamic Republic was ready to shoulder this burden alone, or if we needed aid from other quarters as well. I believe that the method that we suggested is the best one to be followed, and many voices were heard calling upon the state to follow the same one, instead of quarrelling with the homeowners over estimates of the size and cost of their losses.

Regarding the other side of the issue, which concerns the owners of the houses that were destroyed completely, we will contribute to rebuilding them. Of course, we didn't commit to rebuilding them completely, because we will contribute alongside the contribution they will be getting from the government to rebuild.[17] Regarding the implementation of this initiative, whether through communications with the official authorities in Iran or with some religious clerics and popular organizations, I believe that, God willing, we will implement this initiative and we will fulfill this promise. There was a wager on whether Hezbollah would fulfill its promises or not. So far, in our experience, we have never yet promised and failed to deliver, and I believe that the feeling among the brothers in Hezbollah in the south, Bekaa, and Beirut is that, even if we have to use up all our resources, we will implement this step, no matter the cost.

There is a possibility of opening up new fields of assistance, but this step is still being studied with our brothers in the Islamic Republic. The Islamic Republic will announce any development in this field, whether through us or through the government.

---

17 Hezbollah's construction company, Jihad al-Bina, would later assert that it had restored and rebuilt 4,873 damaged homes—or nearly all of the homes affected by Operation Accountability.

8

"WHO IS SAYYED HASSAN NASRALLAH?"

August 31, 1993

In this lengthy interview with the Lebanese newspaper Nida al-Watan, *Nasrallah openly describes his youth, his religious and political development, and the establishment and mission of Hezbollah—all subjects long shrouded in a relative degree of secrecy and ambiguity. On a number of critical party issues brewing at the time, however—the correctness and desirability of Iran's Ayatollah Ali Khameini as the main spiritual and political reference for Shiites, past troubled relations with Syria, and internal divisions within Hezbollah—Nasrallah diplomatically demurs from a more pointed discussion, as he so often would when it came to matters that might exacerbate disunity or provide any sort of a window for Hezbollah's enemies.*

NIDA AL-WATAN: *Who is Sayyed Hassan Nasrallah? Where did he come from? What did he study? And how does he think?*

HN: Hassan Abdelkarim Nasrallah was born on August 31, 1960, in a very poor area of East Beirut, called al-Sharshabouk Quarter, near al-Khodr Mosque and the Karantina.[1] There, under the bridge, is an area by the name of al-Sharshabouk, a quarter in which the best house is a ruin and whose inhabitants were a mixture of Shiites, Maslakh Arabs, Armenians, and Kurds. This is where I lived with my family until 1974, where I spent my childhood and finished my elementary school education at the al-Najah School, which

1 The Karantina-Maslakh district of East Beirut was largely populated by various refugee communities—most notably Palestinians, who gradually gained control of the area through the PLO. A strategic location on the road between Christian East Beirut and the Christian mountain villages to the north, Karantina-Maslakh became a major point of conflict in the first year of the Lebanese Civil War. On January 18, 1976 it was overrun by Christian militias bent on revenging a recent massacre of Christians in the town of Damour, south of Beirut, who killed as many as 1,500 fighters and civilians.

is still there. At that time, this was the highest degree one could earn in that particular area, which meant that I had to go to Sin el-Fil for my secondary education.

Shortly before war broke and we went into exile, we moved to the Sin el-Fil area, though my father continued to go to al-Sharshabouk Quarter on a daily basis to work in the small shop he owned, until the area fell (...) Though I had no political leanings at that time, I had been religious since my early childhood; as you know, the age of religious maturity for us Shiites is 15, but I was already an observant Muslim at the age of nine.

NIDA AL-WATAN: *What was the atmosphere like at home?*

HN: Our home was observant in a traditional way, but I became particularly religious due to the milieu I lived in. During that period, I used to go from al-Sharshabouk Quarter to al-Nabaa to pray at the Usrat al-Taakhi Mosque, in which Sayyed Mohammad Hussein Fadlallah prayed (...).[2] I went there to pray even as a child. Even then, I still did not have particular political leanings until our father took us out of the area, a short time before it fell, to the village of Bazourieh in the south, which is where I originally come from even though I was born elsewhere.[3]

Leftist and nationalist parties were very strong in Bazourieh at the time, and there were no fervent believers or religious youths, like those we call today the "Islamists"; my main interest therefore revolved around the formation of such a group of religious youths. There was a very decent, good, and respected sheikh in our town, by the name of Ali Shamseddin, who has died since (...), so we worked together to found a library at the town's Islamic Center, where the youth could come, read, and receive lessons. It attracted a considerable number of young men and women, and I was the one who gave the lessons.

That year, I completed Grade Eleven in Tyre, joined the Amal Movement, and was only 15 years old when I was given responsibility for the Movement's organization in our town, Bazourieh. The others who held similar positions

2 For Fadlallah, see above, p. 40 n. 8. Fadlallah had centered his activities in the mainly Shiite Nabaa district near to Karantina, which also came under siege by Christian militias in January 1976.

3 The south Lebanon village of Bazourieh lies next to the city of Tyre.

were older than me, more my father's age, and even my uncles were members of that organization. I also became very active in the town's Amal Movement. We met on a weekly basis at the gatherings that Dr. Mostapha Chamran used to hold at the Professional Association in Jabal Amil.[4]

I had a very large appetite for learning, by which I mean religious education and subjects, and had wanted to go to Najaf to study at the religious seminary ever since my childhood—that is, since I was 13, 14, and 15, which was highly unusual. I arrived thus in Najaf on January 15, 1976, at a relatively young age, carrying a bunch of introductory letters from a number of Lebanese scholars.[5]

NIDA AL-WATAN: *There was of course among them a letter from Sayyed Mohammad Hussein Fadlallah?*

HN: No, I could not get a letter from al-Sayyed because I did not succeed in reaching him, since after our exile from Nabaa we went to Bint Jbeil[6] and moved around a lot. I was in touch, at that time, however, with Sayyed Mohammad al-Faroui, a close friend from Tyre, where he still lives, and he gave me several letters to scholars in Najaf. Sayyed al-Faroui was a very close friend of the martyred Imam, Sayyed Mohammad Baqer al-Sadr,[7] and one of the letters was for him personally.

I arrived in Najaf, a city in which I knew no one, around midnight on what was my first trip outside the country. I was very young, and knew only one person there, from the days of Nabaa, the martyred Sheikh Ali Karim. So I went straight to see him and I told him that I was carrying a letter to Sayyed al-Sadr, and wanted to pay him a personal visit.

At that time the Iraqi regime was bringing a lot of pressure to bear on Najaf—in particular on Sayyed Mohammad Baqer, whose movements, home,

4 For Jabal Amil, see above, p. 110 n. 13.

5 For Najaf, see above, p. 110 n. 13.

6 The mainly Shiite south Lebanon town of Bint Jbeil lies 4km to the north of the provisional Israeli–Lebanese border. Long a center of Hezbollah support, it was also the site of Nasrallah's "Victory" speech after the Israeli withdrawal of 2000 (See Statement 15), and an area of considerable fighting during the 2006 Summer War.

7 Ayatollah Mohammad Baqer al-Sadr (1935–80) was a leading Shiite activist and religious authority in Iraq, and the father in-law of the radical Shiite cleric and current Mahdi army leader Moqtada al-Sadr. He was executed by Saddam Hussein in 1980.

and visitors were under surveillance by the intelligence services. Some people avoided going to see him altogether, and some Lebanese students even warned me, since I was a new student, against paying him a visit lest I start my life in Najaf with a black mark on my name. I asked who could take me to see him, and Sheikh Ali said that there was a person with very close ties to Sayyed al-Sadr, by the name of Sayyed Abbas Mussawi,[8] who came to visit him on a regular basis. I said, no problem.

I met Sayyed Abbas Mussawi for the first time in the street while we were on our way to see him, and, maybe because of his dark skin, I thought he was an Iraqi at first. I had already spent two days between Baghdad and Najaf, and had become accustomed to the Iraqi accent, so I started talking to Sayyed Abbas in an Iraqi-tinged Lebanese accent; but he laughed and said, I am Lebanese, not Iraqi, you can relax.

On our way there—for Sayyed Abbas was going to the city mosque—I told him that I had just arrived from Lebanon, was carrying a letter for Sayyed Mohammad Baqer, and wanted the chance to see him. He said, no problem, let us go now. I am giving you all these details so that you can have an idea about Sayyed Abbas' uncomplicated, straightforward, and partic-ular personality. For him it was a simple matter: "Let us go now..."

We went, therefore, to see Sayyed Mohammad Baqer...

I was surprised because I thought, given his wide-ranging responsibilities, a Religious Authority's time was very tight. Sayyed Baqer gave me a whole half-hour, which is quite a lot, during which he asked me about Lebanon, the south, Sayyed Mousa [al-Sadr], who had not been kidnapped yet, the scholars, our activities, and the situation in the country in general. He also asked me what my plans were.

I told him I did not know, and that I was leaving the matter to him; so he turned to Sayyed Abbas and said: take him under your wing. You will be responsible for everything he needs: a place to stay, special clothes, books, teachers ... and let me know if there are any problems. Then he turned to me and said, "You are under Sayyed Abbas's wing"; I actually also remember him asking me if I had any money! I told him, "The money just got me here, to Najaf." So he reached under the mattress (...) It was the habit of people who come to see Religious Authorities to ask for money; the latter,

8 For Mussawi, see Statement 3

therefore, used to stash a certain amount under the mattress, on which they sat on the floor, and would pull some out whenever their visitors needed money. The money never went into the scholars' pockets; that was the tradition.

From that day onwards, I was under the direct supervision of Sayyed Abbas Mussawi—or rather [I was] placed for safekeeping by Sayyed Mohammad Baqer into the hands of Sayyed Abbas.

Sayyed Abbas found me a place to stay and a place to study, and there I met several students and we formed a group together. Studies at a religious seminary are different from academic or ordinary university studies; at the religious seminary studies are not regimented—students can choose their teachers and subject matter. There are no exams or academic years, and the student is personally responsible for the level of education he wants to attain. This means that everything depends on the student's personal initiative.

There is, of course, a generally recognized program of studies, comprising three levels of knowledge: introductory, higher level, and external research, successively. Books and reference material for the first and second levels are required and predefined; the external research stage has no required reading, but needs a professor, the supreme guide, who lectures as the students take notes.

NIDA AL-WATAN: *How long for?*

HN: A student can spend five years or longer on the introductory level, or require only two years. This depends on the student's energy and ability to absorb knowledge. This academic freedom, which heavily relies on research, distinguishes education at the religious seminary from other more regimented academic systems.

We spent almost one-and-a-half academic years in Najaf, during which Sayyed Abbas Mussawi was our main teacher, and the one who chose our other teachers and subjects. But the main subjects we studied, and our whole *raison d'être* during this one-and-a-half years of academic pursuits, were the responsibility of Sayyed Abbas Mussawi, who paid special attention to our group.

NIDA AL-WATAN: *Who were the members of this group?*

HN: There was Sheikh Ali Karim, who was eventually martyred; Sheikh Mohammad Khatoun, who is now the Hezbollah leader in the Bekaa; a brother by the name of Sheikh Abdul-Ilah Dabbouq [laughs as he says "we will show him"], who is now a judge at the Islamic al-Jaafari Court; and another brother by the name of Sheikh Yassin, who is now imam of the Imam Ali Mosque in the city of Baalbek. There were other brethren who are now active out of the country, and it is best if I do not mention their names for their own sakes.

Sayyed Abbas therefore took very special care of this group. This meant that this teacher did not just deliver the lesson and then go on his way, but used to deliver the lesson, engage us in discussions, help us study, come at night to check if we were alright, and give us an exam at the end of every subject and every chapter. In return, we, the members of this group, were as dedicated as he was; we prepared seriously for every exam, and were afraid before each one lest our preparation was not good enough, for we took extra care not to disappoint Sayyed Abbas. We feared him because we loved him, and because his attitude towards us as a group went beyond that of a teacher and his students—he was a father, an educator, a friend, and the authority in charge.

NIDA AL-WATAN: *It did not seem as if he was much older than you?*

HN: No, he was not old; I think he was at most five, six or seven years older than I was. He was martyred when he was only thirty-eight years old. In the religious seminary, however, those who are older than you, no matter by how many years, are from a qualitative point of view far more able and learned than you are. This is why the time we spent learning at the hands of Sayyed Abbas was particularly time-efficient, because it maximized our academic education. Under Sayyed Abbas, our group broke all routines, never took time off, and never rested, because Sayyed Abbas converted us into an active beehive, and made us thirsty for learning. We can say that, qualitatively, those one-and-a-half years were far more educationally fruitful than their actual time value.

NIDA AL-WATAN: *How did this coincidental and remarkable seriousness come about among members of your group?*

HN: This does not mean that we were the serious ones, for youth always searches for someone to look up to and be guided by, and Sayyed Abbas was extraordinary in this respect. He was all of that for us, and we loved his way of doing things, his seriousness, honesty, and sense of responsibility. And because of this particular relationship, our group was accused of having similar ties to the martyr al-Sadr.

NIDA AL-WATAN: *Was your relationship only with the martyr Sayyed Abbas?*

HN: No, we often visited Sayyed Mohammad Baqer al-Sadr; he had a weekly *majlis* [gathering] open to all those who wanted to join, and we often did. But regardless of whether we went to the *majlis* or not, the fact remained that the Lebanese group of students at the Najaf Religious Seminary was in contact with Sayyed Abbas Mussawi, who in turn had a very well established relationship with Sayyed Mohammad Baqer al-Sadr. It therefore follows that our group would have a special relationship also with Sayyed al-Sadr.

About a year later, on the 20th of *Sifr* of the lunar *hijri* year [the Muslim calendar], which is equivalent to July 20, there was a religious occasion by the name of the Fortieth [Day] of Imam al-Hussein. Imam al-Hussein was martyred on the 10th of *Muharram*, and 40 days after that is the 20th of *Sifr*. Every year on this occasion, the Iraqis gather in Najaf and embark on a three-day march, almost completely on foot, to Karbala.[9] Soon after the march started, however, the marchers clashed with members of the Iraqi intelligence services, and Sayyed Mohammad Baqer al-Sadr was arrested and kept for a long time in detention. They also arrested several religious scholars from Najaf and raided various religious schools, including ours; but after three days of such raids, they realized that they were going to find our school continuously empty, since everyone there was participating in the march. They thus expelled all the Lebanese students whom they suspected of involvement in political activities, or of taking a certain position regarding the regime, and so on. A series of arrests of Lebanese students and professors followed, and our school was among the first victims.

9 The Shia consider the Iraqi city of Karbala to be one of their holiest cities, after Mecca, Medina, and Najaf. It is the location of the tomb of Ali, grandson of the Prophet Muhammad, and is a place of pilgrimage, in particular on Ashoura, the anniversary of the battle. For the Battle of Karbala, see above, p. 52 n. 3.

I still remember when intelligence officers came to the school, gathered all the students and asked for our passports. They then divided the passports into four stacks, depending on the date of entry into the country, and started arresting and expelling us by group, according to who had entered most recently into the country: 1978, 1977, 1976, and 1975. I still remember how, after they took the first group—those [who had entered in] 1978—we hurried to close the door behind them, but they told us, "Don't. Keep it open, they will be back shortly" (...) of course, they did not [return] because they were detained for a few days, and then expelled to Lebanon. [The authorities] continued thus, every week expelling a new group, until they reached the 1977 [group]. I managed, however, to escape by the skin of my teeth from being expelled with them—by just fifteen days, since I had entered into Iraq on January 15, 1976. I also managed to escape being arrested with the third group, because it so happened that I and a group of friends were not at the school when the intelligence services came for us. One of the students came looking for us and told us not to go back to school, so I went with a group of friends to Baghdad, and from there continued on to Beirut. We thus managed to escape the fate of all the other students, who were arrested for periods of between ten days to two months, during which time they were interrogated and tortured before being expelled.

The martyr Sayyed Abbas was out of Iraq, on a visit to Lebanon, when these arrests were taking place, so we told him not to go back to Najaf because the authorities were looking for him in particular.

NIDA AL-WATAN: *Your return to Lebanon, therefore, coincided with the first [Israeli] invasion?*

HN: We returned to Lebanon at the end of the first half of 1978, to be exact, without being able to continue our studies in Qom.[10] The Shah's regime was still in power in Iran, and there were after all a group of religious schools in Lebanon. However, based on our very tight relationship with Sayyed Abbas, we left it to him to decide in which of these schools we ought to enroll. Since we needed to complete our education, Sayyed Abbas

10 For Qom, see above, p. 110 n. 13.

thought it best to establish a new school in Baalbek—first because he hails from that region, from Nabi Sheet in particular, and second because it was far from all of the internal turmoil taking place in the country. It would therefore provide students—especially those who were forced to abandon their education—with the necessary stability and security.

We told him that the decision was his (...) and if I remember well he sought, at that time, the approval and blessing of Imam Musa al-Sadr, His Eminence Sayyed Mohammad Hussein Fadlallah, and His Eminence Sheikh Mohammad Mahdi Shamseddin[11] for the establishment of the school. The Baalbek school thus opened its doors with no more than seven or eight students, and Sayyed Abbas became its principal, founder, and teacher.

NIDA AL-WATAN: *What was it called, the religious seminary?*

HN: Sayyed Abbas called it The Awaited Imam's Religious School,[12] and it still bears that name. We completed our studies at the school and were still there when the Israeli invasion of 1978 took place. This meant that when Imam al-Sadr was kidnapped I was still a student pursuing my education, and at the same time a teacher, since, at the religious seminary, students who completed certain subjects and were quite capable could teach them immediately.

We therefore spent this period studying our hearts out at the religious seminary under Sayyed Abbas, away from the general turmoil in the country. This meant that for an entire year after our return to Lebanon and our enrolment in the seminary in Baalbek, we had nothing to do with what was taking place in the country. A short time later, when various activities started taking place in the area, such as lectures, lessons, activities in mosques and *masjids*,[13] and meetings with the people, we held awareness-raising activities and seminars, lectures, and lessons, and my relationships with the people

---

11 Ayatollah Shamseddin (1943–2001) was the head of the Supreme Shia Council of Lebanon, until his death in 2001.

12 A reference to the Twelfth Imam, who adherents of the main Twelver Shia Islam believe went into occultation in the ninth century CE. The missing Imam, it is thought, will return as the Mahdi (the "Guided One") to defeat tyranny and bring justice and peace to the world.

13 The prayer hall area of a mosque complex.

of the region burgeoned—especially with those active in Islamic circles. I became a pioneer in the area, since I was a member of the Amal Movement, which was the only one holding activities in the region, and had held, since my early childhood, a great deal of affection for Imam Mousa al-Sadr. Sayyed Abbas, other brethren and I therefore started cooperating with the Amal Movement in holding awareness-raising and cultural activities in the Bekaa.

I joined the Amal Movement while we were still at the seminary, though Sayyed Abbas did not; and above and beyond the activities we held through the seminary, as a member of Amal I became active at the organizational level in the Bekaa. I kept this up, in addition to my studies, until 1982, and assumed several positions within the Movement, ranging from organizational officer for the First District, to which the Bekaa belongs, to president of the Bekaa District Court.

NIDA AL-WATAN: *They have a court of their own?*

HN: Yes, they have an internal organizational court.

NIDA AL-WATAN: *What happened after that?*

HN: The political official in charge of the Bekaa—another position I held—became a de facto member of Amal's Political Bureau. By now it was already 1982, the year Israel invaded Lebanon. The way Amal dealt with the invasion gave rise to several internal problems, which should best remain unmentioned, since today such talk provokes particular sensitivities.[14]

From the organizational point of view, we in the Bekaa took issue with certain political positions taken by Amal and, at the same time, were very politically involved in thinking about the need for military operations against the occupation. This was when we decided to leave Amal. We therefore left Amal without any problem because, at least as far as we were concerned, the Movement was no longer up to the task required at that particular juncture, and we were seeking an alternative that would allow us to operate the way we wanted to. Thus, after leaving Amal we established the nucleus of a new movement, which soon became known as Hezbollah—although

---

14 See p. 25, n. 5.

when it started it had no name, since no one took the time to find a suitable one for it. We were quite a large group of young men, and we all enrolled in military training camps until the arrival of the Iranian Revolutionary Guards.[15]

NIDA AL-WATAN: *What role did the Iranian Revolutionary Guards play?*

HN: Their role was limited to firing us up with the spirit that prevailed on the front in Iran, but we also benefited from their advanced abilities in our training camps. On the organizational level, they helped us delineate the operational context, and form a new movement and political line all to ourselves.

NIDA AL-WATAN: *Whom do you mean by yourselves?*

HN: I mean the group of young Lebanese men, among whom were Sayyed Abbas Mussawi, Sayyed Jimmy al Tufeili, Sayyed Ibrahim al Amin, and Sheikh Mohammad Yazbek,[16] all of whom were religious scholars from the Bekaa, in addition to another large group of people whose names are known mostly in the Bekaa.

NIDA AL-WATAN: *Given that your new movement did not have a name, an address, or a political line yet, how did you introduce yourselves? Who were you, and who are you? Were you looking for an identity?*

HN: We were looking for a name. But there are people who give the child a name even before he is born—we left the name until after the birth. This way, if he is born too long, we would give him a long name, if he is graceful and delicate, we would certainly not give [him] a rough name (...) so we said, let the baby be born first, let us see what nature, size, and tendencies it has, then we will find a suitable name for it.

NIDA AL-WATAN: *What made you choose the name of Hezbollah for this core entity?*

15 See above, p. 26 n. 8.

16 Al-Amin and Yazbek, alongside Mussawi and Tufeili, were founding members of Hezbollah, and both remain members of the Shura Council.

HN: The nature of the movement that saw the light played a determining role at that time. The movement did not seek worldly pursuits, and both its young and old members had dedicated themselves to God. So what decision could we have reached? What was this movement all about? It was a resistance movement, pure and simple. There was never talk or questions raised about the system in Lebanon or the future of the regime, parliament or the government (...) there was no talk about Lebanese political life. At the time, all these issues were out of context for us. The only reality for us was the fact that there was a country under occupation whose future and fate nobody knew.

We are therefore a movement born as a reaction to the occupation of part of our country; and the rest of Lebanon is now under the threat of a similar fate (...). Even when we were in Baalbek and Israel was in the western Bekaa, there was uncertainty as to whether or not Israel would push further inland and occupy the entire Bekaa Valley. We therefore had certain priorities imposed on us, not only as a consequence of our ideological position vis-à-vis Israel, but also because of the everyday living conditions of the people. You thus had a situation in which there was an occupied country—our own to be exact; Israel the victor that had managed to achieve its grand objectives; [there was] a defeated Arab nation; and there was, of course, us, the young movement getting ready to fight against a legendary army.

Such aspirations need particular kinds of men and youths who do not fear the destruction of their homes, hunger, thirst, wounds or injury (...). There was a need for a jihadi spirit, for a sense of sacrifice, for giving without restraint, and for transcending all calculations, selfishness, and personal temptations. People who are born with such tendencies and have such a spirit deserve the best name of all—a name that befits them best. A group of people who dedicate themselves to God Almighty and decide to become martyrs in the fight against the enemy, in spite of the obvious fact that there is no balance of power either militarily or in fighting abilities, these people deserve to call themselves Hezbollah—the Party of God.

This is how the name came to be (...)

At that time, I was one of the founders, and assumed several positions within Hezbollah while we were still in the Bekaa.

NIDA AL-WATAN: *How did you form the party, and how did Sayyed Nasrallah and others develop within the party? Do any of you still have a personal life or a separate identity from the party?*

HN: After 1982, our youth, years, life, and time became part of Hezbollah.

NIDA AL-WATAN: *Did politics ever take over, or did the military aspect of the resistance remain your only focus?*

HN: The main effort was at the time concentrated on recruiting young men, enrolling them into the military training camps, and organizing them into small groups to enable them to carry out resistance operations against the occupation. This is exactly how things were then; in other words, there were no institutions, no wide-ranging internal organizational structure, or specialized services, [as there are] now. There was only a collective system, which essentially focused on performing two tasks: first, recruiting, training, and organizing young men in groups, and infiltrating into the occupied territories to carry out operations; and second, launching an awareness-raising campaign among the people to lift their morale, re-energize them, instill in them the feeling of enmity towards Israel, and spread among them the policy and objectives of the resistance regarding the occupation. It was necessary to address the people about this issue, using proper mobilizing language rather than giving them theories and political analyses.

This is why, if you go back to the political archives, you will notice that our early rhetoric leaned strongly towards mobilization rather than politics. People at that time needed instigation, not lectures; they also needed freedom (…)

NIDA AL-WATAN: *How many recruits did you have then? Can we know that now, given that some time has passed?*

HN: As far as public support went, we developed a relatively wide base after we started our work in the Bekaa. As to the number of people in our core organization, they were at most 2,000 people, all young men who were ready and willing to follow and persevere on our path, and who sought martyrdom in their confrontation with the occupation.

Also at that time, we started gradually building up our organizational infrastructure, and I assumed several positions within it, the last being at the level of developing the basic cadres. I was in charge of the Bekaa region at a time when we only had a central command, and were present only in three areas of the country, namely the Bekaa, Beirut, and the south. In early 1985 they asked me to leave the Bekaa and take over responsibility for Beirut.

NIDA AL-WATAN: *Was it not strange to have someone in charge of the Bekaa while Sayyed Abbas Mussawi was there?*

HN: Sayyed Abbas was a member of the Central Command.

NIDA AL-WATAN: *So you went to Beirut—why did they take that decision?*

HN: We went to Beirut because our initial organizational efforts focused on the Bekaa, since it was the only area not under occupation. However, when the Israelis withdrew from Beirut, those founders [of Hezbollah] who had gained some experience building the organization and developing its political line in the Bekaa were chosen to start developing the still nascent cadres in Beirut. Since I was responsible for the Bekaa, and therefore well aware of the various plans, policies, programs, and capabilities of the party, in addition to my organizational skills, I was asked to take over responsibility for Beirut.

They asked three of us to go to Beirut: Sayyed Ibrahim al-Amin, myself, and (...).[17] Sayyed Ibrahim al-Amin was required to play a political role, and I myself assumed an organizational role. Sayyed Ibrahim was also the official spokesman for the party when it issued its "Open Letter," containing Hezbollah's first ever complete and comprehensive vision regarding the political situation, the regime in power, the Christians, political parties, the Palestinians, Israel, the United Nations, the emergency forces, and the resistance. All this talk today about a new Hezbollah policy is inaccurate; the letter, which Sayyed Ibrahim read as spokesman on the occasion of the anniversary of Sheikh Ragheb Harb's martyrdom, contained Hezbollah's entire political program.[18] As for the reasons behind choosing me for the organizational and

---

17 Ellipsis in original transcript of interview.
18 For Ragheb Harb, see above, p. 53 n. 8.

semi-founding role in Beirut, it was due to the good relations I had developed with a number of essential cadres in Beirut.

NIDA AL-WATAN: *How did this relationship start, through Amal or... ?*

HN: (...) Partly through Amal, partly not, and some links were developed through the religious seminary in Baalbek. Studying in Baalbek did not mean that we were out of touch with the south or with Beirut.

We launched a movement in Beirut aimed at the youth and the population in general, and the Israeli withdrawal from parts of the south provided us with the opportunity to do the same there; Beirut, however, was the main center of our activity. A period of great activity in the Bekaa, Beirut, and the south took off, and our institutions and secret committees were established. We were thus no longer able to continue working at a simple organizational infrastructure level, comprising a single central command and three regions. We had to build up this basic infrastructure due to the growth and spread of our movement, and instead established what can be best described as an "Executive Committee," at the head of which we appointed a wise member of our command structure. This Committee was responsible for all executive duties within the party with the exception of political relations, including issues relating to organization, jihad, publicity, culture, social affairs, and extra-curricular activities.

I therefore became a member of the Central Command, at a time when that position's existence was not known, and I was simply introduced as the president of the Executive Council. I remained in that position for a time, until I traveled to Qom in order to continue my education at its religious seminary.[19]

NIDA AL-WATAN: *This is rather strange—was there a political crisis of some sort?*

HN: In spite of my involvement in politics, I was very eager to continue my education, and I still feel that way (...). I wish someone else were secretary-general in my place, so that I could fulfill this personal desire. Naturally, press analyses said that internal disagreements were behind my departure for

19 See above, Introduction, p. 7–8.

Qom, but none of that was true; my brothers had actually insisted that I stay on account of the very sensitive nature of my responsibilities, which required experience and awareness. I was afraid to miss the boat, as far as educational opportunities available to me were concerned, and afraid that with age and time I would also lose the necessary mental abilities.

When I left, my intention was to stay a minimum of five years in Qom, which was the minimum number of years necessary to finish my education. That particular year, the party passed through difficult circumstances due to the various sensitive incidents that took place in Lebanon—including the problems between the Amal Movement and the party—and this made it necessary for me to return home.[20] Relationships among us party-members are not simply political, but brotherly, transparent, and existential in nature; I therefore could not morally justify my absence or ignore the difficulties that my brethren were going through, regardless of how eager and convinced I was about the need to pursue my education, and I hastened back to Beirut.

Sheik Naim al-Qassem[21] had been selected as president of the Executive Committee and as a member of the Central Command, so I assisted him in various fields until it was again time for elections in Hezbollah. Sayyed Abbas was elected secretary-general, Sheikh Naim al-Qassem was appointed as the deputy secretary-general, and I returned to my position as president of the Executive Council. On February 16, 1992—on that same day—both Sheikh Ragheb Harb and Sheik Abbas Mussawi were martyred,[22] and I was unanimously elected secretary-general.

NIDA AL-WATAN: *How do you explain this unanimity? Was it due to your personal attributes or to objective circumstances?*

HN: Although what I am about to tell you is one of the party's secrets, I will nevertheless speak about it openly. Members of the *Shura* Council discuss among themselves a number of names regarding the post of secretary-general,

---

20 For a discussion of problems between Amal and Hezbollah, see above, Statement 1.

21 Qassem retained the post of deputy secretary-general of Hezbollah, although he ranked higher than Nasrallah—a development which raised speculation that Qassem was, in effect, passed over for the top post, perhaps because of Nasrallah's allegedly closer ties to Tehran and Khameini.

22 Harb was assassinated on the same day, but eight years before, on February 16, 1984.

to determine whether there are any obstacles to prevent them from occupying that particular position. As far as I was concerned, and from the very beginning, there were no obstacles to my assuming that position. Some of the brethren proposed that I fill that position, and then my name was proposed a second time; we always took into consideration extraordinary circumstances, and my name was always there, regardless of whether or not these extraordinary circumstances had taken place, or whether the legal period had simply elapsed.

NIDA AL-WATAN: *What are the limits of the legal period?*

HN: It is two terms, or a period of between four and five years.

NIDA AL-WATAN: What are the considerations and restrictions that govern the choice of a secretary-general? Should he be the most learned, or the most scholarly?

HN: The secretary-general of Hezbollah sits at the movement's summit, and at the same time plays a political role. Today the party has no official spokesman, so the secretary-general assumes that role; this means that when he expresses an opinion he also commits the party to it. He is also responsible for the supervision of the party's internal activities. He therefore has to have cultural and scientific abilities, political acumen and administrative skills, and he must have the trust of the party's leaders, since they have entrusted him with an important responsibility.

An individual from within, not outside, the leadership structure is chosen for the position, and the command structure should be convinced as a whole that this man's attributes and abilities qualify him for this position of responsibility. This does not mean that he is the only one who possesses these attributes, or that others in the leadership structure are any less capable.

NIDA AL-WATAN: *A relationship undoubtedly exists between Iran and Hezbollah. What is the nature and size of this relationship, and what are its limits?*

HN: First, since Hezbollah is an Islamic movement, it falls under a de facto relationship with a supreme leader known as the "holder of religious leadership, commitment and authority." This person does not necessarily have to be from a particular nationality or tribe: he could be the first or the second [of the] Lebanese martyrs; he could be Sayyed Mohsen al-Hakim, who is an Iraqi; Sayyed Al-Khoei; or Imam al-Khomeini, who is an Iranian; or, one day, maybe even a Pakistani or a Bahraini.[23] You will therefore notice that the Constitution of the Islamic Republic says that the president of the Republic has to be an Iranian, but not necessarily the *wilayat al-faqih*.[24] This means that the *wilayat al-faqih*, who is at the very head of the Islamic Republic and of all the Muslims, can be from the Hijaz, Bahrain, Lebanon, or Iraq; and the president of the Republic, who is an Iranian, would therefore be under his command.

This relationship with this religious supreme leader is very important for our Islamic movement, regardless of whether he is in Najaf or Neauphles-le-Chateau,[25] or whether he is a leader holding sway over an entire country. The point I am trying to make is that our relationship to that leading, scholarly, and legal position is very important to us, regardless of whether the Islamic Republic [of Iran] exists or not. But this relationship does not mean that if this person is in Najaf we have to have a relationship with Iraq, regardless of whether this person has a positive or negative personal relationship with the regime. Right now, this person happens to be in Iran; therefore our relationship now is with someone in Iran. The same principle would apply if this religious and legally appointed supreme leader, the *wilayat al-faqih* in whom we believe, lived in Mecca, for example. The relationship is therefore not subject to geography or nationality; it is a matter of religious scholarship and legality, regardless of where it is located.

From the very beginning, we believed in the *wilayat al-faqih*, the guiding supreme leader, as someone who can lead the Islamic nation towards regaining its identity, its existence as an entity, and its self-esteem. We believed that Imam al-Khomeini, to whom we gave the name of "Imam of the Dispossessed," could have helped the weak and dispossessed of this world get rid of their oppressors, even if they were not Muslims and had not chosen him as their leader, simply because they were persecuted, abandoned, and

23 For al-Hakim and al-Khoei, see above, pp. 110 n. 12 and p. 110 n. 14 respectively.
24 For this concept, see above, p. 26 n. 9.
25 In October 1978, Khomeini took up residence in Neauphles-le-Chateau, France, where he remained until returning triumphantly from exile to Tehran on February 1, 1979.

mistreated. We believed in him as supreme leader and mentor, even when he was still living in exile, and before there was an Islamic Republic in Iran.

Then the Islamic Republic was established, and contrary to [the practice of] other parties that forge relationships with one country or another, Hezbollah did not form any such relationship with a ministry, institution, or state administration. Our relationship was only with the Imam in his capacity as the Imam of all Muslims, from whom we sought guidance and blessings. Today, Ayatollah Sayyed Khameini has succeeded Imam Khomeini,[26] and we still do not deal with him as the leader of Iran or of the Islamic Republic, but simply as the holder of a certain religious status, regardless of his position within the structure of power in Iran.

Contrary to rumors, today, as during Imam al-Khomeini's time, the Iranians do not interfere at all in our movement (...) our leaders are elected by a special body, and not appointed by Iran—not at all. In fact, we believe that the *wilayat al-faqih* does in fact have the right to appoint our leaders, because our movement has voluntarily handed its reins over to him; but what did Khameini the supreme leader say to that? He said, "No, your own Congress should be the one to elect your leaders" (...). Hezbollah's leadership, plans, programs, and the entire movement, are under our orders. We do not receive instructions from any ministry, nor any other authority. The same goes for the supreme leader and the Imam; they do not interfere in our personal affairs—they just formulate the general policy line. For example, both the supreme leader and the Imam, who wields legal authority, believe that we are an occupied country and that, as such, it is our legal right to resist this occupation. As to how we do it, they leave the matter for us to decide whether we throw a bomb or attack a position with Katyushas, and do not interfere at all. Iran, as a state, has nothing to do with this issue; on the other hand, the supreme leader, who has the right to interfere, does not do so at all; he only says that there should be a resistance, and Hezbollah does the rest.

For example, some people linked the vote of no confidence in the government, cast by Hezbollah's deputies in parliament,[27] to the current tensions

---

26 For Khameini, see above, p. 54 n. 9.

27 Hezbollah, as a matter of policy, withheld its support for successive governments, preferring to stay outside of and opposed to any ruling authority constituted under what it argued was an unjust sectarian framework. Hamzeh points out that "It was only Hezbollah that proclaimed its

between Saudi Arabia and Iran (…). Iran learned about our position regarding the government at the same time as everyone else, through the usual media channels. All these internal Lebanese political issues, such as opposition or support, strategy and tactics, are our own business, and we view and deal with them as we see fit.

NIDA AL-WATAN: *Then what happened in Damascus?*

HN: Even when Dr. Wilayati came to Damascus, all he did was ask a few questions, for which he wanted answers to take back home in order to help find a solution. He asked a question and we answered, but in the end we will be the ones to decide.

Hezbollah is therefore an Islamic, Lebanese jihadist movement that has its own independent internal and local decision-making process, and its own independent leadership and cadres. Its relationship is with the supreme leader, who draws general policy lines not only for Hezbollah but for the nation as a whole, of which Hezbollah is only a part. Since this fundamental relationship is with the *wilayat al-faqih*, it is only natural for the Islamic Republic to feel comfortable in its relationship with us, and to be especially interested in mentoring and assisting us in certain cases. It is also natural because the Islamic Republic is the *wilayat al-faqih*'s authority structure, and we have a relationship with him (…) this is the nature of our relationship with Iran.

NIDA AL-WATAN: *How about funding?*

HN: They help us in certain respects, and we also secure our own funding through donations. Donations that go to institutions that support the supreme leader's activities are very generous, while other activities are covered by legitimate funds from religious charitable donations, such as the *Zakat* and

---

opposition to the nomination [of Rafik Hariri as premier], having proposed the name of Ibrahim Bayan (a Sunni from Baalbek loyal to Hezbollah) to fill the post of prime minister. Furthermore, during the vote of confidence on the new government of al-Hariri, Hezbollah's deputies voted against the government's political program, arguing that it neglected the two most important issues: the official recognition of the Islamic Resistance and a time table for the elimination of political confessionalism." Hamzeh, "Lebanon's Hezbollah," accessed online.

Akhmas.[28] Our religious scholars have permission to benefit from legitimate funds donated by Shia religious authorities.

NIDA AL-WATAN: *For example?*

HN: For example, someone who has legal religious authority to donate funds approaches one of the religious scholars or sheikhs, and there are major donors among the world's Shia, whose *Akhmas* add up to enormous amounts. This person can give us the entire sum he wishes to donate, and we will decide what to do with it and whether to use it all or in part. It is the same with the current construction project, for which we obtained a general license, and for individuals whose shares have reached maturity; they can now go to the south and help in the reconstruction. The permission is comprehensive enough for that.

NIDA AL-WATAN: *A final question: the Western media always focus on the "appointment" of the learned scholar, Sayyed Mohammad Hussein Fadlallah,[29] as Hezbollah's supreme spiritual guide, which His Eminence has regularly denied. What is the nature of the party's relationship with Sayyed Fadlallah?*

HN: What His Eminence says is very exact: there is no organizational link between the leadership and decision-making process of the party and His Eminence. However, apart from the organizational aspect, Sayyed Mohammad Hussein Fadlallah has a very special position in what we call the "Islamic scene" in Lebanon—a position he earned thanks to his high level of education, personality, and broadmindedness, and his secular, social, and organizational activities throughout the years.

NIDA AL-WATAN: *You were one of his students in al-Nabaa Quarter. How much were you influenced by him?*

HN: This is true. From this important perspective we can appreciate the

28 *Zakat* is obligatory almsgiving for Muslims, and one of the five pillars of Islam. *Akhmas*, the plural of *Khums*, or "five," is the requirement for Shiites to pay one fifth of their surplus annual income to charity, customarily via religious institutions.
29 For Fadlallah, see above, p. 40 n. 8.

status of Sayyed Mohammad Hussein as far as the Islamic scholars, leaders, cadres, bases, and youth are concerned; they all have a lot of respect, love, and appreciation for him. Hezbollah, however, made no commitment towards him from the organizational point of view, although he holds a lofty position among Muslims, and one feels compelled to consult him and benefit from his wisdom. Sayyed Fadlallah himself does not give his opinion in the expectation that Hezbollah or any other organization will commit to it; neither does Hezbollah feel committed. It can, of course, benefit from his opinion, though the final decision remains solely in the hands of [Hezbollah's] leadership.

Undoubtedly, there is a feeling of common fate between Hezbollah and Sayyed Mohammad Hussein, due to our common spiritual and intellectual way of thinking and the historical relationship that exists between us. This sense of common fate gives the observer the impression that Sayyed Mohammad Fadlallah is no stranger to Hezbollah, and is its spiritual guide. The Sayyed is a highly learned Islamic personality, who has a great deal of influence on the Islamic scene in general; but Hezbollah, its cadres and decision-makers are entirely separate.

NIDA AL-WATAN: *Your participation in the National Assembly—in other words, your entry into the Lebanese political game—has given rise to a sensitive debate within Hezbollah and a lot of speculation from outside the party. What are the reasons behind your decision to participate in the Lebanese body politic?*

HN: The National Assembly issue is one of the items on our priority list, at the top of which lies the resistance; but we also live in a community that has its own political and social life, as well as its own daily worries and problems. We fight on mountain-tops and in the valleys, but live in this community and are a part of it. We are not a foreign army that has come from elsewhere to liberate another people's land; we are part of this people, our own land is occupied, and we want to liberate it.

Once we had succeeded in liberating our territory in 1982, and from then until 1985, we said that we wanted to pursue our resistance and start a process of political openness and participation in Lebanon's political life, and considered this to be one of our responsibilities; because apart from the resistance, solving people's problems, reconstruction, education and culture are also high on our priority list. We shoulder these responsibilities because we are not simply an armed movement; when we said from the very beginning that we are an Islamic jihadist movement, it meant that we also have a civilized social program that goes beyond the mere carrying of a gun.

Based on that, we opened up politically, launched our political movement, established political relationships, and expressed our opinion on several matters through various statements.[30] Then it was time for new elections, and we found that we could make our voices heard by the Lebanese people through the National Assembly and the usual parliamentary press coverage. Furthermore, our relationship with others through parliament would be less complicated than if it was directly with the secretary-general. Relationships with a parliamentarian, for example, would not have the same repercussions as a direct relationship with Hezbollah. We also wanted to make the extent of our public support known to all in response to some foreign speculation that had spread rumors to the effect that Hezbollah is merely a group of armed men in Baalbek, the Southern Suburb, and the south, when it has, in fact, a large popular base. Our presence in parliament could also provide the resistance, in which we strongly believe, with the political support and endorsement it needs.

Our presence in parliament, therefore, provides us with a platform from which we can defend public causes, and gives us the opportunity to serve the people's interests from within the very institution that issues legislation and enacts laws. We are convinced that our participation in enacting laws will be very useful, because we are among those who have the people's interests most at heart. We are also the furthest from factional and partisan self-interest, and the most steadfast in what we believe.

Furthermore, and with all due respect to the deputies, there are probably some who could be bought (I respect the deputies, but this could happen) with $5,000 or $10,000, whereas billions of dollars would not buy our deputies' positions; we have absolute confidence in our brothers in parliament. These are the reasons for which we entered parliament.

---

30 Most notably, of course, through the party's founding statement—the 1985 "An Open Letter to the Downtrodden in Lebanon and in the World."

NIDA AL-WATAN: *Is it true that Christians voted for you in large numbers in the Bekaa?*

HN: We have [voting] tabulations, which I do not have with me now, that show that a certain Christian town, whose name I do not recall, gave our list 304 out of its 365 votes, while another Christian town did not give us a single vote.

NIDA AL-WATAN: *In spite of all the assurances that you have nothing to do with the kidnapping of the hostages, there is still a general perception, inside and outside the country, that Hezbollah is responsible. What is the truth of the matter?*

HN: I cannot of course say that the Islamic scene is a total stranger to the incident, and that the kidnappers were Arab nationalists or communists. In fact, a group of young men had been arrested in Kuwait because they had targeted a number of American and French interests there; some were condemned to death and others sentenced to life imprisonment.[31] Some might even have been handed over to the Americans (...). These detainees had friends and brothers in Islamic circles, but not in Hezbollah, because the party had not yet been established when the incident occurred. Therefore, a group of people did indeed carry out the operation, but the fact remains that they were not members of Hezbollah, and they acted on an individual basis. They believed that this method was the only one available to them to secure the release of their friends, or at least to prevent the death penalty from being carried out or to stop their being handed over to the United States.

Any further speculation would be completely wrong. This group had planned and studied the impact of their action on the political situation. But to say that the incident happened as the result of a decision by Iran, Syria, or Lebanon is completely wrong; the matter is much simpler than people think. But it is possible that certain people's behavior during the Lebanese civil war, which saw tit-for-tat kidnappings between East and West Beirut, has influenced these young men's behavior to some degree. Still, the fact remains that the Americans, French, and Germans can bring a lot of influence to bear on the issue of the detainees in Kuwait, which probably explains

---

31 For kidnapping in Lebanon during the 1980s and 1990s, see above, p. 72 n. 22.

why American, French, and German citizens were kidnapped in Beirut.

No Islamist organization has any connection with this incident, including Hezbollah, none whatsoever; but like everyone else in Lebanon, Hezbollah was privy to information about these kidnapping operations. The only [way] in which Hezbollah has interfered—yes, interfered—is by seeing to it that the release of the hostages is part of a solution to the problem as a whole, and Syria and Iran interfered for this same reason. Our efforts to take advantage of the incident to secure the release of our own detainees in Khiam and other Israeli prisons are our own business.[32] Furthermore, Hezbollah is eager to see the end of this hostage issue, since its fallout ended up entirely on the party's shoulders. Given that there are indeed young men languishing in prison, our interest in the matter did not at all cause us to consider using force against these groups to compel them to release the hostages. However, although we never contemplated using force, we did want various parties to put their efforts behind finding a political solution to the problem.

The truth is that simple, and I believe that any Lebanese citizen who followed what happened in Lebanon since 1974, and then in 1983–84, is aware of how we do things in this country, and would therefore simply accept this scenario. A Westerner, on the other hand, might not (...). In any case, they are free to accept or reject it.

NIDA AL-WATAN: *There were reports in the press recently that Hezbollah might target American and Western interests abroad. Is this based on something you have said?*

HN: Even at the height of the Israeli violence against Lebanese civilians during the Seven-Day War, we never said anything of the sort. We will never use that language in the future either.

NIDA AL-WATAN: *The relationship between Hezbollah and Syria has had many ups and downs, from extreme disagreement to close friendship, so to speak.*

HN: Our relationship with Syria is a strategic one. Hezbollah's strategic cause is its resistance against occupation, for which it has sacrificed a great deal.

---

32 For Khiam see above, p. 97 n. 24.

Since 1982 we have considered the Syrian position as being supportive of the resistance as a right and a practice, which is a supportive and genuine position towards us. In this regard, we agree with the Syrian leadership on the general broad lines; but when an incident takes place between them and us in Baalbek, West Beirut or the Southern Suburb, we look at it as we look at other such incidents that have happened between them and their so-called best friends.[33] We are now in 1993, and we know very well who is genuinely behind the resistance and who is not, and who is disposed to use the resistance as a bargaining chip and who is not (...)

I would like to say, in all honesty, that Syria has a big role to play in Lebanon on both the political and official levels, especially in relation to garnering more support for the resistance and rectifying certain attitudes and convictions. We therefore believe, regardless of the proper protocol to follow or the right number of visits to exchange, that Hezbollah and Syria are standing together in the same genuine, existentialist and jihadist trench. This is why our relationship with the Syrian leadership is important to us.

We have been trying to improve our relations with Syria for a long time now, and especially in recent days, because several issues on which we had not acted before in Lebanon have now been placed on our priority list, because we have become part of the National Assembly. During the Seven-Day War, both our relationship and our trust in each other improved, and we in Hezbollah have noticed that the Syrian rhetoric has become more reassuring.

NIDA AL-WATAN: *What if negotiations are successful and a peace agreement is concluded with Israel? This puts you face to face with the question as to what you really want to achieve through the resistance. Do you want to liberate the south? Do you want to liberate the entire land of Palestine? Or maybe you want to thwart the negotiations, to serve Iran's interests in the region?*

HN: There is more than one aspect to this issue. One of them [is] that resistance is a jihadist activity and a reaction to occupation, which means

33 Nasrallah is most likely referring to the February 24, 1987 killing of 24 Hezbollah fighters in the Basta district of Beirut by Syrian units. The blow to Hezbollah by the Syrian army, which was bent on exercising greater control over West Beirut, marked a low point for relations between the party and Damascus—not to mention Tehran and Damascus.

that there is a resistance against occupation; this resistance had started before negotiations did. We have therefore not launched our resistance movement as a negotiating tool to put pressure on the parties around the table of negotiations. If the Arab negotiator wishes to benefit by using our resistance as a negotiating card, he is free to do so; but when I fight Israel, carry out operations, or launch the Shihine operation, I do not do so in order to weaken or strengthen the people around the negotiating table. I act with the mentality of a resistance fighter.

The objective of the resistance is the liberation of the land. It is true that we do not believe in negotiations, and consider them more than just a mistake; but just as we want to guarantee the future of the resistance on the ground, we also have the best interests of the people at heart. Because we read the future very clearly, the path we have chosen does not involve dragging the region into a war with the intention of ruining the negotiations. Neither do I place my resistance movement at the service of regional or Iranian interests, even if this is our path. The Seven-Day War was a good opportunity for us to drag the region into an all-out war, and we did not do so. One needs to ponder deeply the response to the following question: In whose interest would dragging the region into an all-out war be? Is it in our own people's interest, or the Israeli enemy's?

We do not think about the negotiating table, but about the occupied land and an enemy who threatens the entire region. I want to fight this enemy any way I can, until I achieve victory. In our private discussions, we say that while martyrdom is an individual project, Hezbollah's objective is to achieve victory; there is also an occupied territory that needs to be liberated, and a nation that should not submit to Israel. The individual act of martyrdom should not therefore entail the martyrdom of the entire nation; my ultimate aim as Hezbollah, and my ultimate aim as a nation, is victory, not martyrdom.

If a solution is ever reached, a number of questions will inevitably start being asked regarding the future of the resistance and the negotiations—by the enemy as well as by friends and supporters. We in Hezbollah have the answers to these questions but prefer to keep them to ourselves, for it is not right from strategic or tactical points of view to announce one's program, movements, tactics or strategy if there is not yet a solution (...). It does not make sense to announce them now or in the near future, for I believe that there will be a right time to do this with clarity and precision. We have the answers figured out in multiple scenarios, and we are not at all confused (…) rest assured.

[Conclusion by Nida Al Watan] Sayyed Nasrallah is married to Mrs. Fatima Yassin from Abbasiya, in southern Lebanon, and when we asked him if it was a love match he said, laughing: "Something of this sort." As to how this love blossomed between Baalbek and Abbasiya, and whether it was love by correspondence, Nasrallah said:

You are right to be surprised, but I was not a prisoner in Baalbek, and used to go to the south every now and then. I did not know her at the beginning, but met her through my friendship with her brothers. Her brother is Sheikh Hassan Yassin, who was in the same group with me in Najaf. I gradually got to know her better, thanks to my friendship with her brother.

9

THE APRIL UNDERSTANDING

April 30, 1996

Supported by a joint willingness on the part of Israel and Syria to negotiate, the verbal "Understanding" of 1993 generally held in Lebanon, at least in the sense that the country did not again incur another massive attack by its neighbor. However, as Hezbollah operations against Israeli forces and the SLA[1] within and around the "security zone" intensified in March 1996—perhaps as a means of signifying Assad's dismay over the US-led Sharm al-Sheikh anti-terrorism conference of that month—the situation quickly began to unravel as Israel sought to retaliate widely, both inside and outside of the zone. Although the sequence of causality and blame is difficult to reconstruct in the absence of a written agreement, US peace negotiator Dennis Ross, in his 2004 post-mortem, The Missing Peace, acknowledges that Israeli fire into civilian areas of Lebanon served as the catalyst for the first Hezbollah rocket fire into northern Israel. He reiterates his particular interpretation, however, that the terms of the 1993 Understanding permitted such Israeli action, and that Hezbollah, in any event, had begun to "show far less concern than previously about actually shooting rather than staging attacks from Lebanese civilian areas."[2]

Israel's "Grapes of Wrath" campaign, which followed on April 11, ended sixteen days later with 165 Lebanese civilians killed and 401 wounded, and with widespread damage to civilian infrastructure including highways, bridges, and electrical stations. Sixty-two Israeli civilians were wounded in Israel as a result of Hezbollah rocket fire. Although there were far fewer refugees than in 1993, the Israeli shelling of a UN compound at Qana on April 18, which killed 106 Lebanese villagers, dealt a similarly powerful moral blow to Israeli

---

1 See p. 66, n. 13.
2 Dennis Ross, *The Missing Peace: The Inside Story of the Fight for Middle East Peace* (New York: Farrar, Straus & Giroux, 2004), p. 250.

Prime Minister Shimon Peres's claim to be merely trying to end "Hezbollah terror."[3] More of a blow than Qana, however, was the fact that Peres and the IDF were forced to admit that their enemy was simply not going to run out of rockets, contrary to earlier assessments. In other words, if the IDF campaign continued without a large-scale, sustained ground operation, Hezbollah attacks on targets within Israel would likely continue well beyond the Israeli elections in late May.

Given all this, the US was forced to change its course from supporting Israel's campaign to intervening in the hope of achieving a ceasefire that might simultaneously end the carnage and bolster Peres's increasingly precarious position before voting actually started. (A Labour victory was seen by the Clinton administration as vital for moving the peace process forward.)

Apparently undeterred by its weakened bargaining position, however, the initial US proposal sought to end attacks on Israeli and Lebanese civilians, but also called for Hezbollah to be disarmed. If no attacks took place during a six-month period, Israel would then agree to begin discussions on a full withdrawal from Lebanon.

The maximalist US proposal was roundly rejected by the Lebanese government, Hezbollah, and Syria. Instead, the dynamics of the situation, which had turned so strongly against the US and Israel, shortly resulted in a far different, written agreement, promoted by the French— "The April Understanding."[4] Most significantly, the Understanding affirmed the legitimacy of Hezbollah's military operations in Lebanon, greatly restricted attacks on Lebanese civilians by the Israelis, and placed a modest prohibition on Hezbollah attacks launched directly from civilian areas.

In a surprising turn, though, US Secretary of State Warren Christopher immediately undermined the agreed language by delivering a "side letter" to Peres, which read: "The United States understands that the prohibition refers not only to the firing of weapons, but also to the use of these areas by armed groups as bases from which to carry out attacks." Of course, while a new negotiation over what precisely constituted a "base" might have been joined, no

---

3 Hezbollah would later be criticized by human rights organizations and the UN for the actions of its fighters who were determined to have fired on Israeli forces from positions within several hundred meters of the UN compound.

4 The text of the April Understanding, as posted on the website of the Israeli Ministry of Foreign Affairs, reads as follows: "The United States understands that after discussions with the governments of Israel and Lebanon and in consultation with Syria, Lebanon and Israel will ensure the following: 1. Armed groups in Lebanon will not carry out attacks by Katyusha rockets or by any kind of weapon into Israel. 2. Israel and those cooperating with it will not fire any kind of weapon at civilians or civilian targets in Lebanon. 3. Beyond this, the two parties commit to ensuring that under no circumstances will civilians be the target of attack and that civilian populated areas and industrial and electrical installations will not be used as launching grounds for attacks. 4.

such effort was made. Instead, Israel had language that the original parties had not agreed upon that gave it a far freer hand in the future to fire again into civilian areas in Lebanon—thereby potentially incurring Hezbollah rocket attacks into Israel.

Still, the Understanding itself stood as a remarkable document, especially in relation to US policy in the Middle East. Having designated Hezbollah by name as an enemy of the peace process by Executive Order in 1995, the Clinton administration now recognized—though not in name—the inherent right of Hezbollah to carry out attacks within Lebanon, regardless of any preconditions or the immediate needs of the peace process.

Not surprisingly, for Hezbollah—as Nasrallah makes clear in this interview with the Lebanese daily As-Safir—the Understanding represented a crucial victory, perhaps on a par with the party's improved standing among the Lebanese after it had withstood and responded to massive Israeli firepower during the sixteen-day Grapes of Wrath campaign.

AS-SAFIR: *Some say that this confrontation is the result of a clash between two attempts to bring the situation to a head. On the one hand, there is the American–*

Without violating this understanding, nothing herein shall preclude any party from exercising the right of self-defense. A Monitoring Group is established consisting of the United States, France, Syria, Lebanon and Israel. Its task will be to monitor the application of the understanding stated above. Complaints will be submitted to the Monitoring Group. In the event of a claimed violation of the understanding, the party submitting the complaint will do so within 24 hours. Procedures for dealing with the complaints will be set by the Monitoring Group. The United States will also organize a Consultative Group, to consist of France, the European Union, Russia and other interested parties, for the purpose of assisting in the reconstruction needs of Lebanon. It is recognized that the understanding to bring the current crisis between Lebanon and Israel to an end cannot substitute for a permanent solution. The United States understands the importance of achieving a comprehensive peace in the region. Towards this end, the United States proposes the resumption of negotiations between Syria and Israel and between Lebanon and Israel at a time to be agreed upon, with the objective of reaching comprehensive peace. The United States understands that it is desirable that these negotiations be conducted in a climate of stability and tranquility. This understanding will be announced simultaneously at 1800 hours, April 26, 1996, in all countries concerned. The time set for implementation is 0400 hours, April 27, 1996."

The text of the side letter, also posted on the website of the Israeli Ministry of Foreign Affairs and written by US Secretary of State Warren Christopher to Peres on April 30, 1996, reads: "Dear Mr. Prime Minister: With regard to the right of self-defense referred to in the Understanding dated April 26, 1996, the United States understands that if Hezbollah or any other group in Lebanon acts inconsistently with the principles of the Understanding or launches attacks on Israeli forces in Lebanon, whether that attack has taken the form of firing, ambushes, suicide attacks, roadside explosives, or any other type of attack, Israel retains the right in response to take appropriate self-defense measures against the armed groups responsible for the attack. With regard to the prohibitions on the use of certain areas as launching grounds for attacks, the United States understands that the prohibition refers not only to the firing of weapons, but also to the use of these areas by armed groups as bases from which to carry out attacks."

Israeli desire to implement the Sharm al-Sheikh resolutions,[5] plant the seeds of a security arrangement in the area, and take advantage of the military agreement with Turkey, among other [things]. On the other hand, there is a desire on the part of Hezbollah, Syria, and Iran to put to the test the coalition that saw the light in Sharm al-Sheikh, break the isolation imposed on them, and bring down Shimon Peres. In your opinion, what brought all this about?

HN: Regarding the first part of your question—the Israeli–American wish to escalate the situation—it is a fact and a foregone conclusion, especially after the summit conference of Sharm al-Sheikh, which complicated the search for an Arab and international cover for targeting resistance movements in the region, which they call terrorist organizations. All of us in the region know that it is precisely this refusal to provide cover for an attack on the region, and the targeting of its resistance movements, that prevented Syria and Lebanon from taking part in this conference. Thus, as soon as it obtained the necessary cover from Sharm al-Sheikh, Israel launched wide-ranging operations against the region's resistance movements. The targeted organizations are those movements that carry out high-level jihadist operations against Israel—namely Hamas, Islamic Jihad in Palestine, and Hezbollah in Lebanon, although we do not want to minimize the efforts of other smaller groups.

The Israeli enemy, in cooperation with Yasser Arafat, the head of the Palestine National Authority, has launched brutal attacks—though we cannot say fatal—against Hamas and Islamic Jihad in Palestine,[6] and they have yet to target the resistance in Lebanon. This American–Israeli decision enjoys some hard-earned cover and support from Sharm al-Sheikh, and their operations

5 The March 13, 1996 "Summit of Peacemakers," as the conference at the Egyptian Red Sea resort of Sharm al-Sheikh was known, ended with a declaration by the 29 world leaders (including 14 Arab leaders) that strongly condemned "all acts of terror in all its abhorrent forms … including recent terrorist attacks in Israel." A working group on terrorism was also created, in order to enforce the parties' aim of bringing the "instigators of such [terrorist] acts to justice."

6 The Palestinian Hamas and Islamic Jihad movements had already taken responsibility for numerous attacks on Israeli civilians by the time that Islamic Jihad claimed responsibility for four suicide bombings, in nine days during February 1996—bombings that had killed 59 Israelis. As both movements were headquartered in Damascus, the US and Israel demanded that Assad crack down immediately, in order to prove his commitment to the ongoing Israeli–Syrian peace negotiations. As a result of his unwillingness to do so, Syria was excluded from the Sharm al-Sheikh conference.

were timed to take place prior to the Israeli parliamentary elections, so that Shimon Perez can use them to boost his chances in the elections, as proof that he is a man of war, peace, and security.

What I want to say is that the desire for war is purely American–Israeli in nature, because on the other side of the equation neither the Lebanese resistance, Syria nor Iran have any desire to take part in it. The war we are keen to fight is the guerrilla war the Islamic Resistance is waging in the occupied territories. In our opinion, this guerrilla war is far more important and effective, and has more impact on the enemy and its plans and morale, than this recent despicable tit-for-tat war.

The war we want is the kind that makes the enemy bleed slowly, puts it under pressure, and forces it to leave our country. So it is incorrect to say that the resistance, Syria, or anyone else involved in Lebanon, had any desire to take part in such a war or bring the situation to a head.

AS-SAFIR: *What are Israel's objectives in launching such a war?*

HN: In fact everyone knows what these objectives are, and none of us can add anything new at this point. The objective of the operation is mainly to target the resistance's military infrastructure, isolate it popularly and politically, and eventually get rid of it once and for all: this is what the meeting in Sharm al-Sheikh was all about. However, for the enemy to say after the fact that these were not his objectives is a repetition of what took place in the so-called Operation Accountability, which started with very bombastic and wide-ranging objectives and ended with the July Understanding.[7] We believe that this was indeed the main objective of the operation, based on what they themselves declared in the early days of the war. By targeting the resistance the way they did, they hoped to damage its infrastructure, paralyze its movement in the south and in the western Bekaa, and stop the launching of Katyusha rockets, which we launch only in response to their own attacks. Their ultimate aim is to use these operations to foster disquiet among the [Lebanese] people, and force them to turn against the resistance and blame it for all that has befallen them. They hoped the operations would also put pressure on the Lebanese authorities, given that they probably have their

7 For the 1993 understanding, and for Operation Accountability, see Statement 7.

own calculations that might or might not be similar to those of the resistance. This pressure, added to the strikes that the military infrastructure of the resistance would sustain, was supposed to bring about the demise of the resistance, or to escalate the situation to a point at which Lebanon would completely surrender to Israel.

They hoped that the successful achievement of this objective would lead to the political isolation of Lebanon, force it to surrender, isolate it and impose on it a separate peace treaty, and thus complete the isolation of Syria. This would enable Peres and the Americans to conclude a settlement based on their own aspirations in the area; and if at some point in the future Syria wished to join in, it would be welcome—but only on Israel's conditions. If not, it would remain isolated in the region.

From the military point of view, Israel launched early today, Thursday, an air raid on a location in Baalbek by the name of Tallet al-Kayal, based on the belief that it contained warehouses and that a large number of *mujahidin* were inside. It also shelled a number of buildings in Bousoir, also on the assumption that there were weapons and Hezbollah's *mujahidin* inside; and on the heart of the Southern Suburb of Beirut, believing that it was actually targeting Hezbollah's leadership headquarters. The aim of the first strike was not to stop the Katyushas, but to strike at Hezbollah's military infrastructure and paralyze its resistance activities. In response to your question, I would say that we were able, on that first day, to absorb the initial strike, because Tallet al-Kayyal is not a military base, there were no *mujahidin* inside, and no one was killed. The buildings they struck in Bousoir were empty, and the location they shelled in the Southern Suburb is the home of ordinary people who are not even members of Hezbollah, let alone part of its leadership. Although it is true that in the area where the house is located there are various leadership headquarters, and the headquarters of the general secretariat are adjacent or just opposite the targeted building, the fact remains that they struck a building that belongs to ordinary people.[8]

---

8 Although the "rules of the game" embodied in the April Understanding were meant to restrict military conflict only to non-civilian and/or depopulated areas (including areas free of certain civilian infrastructure), human rights groups would repeatedly criticize the logic promulgated here by Nasrallah which, they argued, violated international law that, "requires [Hezbollah's] forces 'to the maximum extent feasible … avoid locating military objectives within or near densely

What was their first strike, then? Useless. And usually the side that loses the first strikes gets bogged down in the "routine" of the war. Naturally, Hezbollah's leadership took the necessary precautions and placed the resistance on the highest level of alert. In fact, July 1993 was a very good lesson for us as far as confronting this kind of aggression is concerned, because we pinpointed our strengths and weaknesses at the beginning of the war, and were therefore ready when the confrontation came.

Going back to the Israelis themselves, in my opinion they did not estimate correctly how much time the operation would require, and even the information they had proved to be wrong, as they themselves have since admitted. They might have expected the operation to confound Hezbollah and make it lose the ability to act; they thought that their concentrated and intense air strikes, and filling the skies with military aircraft, would prevent the *mujahidin* from firing Katyushas from here or there, and put an end to the rocket-launching. They believed that the resistance owns a limited number of rockets, and that on the first, second, or fifth day they would run out. The fact that they take this factor into account at all is not an indication of Israeli military strength, because those who believe that the firing of Katyushas will end only when there are no more left to launch are not depending on their own strength, but on the weakness of their enemy. All Israel's assumptions were wrong (...)

AS-SAFIR: *Could one divide this war into stages, both politically and on the ground?*

---

populated areas.' This rule," one 1997 Human Rights Watch report continued, "clearly encompasses the positioning of mortars and Katyusha rocket launchers within or in close proximity to concentrations of civilians, including displaced civilians sheltered on U.N. bases" – just as it does the positioning of leadership facilities and operational bases even if actual firing from such areas does not take place and even though a civilian area may be under direct threat from invading and/or attacking forces. See Human Rights Watch, "Military Operations by Lebanese Guerilla Forces," September 1997, accessed online.

Human rights groups would further argue over the years that, quite apart from the April Understanding, Hezbollah was bound by the requirements of international humanitarian law prohibiting the targeting of civilians or civilian infrastructure, even if Israel violated such law. As one 2006 Amnesty international report put it, "The fact that Israel in its attacks in Lebanon also committed violations of international humanitarian law amounting to war crimes, including indiscriminate and disproportionate attacks, is not an acceptable justification for Hezbollah violating the rules of war, whether as a deterrent or as a means of retaliation or retribution." Amnesty International, "Israel/Lebanon under fire: Hizbullah's attacks on northern Israel," September 14, 2006, accessed online.

HN: We could divide the unfolding events into two stages—before and after the massacres took place. From the Israeli military standpoint, however, nothing encourages us to speak about stages.

AS-SAFIR: *We finally come to the recent agreement. Can you give us an estimate, from the resistance's point of view, of the gains and losses, and of the restrictions that this Understanding places on the resistance's activities?*

HN: We could say, first of all, that the fact that this Understanding exists at all means that most of Israel's objectives behind the operation—to be on the safe side I do not say all of them—failed the moment Israel accepted the agreement. Striking Hezbollah has failed; ending the resistance by military means has failed; isolating Lebanon and leading it on its own from war straight to the negotiating table is over; the isolation of Syria is over; and even the portrayal of the Lebanese resistance as terrorists is over. The whole world now accepts the fact that the war in Lebanon is between Israel and resistance fighters defending their territory. When we read the text of the Understanding, we therefore arrive at the conclusion that the situation is effectively over.

I do not know whether you have noticed, but Israel's Foreign Minister Ehud Barak, the Chief of Staff Amnon Shahak,[9] and Peres denied in the past two days that Israel's objective was to disarm and deal a blow to Hezbollah, and impose a separate peace on Lebanon. Records of press conferences held in the first two days of war still exist, and you can go and have a look. It is normal for each side to view the Understanding from its own perspective, and to consider it a great feat of success. Similarly, if one side or the other wants to escape from applying its main terms, it could claim that a secret imperative allows it to do what the Understanding does not.

Here is the official Arabic-language translation of the Understanding, although the English-language version is the main one. I would like to say at the outset that we took part in writing the terms of the Understanding, although we have nothing to do with the text itself. Based on that, we see

9 Ehud Barak (1942–) would later become the tenth prime minister of Israel, from 1999 to 2000—a period that arguably represented the peak of Arab–Israeli peace efforts. Amnon Lipkin-Shahak (1944–) had succeeded Barak in 1995 as the fifteenth chief of general staff.

this Understanding as an agreement between the Lebanese government and the government of the Israeli entity.

The Understanding says the following: first, "Armed groups in Lebanon will not carry out attacks by Katyusha rockets or by any kind of weapon into Israel" (although we have reservations about the wording of this text, this provision was also included in the July Understanding); second, "Israel and those cooperating with it will not fire any kind of weapon at civilians or civilian targets in Lebanon". The phrase "and those cooperating with it" was not included in the July Understanding, and was added to this one. This agreement is more comprehensive than the July Understanding, and more to the advantage of Lebanon and its people. Why do I say this? I say it because the first agreement focuses on preventing the shelling of towns and villages, which means that if they strike a van carrying students to school, they can say that it is not a village, but a road. The same goes for a group of farmers working their field, because the Israelis can say that the field is not a village or an inhabited area. We have here two central points, civilians, and civilian targets that include vehicles on roads, ambulances and non-military installations (factories, electricity grids, and so on).

These two provisions therefore forbid the resistance from launching Katyushas and other such weapons into the occupied Palestinian territories, and forbid the Israeli enemy from shelling civilians and civilian targets. These two provisions, the main ones in the Understanding, are bolstered by the paragraph that says, "Beyond this, the two parties commit to ensuring that under no circumstances will civilians be the target of attack, and that civilian populated areas and industrial and electrical installations will not be used as launching grounds for attacks." This means that, when they launch an attack, the resistance, the Israelis, and Lahd's militia[10] should ensure that civilians are not targeted—and the "and" here means that both sides are bound by it. In other words, we not only have to desist from launching rockets from inhabited areas, but both the Israelis and Lahd's fighters cannot place artillery or rocket launchers in the heart of Marjayoun [in south Lebanon] or Kiryat Shmona [in northern Israel].[11]

10 For Antoine Lahd, see above, p. 97 n. 23.
11 Here, Nasrallah appears to offer an interpretation that would allow Hezbollah to place weapons within populated areas – or, in other words, to stage or base attacks from populated areas without actually firing from these same areas—but that Israel and its proxy, the SLA, were prohibited

There is some disagreement surrounding the wording of the provision relating to the launching of attacks, and the translation that the Israelis have adopted does not have either the term "to launch" or "the launching." It just said "Katyusha rocket launch sites,"[12] and made the life of the Lebanese easier; even those who used the term "the launching" when talking about the issue, admitted later that "to launch" was the right word. Another provision states, "Without violating this understanding, nothing herein shall preclude any party from exercising the right of self-defense." Shahak is trying here to confound the issue by saying that if occupation troops in the frontier zone are the target of a military operation, he has the right to retaliate by striking Hezbollah anywhere. Although the provision starts with the [phrase] "Without violating the Understanding," this is a violation of the Understanding, because although it allows for the right of self-defense, it is only subject to the terms of the first three provisions. What he calls "self-defense" we do not recognize as such, because an occupier has no right of self-defense; all he is required to do is withdraw. If he wishes to defend himself, he should only do it within the context of this Understanding.

If we want to evaluate the pros and cons of these provisions, and the concomitant establishment of a monitoring group, we can talk here about two objectives. First, these provisions do not constrain anyone in the resistance—resistance activities will continue, and [their] freedom of movement is maintained, as far as liberating the occupied territories is concerned. We can consider the provision that forbids the launching of attacks from within inhabited areas as being a constraining factor, but I would like you to know that we voluntarily imposed this condition on ourselves years ago. We committed ourselves from the very beginning not to use inhabited areas for launching missiles, or any other such purpose, because these villages are after all are our own. We cannot play the pretend game and say that a Japanese army came to fight in south Lebanon; we are Lebanese, our resistance fighters

---

from doing so. Christopher's side letter, of course, states that "the [Understanding's] prohibition refers not only to the firing of weapons, but also to the use of these areas by armed groups as bases from which to carry out attacks." Both sides, therefore, held interpretations, buttressed by the fungibility of the term "launching," that prohibited the other side from using civilian-populated areas as staging grounds for attacks.

12 Although an earlier Israeli version of the Understanding may have used this term, the version made available by the Israeli Ministry of Foreign Affairs corresponds to the accepted international version.

are Lebanese young men who hail from these same villages, and therefore care more about their families and their children than does the resistance—which itself cares a great deal. Nothing in the Understanding prevents us going to war, or resisting, to liberate our land, which means that the right to resist to free one's occupied land is guaranteed and unequivocal.

Our second objective is the protection of civilians: before the July Understanding, no one bothered about the Lebanese civilians—neither America, France, Russia, the European Union, the Arab League or the United Nations. It was nobody's business; we never even heard condemnations of civilian massacres in the south. The resistance used Katyushas in order to put pressure on the Israelis, and tell them that when Lebanese civilians are in danger, your civilians will also be in danger. You might say, and correctly so, that there is no parity in rocket or firepower between the two sides; but issuing threats, forcing Israeli civilians into underground shelters, wounding several of them, and damaging their factories are in themselves pressure factors. Three years after the Understanding was signed,[13] Likud accused the Labour Party in Israel of tying the hands of the army, which was in fact true, because at certain times the Israelis did try to avoid civilian casualties, whereas before that point they had never hesitated to strike at entire villages.

The resistance does not have a category of operations known as "launching a Katyusha rocket," because these launchings are not operations per se, but purely reactive strikes. The resistance attacks a given target, executes a martyrdom operation, and plants an explosive device (...) but it only uses Katyushas to protect civilians and deter the Israelis from attacking them. The July Understanding established the principle that no one in the world can speak anymore about Israeli civilians and ignore Lebanese civilians. We would never approve any formula, no matter the price, that provides security to Israeli civilians in northern Palestine and disregards the security needs of civilians in Lebanon. The Understanding states that both sides want to avoid civilian casualties—and we agree, because we do not attack civilian targets as a matter of principle, and in any case do not need to do so. From this particular point of view, the Understanding is totally in line with our objectives.

We nevertheless asked for guarantees. In the past, we used to say that

---

13 The 1993 Understanding was, of course, not signed since it was an unwritten agreement.

Israel had violated the Understanding, or vice versa; no one could guarantee this kind of Understanding, and they all said that they were not a party to it—even Syria. Today, however, there is a guarantor and a monitoring group; there is also the United States, which is in fact the same as having two Israels, and there are France, Syria, and Lebanon. Today, this group is required to assume responsibility for any confrontation or violation that takes place, and we state that we will not be the ones to violate this Understanding. We believe that the ability to protect our civilians means a considerable victory for us, and a feat not witnessed in Lebanon for the past ten years.

The protection of our civilians is now guaranteed at the military level, no matter what, which means that if a jihadist detonates the explosive he carries in an Israeli military convoy and kills and wounds dozens of soldiers, the Israelis have no right to respond by targeting civilians in Lebanon. We will be very careful not to violate this very important achievement, and we have no compulsion or obsession whatsoever regarding the use of Katyusha rockets. We can therefore say that this Understanding is a new attempt at ensuring the protection of Lebanese civilians, and that we are bound by it and agree to its terms. As for the movement of the resistance, it remains intact.

AS-SAFIR: *When you compare this latest Understanding with the one concluded in July [1993], you notice that Lebanon has a larger role to play in it, such as being part of the monitoring group. Does this not require the drawing of a new, different or more developed formula to reconfigure the relationship between the party and the state, including the government, army, and the security forces, among others? Is it not necessary to place this issue on the agenda of discussions between the party and the state?*

HN: We would like to underline the fact that cooperation between Hezbollah and the state of Lebanon, with its various institutions, is a national imperative and a higher priority than this Understanding; in other words, it is not the Understanding itself that makes this cooperation necessary. We have been calling for many years now for such cooperation between Hezbollah and the state, especially after the parliamentary elections and our entry into parliament (although we have been for a long time in the opposition, due to our attitude to various state policies). Our hand has always been extended to the state, and we have never tried to encroach on its domain, whether politically, economically or socially. Like any other movement, party or political force active on the political, social, cultural, intellectual, economic, and humanitarian scenes, our movement is part of this country. We might be different in the sense that we are fighting a resistance war; but there were always several resistance groups in Lebanon working on multiple levels, including direct jihadist and military activities, although Hezbollah today is the only force still active as a resistance movement. We have no problem whatsoever in cooperating, coordinating, and opening ourselves up to the state on all these levels, and we have never been remiss in this domain. The state and its institutions, however, have their own considerations to factor in, and we have resolved not to interfere in them, because we are careful not to get involved in polemics.

Regarding the resistance per se, we are rather sensitive about this subject. The idea that the resistance could be subject to the central authority's decision-making process is not, in my opinion, in the interest of the state authorities themselves. If you, for example, plant an explosive device today, and it explodes and kills Israelis, America and Israel would blame Hezbollah; but if the resistance is under the authority of the state, the blame would automatically shift to the Lebanese government and army. First, we notice how the Israeli enemy announces his intention, nowadays, to avoid targeting the army—although this army took an honorable stand during the war, and contributed to the defense of the country. As things stand, the Israelis cannot blame the actions of the resistance on the Lebanese army and the state, and the latter has been very clever in washing its hands of us, under the pretext that Hezbollah does not listen to it anyway (...) and this, undoubtedly, decreases the pressure on the political authorities.

Second, the real significance of the resistance lies in its ability to slowly bleed the enemy and put pressure on it, either to force it to withdraw or to gain a bargaining chip in the negotiations. However—in spite of our position, in principle, regarding these negotiations—we have always said that we would not be angry or distressed if Lebanon or Syria uses the pressure the resistance puts on Israel as a bargaining chip in the negotiations.

We want our resistance movement to be effective and vibrant, and in order for it to be so, it has to stay active day in and day out. But if we link the resistance to the political authority of the state, [the state's directions to it] would be along the lines of: "Young men, there will be no operations today, too many things happening"; or "Young men, tomorrow's operation would not be helpful on account of the regional situation." How can the resistance remain effective under such circumstances? We believe that if the resistance depended on the political authority of the state, there would be no resistance on the ground at all, because under such conditions resistance would simply be pro forma—a resistance in name only, staged for publicity purposes, rather than genuine, serious, and effective.

We believe, a priori and as of now, that the highest national interest requires that the resistance be effective, free, and unfettered. There are checks and balances to which the resistance has committed itself for years now. In other words, we do not need anyone to impose restrictions on us, because the Lebanese people are our people, the destroyed homes are our homes, the dispossessed are our families, and we do not want our sons to die in vain. For example, we never carry out indiscriminate martyrdom operations; we have hundreds of would-be martyrs, and I come under pressure, every day, from young men eager to go out on martyrdom operations. I could easily tell any of them: take this explosive device inside the occupied zone, and when you meet two individuals from Lahd's group, or an Israeli, detonate it. We do not execute operations of this kind; if the operation is not productive and effective, and [doesn't] cause the enemy to bleed, we cannot legally, religiously, morally or humanely justify giving an explosive device to our brothers and telling them, "Go and become martyrs, no matter how"!

Even when we perform jihad and seek martyrdom, we do so only in order to achieve victory; we seek martyrdom and victory as a great reward for our people and nation, and to this end the resistance saw fit to impose certain restrictions on itself. The survival of the resistance is in the national interest, and I believe that we have put this issue to rest in the past couple of days.

AS-SAFIR: *Within the context of your relationship with the state, about which you have just spoken, and the restrictions to which the resistance has committed itself and which were spelled out in the Understanding, do you believe that it is possible to work out a joint policy with the state regarding issues relevant to the frontier zone and its inhabitants?*

HN: I have a suggestion to make: Why does the state not form a resistance force of its own? Many occupied countries, for one reason or another, have chosen not to involve their military in the fighting, and have instead formed a popular force of sorts, and have financed, protected, and managed it. Let the state form a popular, not official, resistance force, which it would personally finance and run, and for whose actions it would assume responsibility. If this is what they mean by harmonization, and we like the outcome, we would have no problem with that; we might even tell it, "Come and adopt us, give us weapons, money and political cover." Our main concern is not whether we are under the jurisdiction of the state or not; it is whether we have a genuine resistance or not.

AS-SAFIR: *I have another suggestion: based on what we recently witnessed in Lebanon, generally speaking, and on the actions of the armed resistance, including the minimum level of internal cohesion and mobilization to provide relief, which now exists (...) Is there any chance of opening another door—besides the idea of the armed resistance force—to encourage the inhabitants of the frontier zone to form some kind of resistance group, even something short of an armed resistance? This way, the state would not have to establish an armed group per se, but would compel the inhabitants of the frontier zone to confront Israel with the aim of liberating themselves and rejoining the motherland.*

HN: We have gone even further than this. We proposed that no conditions be imposed on the inhabitants of the occupied zone, and called upon the state to shoulder its responsibilities towards this area and its people. We even proposed that those who went too far in normalizing their relations with Israel come back to their homeland. The state is responsible for the people of the frontier zone, even under occupation.

If our party's humanitarian institutions were able to move freely within the frontier zone, we would have mobilized our efforts and reached the people inside it. As you well know, however, not only are Hezbollah's fighters not allowed to move freely within that zone, but the area's inhabitants themselves are not allowed to talk about culture or intellectual matters, and if they do they are incarcerated in Khiam Prison.[14] At the end of the day, the state and its institutions are present, and we have always asked them to

14 For Khiam see above, p. 97 n. 24.

give priority to the occupied frontier zone until such time as the inhabitants are able to stand fast and do not have to seek employment with the Jews, or the Israeli Administrative Authority. This is the responsibility of the state.

AS-SAFIR: *A large majority of the Lebanese people favor giving succor and assistance to the displaced, there is a smaller majority, but a majority nevertheless, that supports the idea of resistance, and a minority that supports Hezbollah itself. These together led to the formation of a large movement, which as a whole reinforced the success of the resistance on the ground, its steadfastness and continuity. It also produced a collective will to provide good quality relief and assistance work. Concomitantly, there were political and diplomatic efforts by the state of Lebanon that contributed, in one way or another, to the military aspect. We are witnessing, therefore, a slew of complementary elements that together produce a positive scenario for Lebanon, of the kind the country has not witnessed in the past 25 years. If Israel's aim was to isolate the party from its public, in areas where resistance was taking place, then the opposite has happened, and the party is now very much part of Lebanese public life. The party has also become more tolerant, due to the need to reduce people's suffering; [it] has become less belligerent and more compassionate. How do you assess this general situation in Lebanon, which imposes certain modes of behavior on the party?*

HN: I would like to mention two points here: the first is the general point, which refers to before and after the event, and the second refers to the impact of this event, within the context that you yourself have mentioned.

The general point is that when we talk about "Lebanonization"—i.e. whether Hezbollah is becoming more Lebanese or not—the question that poses itself is, How do we make Hezbollah more Lebanese than it already is? Therein lies the problem: What does the "Lebanonization" of Hezbollah mean? We could ask the question differently: What is non-Lebanese about Hezbollah, and needs to become Lebanese? What then is the yardstick for being Lebanese? We understand it to mean the person, and the degree of his patriotism; but does his being a Muslim detract from his Lebanese identity? Does his being a Christian, or his belonging to a certain religion or political ideology, detract from his being Lebanese? If this is the case, then the patriarchs and bishops—even the secular Christians who assembled at the Vatican and prayed for Lebanon—are providing proof of a non-Lebanese identity. The Christians would therefore qualify as Vatican citizens, not

Lebanese citizens, because this is where they went to solve their problems. It would also mean that the communist, who follows Karl Marx and Lenin's ideology, is in contradiction with his Lebanese identity; if, in this sense, the communist is not Lebanese, then the nationalist is also not Lebanese. Thus, if we say that being an Islamist does not qualify one to be a Lebanese or a patriot, the principle should also apply to everyone else. Therefore, we do not need to make Hezbollah more Lebanese than it already is. At the same time, we believe that the highest form of patriotism is when one sheds his blood for his country—and we have fought the enemy in Beirut, the western Bekaa, Sidon, Tyre, Nabatieh; and now, in Marjayoun, Bint Jbeil, Mys al-Jabal, Jezzine, and Maroun al-Ras since 1982, and fought for these Lebanese villages until their liberation in 1985. The people recognize this liberation, the pressure on Israel, and the war of attrition as great feats by the resistance.

Can anyone speak about significant Lebanese diplomatic efforts during that period? Lebanese diplomacy at the time was focusing on something else. Are these not Lebanese areas, or are they Syrian or Iranian areas? The areas we are fighting to liberate are purely Lebanese; the individual shedding his blood for his nation, his land, and the restitution of the land, is the most loyal and patriotic individual ever. Given the accusations leveled at Hezbollah, I can easily claim that our Lebanese patriotism is superior, and our identity more genuine, than all other patriots in the country, because we have shown proof of the highest form of loyalty to the land, the motherland, and the people. What is a motherland? It is the land and the people who live on it; it is the harmony and close ties between the people of this land that allow us to form a community.

While we do not speak in Farsi, many Lebanese Christians speak in French. Why do we continue to say that they are Lebanese rather than French citizens? What does "Lebanonization" mean? In the final analysis, it is the mere fact of belonging to the land, the people, the motherland, and history. We are not marginal to the history of this area, rather the contrary; we believe that our scholars in Jabal Amil brought ideology and culture to many Muslim countries.[15] If one means the language, then we speak Arabic with a Lebanese accent—what does "Lebanonization" mean then? There is an

15 For Jabal Amil see above p. 110 n. 13.

opportunity for openness, but it has nothing to do with "Lebanonization" or the lack of it. Many Lebanese have turned inward, but being open or closed-up is one thing, and the issue of "Lebanonization" is another.

This is before the event. As for after the event, it is evident to all that the Lebanese people are open towards each other. They share common feelings and values, and therefore have what it takes to from a single, cohesive community in the face of aggression. I do not deny that this will further encourage Hezbollah to be more open, to forge stronger relations with other groups, and to be more forthcoming in interacting with various sectors of the Lebanese population. This would be a factor of assurance, not a founding factor, because the latter already exists.

AS-SAFIR: *The composition and status of the monitoring group are rather murky and unclear. Is it military in nature, or not? Will it convene, and does it already have the monitors, or not? Are you aware of its composition? It has an American–Israeli component and a Syrian–Lebanese component, and maybe France will play the role of arbiter. Do you have intimate knowledge regarding its role and performance?*

HN: It appears that the negotiations relevant to the adoption of the Understanding did not have enough time to go into the details, which means that it is too soon to ask about such details. But I believe that there is a degree of murkiness even as far as the group's members are concerned, which is why they took a short cut and said that the monitoring group would meet and set its own modus operandi. I do not think they have done that yet, and I believe there would be several opinions on the matter.

AS-SAFIR: *Do you draw a connection between the Understanding and the push to resume negotiations?*

HN: The Understanding does not have to lead to the resumption of negotiations, even though the Americans would like this to be the case. The Americans would definitely like bilateral negotiations to resume, however. Israel's considerations, as far as the negotiations are concerned, are rather complicated now, especially given that they were the ones who suspended them, and not the Syrian and Lebanese; Shimon Peres now has his election campaign to worry about. If a resumption of the negotiations serves Peres's election campaign, I believe that the Americans and Israelis will try to reconvene them before the elections take place.

AS-SAFIR: *Did the party assess the official and public mood in Arab and Muslim countries? If so, what was the result, and what can you do on the public level to forge closer ties with groups from within and outside Islamic circles that expressed support for you? Do you have an idea about what needs to be done?*

HN: During the war, we did several assessments of this kind, but I cannot say yet that we have had the opportunity to sit down and calmly review the results. However, now that the war is over, we have a major task on our hands assisting the returning refugees, healing the wounds, and taking part in rebuilding the country.

The assessments revealed a generally positive public and official reaction, which at times was even excellent. If we first consider the official reaction, we can safely say that it was good, as was the attitude of the Arab foreign ministers who condemned Israel and issued a good statement in this regard. In fact, we did not expect such a reaction on their part, and this is a good omen. We heard many good statements coming from various countries around the world, including a condemnation of Israel by the United Nations, in spite of American efforts to prevent it, or at least compel them to condemn . both sides—i.e. the killer and the victim—and this is also a good omen. In any case, official reactions were in general positive, of a high caliber, and much better than what we had in July [1993].

AS-SAFIR: *Better than what Sharm al-Sheikh predicted?*

HN: Certainly, we consider this to be one of the important results of this war, although it was not in itself one of our aims, given that we were not the ones who started the war. This is why I speak about results and not about objectives. Among the most important results is the fact that Sharm al-Sheikh has no longer any taste, color or odor, and the little that is left of it lacks vigor and spirit.

What they really wanted, even at the official level, was to isolate Syria and Lebanon because they had boycotted Sharm al-Sheikh. What happened, however, was that foreign ministers from around the world gathered in

Damascus and on the Damascus–Beirut road. Furthermore, leaders of important nations were in touch with President Assad by phone, which means that this war has proved that it is impossible to decide on this region's fate without Syria and Lebanon. Even if they hold 1,000 Sharm al-Sheikhs, they will still not be able to decide the fate of this region without us.

On the public level, the reaction in Lebanon was excellent. If we said today that we have a strong-willed people in Lebanon, and a resisting and proud population, it would not be just a compliment to them. Some individuals confer on the people certain adjectives in order to rouse and rally them; today, however, when we use those same adjectives, we do not only mean to rouse and rally them but also to call them by their rightful name.

Regarding the Arab people, and based on the information we received, we believe that there was a high level of understanding of what is at stake, even among those who did not take part in the demonstrations. As you well know, some Arab countries do not even allow their citizens to demonstrate, and the same can be said about the Islamic world. I can also say that the media, even the foreign [media], played a major role in carrying a vivid image of what was really taking place in Lebanon.

We have all seen the large and spontaneous demonstrations and the positive popular attitude in Turkey, which has a military pact with Israel, as well as in Egypt, which is supposed to have a, by now, long-standing peace treaty and a normalization of relations with Israel. I also believe that watching all these positive reactions, in Lebanon and throughout the world, including at the official level, compelled Israel to halt the operations that had done so much harm to Shimon Peres, to the Labour Party, to the regional settlement plan,[16] and to American aspirations in the region. America and Israel arrived at the conclusion that pursuing their military activities would only increase the harm already done to their strategic aspirations in the region. Had it not been for this high positive level of public and official reaction, America and Israel would not have wanted so badly to put the issue to rest.

16 Nasrallah is presumably referring to the Clinton administration's efforts to achieve peace along the Palestinian and Syrian tracks—efforts bolstered by the 1993 Oslo Agreement and the ongoing (though at this point frozen) negotiations with Syria that focused on returning the occupied Golan Heights, as well as the 1994 Jordan–Israel peace agreement.

AS-SAFIR: *The confrontation produced a number of clear results—namely the severe blow dealt to Sharm al-Sheikh, which makes it difficult for it to continue as it had started. There is also the presence of the French in the settlement, which, for the first time in ten years, breaks America's role as sole broker in the region. Do you believe that France's presence is temporary, and will end at a later stage, when the [regional] settlement issue is on the table once again? There is another unexpected result: Peres's particular view of the Middle East was dealt a severe blow, and he is now forced to back down from his once lofty ambitions. My question is, How do you assess the role of France and the chances for its role to survive? And [has] a decision been taken to find a formula for it to continue, or to give it the right support that would allow it to remain effective and active? I believe that without local support, France would not be able to continue playing a role. My second question is, What will be the fate of the moribund Middle East Initiative, as they announced it in Sharm al-Sheikh, from the economic and security points of view?*

HN: Since the very first day, we were among those who said, during our talks in Damascus and Beirut, that the larger the number of guarantor countries [to the Understanding], the better. It is in the interest of Lebanon, Syria, and the people of the region to break America's unilateral role. We can discuss the history of those other countries, but breaking America's unilateral role is in itself a worthy objective, regardless of the balance of power between the countries that have recently entered into the fray, and the extent to which they care about Lebanon's, or the Arabs', interests. This is why we asked that France play a role, and that the European Union be present or send a representative. We even asked for Russia to be part of the monitoring group—because the larger the number of guarantors, the more advantageous is the situation for the Lebanese people. The European Union—if we put aside Britain's remarks—has insisted that France be present, and I believe that this is how France ultimately became part of the monitoring group, and why Russia was excluded.

The French have to realize, in the final analysis, that the only way they can exercise their role is by being equitable, and that if they stand on the side of Syria, Lebanon, and the Arab counties they will end up playing an increasingly larger role. If they prove to be fair and balanced, they will be able to maintain their role in the region, regardless of the fact that the Israelis do not want France to play a role, and had even insulted their foreign minister in the past. [It] was the obstinate insistence of the foreign minister that allowed him to continue his diplomatic drive in the region. France, however, ought to be aware that only Syria, Lebanon, and the Arab countries can endorse and boost its role in the region, and that this is why they expect its position to be balanced and impartial. The fact that America is no longer the sole broker should at the very least reduce the pressure and the siege that Israel imposes on the region.

AS-SAFIR: *What about the negotiations?*

HN: The Understanding necessarily has to lead to specific negotiations, but the fact that the French have succeeded in achieving an important step forward does not mean that other steps will follow. The United States wants to continue holding on to the peace negotiations file, and will not allow anyone else to play a role; it has already distanced Russia, which it recognizes as a sponsor, and I do not think that it would allow France or anyone else to take part in the negotiations.

I have already said that this operation has caused a great deal of political, cultural, and psychological harm, as well [harm to] security, to the New Middle East Initiative, and therefore Shimon Peres will have to wait a long time—much longer than anticipated—to see his dream realized. I cannot say, however, that this plan has completely failed, only that it has suffered a considerable setback.

AS-SAFIR: *How does Hezbollah define the role of Syria and Iran in the recent war?*

HN: Although it is true that the Lebanese government took part in the negotiations, we know—and they know—very well that the real strong negotiator, the one that cool-headedly, courageously and expertly managed the negotiations, was President Assad. He knew all that was going on in the region, and was able to calculate the precise losses and gains. The results achieved by this agreement are above all due to the role and efforts of President Assad, who maintained an ongoing and direct dialogue with the parties. We also know that he always has defended Lebanon and supported the resistance, [and always will,] and this makes him in the end not a mediator but a full party to the negotiations.[17]

The role Syria played has helped Lebanon a great deal in confronting this aggression and its fallout, whether through its contacts with Arab countries or by employing its relationships abroad and within the Arab League. We cannot deny the fact that Syria has used all its political and diplomatic clout and experience in support of Lebanon's political and diplomatic efforts. Iran also placed its entire weight behind Lebanon, and used its contacts with the Europeans, the Russians, and all other countries that could potentially have an impact on the situation.

It is this political and moral support by Syria and Iran that have allowed Lebanon to feel that it is not alone or abandoned, and that there are those who speak its language and act the same way it does.

AS-SAFIR: *Returning to the domestic situation, and in particular to preparations underway by Hezbollah to give assistance to the returnees and provide them with relief services, the state undoubtedly has a role to play—but what role will the party play in this domain?*

HN: We have mobilized all our institutions in the south, including doctors, clinics, engineers, tractors, and reconstruction tools, and they are now ready. First of all, roads that were cut by the Israelis have to be repaired. As for damaged houses, our young men are supposed to have contacted their owners and proposed that each family rent a house in the same village, or in a nearby one, and that we will pay rent for a six-month period, until their own homes have been rebuilt. If at this point the rebuilding is not over, we will pay their rent for another full year, because we do not want our people to live in tents.

We shall soon embark on a large-scale rebuilding campaign, as we did in July [1993], and in the next few hours I will receive a comprehensive estimate of the overall amount of damage in various villages.

17 Assad, of course, was more than just a full party in the negotiations. Although he himself would periodically warn US officials that his control over Hezbollah was limited, given the party's influence on the ground as well as its relationship with Iran, Assad nevertheless exercised a preponderance of power over Lebanon (where his tens of thousands of his troops and intelligence agents remained) and, arguably to a lesser extent, over Hezbollah. Indeed, as a critical regional player as well, he was often the first and last voice in any negotiations in which the US involved him, especially as far as Lebanon was concerned.

AS-SAFIR: *Today, the party is in a position to use its regional and international clout domestically, and this could provoke some local sensitivities. How do you demonstrate your new clout locally, without stirring up domestic sensitivities?*

HN: It is undoubtedly a difficult and complicated operation. Usually, people who wield a lot of power in the country have no choice but to put up with various sensitivities, even if they do not stir things up themselves, which is why we are very careful. Official Lebanese assessments of what happened differ, but an assessment of official and public opinion in Syria shows that most consider it a major victory. There are those who complain when we talk about losses; in fact, we call them sacrifices rather than losses, for what is the alternative? The alternative to the loss of an electricity grid, or a number of houses, could be the loss of the entire country. It is therefore not a matter of Katyushas or explosives; the Israelis ultimately want to submit Lebanon to their will politically, economically, and in matters of security. Lebanon, therefore, has two choices: either it surrenders and submits to Israel's will, and this will lead to immeasurable losses at all levels; or it resists and offers sacrifices, no matter how big, since these would be nothing compared to the great feat that would be achieved by Lebanon if it manages to stay out from under Israel's thumb.

We believe that what happened was a great victory, and that it was above all a victory for the Lebanese people—for Lebanon, Syria, the Arabs, and Muslims. It is a victory that we consider a lesson and an example to all those at the receiving end of Israel's and America's belligerence. We do not deal, however, with this wonderful victory with a sectarian mindset, and do not consider it a reason for rejoicing, but see it as a gloomy occasion; Israel did not achieve its objectives.

People could say that we have failed to achieve tangible results. We did not have objectives to achieve, however, but rather clear principles regarding the need to pursue our resistance, protect civilians, and not submit to Israel's dictates—and we have achieved that. The pictures of children whose heads were severed and whose bodies were torn to pieces do not leave our mind, and never will; we are not people who forget easily.

We believe that what we have here is a victory, and intend to preserve it. To this end we are prepared to tolerate, to a certain degree, those who take advantage of the situation locally, even at our expense—to tolerate some of the complications and doubts that will come our way, and deal with them realistically, objectively, and carefully. Armed with this spirit, we believe that we will be able, as much as possible, to create a new balance between our new influence and local sensitivities. One of the assessments, which I believe to be true, shows that had the Israelis been able to stop the Katyusha rockets after three, four, or sixteen days, Warren Christopher would not have come to the region. Political, diplomatic, and popular efforts have succeeded in setting the stage and creating the right atmosphere for both Israel's military failure and the resistance's military resilience. However, we want to go beyond that and reiterate that our aim, above all, is to preserve this patriotic spirit, rather than claim our share and our gains from this war. In any case, we did not take part in this war to reap advantages or score electoral points; this achievement in itself was our sole objective.

10

THE MARTYRDOM OF SAYYED HADI NASRALLAH

September 13, 1997

Nasrallah was set to deliver this speech in commemoration of September 13, 1993— the date when nine Hezbollah supporters protesting against the Oslo Accords were killed by the Lebanese army and security forces. The purpose of the event was superseded, however, by the announcement hours before that Nasrallah's eldest son, Hadi, and two of his companions, Haitham Mughnieh and Ali Kawtharani, had been killed the previous day while fighting the Israeli army in the "security zone." Although Israel took possession of the bodies in the aftermath of the engagement, Nasrallah later publicly refused to broker a special deal for Hadi's return, saying: "Let them bury him with his companions in Palestine." Nine months later, Hadi's body was swapped for the remains of Israeli commandos taken one week before Hadi had been killed. Also returned to Lebanon were the bodies of all those who fell with Hadi, as well as dozens of prisoners held by Israel and its proxy South Lebanon army.

Shortly after this speech, and in response to the overwhelming, cross-sectarian outpouring of emotion that it evoked, Hezbollah established the Lebanese Brigade for Resisting Occupation, a unit composed of volunteers from across Lebanon's confessional divide, including Sunnis, Druze, and Christians charged with helping to dislodge Israel from occupied Lebanese land.

We meet today to commemorate our dear oppressed martyrs, and to honor the memory of our sisters and brothers who were unjustly and aggressively killed on September 13, the day of the great betrayal of Jerusalem, of Palestine, and of the nation. There was also the carnage. We meet here to reaffirm that we shall not forget our martyrs, not forget our martyrs, not forget our martyrs. We meet here today on this occasion bearing with us to this platform, to everyone, and to this occasion of our victory, our self-esteem and our pride; bearing with us our glory, strength, and determination to pursue the path; and bearing with us the sincerity of our commitment to the martyrs, the *mujahidin*, the nation, and the Imam. However, before we speak about the carnage of September 13, we will speak about the state we are in—a state intimately linked to the martyrs of that carnage and no stranger to it; no stranger to the blood and patience of September 13, and no stranger to the courage and wisdom displayed on September 13.

Here I will stand and say: we commemorate today this occasion while in our hands, in our grasp and on our faces—not only Hezbollah's and the Islamic Resistance's faces, but those of all the Lebanese, Arabs, and Muslims, and of every honorable person in this world—[we display] the joy of the victory accomplished by the pure and brave *mujahidin* at the gates of the town of Ansariya.[1] For the first time in the Jewish entity's history (in the press conference we said that it may have been the first time, and now we say it was indeed for the first time) the crème de la crème of the Israeli naval commandos cross over to carry out an operation in the south—not in Tunis, Entebbe, the depths of Beirut, or the capitals of Europe,[2] but in the south, only a few kilometers away from their own country—and then are soundly defeated, outmaneuvered, destroyed and humiliated by our God, who sent us victory as the token of his esteem and generosity. It was a great victory for the nation: the enemy left behind the remains of its soldiers and departed, shamed and humiliated, and we, over here, were left with our pride, glory, victory, and faith in God, on whom we relied, in whom we trusted, and to whom we gave thanks; and which left us with our belief in the righteousness of our chosen path.

How can a small group of *mujahidin* humiliate the entity that has humiliated the Arabs and Muslims for 50 years, incapacitate the very entity that has incapacitated the Arabs and Muslims for 50 years, and defeat the entity that has defeated the Arabs and Muslims for 50 years? Isn't that proof as bright as the sun, and as clear as only the truth can be? This victory calls

---

1 The September 5, 1997 Hezbollah operation at Ansariya, near the southern port city of Sidon (and therefore outside both the "security zone" and the territory controlled by the SLA) resulted in the ambush of an elite Israeli commando unit. The ensuing clash left numerous dead and wounded on both sides, with Hezbollah succeeding in gathering Israeli body parts that were later used in the prisoner–body exchange that saw Hadi's body, among others, returned to Lebanon for burial.

2 Nasrallah is referring to the series of high-profile Israeli commando raids deep into foreign and enemy territory through the 1970s and 1980s that, at the time, seemed to confirm Israel's daring, global reach vis-à-vis its opponents.

out to all our Lebanese people and to all the Arabs, but mainly to Palestine, which is moaning under the weight of what took place on September 13, and the humiliating and treacherous agreement;[3] moaning under the weight of the whip, hunger, siege, humiliation and brutality.

The message of the incident at Ansariya is clear to the whole nation and to the Palestinian people: it tells this oppressed and struggling people in Palestine once again that the path to victory and justice and the path to the future is the one chosen by the great *mujahidin* and martyrs in Jerusalem, Tel Aviv, and across the sacred land of Palestine. Everyone should understand this message, and should also know that our enemy is weaker than we think, and lowlier than we think. If we search the entire globe for a more cowardly, lowly, weak, and frail individual in his spirit, mind, ideology, and religion, we will never find anyone like the Jew—and I am not saying the Israeli: we have to know the enemy we are fighting. Then there was this great victory and the ensuing need for the resistance to pursue its jihad, operations, and confrontation. The resistance is not only there to protect village gates, but first and foremost to break into the occupied land and set up a trap here and a bomb there, and for its martyrs to blow themselves up either here or there. It was therefore only natural that these operations and confrontations should continue, chief among them yesterday's honorable and heroic confrontation during which the *mujahidin* of the Islamic Resistance in Iqlim al-Tuffah fought alongside officers and soldiers from the Lebanese army. The resistance lost martyrs, and so did the army, and these martyrs bore witness to how this resistance, steadfastness, presence, and honor were displayed on the field. They are also the real witnesses to life. The blood of the resistance and of the army's martyrs is calling out, and the echo of their voice is reverberating in all ears. Let no one believe that this nation has died; look at how life goes on in Lebanon, clamoring with will power and blood, jihad and martyrdom; such a nation can never die.

On this occasion I wish to express to my brothers and kin, the families of the Islamic Resistance's martyrs and those of the Lebanese army's martyrs, my warmest congratulations for this God-given, humane, and national badge of honor earned in yesterday's confrontations. Allow me here to digress from

---

3 The agreement is presumably the Gaza–Jericho agreement that resulted from Oslo (for details, see above, p. 100 n. 1).

the text of the September 13 speech—because the nature of the incident imposes it on us—by saying that my son the martyr had chosen this path of his own free will. I would also like to say to the enemy and the friend alike: do not ever believe that because this boy's father is the secretary-general, that he exerted pressure on him and sent him to the jihad, even though this particular point is in itself one of the good aspects of jihad. This young man, like all the martyred *mujahidin* of the resistance, the *mujahidin* who are still on the lines of confrontation, some of whom are on frontlines as we speak—and like all these honorable and pure individuals—he consciously, willingly, and independently chose this path. If I, his mother or any martyr's father have played any role in this, it was to facilitate and not object to or prevent this or any other young man from going where he wished, or doing what he thought was right. This is something I wish to make clear from the very beginning.

Secondly, the Israelis might think that they have scored a victory by killing the son of the secretary-general. They did not kill the son of the secretary-general while he was walking in Haret Hreik;[4] neither was it a security operation or similar accomplishment; nor was he killed in Entebbe while hijacking a plane. This *mujahid* was with his brothers in arms on the frontlines with the enemy; he went to them, they did not come to him; he went to them on his own two feet, armed with his gun and his willpower. This is the difference: it is not and could not be construed as a victory for the enemy. This is a victory and an honor for Hezbollah; this is a victory for the principle of resistance in Lebanon. Where is the victory?

In the past, we used to take pride—and still do and forever will—in the fact that ours is a forward march, a resistance force and a jihadi movement, some of whose leaders and great men, like the martyr Sheikh Ragheb Harb, have been martyred. We used to hold our heads high for the fact that our leader, master, and beloved secretary-general, Sayyed Abbas Mussawi,[5] his wife, and his child were among our martyrs. Today, however, we wish to tell this enemy: we are not a resistance movement whose leaders want to enjoy their private lives and fight you through the sons

4 A now heavily Shiite area of the Southern Suburb, where Sayyed Fadlallah lives and where the Hezbollah-affiliated Al-Manar TV is located. The area also bears indications of its majority Christian past, with the Maronite church of Haret Hreik still serving as a place of worship.

5 For Ragheb Harb, see above, p. 53 n. 8; for Mussawi, see Statement 3.

of their loyal followers and their good and true supporters from among the ordinary citizens. The martyr Hadi's martyrdom is the proof that we in Hezbollah's leadership do not spare our own sons; we take pride in them when they go to the frontlines, and hold our heads high when they fall as martyrs.

This is the true worth of Hezbollah's Islamic Resistance. I say in all sincerity that among my brethren in the leadership, who shoulder important and major responsibilities in this forward march, there are those who have the will and desire for martyrdom, and are utterly determined to carry out a martyrdom operation. But we prevent them from doing so. I tell you, some might believe that as far as some of those leaders are concerned, the spilling of these pure martyrs' blood means that the issue of jihad and martyrdom has now been put to rest, and that the matter has been given to others to deal with. In the name of this pure blood I tell you: some of these same men come to me privately crying and asking for permission to carry out an operation. We will remain in the best of situations as long as our men, women, leaders, and *mujahidin* are armed with this spirit. Here, I would like also to tell the enemy: you have to understand the real meaning of the message in Sayyed Hadi's and his brothers' martyrdom. We, the men, women, and children at all levels in Hezbollah, are determined to pursue the path of Sayyed Abbas, Sheikh Ragheb, and Imam al-Khomeini, and are determined to pursue the path of jihad no matter what the challenge, the danger and the sacrifice. This is a promise, an oath, and an acclamation from which we shall never retreat. Tonight, this is a message of martyrdom and of these good martyrs.

I thank God Almighty for his bounty in turning his gaze upon my family and choosing a martyr from among them, and for accepting me and my family as members of the blessed and sacred group of martyrs' families. I used to feel embarrassed in front of the martyrs' fathers, mothers, wives, and children when I visited them, and still do. Thank God for having accepted me and my family as consolers to these martyrs' families —not only to those whose loved ones have been martyred, but also to those whose loved ones' bodies are still in enemy hands. I wish to tell these families: there is now something in common between us in this domain.

This is one of God's great bounties that have made our burden so heavy, for we do not know how to thank him. Do we thank him for the honorable victory in Ansariya, or the honor of martyrdom in Iqlim al-Tuffah in Jabal al-Rafie? What should we thank him for? For his gift of faith, the righteous path, the power and the jihad; or for the gift of living in this era that boasts learned men, leaders, men and women known for their loyalty, their faithful execution of the trust and their allegiance, such as yourselves?

Let me go back to the martyrs of September 13, and say that our pride today comes as a result of this spilled blood, and that our path will continue because of it. Their testimony is now an historical record, which says that on September 13, people from Lebanon went out and traced with the blood of their martyrdom for all generations to come—it is neither a coincidence nor happenstance that these martyrs are both men and women—with the blood of these men and women, that they are people who, like their fathers, grandfathers, nation, and Prophet before them, reject injustice and humiliation and refuse to turn their eye to treachery. And what a treachery Oslo was— the treachery of having abandoned Jerusalem and Palestine, and wasted the sacrifice, the pain and the suffering that the Arab and Muslim people have endured for 50 years.

It is in the face of such treachery that these martyrs fell and wrote with their own blood: we reject these humiliating agreements and reject the humiliation of our nation, occupation, disgrace and arrogance. The land is our land and the holy sites belong to our nation; we want to live with honor and freedom in our region of the world. We do not want to beg for peace or security, neither from a savage racist nor from a crazy old crony who comes to this region to talk about peace. We want to forge our nation's peace with our own blood, guns, body parts, and bones; this is the peace we believe in and seek. We have to ponder at greater length the greatness and importance of this incident, the incident of the martyrdom of September 13 and the blood of these martyrs.

Here also, I would like to caution and say that on September 13, and precisely under the airport bridge, elements of more than one security service deliberately opened fire on the demonstrators, killing a number of brothers and sisters, and wounding many others. We tended our wounds and waited patiently. Someone might ask us today what was the most courageous position ever taken by Hezbollah—the July War, or maybe the April War? No, the most courageous position in all of Hezbollah's history was taken on September 13, and required awareness, wisdom, courage, daring, a clear assessment of the future, and a serious assumption of responsibility on the part of its leadership. That is where courage comes into play: it is easy for someone to open fire on others, but it is difficult to bear your wounds and walk away. One of the easiest things we could have done on September 13 was allow ourselves to be dragged into civil strife, take the people with us into the battle, and act like the sheikh of the tribe who musters its forces and seeks revenge. But the leadership took the most courageous, wise, and farsighted position ever in this regard—and here I do not wish to laud myself, since I am just one of a large group of decision-makers, and the youngest and weakest among them. This was the greatest and most courageous decision we have ever taken, and we shall forever be proud of the fact that on September 13 we were patient, carried our martyrs and buried them, and took our wounded to the hospitals to be treated. We were patient then, and are still pressing on the open wound, which will remain open; nothing will heal the wound we incurred on September 13, and we will keep pressing on it until God tells us otherwise.

Among the objectives of the September 13 incident, or rather its expected results after elements of the Lebanese army and security forces opened fire on the people, was that Hezbollah would not abide such a massacre, would take up arms, and that Lebanon would once again become a battleground. Hezbollah was supposed to open fire on the Lebanese army, which was supposed to fire back, thus dragging Lebanon into a civil conflict whose conclusion no one knew. But your patience, awareness, commitment, and determination took us to a point at which the army no was longer firing on Hezbollah, and Hezbollah was no longer firing at the army, but both firing together at Lebanon and the nation's enemy, Israel. They wanted one of us to kill the other; but with patience, wisdom, and God's guidance we started firing together at the nation's enemy, and together we fell as martyrs, received congratulations, and consoled each other.

This is a great victory for those who know what sedition—a condition whose beginning and end no one knows—would mean for Lebanon. This is a blessing brought forth by these martyrs' blood, and by their unjust treatment. We are saying to the people, to all the citizens and political forces:

let us transcend our wounds, these mistakes and these crimes, and let us heal our wounds and unite in the face of our enemy. We have only two choices ahead of us: either we heal our wounds, or we disappear from existence. Healing our wounds means that we cooperate and help one another defeat and humiliate the enemy, and make our nation victorious. On the other hand, reopening our wounds means that one of us would kill the other, and thus allow the Israeli enemy to come for a picnic in Lebanon, and that people will give up on us as they did in the invasion of 1982. In that 1982 invasion a shameful thing happened when roses were thrown at the advancing Israelis.[6] Do we say that the people who did this are treacherous and enemy agents? No. But the events that took place in Lebanon led many to view the Israeli enemy as the savior. We have to take advantage of all these mistakes and learn from them.

Lest anyone believe that the file has been closed, I wish to confirm that the September 13 file, like the wound of September 13, is still open, until God decides what we should do about it. This file, therefore, will not be closed, although we are in the process of healing our wound, picking up our file and leaving; the wound, however, remains in our heart and our mind. Whenever we remember one of our sisters or one of our brothers who fell as martyrs under the airport bridge, we feel pain as if we can still see them falling before our eyes. But the great mind, great heart, great willpower, and great degree of awareness with which you all dealt with the incident at the time will be carried forward, because we are soldiers and leaders in this great battle.

Today we wage the nation's battle, and fight on its behalf; and today these martyrs are this nation's pride and joy. I believe that, after the confrontation at Ansariya, any Lebanese who still does not agree with the resistance, and considers it a terrorist, violent, and extremist movement, deep inside and in front of others, nevertheless still feels proud to be a Lebanese, as every Arab is proud to be an Arab and every Muslim is proud to be a Muslim.

Look at the faces of the enemy's leaders, hear their words, and see their shame and humiliation. As for us, we were and still are holding wedding ceremonies for our martyrs, rejoicing in them and envying them their lofty

6 See in particular the account given by Robert Fisk, *Pity the Nation: The Abduction of Lebanon* (New York: Thunder's Mouth Press, 2002), pp. 236–7.

status, their badge of honor and their good fortune. We congratulate them on this honorable fate, take pride in them, and are more worthy and proud for having known them.

We pledge ourselves to the martyrs of September 13, who know now that the agreement they went out to fight against is faltering under the weight of the many blows it is receiving. This agreement will have no tomorrow, for there will be neither reconciliation in this region with the Israeli enemy nor peace with the furious invaders and occupiers. We tell Albright:[7] there will indeed be a merciless war against terrorism in this region; but then who is the terrorist? Israel is the terrorist, from the top of its head to its toes, and there will be no peace in this region as long as this terrorism exists.

We pledge ourselves to these martyrs. We will persevere on their path, preserve their blood, and heal their wound until God makes his will manifest. To all the resistance's martyrs we also pledge ourselves, and renew the covenant; no matter how much we offer or how much we give, we still feel that we are giving too little, that we are still not up to par, still at the beginning of the road. If we are true to our God and commit to Him, our good intentions, the path of jihad will still be rife with more victory, honor, and pride. The battle taking place in the south and the western Bekaa today is another kind of battle—a different story, of a different nature. Before being a battle with guns and weapons, it is a battle of ideology, faith, loyalty, truth, reliance on God, aspiration to martyrdom, renunciation of worldly pleasures, the love of others, and the desire to serve them. Generations of our people might still have to carry the gun; we might lose a generation of those who are armed with this kind of faith, love, willpower, resolve, and companionship with death, because this generation has learned well from its imam and leader, the Prince of the Faithful (...): "Ali bin Abi Taleb has sought familiarity with death since he was an infant suckling at his mother's breast."[8] This phrase, thanks be to God, has now taken on a new significance and a new value for me, unlike before. Imam Zein al-Abidin[9] (...) has given us a slogan which I used to quote to you, a slogan we carried with

7. Madeleine Albright succeeded Warren Christopher as US Secretary of State in January 1997.
8. The full name of Muhammad's cousin, and, according to Shia, the first rightly guided Caliph (for further details, see above, p. 52 n. 3).
9. Imam Zein al-Abidin (658–713 CE) was the fourth Shia Imam, after Hussein.

us and went forth with. Today, when someone speaks to me about the martyrdom of Sayyed Hadi, the descendent of the Hashemites,[10] I tell him what Zein al-Abidin has said: "Killing is for us a habit and our martyrdom is God's sign of love for us."

---

10 As a sayyed—an honorific title especially employed by Shia when naming males accepted as descendants of the Prophet Muhammad, through his daughter Fatima Zahra—Hadi was also therefore a Hashemite, i.e. a descendent of Hashim ibn Abed al Manaf, the great-grandfather of the Prophet.

11

ON CONDITIONAL WITHDRAWAL

March 29, 1998

Ever since the first major IDF withdrawal under fire in 1985, successive Israeli governments had premised any further territorial withdrawals in Lebanon on a series of demands and tests that invariably emphasized ending Hezbollah's increasingly effective military operations in south Lebanon—as well as ending, once and for all, its armed presence in the whole of the country.

The following interview, conducted by the Lebanese newspaper Al-Moharrer and headlined, "Nasrallah: No political rewards for the enemy in return for the occupation," came shortly after Israeli Premier Benjamin Netanyahu had belatedly announced that his country would finally recognize and implement United Nations Security Council Resolution 425, almost 20 years after its issuance following the first Israeli invasion of Lebanon. Netanyahu's "offer," however, was little different from past Israeli statements: withdrawal from the 1000 square km "security zone" in south Lebanon would be conditional, despite the fact that 425 plainly called upon Israel "immediately to cease its military action against Lebanese territorial integrity and withdraw forthwith its forces from all Lebanese territory."[1] As Israeli Defense Minister Yitzhak Mordechai made clear to one Arab newspaper in January 1998, the actual implementation of 425 would only come after a crackdown on terrorism, which effectively meant disarming Hezbollah; ceasing attacks against Israeli forces and their proxy, the SLA;[2] establishing neighborly relations on both sides of the border; and cooperation being joined between the IDF and Lebanon on terrorism generally in the region. As Israeli scholar Daniel Sobelmen would later point out, "In effect, there was nothing fundamentally new in Mordechai's statement."[3]

---

1 The full text of UNSCR 425 can be found at: http://www.un.org/Depts/dpa/qpalnew/resolutions_new_qpal.htm

2 For the SLA, see above, p. 66 n. 13.

3 Daniel Sobelman, *New Rules of the Game* (Tel Aviv: Jaffe Center, January 2004), p. 25.

179

What was new about Netanyahu's "acceptance" of 425, however, was that it highlighted the growing opposition within Israel to the IDF's continued occupation of and control over south Lebanon. As Nasrallah would repeatedly claim, Hezbollah's military operations, now filmed and viewed in Israel and the Occupied Territories, were having a powerful effect on public opinion and, he argued, IDF morale—in the process improving Lebanon's bargaining position amid continued movement towards a regional settlement of the Arab–Israeli conflict. Two years later, when Israeli forces finally withdrew unconditionally, Nasrallah would claim that, despite the terrible toll in lives and property damage, the logic of violent resistance to Israel had indeed bettered Lebanon's overall position, much as he and other Hezbollah leaders had long claimed it would.

But Netanyahu's move also represented a renewed attempt at promoting a "Lebanon first" approach to the Arab–Israeli conflict as a whole. The strategy shrewdly sought to remove the link between the Lebanese–Israeli and Syrian–Israeli negotiating tracks—thereby diminishing Syria's ability to use Hezbollah and Lebanon as a bargaining chip, or a bleeding wound, in regaining the Golan Heights. Syria, of course, had little choice but to reject the proposal, but even so, "Lebanon first" placed the Syrians in a serious dilemma: by potentially accepting to disarm Hezbollah, Damascus would deprive themselves of the one military instrument they were able to exercise against Israel; by refusing to do so, they appeared to be uncompromising and, in the eyes of many in Washington, to be backing a terrorist organization.

Perhaps more importantly, though, from the standpoint of Hezbollah, Netanyahu's dual-track approach—acceptance of 425 on the one hand, and a "Lebanon First" push on the other—also threatened to undermine popular support for the resistance, especially among those Lebanese who saw their own immediate, national needs as far more pressing than those of Syria. Although Israel's various conditions, as well as Syria's grip on the country as a whole, certainly eased his task, Nasrallah's public stance against any sort of compromise would only become more precarious in the coming two years, as Syria itself increasingly moved towards a final settlement with Israel—one presumably premised on the end of Hezbollah's militancy.

AL-MOHARRER: *Foreign political circles are putting forward suggestions of implementing Resolution 425, which states that Israel must withdraw from the occupied Lebanese south. These plans are connected to security arrangements whose implementation is requested in two stages: A: deployment of United Nations forces between Lebanon and Israel in the occupied territories, and B: disarmament of Hezbollah. The first question is: Do you believe that Israel is serious in its suggestions, or does it aim to shift attention away from its actions and arouse internal controversy in Lebanon? The second question is: What is your attitude towards this suggestion in both of its stages? In your opinion, is there any connection between the Resolution's implementation and any Lebanese or international security arrangements? And what are the limitations of these arrangements?*

HN: For years now, the Israeli enemy has felt that it is drowning in a swamp of blood in south Lebanon and the Bekaa. This has sapped its strength and dealt a blow to its political and military ego. It is now looking for a solution, which it was forced towards by two factors: the resistance, with its continuity, growth, and determination; and the steadfastness of the Lebanese people in all of its factions in the face of occupation and aggression. These two factors are forcing it to discuss a retreat that it has to seek—but it doesn't want to withdraw without achieving political and military gains, even if they are minimal. Withdrawing without any conditions or terms is a dangerous precedent for Israel, and implies that the mythical army was defeated at the hands of the Lebanese people's resistance. It would also set an excellent standard for the Palestinian people, as well as others. Thus (...) the Israeli enemy is looking for a way to exit this swamp that would enable it at the same time to achieve whatever gains it can achieve by pitching new formulas for its withdrawal. Of course, there is a new suggestion on the issue of the retreat. Before the resistance's steadfastness forced it to seek the minimum, the enemy was asking for a peace treaty with Lebanon and a Lebanese commitment to normalize relations. Today it is backtracking from these two demands, not because it respects international legitimacy or human rights, but because of the attrition on the battlefield. [It] found in Resolution 425—which had been long forgotten, and which [it] remembered only 20 years after it was issued—an exit from its crisis. Because it wants to withdraw and at the same time achieve whatever gains it can, it put these terms for the implementation of the Resolution under the guise of "security arrangements", while hiding many things behind this heading.

However, suggesting the implementation of Resolution 425 today is not just an Israeli maneuver—if we believed this explanation, then we would be ignoring the importance of the pressure applied by the resistance and the steadfastness of the Lebanese in forcing it to remember the Security Council

Resolution and bring it out of oblivion 20 years after it was issued. The Israeli enemy is struggling and maneuvering at the same time. If it makes any gains at all, then it will have achieved some of its goals; if it fails, then it will have gained something else connected to improving its image in the eyes of the world. The new suggestion to implement the Resolution gives a different image than the conceited Netanyahu—who knows nothing other than refusal—wants to project. It presents him to the world in the guise of one who wants to withdraw and implement the Security Council Resolution, but is frustrated by Lebanon's refusal to do so. It is a serious attempt and a devious plot at the same time. If he is not able to impose his terms for withdrawal, then he will at least have polished his image in front of the world.

This is the general situation as it stands. Regarding our attitude towards this suggestion—the withdrawal terms and arrangements—it is clear: we reject completely any formula that talks about security arrangements and terms. We don't accept that the Israeli enemy should receive any rewards or gains for occupying our land. We call on the Lebanese authorities to present a complaint against the Israeli enemy, and to call for its generals to be brought to trial for their aggression, for the massacres that they committed against our people, and for the rights and freedom that they stole from them. We call upon the Lebanese authorities to explore every avenue in calling for compensations to be paid to our displaced people in the south, who are threatened and whose lands and rights are stolen. I say to everyone: there is a bare minimum of dignity and logic in the face of the occupation, which is not to present the enemy with political rewards in return for its occupation. What I am clearly calling for is an unconditional withdrawal. The enemy has to withdraw or we will keep fighting it until we force it to do so. There are those who believe that Israel's suggestion entails only withdrawal. If this is so—and I have my reservations about Resolution 425—then let the enemy withdraw without any conditions, and it will thus achieve a common goal for us all.

AL-MOHARRER: *Are you a resistance only, or are you also a political party? Is the justification for your existence and activities only the liberation of the south, or will you become part of Lebanese political life?*

HN: It is beyond doubt that we are a resistance, and this has been testified to by martyrdom and blood. At the same time, we are a political, social, economic, and cultural movement. Those who know Lebanon well and who have lived inside it know this truth, and touch it. We have members in parliament, and we have political alliances with various factions and movements.[4] We also have political attitudes towards all the political, economic, and social developments on the ground.

AL-MOHARRER: *Do you consider yourselves a Lebanese party or an Islamic party, in the sense that your activities and goals transcend the borders of Lebanon?*

HN: We are an Islamic party because we follow an Islamic ideology. What takes place on the Islamic and Arabic scenes concerns us, because we are part of this world. In this sense, we are an Islamic party. But we are also a Lebanese party regarding our organizational structure. The members of our party are Lebanese, and Lebanon is the home in which we live and for which we fight. Here we must present a clarification: we are a non-sectarian Islamic party, and we are a Lebanese party that is not isolated within the borders of this country.

AL-MOHARRER: *What is the nature of your relationship, as a resistance and as a political party, with Iran? Is it an organizational relationship or just a general relationship that stems from your being an Islamic party? Is their any relationship between yourselves and any Islamic organization outside Lebanon?*

HN: Our relationship with Iran is not organizational in the usual sense. Iran is an Islamic state that believes in Islam and works to implement it. We as an Islamic movement respect any regime that endorses Islam and the struggle with the Israeli enemy, which is our central cause. We in Lebanon live this struggle, and we fight against the occupation. Thus we see in Iran both the state ruled by Islam and the state that supports the Muslims, Arabs, and Palestinians. However, in our relationship with Iran

---

4 As a result of the 1996 parliamentary elections, which saw an end to the previous boycott by many Christians, Hezbollah held nine seats in total—down from the 12 seats it had won after the 1992 elections.

we make a distinction between two positions: that of the regime and that of the religious reference. Our relationship with the regime is one of cooperation, as we have many friends among its cadres and we communicate with them. But the regime doesn't constitute for us a political and religious reference. Here we are a totally independent movement from the political regime in Iran.

There is another position in Iran, which is that of the religious authority whose high rank and influence provide religiously founded legitimacy to our struggle. Regarding the relationship with other Islamic organizations and movements, we have relationships and agreements with some of them. There is, for example, a relationship with the Islamic movements in Palestine—Hamas and Islamic Jihad—and with the National Islamic Front in Sudan. We also have acquaintance with Islamic movements in Afghanistan. But because of the nature of our arena and the struggle, these relationships are not developed to the level of coordination and alliance. We can certainly say that we share common concerns and empathize with each other.

AL-MOHARRER: *If the south was liberated through your own efforts or through external pressure, or both, would you set aside your weapons? [In other words,] when will you set aside your weapons, and what are the subjective conditions for this? Are they Lebanese, Arab or Islamic?*

HN: The answer to this question is linked to the whole issue [of] the future of the armed resistance after the Israeli withdrawal, and whether it will continue its operations or not—that is to say, whether or not it will give up its weapons. This is linked to the situation beyond an Israeli withdrawal, and we prefer to talk about it after the withdrawal, not before, for the simple reason that we don't want to link the withdrawal to this issue or vice versa, so that it won't become a condition for withdrawal.

AL-MOHARRER: *Many of your enemies consider you the dark horse in any project for peace. Do you believe that this is due to the fact that you are an armed party, or to your strategic relationship with Syria?*

HN: Both.

AL-MOHARRER: *Do you link your patriotic attitude towards liberating south Lebanon to the liberation of the Golan Heights? In other words, are you part of the national Lebanese struggle, or part of a more comprehensive struggle against the Israeli project in the region?*

HN: There is a common misunderstanding [here]. Some believe that the Islamic Resistance in Lebanon rejects a withdrawal from the occupied Lebanese south unless it coincides with a withdrawal from the occupied Syrian Golan Heights. This is incorrect. If Israel withdraws tomorrow from Lebanon, do we tell it, you must not do so unless it coincides with a withdrawal from the Golan? Never. President al-Assad has always made it clear that Syria would be very pleased with an Israeli withdrawal from south Lebanon. You have of course heard the latest statements issued by the Syrian foreign minister, Farouk al Sharra, where he said that when Israel withdraws from Lebanon, we will organize celebrations, along with Lebanon and Hezbollah.

But there is something that needs clarification. The resistance here is fighting to liberate Lebanese lands. The rest—whether Golan or elsewhere— is part of the hidden file of which we spoke earlier. It is a fact that what is taking place in Golan is occupation, and we believe that its liberation is part of a whole. For us, all of Palestine is occupied territory, and Israel is an illegitimate and illegal occupying and thieving state that enjoys some strength. We must all cooperate today to prevent this thief from taking over all of our region, from placing its hand over all of its resources and holy shrines, and from erasing both its past and its future.

There remains one point: Will the Islamic Resistance fight to liberate Golan or Palestine? We will withhold the answer to this question until a future date, because we don't like to give a commitment, whether positive or negative, on which Israel will base an attitude.

AL-MOHARRER: *Is your attitude towards Israel the same as towards Jews and Judaism, or is it restricted to Israeli aggression or to Israel's aggressive existence in the first place?*

HN: Most assuredly our attitude towards Israel is not an attitude towards Jews or Judaism. Since the West doesn't want to understand that Hezbollah is anything other than an exact copy of Iran, let us consider Iran's attitude towards the Jews. They enjoy there all their political, social, and economic rights, for they are citizens, and have representatives in the legislative authority.[5] Thus our war is not against Judaism or Jews but against Zionism, which created its racial state in Israel.

Let us [be clear] that Islamic intellectualism and religion have throughout Islamic history never laid the foundation for a hostile attitude against Judaism and Jews. The war between ourselves and Israel is a war against Zionism and its plans, and not against Judaism as a religion or against those who believe in that religion.

5 Iran's Jewish population may have been as high as 140,000 persons in 1948. However, as a result of emigration to the new state of Israel, as well as relatively heavy emigration following the 1979 Revolution, Iran's Jewish population is currently thought to number between 25,000 and 40,000 persons. Although officially recognized as a religious minority group, Jews in the Islamic Republic of Iran, like other religious minorities, suffer from officially sanctioned discrimination in a number of social, political, and economic domains. Iran nevertheless still accounts for the largest Jewish population in any Muslim country—a population represented by one member of the Iranian parliament—and is home to eleven synagogues, as well as several educational and charitable organizations.

12

ON JEWS

May 7, 1998

The following speech at a party rally in Beirut, broadcast live on the nascent Hezbollah-affiliated Al-Manar television station, contains a series of publicly pronounced vilifications directed against Jews as Jews. Perhaps not surprisingly, the first several lines of the speech, which describe "Zionist Jews" as "the descendents of apes and pigs" (the Zionist qualification is quickly dropped thereafter), was among the most widely circulated quotes attributed to Nasrallah by the English-language media during the 2006 Hezbollah–Lebanon war—submitted as evidence, along with a handful of other quotes referring to Jews, of Nasrallah's and Hezbollah's apparently uncompromising and totalizing hatred of adherents of the Jewish faith.

The careful reader and analyst should of course note that Nasrallah's rhetoric here directly contradicts the previous statement, where he points to the experience of Iran's Jewish community as evidence that "our war is not against Judaism or Jews but against Zionism which created its racial state in Israel." As several scholars have suggested, this apparent contradiction enormously complicates the potential for any kind of future reconciliation or normalization between the two sides (though it should be said that it does not preclude a potentially containable, non-violent level of hostility). For although Nasrallah at times suggests that Hezbollah could live side by side with Jews—of course only under Hezbollah's particular vision of a unified Palestinian state where many Jews would be forced to leave—this statement, in particular, suggests that Hezbollah's skepticism of Judaism, exacerbated over 16 bloody years of fighting the state of Israel, may have run so deep as to become dangerously mired in what amounts to racial hatred.

Of course, there may also have been a more immediate element of populist politicking in the statement that follows. In an effort to offset the effects of its previous loss of three parliamentary seats in 1996, the party vigorously appealed to its base ahead of the country's first municipal elections in late May 1998. At the same time, the regional situation, too, appeared to be moving Hezbollah into an ever more radical overall stance. Only one month before this speech, amid a general air of accommodation created by Mohammed Khatami's 1997 presidential win in Iran, the country's culture and Islamic guidance minister, Ayatollah Mohajerani, had declared that "if Israel withdraws from south Lebanon with guarantees for fixed and secure borders, there will be no further need for Hezbollah's resistance operation there"[1]—a suggestion angrily rejected by Nasrallah.

With Syrian and Israeli negotiations still frozen, but looming nonetheless, a worsening political split in Tehran reverberating in Lebanon, and the process of Israeli–Palestinian negotiations well on their way to October's Wye River Accords, Nasrallah's words may therefore indicate, perhaps more than anything, the party's creeping realization and fear that regional normalization might soon be imposed on the party, regardless of its concerns about Israel— or Jews, for that matter.

(...) Very regrettably, the 10th of *Muharram* [the day of Ashoura][2] this year coincides with the fiftieth anniversary of the historic catastrophe and tragic event: namely, the establishment of the state of the Zionist Jews, the descendants of apes and pigs, on the land of Palestine and the holiest of our holy places. This enemy celebrates its overwhelming victory. A few million vagabonds from all over the world, brought together by their Talmud and Jewish fanaticism, are celebrating their victory over the nation of 1.4 billion Muslims. This is why I say that it is a tragic, painful, and bitter thing that a small number of people gather in Palestine, dancing and holding celebrations in Al-Aqsa Mosque and the holy city to celebrate their great victory over the nation of Muhammad. When this Muslim nation was small, the Jews were unable to defeat it, and the Jews of Bani al-Nudayr, Bani Qurayzah, and Khaybar[3] were forced out of their castles and fortresses.

Over the past 50 years, the Jews have succeeded in defeating the nation of 1.4 billion Muslims and the nation of hundreds of millions of Arabs. Fifty years have passed and the enemy is still wagering on its superiority, backed by the US administration. Here, I would like you to know that

1 Magnus Ranstorp, "Between a Rock and a Hard Place," St. Andrews Working Paper, October 2000, p. 20.

2 For the significance of this date in the Shia calendar, see above, p. 52 n. 3.

3 Jewish tribes in central Arabia that clashed with the Prophet and his followers, and who eventually submitted to the rule of Islam.

the historical position of this administration towards Israel is based not only on interests and political and economic considerations, but also on ideology. It is [based] more [on] ideological commitment than political interests.

They bet that, with time, they will be able to impose peace on the Arab countries and on the Palestinians by giving them a very low percentage of the West Bank. They do not want any discussion on the issue of Jerusalem. They imagine they can impose peace on Syria, which would enable them to keep part of the Golan Heights, and that they can impose a peace on Lebanon under which the Lebanese state and army would turn into guards to protect the Israeli border, while the *mujahidin* and honorable people are punished, and the collaborators and traitors are awarded medals.

But despite all these Jewish ambitions, we in this nation say that the dreams of the Israelis have come to an end. The blood that will not be defeated by the sword that has been unleashed in southern Lebanon, western Bekaa and Palestine —today, this blood is boiling in the veins of Arabs and Muslims. The dreams of the Israelis are over. We promise and warn them that their dreams are over, and that the time has come for them to wake from their dreams and face reality, a reality in which people refuse to live in humiliation, and view life with the Zionist Jews as nonsense; a reality in which every man, young and old, loves to blow himself up to tear apart the bodies of the invading, occupying Jews.

This nation has a message, a religion, a culture, and tremendous capabilities. All that this nation needed was to regain its freedom and will. Now it is regaining them through the blood of the young martyrs of this nation. We therefore tell all those who have held conferences and discussed the tragedy for the past 50 years: do not despair, do not be pessimistic, and do not become hostages to theories and your imagination. Come and join us in the real world, the world of jihad and martyrdom, and you will see that we are able to change the equation.

I would like to draw attention to the grave nature of this usurping entity in Palestine, this cancerous growth and harmful microbe, this entity without borders. Israel's borders stop where its arm, tanks, and spears can reach. Israel's borders extend to river sources and sea basins, and any place where there is a trace of an old Talmud or a stone on which an old Jewish rabbi sat. That is the land of Israel. The waters of the Nile and the Euphrates, the mountains of Yemen, and the land of Khaybar are part of Israel's land.[4] Is this not the dream? But let us return to Khaybar: the army of Muhammad has returned carrying the Message [of Islam], history, religion, and culture, full of resolve and determination, with its leaders being martyrdom-seekers, just like Ali and Hussein, may God's peace and prayers be upon them. So wait for the dream of the Khaybarites to collapse, just as Khaybar collapsed.[5]

Far from despair, a state of vigilance and readiness exists among the nation. There is a great respect for *jihad*, *mujahidin*, martyrs and the option of *jihad*. There is a rejection of normalization with the enemy. This is even true in Egypt, which signed a peace agreement [with Israel] 20 years ago. The same applies to Jordan, whose king bows down every morning and evening on the Jews' doorsteps.

Hope in Lebanon grows with the presence of the Islamic Resistance and with the *intifada*, which erupted in Palestine,[6] and which, God willing, will return to the land of Palestine. Hope increases with the great political steadfastness in Syria, led by President Hafez al-Assad, and in the Islamic Republic [of Iran], led by His Eminence Ayatollah Khameini, the guardian of the Muslims' cause, may his shadow be extended. We tell Netanyahu: let Arafat bargain with you over 1 per cent or 0.5 per cent. If Netanyahu's decision to raise the ratio of the withdrawal from the West Bank from 9 to 10 per cent requires the mediation of heads of states, prime ministers, and foreign ministers of major powers, compare this with Arafat, who immediately accepted a reduction from 30 per cent to 13 per cent because of his humiliation, loss, disgrace, and relinquishment of *jihad*. But this nation will not accept from Netanyahu 1 per cent, 9 per cent, or 30 per cent. This nation will only accept every inch of the sacred land of Palestine (...)[7]

---

4 For the concept of "Greater Israel", see above, p. 95 n. 20.

5 Khaybar, in the modern state of Saudi Arabia, was an oasis community north of Medina inhabited by Jews. The Prophet Muhammad conquered it in 628 CE.

6 For the first Palestinian *intifada*, see above, p. 95 n. 18.

7 Nasrallah is referring to the vigorous US–Israeli–Palestinian negotiations over the percentage of land that would be included in Further Redeployments (FRDs) of Israeli forces, as called for

Regarding the Israeli proposal for Lebanon, I would like to point out that the Zionists seek to drive a wedge among the Lebanese concerning Resolution 425, with its security conditions. The Zionists are also trying to drive a wedge between the Lebanese and Syrians, between the Syrians and Iranians, and between the resistance and the state. The Zionists are spreading rumors, suspicion, and lies.

Regarding some statements and analyses that have reported that Iran has facilitated the Israeli proposal, I would like to stress that all these things are sheer lies, aimed at launching psychological warfare, driving a wedge, and making both Syria and Lebanon feel that they are besieged and isolated in their confrontation. Iran not only calls for the unconditional withdrawal of the Israeli forces from Lebanon, but also calls for the elimination of Israel. This is evident in Iran's firm ideological, religious, and political stance, which is the stance of the imam and leader. Iran's stance is too lofty to be harmed by lies and accusations.

Regarding Hezbollah's stance, some circles have said that a certain political deal has been made. I would like to say that Hezbollah's stance and [its] pride are far too lofty to allow it to participate in this kind of deal. I want to declare here that during the April [1996] war,[8] the foreign ministers of great countries contacted us and suggested ideas sweetened with many political incentives. They said they would recognize us as a big political party in Lebanon, and as an important political factor in the Lebanese equation. They also said that the doors of financial and material assistance would open for our institutions, and that we would be recognized by the highest authorities in the world in return for abandoning our resistance and stabbing our friends in Syria in the back. But we categorically rejected all this, because we are the sons of Abu Abdullah al-Hussein,[9] who know nothing of treason and who do not sell out their religion for the entire world.

If any Lebanese, Syrian or Arab is apprehensive about the conflict with

---

by the 1995 Interim Agreement and the 1997 Hebron Protocol. Under the eventual formula worked out at Wye River, the first and second FRD was to have consisted of the transfer to the Palestinian Authority (under either full Palestinian control or mixed Israeli military/Palestinian civil control) of 13 per cent of the territory that had previously been under full Israeli control.

8 See Statement 9 on the April Understanding.

9 The son of Ali, the first Shia Imam. For further details of Hussein, see above, p. 52.

the Zionist enemy, then we are not. This struggle is our religion, prayer, fasting, pilgrimage and life. It is our Hussein and Zeinab, and our infants. We will never bargain over it, regardless of the proposed deals or temptations.

Like Hussein, we call on the traitors, the agents, and those led astray—the Lebanese agents in Antoine Lahd's militia[10]—to repent. We have been urging them to do so for a long time. To make it easier for them, we submitted a draft bill to the Chamber of Deputies, pardoning and giving immunity from trial to anyone who repents and flees from the agents' army within three months. We presented this draft bill several months ago—that is, before Israel woke up to Resolution 425, with its security conditions. Our objective was to help dismantle Antoine Lahd's militia, and save these poor young Lebanese men from death. Unfortunately, this draft bill remained filed away until it appeared at a moment when there was talk about deals, suspicions, and hints of accusations.

We reiterate our call to the agents to repent and rejoin their kinsfolk and homeland. We do not tell them to come and join Hussein's group [Hezbollah] so as to be killed or martyred, but tell them to leave the killers and the corrupt, return to [their] homes, and live in peace and safety. We hope that the parliament will settle this matter soon. I declare to you that, if the draft law isn't discussed soon in the parliament, then the coalition of the resistance will—regrettably—have to retract it. This will waste a chance to dismantle the Lahd militia, but the resistance will have to withdraw the draft so that it won't be misused one day, when deals are made at the expense of Lebanon and the resistance.

I would like to remind the [Lebanese] government that, although the people are occupied with the municipal elections, the regional incidents, the Israeli suggestion, and the resistance, all this won't make them forget that the authorities are responsible for the difficult economic situation. This matter is the responsibility of the authorities, and they should never ignore this momentous reality in Lebanon. I would also like to ask the people to participate strongly in the municipal elections, [and] to choose the fittest candidates, so that the people can participate in their own development and the treatment of their economic ailments, so long as this government continues to ignore all their suffering and pains.

10 For Lahd and the SLA, see above, p. 66 n. 13.

In conclusion, and as on every 10th of *Muharram*, we renew the slogan against the Great Satan. As we did last year, we shout: Death to America! We shout in the face of the killers of prophets and the descendants of the apes and pigs: We hope we will not see you next year. The shout remains: Death to Israel!

13

TOWARDS LIBERATION

June 21, 1999

Amid increasing signals of an impending Israeli withdrawal from south Lebanon, speculation flourished both within and outside Lebanon that Hezbollah's primary raison d'être *would soon be removed. Such a scenario did not, however, appear to be particularly worrisome to Nasrallah in the statement that follows. After all, the party had by this time already built up a substantial political machine, alongside an effective network of social services, an array of revenue-generating entities, including the increasingly formidable construction company, Jihad al-Bina, and an expansive framework for allocating charitable contributions from across the world. Moreover, repeated Israeli air strikes during the previous seven years—sometimes directed at non-Hezbollah, non-Shiite areas and infrastructure—had only bolstered the view in Lebanon that, even after a withdrawal from the south, Israel would continue to represent a threat to the country. The real problem for Hezbollah, then, was that an overall regional normalization with Israel appeared closer at hand than ever before, especially along the all-important Syrian track.*

Indeed, just before this interview with the government-controlled Syrian daily Teshreen— *one of Assad's primary mouthpieces—Syrian Ambassador to Washington Walid Mualim told the journal* Middle East Insight *that "Hezbollah is the national resistance movement of Syria and Lebanon. Hezbollah's [leadership] understands that every agreement accepted by Syria, Israel, and Lebanon will obligate it as well."[1] Mualim's clear signal that Hezbollah's right to bear and use arms, hitherto effectively guaranteed (and to a certain extent contained) by Syria's control over Lebanon, would end if a peace agreement was signed, provided an ultimatum which Hezbollah, despite its substantial guerrilla capacity, could do little to resist.*

Still, renewed Syrian–Israeli negotiations, after several years of inactivity, were yet to come, restarting "where they left off," according to Assad's dictum, only in December 1999. In

1 Sobelman, *New Rules of the Game*, p. 28.

past rounds of discussion, however, an agreement had proved elusive. Ehud Barak's victory in the May 1999 Israeli elections, though—laden as it was with the promise to withdraw from Lebanon within one year and conclude a peace agreement with Syria—had pointed an energetic way forward; and Mualim, not to mention Assad, with his public description of Barak as a "strong and sincere man," had made it clear that the opportunities presented by Barak would be taken up with equal vigor.

Nasrallah accordingly presents a somewhat scaled-back set of "minimum demands," short of what he expected from any peace agreement: "Israeli withdrawal from south Lebanon and the western Bekaa; withdrawal from the Golan Heights; and the return of Palestinian refugees to their country, because Lebanon rejects the plan to settle Palestinian refugees in Lebanon."

His focus is, however, primarily on the domestic factors associated with an Israeli withdrawal. In this, he eagerly points to Hezbollah's reaction to the largely uneventful pullout of Lahd's SLA from the mainly Christian southern city of Jezzine on the night of June 1—an event which defied expectations of a Shiite-led bloodbath, and which represented a major public opinion coup for the party in the eyes of multi-confessional Lebanon. "Even the Israelis," Nasrallah proudly tells his interviewer, in a further pitch to the Lebanese public, "said that Hezbollah was demonstrating what an eventual unilateral Israeli retreat from south Lebanon would look like."

TESHREEN: *Are we on the threshold of a new phase, now that Barak has won power in Israel?*

HN: There is no doubt that the next phase, following Barak's election, will be a very sensitive one, especially given that a number of Arab governments are pinning their hopes on the enemy once again. We also expect, and it is only natural for us to do so, the American administration to start applying pressure on involved parties in the region, and especially on Lebanon and Syria, to give concessions under the pretext that Barak's administration now needs help to succeed. They also tell them that they should give the so-called moderate wing in Israel a chance, although it is not exactly moderate as far as Israel is concerned. This is the situation in which we find ourselves and, in my opinion, it is no worse than the Madrid Conference or the Oslo Agreement.[2] As far as Lebanon and Syria are concerned, they are in a better

2 For Madrid, see above, p. 93 n. 14; for Oslo, see above, p. 100 n. 1.

situation now, and therefore have a better chance of holding fast and not submitting to the enemy's will.

TESHREEN: *Why did the Israelis withdraw from Jezzine?³ Do you believe that they want to foment sedition and provoke discord and infighting in Lebanon as soon as they leave?*

HN: Certainly, the Israeli enemy's intentions are beyond doubt and always bad and satanic; but, in fact, when we look at the Jezzine experience, we have to keep in mind that everything is possible, and see the events in Jezzine in a positive light. According to specific information at my disposal, Antoine Lahd's militia had reached a point where they could no longer remain in Jezzine, and had two possible courses of action to take. Either the Israeli troops enter the area—which they had not previously done, instead relying on the presence of their security apparatus and agents in the area—and reinforce the militia by deploying in various positions and helping defend them, or Lahd's militia leaves the area entirely.

The first course of action is not possible, because Israeli public opinion would not have accepted Israel's expansion into new areas of Lebanon, or the ensuing increase in [Israeli] casualties due to the nature of the terrain there. Furthermore, the Israeli defense minister has already said that they want to reduce the number of forces in Lebanon, and a deployment of forces in Jezzine would have meant putting additional forces on the ground.

Now that the first course of action has been debunked, the second—a total withdrawal from the area—becomes inescapable. Antoine Lahd had asked to withdraw from Jezzine before the Israeli elections, and had insisted on it, but the Netanyahu government asked him to delay doing so until after the elections. Netanyahu considered any withdrawal from Jezzine to be a defeat for him personally, and therefore a move that would negatively affect his already poor chances of re-election. This is why—as soon as the elections were over, and before Barak even had time to assume the premiership and form a new government—Lahd's militia announced its intention to withdraw. This withdrawal actually proved extremely humiliating for them,

---

3 The southern city of Jezzine lies roughly equidistant between Beirut and the provisional Israeli–Lebanese border.

because our resistance fighters did not allow them to do so in peace; they pursued them, destroyed their weapons, and inflicted heavy human losses on them. Even the Israelis condemned the way this humiliating withdrawal had proceeded, and said that Hezbollah was demonstrating what an eventual unilateral Israeli retreat from south Lebanon would look like.

In fact, Antoine Lahd's militia withdrew from Jezzine, on the one hand, because they could no longer afford to stay there due to the resistance's activities and, on the other, [because] the enemy's government had tried to reach an agreement with the Lebanese government that would have allowed it to withdraw based on a partial settlement. This agreement, which they called "the Jezzine first option,"[4] would have required the Lebanese government to put special security arrangements in place and make a number of commitments to Israel, and a lot of pressure was brought to bear on it, and on the Syrian government, to go along with it. But the steadfast official positions, in both Lebanon and Syria, prevented this partial agreement from seeing the light; and when the Israelis and Antoine Lahd realized that they had failed to impose their will on the Lebanese government, they had no choice but to withdraw.

They hoped to be able to foment sedition, dissent, conflict, and infighting in Lebanon after their withdrawal, and in my opinion it was the resistance's alertness and wise stance, the official Lebanese position, and the understanding between the resistance and the state, that had actually thwarted Israel's and Antoine Lahd's plans.

What we have witnessed in the past few weeks, therefore, is the liberation of another part of Lebanon's territory, and today Jezzine is enjoying a period of peace and security, without a single problem on the horizon. As far as Jezzine's inhabitants were concerned, the much-talked-about fears in the first few days proved to be mere figments of the Israelis' and their agents' imaginations.

TESHREEN: *There are calls for mercy, and for pardoning those members of Lahd's militia who surrendered to the Lebanese authorities. What is your position towards these individuals, especially in view of the fact that you submitted a proposal to parliament that involves possible pardons?*

4 See above, p. 101 n. 3.

HN: We draw a distinction between two groups of enemy agents: the first includes those young men who remained enemy agents and members of an agent militia up to the very end, and chose to stay behind with their families when the bulk of this militia withdrew from the area. We do not consider these people as having repented their actions, because they stayed in this agent militia and serviced the enemy until the last moment—the last possible chance and the last shot. These men should be held accountable for serving as enemy agents and committing treason, and calls for pardoning or showing them mercy are unfair and based only on sectarian, electoral or political considerations. For the sake of Lebanon's national interest, these people ought to be punished and tried according to this country's laws, and this is what we have demanded. As for excusing them by saying that they had joined the militia in order to earn their daily bread, I am very sorry to hear such words coming from the mouths of people who hold prominent political and religious positions in Lebanon.

If we pardon these enemy agents after they have betrayed their country, and carried arms with the enemy against their compatriots, simply because they wanted to earn their daily bread, then we have to pardon all the thieves in Lebanon, or 90 per cent of those who are currently in Lebanese jails or are being tried for theft in Lebanese courts; 90 per cent of all thefts in Lebanon are committed for reasons of daily survival, and being a foreign agent and committing treason are far more serious crimes than theft. One robs a bank or steals a piece of jewelry, and the other betrays a country and consorts with an enemy, which threatens this country and this nation. Therefore, if we are required to pardon enemy agents and absolve them of their guilt for reasons of daily survival, then we have to pardon all thieves, murderers, and criminals in Lebanon who have received heavy sentences for their abominable crimes. We say no: those who chose to remain enemy agents until the very last moment should be punished in the same way that agents are anywhere else.

The second group includes those who have given up their activities as enemy agents and remained in the occupied areas, including Jezzine, but have in the past few years ended their relationship with the Israeli enemy; these deserve different treatment. As for those enemy agents who are still in the occupied areas, we call upon them to give up their treasonous activities and surrender to the resistance or the Lebanese army. We promise to work with the legal authorities to reduce their sentences substantially, and possibly hand down a minimal sentence on them, although we had requested that those who fled from the militia within a specific period be granted a full pardon.

People have incorrectly interpreted one of our important proposals—and although the relevant text is amply clear, they are still interpreting it the wrong way: the pardon proposal we submitted to the National Assembly did not mean that all enemy agents ought to be pardoned. We were saying that those who did not kill people (military elements, officers, and [presumably, associated] individuals) or whose crimes did not exceed a certain acceptable limit, could be granted a pardon if they escaped from the militia and surrendered to the resistance or the Lebanese army within a period of three months after the law has been enacted. The aim behind this proposal is to give those Lebanese individuals who want to abandon their activities as enemy agents, help dismantle Lahd's militia, and unmask Israeli schemes in Lebanon, the chance to do so. In this case, we would support granting those people a pardon, reducing their sentences, and rehabilitating them; but this offer only extends to those who abandon their service to Israel, not to those who stay in its service until the last moment.

TESHREEN: *Do you, therefore, believe that the Jezzine withdrawal was the result of the resistance's activities, and not of other reasons?*

HN: Of course, there are no other reasons.

TESHREEN: *Why did the Israelis shift gears and choose this particular time to withdraw, given that the resistance has been going on for years?*

HN: The Israelis did not change the way they think; when they occupy an area, they hold onto it until their last breath, and leave it only for a hefty price. When they withdraw without preconditions and without asking for a hefty price, it means that they came under pressure and were badly hurt. Although the resistance has been [in south Lebanon] for many years, the cumulative effect of its operations on the one hand, and Israeli losses and the fate of their agents in south Lebanon on the other, took their toll. Let me say, in this context, that one should not measure the impact of events in south Lebanon based only on the number of operations or of Israelis killed and wounded, for there is something more important than that—namely the psychological aspect. This factor is very important for the Israeli military establishment, which relies on its ability and power to hurt the enemy (...) and what happened has debunked the myth of the army that cannot be defeated, and dealt a severe blow to the high morale that the Israeli military boasts about.

For example, in the Ansariya operation,[5] the Israeli soldiers fell into a trap set by the resistance deep into the liberated area, which means that the resistance was waiting for them to arrive, in spite of the diligence and meticulousness with which they had planned their operation—at the highest military echelons—and the precision of its execution. Thus, the fact that this operation failed, as did many others they attempted behind our lines, is a very considerable psychological coup against the Israeli military establishment. Furthermore, all the measures that Israel put in place on the frontlines[6] failed to stop the Lebanese resistance fighters from reaching the Lebanese–Palestinian border, and many of our operations were actually carried out close to that border. We filmed those operations and showed them on television, which prompted the Israeli Commander of the Northern Region to declare: "Hezbollah can infiltrate our lines but we cannot infiltrate theirs; Hezbollah knows what is going on here, but we do not know what is going on there." A few days later, we read in the newspapers that Shaul Mofaz, Commander of the Israeli army, had said that there was not a single army in world capable of defeating Hezbollah.[7] But when his officers and soldiers, hunkering down on the frontlines, hear this admission their morale will undoubtedly sink even lower, because what he is in fact telling them is "It is not just us; no other army can defeat Hezbollah."

What is important, in the final analysis, is that the Israeli army has humiliated itself and lost its strongman image, and you know as well as I do that this army's strength resides mostly in its aura, well before its size and the lethality

---

5 See above, p. 170 n. 1.

6 Nasrallah is presumably referring to the frontline between "liberated" south Lebanon and the combined territory held by Israel (the "security zone") and the SLA.

7 Shaul Mofaz (1948–) was appointed Israel's chief of general staff in 1998. His tenure was noted for his tough tactics against Palestinian guerrilla warfare in the Occupied Territories.

of its weapons, [an aura] it heavily banks on. This is why I say that the Israelis have endured a lot in Lebanon. I read something that Uri Lubrani, the expert and coordinator of Israeli affairs in southern Lebanon, has written recently, to the effect that Israel had no way out of Lebanon except through an understanding with Syria. He said that Israel had to admit that the only solution to the catastrophe in which it finds itself in Lebanon (he considers their situation in Lebanon to be a catastrophe) is by negotiating with, and paying a heavy price to, Syria, if the objective is to extricate Israel from the quagmire in Lebanon.

TESHREEN: *What is the secret behind the resistance's success, and behind this large number of successful operations that inflicted such heavy losses on the Israelis? Did your intelligence information play a role in this success?*

HN: In my opinion, and based on my close observation of the resistance's operations over the past 17 years, more important elements than mere technical details have led to the success of the Islamic Resistance, and the most important of them all is loyalty. This group of fighters does not go to war in order to flex their military muscles, score a publicity coup or achieve material advantages; they fight and do jihad with serious intent and a deep conviction that the only way to regain their usurped territory is by waging war on the enemy. This serious intent is the culmination of disciplined behavior, such as maintaining confidentiality and secrecy, which makes it impossible for the enemy to infiltrate the resistance. When a group of resistance fighters enters an enemy location, the local inhabitants do not feel their presence; neither do the army or other resistance groups. They do their job quietly and in secret, and the success of their operations is commensurate with the secrecy of their movements. Our fighters go in and out, in and out of the occupied areas, and the enemy never has prior knowledge of their movements.

Secondly, the fact that the resistance cares about the people on the Lebanese side of the border has helped them carry out their operations with a greater degree of precision, and has made the people like them and feel the need to protect them. Had they cared less about the fate of the local population, which has been on the receiving end of Israeli shelling and attacks, the people would have just wanted to get rid of the *mujahidin*, and would have blamed them for all their woes. This mutual affection and cooperation between the *mujahidin* and the local inhabitants has given the resistance a lot of leeway as far as its movements are concerned.

Thirdly, constant improvement and creativity. Fighters in south Lebanon and the western Bekaa Valley do not see themselves as mere receivers of orders; even local resistance commanders consider it part of their responsibilities to sit and think together, study various options, and figure out what the best courses of action are, and how to improve the resistance's operations. There is no single group charged with figuring out how to improve our operations—it is everybody's responsibility to do so. Shaul Mofaz recognized as much when he said that he was facing a group of fighters that depended on creativity to develop their operations and tactics.

In any case, though such descriptions are a source of strength for us, the most important remains what makes us serious, loyal, and faithful: the *mujahidin* are, in fact, individuals who seek martyrdom. There are two categories of fighters in the south: fighters and officers whose objective is eventually to go back home; and those whose objective is martyrdom, pure and simple. The latter have a far higher morale on the battlefield, and regardless of the kind of weapons they carry, their faith and spirit make them strong and steadfast, and allow them to deal the enemy a severe blow. How else do you explain the fact that when Israeli warplanes bomb a road that one or two *mujahidin* have used, or drop 20 missiles on an artillery site, the *mujahidin* return to those same sites as soon as the raids are over to launch a counterattack?

TESHREEN: *We would like to turn now to the April Understanding.[8] Israel has violated this understanding dozens of times. How has the resistance responded to that, and how will it do so in the future?*

HN: We believe that the Understanding was motivated mainly by Israel's fears that their settlements in northern Palestine would be shelled by Katyusha rockets. However, although they are violating this Understanding, we do not respond to every one of these violations, because if we did it would upset all existing considerations. From time to time, and especially when

8 For the April Understanding, see Statement 9.

Lebanese civilians are targeted, we shell their settlements, breathe life into the Understanding once again, and impose a measure of self-restraint on those Israeli soldiers and officers who do not hesitate to target civilians. This, in my opinion, is the only way to keep the April Understanding alive.

TESHREEN: *The April Understanding is therefore useful to you. How do you make use of it?*

HN: In general, the Understanding has provided a good measure of safety to the civilian population, which is what we were looking for in the first place, in spite of Israeli violations.

TESHREEN: *Our next question concerns Hezbollah's future. What would this future be if a just and comprehensive peace is established in the region?*

HN: What Lebanon wants officially is now clear to all. It has three minimum demands: Israeli withdrawal from south Lebanon and the western Bekaa; withdrawal from the Golan Heights; and the return of Palestinian refugees to their country, because Lebanon rejects the plan to settle Palestinian refugees in Lebanon. One cannot look at the situation from a narrow angle: there are now around 400,000 Palestinians in Lebanon, and these people should have the right to return to their homes and reclaim their property.[9]

If this happens, then there are two factors to consider when talking about Hezbollah's future: the first is the political factor. I am not worried, in this context, as far as the future is concerned, although some would like to provoke people's insecurities and fears. The situation is not what they think, for although it is true that Hezbollah is above all a resistance movement, and has *mujahidin* who sacrifice themselves, it is also a large Lebanese, popular and political Shia mass movement that has representatives in the National Assembly and participates in municipal elections.

We are very concerned about what takes place in our country in the local, media, political, social, and cultural domains, and regardless of whether it is

9 By 2007, the United Nations Relief and Works Agency for Palestine Refugees in the Near East reported that there were 405,425 registered Palestinian refugees living in twelve camps across Lebanon—the result of widespread flight and exile following the 1948 and 1967 Arab–Israeli conflicts. See http://www.un.org/unrwa/publications/index.html.

large or minor. We are citizens of this country and therefore care about its future. In my opinion, Hezbollah has a good and prosperous future, and I am not worried at all from this point of view. I also expect the Lebanese people to recognize Hezbollah's jihadist role, and the state to appreciate the favor that Hezbollah has rendered to this country.

As for the military factor—in other words our field operations—we do not usually speak about this topic in public, and I believe that keeping it secret and under wraps, regardless of the reality on the ground, is in the interest of both Lebanon and Syria.

TESHREEN: *You regularly express your appreciation for President Hafez al-Assad's positions and his role in ending Israeli hegemony over Lebanon. What is the secret behind this deep appreciation and respect?*

HN: To express my real thoughts, and reflect an accurate measure of my feelings towards President Assad, I will give you a very simple example. When Israel invaded and occupied large parts of the Bekaa Valley, Mount Lebanon, and Lebanon's capital city in 1982, a contingent of multinational forces arrived to bolster this occupation, and many Lebanese groups opted to cooperate with it.[10] Israel succeeded in imposing a president of the republic and the humiliating May 17 Agreement on Lebanon.[11] Had there not been in the region a state by the name of Syria, led by a president of the stature of Hafez al-Assad, Lebanon would still be wallowing in the Israeli era.

10 The Multinational Force, made up of British, French, US, and Italian "peacekeeping" soldiers, was greeted upon its arrival in August 21, 1982, with far greater acceptance by various Lebanese parties than had been the conquering Israelis, then entrenched around mostly Muslim West Beirut, as well as the southern half of Lebanon itself. Originally sent to the country in order to expedite the withdrawal of PLO forces from Lebanon, and thereafter protect the remaining Palestinian refugees, the Multinational Force nevertheless hastily began pulling out from Lebanon almost as soon as Yasser Arafat and many of his fighters had left the country. When Phalange leader and recently elected Lebanese President Bashir Gemayel was assassinated—on September 14, 1982—Phalangists, under the watch of the Israeli troops who had just recently entered West Beirut, stormed through two of the capital's Palestinian refugee camps—Sabra and Chatila—massacring, by some accounts, hundreds of Palestinians and Lebanese, including women and children (for one seminal account, see Robert Fisk, *Pity the Nation*, pp. 359–400). After a series of deadly suicide bombings, constant attacks, and increasing interventions into what was by then a full-blown civil war, the Multinational Force withdrew at the end of March, 1984.

11 Among several objectives and stipulations, the May 17, 1983, peace agreement between Lebanon and Israel was designed to end the state of war between the two countries, while providing

I think this example gives you the right idea. In other words, had it not been for Syria, its steadfastness and the iron will of President Hafez al-Assad in the face of this American–Israeli onslaught, and had Syria not opted to adopt and protect the resistance and support its fighters, we would not have achieved what we did in Lebanon. It was the Lebanese *intifada* and the resistance that forced the Israelis to withdraw in 1985, followed by the withdrawal of the multinational [forces]. They are the ones who brought about the demise of the May 17 Agreement and the end of the regime that Israel had established in Lebanon. The Lebanese resistance and the handful of Palestinian factions would not have succeeded in doing what they did, had there not been a presence to protect, support, defend, and strengthen them, as President al-Assad's leadership has done. What is also beyond doubt is that Iran also adopted a politically supportive position towards the *mujahidin*, although the special role that Syria played was the most direct and closest to where the action was.

It is only fair to say that the efforts that Syria exerted in Lebanon—efforts that have led to peace and security in the region—have been a major factor in reactivating the resistance and freeing the hands of many parties to refocus on fighting the Israeli enemy. The civil war drained everybody's energies and preoccupied the Lebanese people; it was the country's political stability and security, the resurgence of the state and its institutions, and the end of internal strife that made it possible for people to devote time to the resistance, and provided the right climate for building a consensus around it. We in Lebanon know very well that, after God Almighty, it is thanks to President Assad, to Syria, and to the Syrian army that we have durable security in this country.

---

for a phased withdrawal of Israeli forces. Such a withdrawal was premised on the Lebanese army, already badly split by years of escalating civil war, establishing a tightly controlled security zone in the south. Although the agreement was signed by Phalange leader and Lebanese President Amine Gemayel almost one year after the June 1982 Israel invasion of Lebanon, it was effectively abrogated only one year later, after the withdrawal of the Multinational Force and the collapse of the army forced Gemayel to travel to Damascus to make amends with the regime that many held responsible for the earlier assassination of his brother, President Bashir Gemayel, in September 1982. For Hezbollah, the agreement—especially its call for an end to any "hostile propaganda"—epitomized the maximalist demands that Israel, it argued, would always pursue in the absence of any countervailing power on the ground.

TESHREEN: *Did you find Israeli soldiers to be strong and courageous, or the contrary?*

HN: Based on my experience, I would say first of all that Israeli soldiers only fight when they have material superiority—in other words, when they can muster large numbers of troops and move in units of 15 or 20 soldiers at a time. Although this method of security in numbers makes them better targets, the fact that they use [it] at all means that the Israeli soldier is fearful and cowardly.

Second, their defensive readiness and the readiness of their helicopters to ferry casualties. Whenever there is an engagement between one such Israeli unit and the resistance, Israeli artillery intervenes and starts pounding enemy positions, and helicopters appear overhead to cover it, although a typical battle would involve between 20 Israeli soldiers and only three to four resistance fighters. According to the *mujahidin*, when an Israeli soldier is wounded his unit's position quickly becomes obvious, thanks to all the screaming and wailing, which the *mujahidin* make fun of. For example, in the recent confrontation that took place in Iqlim al-Tuffah,[12] they started screaming even though their unit was a large one, and ours was small, and in spite of the fact that our unit leader had been twice wounded in the leg, which could not but have affected his small unit. The *mujahidin* are well able to inflict losses on the Israelis.

I am not underestimating the Israeli soldier's abilities; I am just saying that he hides behind his technology, his artillery, his helicopters, and his heavy gunfire, and the human element comes last in Israeli military estimates. This is why I know that it is possible to defeat Israeli soldiers if we know how to use the elements of the battle on the ground to our advantage.

TESHREEN: *As the secretary-general of Hezbollah and a politician, how do you visualize the Zionist entity's present and future?*

HN: At this particular point in time, when many are talking about the need to accept the status quo, to live with it and acquiescing to any kind of settlement with Israel, my view is realistic, if somewhat different. Israel is an illegal and usurper entity built on false pretences, on massacres, and on

12 See above, p. 98 n. 28.

delusions, and has therefore no chance for survival. Certain characteristics, innate to the nature of aggressive and arrogant peoples, have prevailed throughout the history of humanity. In this context, I read some of Netanyahu's desperate statements that say that the Israeli people are sick and tired of Zionism, and that they only care about their own personal lives. I consider this statement as a confirmation of my belief that the Israeli entity's nature is one that cannot change, and that although they are incapable of change, they are capable of regression. Today the Zionist society is ethnically (Sephardim and Ashkenazi), religiously (extremists, centrists, and secularists), and politically torn. Israel has never had a Knesset as badly torn as the current one, in which many groups have barely three or four seats each; this means that the Israeli street is itself badly divided, and that the system does not function as it did before.[13] Many Mossad operations, for example, have proved to be total failures, and the chief of staff himself has said that there is not a single army in the world—he did not say in the Middle East only!—capable of defeating the resistance.

The Israelis are scared of war and scared of peace; or at the very least, they do not want peace as much as some Arabs want it. This is the typical behavior of a people that isolates itself, and of a racist people who live in fear of being done in.

TESHREEN: *Your military operations are ongoing. Do you think the Israelis will pull out from the south? When will you escalate and intensify your operations, and when will you do the opposite?*

HN: Any withdrawal from south Lebanon must be unconditional, because the Israelis have to pay the price for their occupation and, as I said before, the official Lebanese position rejects giving Israel any security guarantees. We want a total withdrawal from south Lebanon and the Golan Heights, and the return of the refugees; but since Israel will not get the security guarantees it seeks, it will find it difficult to withdraw without them. The only

---

13 Although the Israeli public and the Knesset were indeed deeply divided, partly reflecting divisions over peace negotiations, Barak had won the Israeli Premiership with 55.9 percent of the votes, compared to 43.9 percent polled by Netanyahu, in what the US Cable News Network at the time termed "a landslide triumph by Israeli standards," and one that exceeded almost all pre-election forecasts.

way they can be made to take a gamble and withdraw without guarantees is for the resistance to inflict heavy losses on them; and the Israelis know very well, as Lubrani has said, that the only way they can withdraw without taking a gamble is by negotiating with Syria and paying the price of this withdrawal.

As for the second part of your question, in reality any escalation or reduction in the number of the resistance's operations is not contingent upon a political decision, but rather upon the situation on the ground, and the readiness of some of our operations. You and I assume that, because we do not hear of them, these operations do not exist; in fact, there are ongoing operations, landmine explosions and traps in the occupied territories all the time, and we can often clearly hear the sound of an explosive device hitting an Israeli patrol. Sometimes no Israeli patrols pass by, and the *mujahidin* do not detonate their explosives. People talk about the operations they hear about, and whether or not they are escalating; on the ground, however, these decisions depend on the results of operations. Furthermore, an escalation or reduction in the number of operations does not necessarily depend on the resistance, which is continually setting traps for the Israelis, but on the Israelis themselves who, for one reason or another, decide to reduce their movements; sometimes days will pass without any of their patrols passing along a certain road. They often avoid certain routes, and sometimes senior officers wear civilian clothes, drive taxicabs and place chicken coops and vegetable crates on top of them to trick the resistance into believing that they are just civilians, and [to have them] refrain from opening fire. The situation therefore depends on circumstances on the ground, rather than on political decisions.

TESHREEN: *Finally, would you like to add anything to what you have already said?*

HN: I would like to say that there is not a big difference between Barak and Netanyahu. In statements after his victory in the elections, Barak said that Jerusalem was the eternal capital of Israel, that settlements in the West Bank and Gaza Strip will be maintained, that there will be no return to the 1967 borders, and that no troops, except Israeli, will be stationed west of the Jordan River. What have they left to negotiate over in any eventual final status talks?

Netanyahu failed to win in the elections because of his own performance, not because of his policies, and Barak professes exactly those same policies: he says that he will continue on the same track, and that he is not willing to pay the price for peace. We expect an escalation in the south and more Israeli security operations, and should therefore be ready for them.

II

REPOSITIONING, 2000–2004

14

"A PEACEFUL RESOLUTION IS
A VICTORY FOR THE RESISTANCE"

February 16, 2000

Only weeks before a climactic meeting between US President Bill Clinton and Hafez al-Assad in Geneva, to finalize what would have effectively been a three-country peace agreement, Nasrallah placidly told one of the most revered, pro-government dailies in the Arab world, Egypt's Al-Ahram, that "we carry on with our normal lives, here in Lebanon, where we have our own institutions and parliamentarians, and where we intend to be more engaged in the country's political life." Insisting that "Israel will remain, in our minds and plans, an illegitimate, illegal, aberrant, and cancerous entity," Nasrallah reiterates that "normalization" will be resisted, but acknowledges, in effect, that violence would no longer be a modus vivendi *for the party in the future. In claiming an important victory in preventing Israel's wider territorial ambitions in Lebanon, he also provides a harbinger of sorts for the second* intifada, *which was only months away, suggesting that "the experience we went through could be a good example for the Palestinian people, especially when they compare the results of the final status talks with those achieved by Lebanon and Syria thanks to their steadfast attitude, over many years, until they achieved their national objectives."*

AL-AHRAM: *How did the name "Hezbollah" come about, and does it mean that all those who do not belong to it are from the Devil's prty?*

HN: God gave this name to the people who obey Him and his Messenger, and since we claim to be among this group of people, we believe we have the right to use this name. However, this does not mean that we never make mistakes, and never fail or lose.

AL-AHRAM: *What do you think about recent developments including the Israeli shelling of civilian installations?*

HN: What the Israeli enemy has done recently is launch revenge operations;[1] now that the measures they put in place to stop the resistance's operations have failed, they are incapable of confronting the fighters in south Lebanon. They do not dare launch ground operations either, because they would incur many casualties if they did; they therefore bombard the area from the air to wreak vengeance on Lebanon and its people. We were very sorry to hear Barak[2] threaten Lebanon and the resistance while still in Cairo, and then repeat those same threats the next day in Amman.

AL-AHRAM: *When we asked about that, they told us that Barak's statement came as an answer to the last question, posed in Hebrew, at the press conference given by [Egyptian] President [Hosni] Mubarak and Barak. Anyway, no one attracted the president's attention, and Egypt has already strongly rejected Israel's aggression and condemned it in front of the whole world.*

HN: In any case, the Israelis tried to impose a new fait accompli on the ground, to safeguard the occupation in the south, by targeting Lebanon's infrastructure. In the past, when they shelled our civilians, we retaliated by shelling their settlements in order to protect our civilians; now they are shelling our infrastructure to protect the occupation troops. What is the aim behind this latest move? The Israelis want to maintain their army in the south, but do not want the resistance to fire on it; they are actually saying that if we do, they would simply destroy Lebanon's infrastructure. They also want the resistance to become the guardians of the occupation, in the future, which is an illogical proposition. We see it as our natural right to fire Katyushas at their settlements in response to their recent bombardment of our electricity grids. Before they launched their latest air raids, Barak went personally to the north, met with the settlers' representatives, and asked them to go down to the shelters; and according to my information 70 per cent of them where evacuated from the area, and

---

1 In January 2000, Hezbollah fighters killed seven Israeli soldiers and wounded scores of others, during a bloody three-week period. Israel's ostensible response, designed primarily to put pressure on the Lebanese government to rein in Hezbollah, was to bomb three Lebanese power plants, which cut 50 per cent of the country's electricity supply, and wounded 20 Lebanese civilians.

2 Statements from the Barak government had repeatedly underlined that dire consequences "that would not spare Lebanese civilians" and "that would surprise the terrorists" would follow Hezbollah attacks against Israeli forces in the "security zone." Harik, *Hezbollah*, p. 124.

30,000 Zionists were either displaced or went into hiding ahead of the resistance's counterattack.

Thanks to the publicity campaign that accompanied their recent operations, we are now pursuing two objectives: first, to foil the fait accompli that they are trying to impose on the ground. Israel says that it wants to protect its troops by targeting Lebanon's infrastructure, and that this bombardment is their way of applying pressure on the resistance to stop their operations. We said in response that our operations would continue, because they are the right tool to foil their 'troop protection vs. the bombardment of installations' plan. Based on that, on the very day that followed the Israeli operations, we shelled the occupying troops and killed a number of them and their Lebanese agents. We did the same on Thursday against Antoine Lahd's troops, and yet again today, Friday, killing one Israeli and wounding three others. Some sources say that two Israelis have died. To put an end to these attacks, we are determined to continue mounting operations, regardless of the measures the enemy chooses to put in place, or the pressures it chooses to exert. I do not believe that Lebanon's government and people would accept that the occupation stays, unmolested, on its territory; as Lebanese, therefore, we have no other choice but to expel the occupiers from our country.

Our second objective is to protect Lebanon's infrastructure and population. Based on that, we believe that it is in Lebanon's national interest, and the interest of the resistance, that we restrain ourselves while reserving the right to respond when we see fit. We believe that Israel's main intention was to provoke Hezbollah into responding violently, and that our self-restraint de-stabilized their entire plan. Although we will not use our Katyushas at this time, we reserve the right to respond at a time and in a manner of our own choosing; all options are still on the table. Settlers in the north should expect our revenge to come at any moment. I also believe that the position we took will keep Israel in a constant state of anxiety, because they know that our operations will continue as long its occupation troops are still on our territory.

Regardless of their intellectual, religious or political affiliations, Lebanon's government, people, and army have expressed their support for the resistance, and for putting an end to the occupation. Lebanon has no problem regarding this issue, because it is not only the resistance's right to fight occupation, but also the right of the Lebanese people. This was made evident in July 1993, in 1996, in the June attack of a few months ago, and in this recent attack.

Last Monday, Israel said that the ball was now in our court; but now that Hezbollah has exercised self-restraint, including the operations it carried out in the occupied territories, the ball is now in the Israeli court again. Israel has to decide in which direction it wants the region to go: Does it want the conflict in the south to remain subject to the rules of the April Understanding,[3] or does it want those rules to change? In any case, we are ready for all eventualities.

AL-AHRAM: *In light of what took place at the April Understanding committee meeting today, Friday, do you expect Israel to carry out an operation, or operations, now that the ball is once again in its court? Will the reactions and counter-reactions persist, and is this what is required at this point?*

HN: First, Israeli negotiators did not take part in the April Understanding talks, and therefore it is not correct to say that they withdrew from them; they actually arrived late, and did not even go into the hall where the meeting was taking place. They behaved in a very arrogant and dismissive manner at a time when the [monitoring] committee was meeting to condemn their aggression against Lebanon. They wanted to impose their conditions and control the meeting's proceedings, even its general atmosphere. But one should not view the situation as [one in which] one party strikes, the other responds, and vice versa: people should realize that Israel occupies Lebanese territory, and that Lebanon is trying to end this occupation and recuperate what belongs to it. There is no need for us to go over the details, or the rules of the game, all over again.

Israeli extremists, like the deputy defense minister,[4] say that we violated their national territory; we believe, however, that the territory they are talking about is occupied Palestine. Their real land is Ethiopia, as far as the Falashas are concerned,[5] and Russia, as far as the Russian émigrés are

3 For the April Understanding see Statement 9.

4 Israeli Deputy Defense Minister Ephraim Sneh (1944–) is generally considered a "hawkish" member of the Israeli Labour Party.

5 The Falashas are the African Jews of Ethiopia, who came to prominence in 1984 when

concerned, and there will be a time when these people will really feel nostalgia for their original homeland. Israel's deputy defense minister told the press that the Israeli people thought that if they just said a few words, launched a few military operations, and changed the rules of the game, they would be able to prevent their soldiers from suffering additional casualties and be able to solve Israel's problems by diplomatic means. This opinion differs fundamentally from what Barak, Sharon, and Mofaz stated earlier—for after Sharon, Mofaz, and a number of other ministers announced the demise of the April Understanding, they have now changed their tone and are saying that they want to keep the April Understanding as it is. This change in attitude has undoubtedly come about as a reaction to the resistance's operations and the steadfastness of the Lebanese position.

Accusations to the effect that Hezbollah has violated the April Understanding are unfair and incorrect, and a ploy to boost the morale of the Israeli soldiers who, in the past few days, have suffered considerable casualties. Today, Friday, they admitted the death of 19 Israelis in 1999 when, in fact, there were eight Israelis dead and 20 wounded in the past 15 days alone. Saying that Hezbollah has violated the April Understanding is just an excuse for Israel to do that itself. All Hezbollah's operations were carried out within the boundaries of the April Understanding, and nothing whatsoever outside it. Let me reiterate that, at the end of the day, Israel has no choice but to get out of Lebanon.

AL-AHRAM: *When is it the right time to reduce the intensity of the resistance's operations, and when is it the time to go full speed ahead?*

HN: The importance of the resistance in south Lebanon comes from the fact that it is an effective and serious movement, that it has earnest intentions, and has caused the occupation to bleed profusely. Barely three months after Israel invaded and occupied large areas of Lebanon, we were able to expel the Israeli troops from the capital, the suburbs, Mount Lebanon, Sidon, Tyre, Nabatieh, and the western Bekaa, and force them to hide behind the hills known now as the frontier zone. This came as the result of resistance oper-

---

12,000 of them were airlifted to Israel from refugee camps in the Sudan, in an Israeli military effort known as Operation Moses.

ations rather than diplomatic or political endeavors, and culminated in the Israeli people putting pressure on their government to withdraw, and in the latter doing just that.

From that time on, and in spite of the difficulties that Lebanon has experienced—difficulties that ended only with the signature of the Taif Agreement[6]—the resistance started substantially regaining its vigor. It currently relies on operations rather than on launching Katyushas, which are a weapon of choice for targeting specific objectives. This is why we do not consider launching Katyushas to be part of the resistance's operations, but only a defensive measure. Ground operations, on the other hand, depend on circumstances; we do not tell the resistance "Do this or do that," because if we did it would no longer be serious and effective. So far, our resistance in south Lebanon has been both serious and effective precisely because it is genuine and produces high-quality results that put the Israelis under pressure. In this context, an opinion poll, published the day before yesterday, Wednesday, revealed that 83 percent of Israelis support withdrawal from Lebanon, which means that the Israeli public now wants to leave Lebanon as a direct result of the resistance's activities.

AL-AHRAM: *Barak said that Israel would withdraw next July from Lebanon. Are your recent operations therefore just a tactical maneuver, given that you have not carried out any operations in the past five months?*

HN: It is clear that Barak, as the result of pressure brought to bear on him by the resistance, now wants to withdraw from Lebanon according to his own conditions, and wants to punish it for resisting; this is what we are afraid of, and need to prepare for. The responsibility falls here on the shoulders of the Arab governments and the international community: if the enemy wants to leave, then he should do so without destroying the country in the process.

AL-AHRAM: *Is the current position of the resistance a strategic position, or is it a tactical one to help advance the negotiations on the Syrian track—especially given that the resistance has not carried out any operations in the past five months, and that the Israelis have said that they will withdraw come next July, or even earlier*

6 For the Taif Accord, see above, p. 63 n. 10.

than that? Why did the resistance not execute these operations at a more opportune time, when the rewards could have been greater?

HN: If we had carried out operations, they would have said that Hezbollah is working on Iran's orders to foil the Israeli–Syrian negotiations; and if we ceased our operations, they would have said that Hezbollah did so upon orders from Syria to facilitate the negotiations. On the other hand, if the negotiations stalled, and we carried out operations, they would have said that Syria was putting pressure on Israel to accept its conditions. This is all mere imagination, and those who think this way do not know what is really taking place in south Lebanon, what the resistance is all about, what is its identity or the extent of its willpower. I would like you all to read what Shaul Mofaz wrote, [saying that] the resistance's operations have increased but that their own casualties have decreased, thanks to the measures they had put in place against it. This means that, far from decreasing, the operations of the resistance have actually increased, from the point of view of setting traps and planting explosive devises, more than anytime before, as demonstrated by the martyrdom of many of our fighters in the past five months while trying, with their minds and blood, to circumvent the enemy's measures. We executed operations while the negotiations were going on, the only difference being that we did not achieve all that we were aiming for, due to the measures that the enemy had put in place. But once we succeeded in circumventing these measures, we started hitting the target.

I have to say, in all honesty, that the Syrians did not talk to us before they went to the negotiations or afterwards, and never shared any information with us about them. Syria has it own principled, steady, and public position; [it] really knows what the resistance and its operations in south Lebanon are all about, and has full confidence in its wisdom and intellect.

There are people in the Arab world who do not believe that there are young men in Lebanon who have taken it upon themselves honestly and truly to end the occupation and liberate the occupied Lebanese territories without having regional or international ulterior motives. These young men believe that ending the occupations is a sacred duty tightly linked to their religion, prayers, and fasting, and to the thereafter; this is what the resistance in south Lebanon is all about.

I do not agree with calls, from some quarters and by some of our brothers, for the resistance to cease its operations until the April Understanding [monitoring] committee has held its meeting. Our brethren should be allowed to go on killing Israeli soldiers, any time they choose, regardless of whether the Understanding Committee is holding a meeting or not, because the Understanding is intended to protect civilians, not Israeli soldiers.

AL-AHRAM: *In spite of the resistance's legitimacy, does Hezbollah take into consideration, when making decisions, the suffering of the people as the result of Israeli targeting of civilian and economic installations?*

HN: We have no other choice. The only alternative is for our territory to remain under Israeli occupation, and for Israel to impose its conditions on us. It is the fate of the Lebanese people to resist and endure the burden of this resistance; the Israelis cannot last for long in this situation. I am not claiming, however, that we have a balance of power or military parity on the ground, but I do know that this kind of warfare is very costly to the Israelis; and although I do not want to issue threats, allow us to work rather than talk.

AL-AHRAM: *Do you have a vision of a future settlement? Could the door be open for such an eventuality?*

HN: Of course, the door could be open, and the proof is the meeting held in Washington between the Syrians and Israelis around the negotiating table, at a time when no one expected such a meeting to take place—especially at this particular time and in this manner.[7] We do take into consideration international efforts to find a solution in the region, and determine our plans and movements with this possibility in mind. We actually estimate that a peaceful resolution is a victory for the resistance and its logic. The experience we went through could be a good example for the Palestinian people, especially when they compare the results of the final status talks with those achieved by Lebanon and Syria thanks to their steadfast attitude, over many years, until they achieved their national objectives.

7 A reference to the US-mediated negotiations in Washington in December 1999 between Barak and Syrian Foreign Minister Farouk al-Sharaa.

At the same time, we carry on with our normal lives, here in Lebanon, where we have our own institutions and parliamentarians, and where we intend to be more engaged in the country's political life. Israel will remain, in our minds and plans, an illegitimate, illegal, aberrant, and cancerous entity, which we therefore cannot recognize. We will instead work with others to combat normalization with it, because fighting normalization will impede its development into a regional superpower. Just as the wars of 1973 and 1982, the impact of the Lebanese resistance and of Israel's failure to occupy Lebanon [have together led] to the demise of the military aspect of the Greater Israel plan, combating normalization would lead to the demise of the political, economic, and cultural aspects of the Greater Israel plan.[8]

As for the future of the armed struggle, we had better leave that subject aside for now because, regardless of whether my answer to your question is positive or negative, keeping such matters secret is in Lebanon's best interest.

AL-AHRAM: *Why is Hezbollah alone on the battlefield, and what do you tell those who say that Hezbollah evolved out of the Amal Movement?*

HN: Lebanon's demands are clear: they want the restitution of their occupied territories; the repatriation of the Palestinian refugees, which is as important; and compensation for Lebanon. In its current social configuration, and given the nature of its problems, Lebanon cannot accommodate the Palestinian refugees on its territory. Hezbollah's rejection of the option of settling the Palestinians in Lebanon is not politically or ideologically motivated, but rather based on a sincere belief that settling the Palestinians in Lebanon, Syria or Jordan would mean the total abandonment of Palestine, [which] is neither acceptable nor logical. What we are saying is that it is not enough to reject the option of settling the Palestinians in Lebanon: we should also reject their displacement and exile all over the world. The only acceptable option for us is their return to their homeland and the restitution of their rights.

In 1982, when the Islamic Resistance first started its activities, Lebanese parties already active in the field had chosen various descriptive names for

---

8 For the concept of Greater Israel, see above, p. 95 n. 20.

themselves—for example, leftist parties were known collectively as the National Resistance Front; and when the Amal Movement was still carrying out resistance operations, it was known under the name Lebanese Resistance Cohorts. When there were internal problems, the Amal Movement insisted on saying that it was the one carrying out the resistance operations. Given that these names were descriptive of operations against the Israeli enemy, Imam al-Sadr[9] used the name Lebanese Resistance Cohorts in reference to operations against the occupation. For more than one-and-a-half years, however, Hezbollah carried out operations without claiming responsibility for them, whether as Amal or as the Islamic Resistance Movement (i.e. Hezbollah), because it did not seek political or media attention; it was this anonymity that had, for a time, provided protection for the party's fighters. But when it became clear that this group was different from all the others, the Islamic Resistance made its existence publicly known in 1982.

In fact, the name Islamic Resistance refers to the military operations that Hezbollah's fighters carry out against the Israeli occupation. It is worth mentioning here that we draw a distinction between the Islamic Resistance and the National Resistance Front—namely, the fact that one refers to the fighters' religious affiliation and the other to their sectarian affiliation. When we speak about the Islamic Resistance, we are actually referring to the fighters' intellectual and ideological, rather than sectarian identity. What compels these fighters to go south and resist is their faith in God, in judgment day, in answering God's summons to fight the occupiers, and in the expectation of going to paradise. When you ask some young men to go and defend their country, they will tell you "Why should we? Our country has done nothing for us." There are also those who loot, pillage, and commit other such acts, and when you tell them to go and defend the Arabs, they will tell you: "The Arabs are trying to further their narrow regional interests." What I am trying to say is that they tried for years to motivate the people using purely nationalistic and popular language, but failed to forge *mujahidin* like those currently fighting in Lebanon. It is impossible for people to imagine that there are young men who have no aircraft, missiles or tanks, and live in the wild, and yet wage war against the strongest army in the Middle East. The only dogma that could inspire such devotion is Islam. Given that Islam

---

9 For Sadr, see above, p. 26 n. 6.

is its motivator, it is therefore only natural for this resistance movement to give itself a name that fits it to a tee.

Ever since the movement's inception, the name "Islamic Resistance" has never had a sectarian connotation or referred to anyone in particular in this country. The Islamic Resistance does not only fight to defend Muslims, or Muslim areas, but rather all of Lebanon: its villages and citizens, be they Muslims or Christians. We have gone well beyond this issue in Lebanon. A more important issue for Lebanon is all the talk about growing fears regarding the increasing power of Hezbollah because of its armed resistance, when, in reality, the situation on the ground does not justify those fears. One could say that Hezbollah is able to defeat Israel and achieve victory, or that it could very well play a role in the political equation of the region. However, when we deal with the Lebanese domestic equation, we inevitably have to take into consideration Lebanon's contradictions and particular calculations. Those who speak about such fears therefore know that they are exaggerating quite a bit, and that their fears are not justified.

Before 1982, a number of Hezbollah's leaders and cadres belonged to the Amal Movement, and another group were members of other Islamic organizations of various names and shapes, including student associations and committees. But there was no central body to unite all these movements under a single umbrella. When the Israelis invaded Lebanon in 1982, a disagreement took place within the Amal Movement regarding the manner in which this invasion had to be dealt with; as a result, we decided to split from Amal. We joined ranks with the other leaders and cadres who were not in Amal, and together started a new movement to confront occupation and expel it from Lebanon. We chose the path of jihad and did not care at all about holding conferences, issuing founding statements, or even finding a name for our new movement.

As for the name "Islamic Resistance", it came about only one-and-a-half years later, and it is therefore not accurate to say that Hezbollah was born and formed from within the Amal Movement, or that it emerged from under its cloak.

AL-AHRAM: *What is the nature of your relationship with Syria and Iran?*

HN: We are a Lebanese Islamic jihadist movement that has its own cause, ideology, and plans, as well as its own leadership and elected cadres; and Syria is a sister country, and a friend, with whom we share a common fate. We say that very earnestly, not to placate the Syrians but to state a fact, because our hopes are pinned on the unity of purpose among the Arabs and the common fate of the entire Islamic nation. At a time when the rest of our Arab brothers are busy pursuing their own interests, our friendship, brotherly relations, mutual trust, cooperation, and exchange of views with Syria are as strong as ever. But in the pursuit of the national and popular interests, Hezbollah makes its decisions alone and as it sees fit, and Israel's portrayal of Hezbollah as a Syrian tool is completely wrong.

As for our relations with Iran, the Islamic Republic of Iran is a country we deeply respect, and believe to be a genuine and true Islamic state with no links to any of the world's powers, and a wonderful example of an Islamic regime, especially in comparison to other Islamic countries. When the Islamic Revolution achieved victory in Iran, it took a decision to help the Palestinian people in their fight to regain their Israeli-occupied land. The Islamic Republic of Iran is a strong state that stands on the side of the Arabs, against Zionist and other ambitions in the region. After the Israeli invasion of Lebanon in 1982, our relationship with it started developing fast. Thus, in spite of being occupied fighting a war that Iraqi President Saddam Hussein had imposed on it, Iran was the only country in the world that sent armed troops to fight the Israeli occupation, on the side of Syria and Lebanon. When it became clear that the situation in Lebanon would not assume regional proportions, the Iranian troops went back home, leaving behind a few Revolutionary Guards to help train and morally motivate the Lebanese fighters against the occupation.[10] This was of tremendous help to the resistance in regaining its self-confidence after its morale had almost plummeted to the ground, as the result of all the talk about our entering into the Israeli era without the chance of ever leaving it. Since that time, Iran has supported us politically and stood at the Lebanese government and people's side; and although Iran might disagree with the Lebanese government over certain issues, it will always be at its side, and on Syria's side, in the confrontation with the Israeli enemy.

---

10 For the presence of Iranian Revolutionary Guards in the Bekaa valley in the early 1980s, see Fisk, *Pity the Nation*, pp. 468–70.

However, to say that the relationship between Hezbollah and the regime of the Islamic Republic of Iran is that of master and servant is wrong: Iran does not interfere at all in our internal affairs, and pursues its own policies regarding the Lebanese government. For example, at a time when we were opposed to [Premier] Rafik Hariri's government,[11] the latter had very good relations with Iran and paid several visits to Tehran. It was in Iran's interest, as a state, to have good relations with the Hariri government, and this by no means meant that we had to support that government. We are not like those parties that have relationships with other countries and act accordingly; when I oppose the government, I do so based purely on local Lebanese considerations that have to do with the economy, foreign policy, financial affairs, or other such issues.

I would also like to tell you that Iran's support for Lebanon and Syria is based on ideological and intellectual considerations, rather than on political interest. For example, Iran received several messages from the United States, through Japan, Switzerland, and other European parties, asking for two things: that it keep silent about the peace settlement in the region, even if it opposed it, and that it end its support for resistance activities in the region—by which, of course, they mean Hezbollah, Hamas, and Islamic Jihad. In return, the Americans would bring about a détente in Iranian–American relations, stop the activities of the Iranian opposition group, Mujahidin Khalq, lift the economic sanctions on Iran, recognize Iran's regional role in Central Asia, and solve the problem of the three disputed islands.[12] Does Iran have bigger or more important political interests than that? Will it ever receive a better offer? I believe the answer is no.

Iran cannot keep silent regarding the peace settlement issue, because—on the very first day the Revolution assumed power, on February 11, 1979— it took a clear position in favor of Palestine and Jerusalem. It will not back out of it now, because it sees it as a religious and ideological duty to support jihadist movements.

---

11 See p. 134, n. 27.
12 The Mujahidin Khalq is an Iranian politico-military exile organization, based mainly in Iraq, which has long fought the government of the Islamic Republic of Iran. The US and the European Union, among others, list the Mujahidin Khalq as a terrorist organization. The three islands Nasrallah is referring to are located in the Lower Persian Gulf—Abu Musa, Tunb, and Lesser Tunb—and were seized in 1971 by the Shah of Iran. All three are currently claimed by the United Arab Emirates.

AL-AHRAM: *Did you try, one way or another, directly or indirectly, to forge a relationship with Egypt?*

HN: Above all, such a relationship would depend on the extent to which Egypt has a role to play in south Lebanon. Let me say first that Hezbollah has its own clear policies and firm position regarding the Israeli occupation and the need to confront it—not only as far as its foreign policy is concerned, but also in its relations with other political power-centers in the country. The closer various parties come to those policies, the closer will be the relationship Hezbollah will forge with them; in fact, Hezbollah sees it as its duty to forge close ties with these parties. I would like Egypt to play a role in south Lebanon, and shoulder a considerable national responsibility. Although I do not wish to interfere in Egypt's internal affairs, or in its policies and problems, from 1982 until today Lebanon's problems have made it feel all alone and abandoned to its fate. We are not asking Egypt to position missiles, artillery or military barracks against Israel; we did not even ask the Syrians, who support us, to do that. The Lebanese people have various other needs that Egypt could fulfill. Lebanon does not feel that Egypt is ready to play such a role, and no negotiations have so far taken place between us and any Egyptian official party. No one in Egypt tried to talk to us, and I cannot remember if contacts with Egypt ever took place at all.

AL-AHRAM: *You spoke about sharing a common fate with Syria at a time when Syria has a particular position on groups with ideologies similar to Hezbollah's within Syria itself. Is there an ideological rift between you and the Syrians?*[13]

HN: Our Syrian brothers have a particular ability to distinguish between Islamist and non-Islamist groups; they do not judge various parties based on their name. For example, just as the Nationalist Movement comprises several

13 The interviewer is referring to the Muslim Brotherhood organization officially banned in Syria. After a brutal crackdown by Hafez al-Assad in the Syrian city of Hama in 1982, which may have killed as many as 10,000 Syrians, membership in the Sunni Islamist organization became punishable by death. In Egypt, the group had long been banned, but it was increasingly tolerated by the authorities during the presidential reign of Hosni Mubarak in the 1980s, and through to the present day, although arrests, torture, and official suppression continue.

contradictory opinions, formulas, and programs, Islamic movements in different countries have different policies, programs and visions. Based on that, Syria views Hezbollah in a different light. If you look at the map of the Muslim world, you will find that Islamic regimes differ from one another. For example, you cannot see the regime in the Islamic Republic of Iran the same way you do other Islamic regimes, like that of the Taliban in Afghanistan;[14] one is democratic, and the other is not. Likewise, you cannot generalize by applying the criteria of one Islamist regime to all the others; our Syrian brethren could have their own views regarding Islamist movements such as the Palestinian Islamic Jihad, Hamas, and the Muslim Brotherhood Association. When an Islamist movement says, "My plans, objectives, and priorities are to resist against the Israeli occupation in Palestine," the Syrians have no problem establishing a genuine relationship with it. We agree with the Syrians on a number of fundamental political and strategic issues with regard to the fate of Lebanon, Syria, and the region as a whole, in spite of the fact that the Arab Baath Socialist Party[15] and Hezbollah each have their own different ideologies. I feel a certain affinity with Syria, not only in the political domain, but also on many other levels, including psychologically and emotionally, thanks to our shared interests and fate.

AL-AHRAM: *Hezbollah has its own ideas and plans. Where does Hezbollah's interest lie as far as maintaining, or ending, political sectarianism in Lebanon is concerned?*

HN: The situation in Lebanon is complicated to some extent. In theory, we are working to end political sectarianism in Lebanon. The problem is that political sectarianism benefits the Lebanese Christians, based on the fact that the country has a Muslim majority. So, when we call for the abolition of political sectarianism in Lebanon, the first thing that comes to our Christian brothers' minds is that we are advocating an open democratic system that would automatically lead to Muslim domination of the National Assembly and the state administration. We respect their fears, and feel that it is necessary

14 Indeed, the puritanical Sunni Taliban regime then controlling the majority of Afghanistan fought a series of running battles with Shia minorities in the country, as well as with the Iranian government itself, regarding both as apostates to be eliminated.

15 A reference to the secular party organization which provided the backbone for Hafez al-Assad's ascendancy to power in Syria, beginning with the Baath-led coup of 1966.

to deal with various Lebanese domestic issues with a great deal of empathy and understanding; we want to get rid of political sectarianism, which is a backward and tribal system, and replace it with a modern one that would govern the country and preserve internal cohesion. In this context, and to allay the fears of our Christian brothers, we call for the formation of a Higher National Council, as was provided for in the Constitution, with a mission to abolish sectarianism. So far, no one has taken up or discussed this call in any serious way, and all that is taking place right now in this regard is only for press and election sloganeering purposes. We are not calling for the abolition of direct political sectarianism; this could happen at a later stage, and could take up to 30 more years to happen.

AL AHRAM: *How about the coordination with Syria?*

HN: We coordinate with Syria in the general sense, but we coordinate with no one regarding all that has to do with the resistance and the relevant details of its activities—neither with Syria nor the Lebanese government.[16] In this respect, Hezbollah, the Lebanese government, and Syria are in agreement regarding the legitimacy of the resistance against occupation. On the other hand, what takes place in south Lebanon is governed by the terms of the April Understanding, and Hezbollah reiterates its commitment to this Understanding on a regular basis to the Syrian and Lebanese governments. The Lebanese government is not responsible for the actions of the resistance, because we do not coordinate our plans with it; this situation serves the interest of the resistance well, as well as that of the Lebanese government. Had the resistance been under the control of the Lebanese government, it would have been better for it to send the Lebanese army to fight in the south instead of relying on the

---

16 Although Nasrallah undoubtedly plays down the degree to which there was "general" coordination with Syria, especially in regard to the timing of military operations, his response to the question of Syrian involvement in the specifics of Hezbollah's planning and implementation is generally plausible. Hezbollah and Nasrallah have long maintained that fighters operate with a large degree of autonomy, even from the central party leadership, engaging targets of opportunity when possible, and according to the fighters' immediate context. Additionally, as Dennis Ross points out, Assad had made it clear to Israel and the US that Syria would not put itself in a position of engaging Hezbollah if Israeli actions, such as the shelling of civilian areas or actual incursions, created a rationale for Hezbollah responses. "If we exert efforts and they [the IDF] don't stop shooting, then the resistance will turn their guns on us." Ross, *The Missing Peace*, p. 233.

resistance. In this case, the responsibility for all that took place would have fallen on the shoulders of the Lebanese government. Under the present circumstances, no one can blame the government for the actions of the resistance; furthermore, the situation as it is now makes the resistance more effective, genuine, and fit for the task of liberating the occupied territories.

At the same time, as everyone knows, we are careful not to encroach on the government's responsibilities or maintain direct contacts with anyone— be it France, Iran or Syria. This is in the best interests of both the country and the resistance. It is also in the interest of the resistance to refrain from direct political contacts; the Lebanese government formulated the April Understanding, and Lebanese delegates at the talks represented the government, not the resistance. It is true, however, that we were consulted regarding the terms of the Understanding, and that we had certain reservations concerning some of the terms that the government had agreed upon. Nevertheless, we agreed to commit to the spirit, if not the terms, of the April Understanding. For example, we do not agree on the term "armed groups," for we are the most honorable resistance force in the world; we also do not recognize anything by the name of "Israel's borders," but rather [recognize the] borders of occupied northern Palestine. In the same vein, as far as we are concerned, the international borders are the Lebanese–Palestinian borders. These were our reservations on the April Understanding.

AL-AHRAM: *What kind of budget do you have, and what are your sources of income?*

HN: The figures one reads in the media are incorrect; it is not true that we receive between $100 million and $150 million per annum.[17] We have several sources of income. There is first our social obligation to the families of the martyrs and the wounded, and this expense is shouldered by a semi-official Iranian organization that attends to the families of martyrs, prisoners, and the wounded. A non-Iranian organization assumes responsibility for reconstruction and rehabilitation work, such as the rebuilding of bridges and destroyed areas.[18] Hezbollah's second source of financing—i.e. the political aspect—

17 See p. 92, n. 12.
18 The Lebanon-based Jihad al-Bina Developmental Organization, under the direct control of the party, was established in September 1988.

comes from donations from inside and outside Lebanon, while the third source is the *Khoms* and *Zakat*[19] that come to us from the four Muslim denominations. Although the *Khoms* is limited to profit from war, in the Jaafari denomination, it could also be part of the profit from trade; in this context, various Shia religious authorities have given us special permission to receive *Khoms* in aid to the resistance.

Without a doubt, this particular source of financing solves a very big problem for us from the point of view of the *mujahidin*'s daily expenses and weapon purchases, which are not Iranian, but bought on the open market. Anyone can purchase the weapons we have in our possession, as long as they have the right amount of money. It is not worth endangering any particular country by exposing it to accusations of arming the Islamic Resistance, although such an accusation should rather be a source of honor.

AL-AHRAM: *Some people believe that Hezbollah is confronting the world without any means of ensuring its eventual victory. It is well known that Shia ideology urges* taqiyya,[20] *and warns against getting involved in something without first ensuring that the elements for success are actually there. At the same time, there are international and regional factors that support the theory of an eventual peaceful settlement in the Middle East. What would you say to those who believe that your current actions are not based on clear religious justification?*

HN: *Taqiyya* in our Shia dogma signifies the desire to preserve our own specificities and religious teachings when we live in an Islamic community. If, however, our attempts to preserve our specificities would lead to sedition, infighting, and warfare among Muslims, then we should practice *taqiyya*, to help us protect our specificities without the need to flaunt them to the world. The Shia have practiced *taqiyya* since the Umayyad and Abbasid eras, and up to the Mameluke and Ottoman eras.[21] Shiism is not an inward-looking sect, and while *taqiyya*'s rightful place is within national, popular, and Islamic communities, it is not suited for places where there is colonialism

---

19 For *Khoms* and *Zakat*, see above, p. 136 n. 29.

20 *Taqiyya* is an Islamic dispensation that allows Muslims to conceal their faith if threatened by persecution. *Taqiyya* is generally seen as a Shia practice; some Sunnis view it as a deceptive and hypocritical act.

21 In other words, since the beginning of Shiism. See p. 75, n. 28 and p. 52, n. 3..

or occupation. For example, when the British invaded Iraq, Shia everywhere were required to do jihad in defense of Iraq, on the side of the Ottoman Empire, which was oppressing them and putting them in jail. All religious texts endorse the principle of Muslims going to war in defense of Muslim lands, even without the Caliph's or the Imam's permission. Muslims are also allowed to use any means at their disposal, for there are no conditions regarding weapons to use or troop numbers when a country is under threat.

On the other hand, when Hezbollah started its resistance activities in the early 1980s, Israel was occupying large parts of Lebanon, and American and multinational troops were present on Lebanese soil. Lebanon's political regime was pro-Israel, Israel appointed the president of the republic and the prime minister, and the Lebanese army was loyal to that pro-Israel regime. At the same time, part of the Lebanese community was collaborating with Israel militarily and politically, which meant that our situation was much more difficult than it is now. The international situation was not much better than it is now either; nor was the state of the Arabs.

In spite of all these difficulties, the resistance has achieved several considerable victories over the past 17 years. Some people ignore important factors that we believe have brought us this victory—namely that God is the final arbiter in this world, and that his will always prevails. In the Quran, God promises the *mujahidin* victory if they do jihad and go to war, and they are doing exactly that. Ever since we started the resistance in 1982, and up to today, we rely on the fact that God will grant us victory if we obey him. Only God can grant the young men of the resistance peace of mind, and although we have no missiles or aircraft to shell Tel Aviv with, the Israelis live in constant fear of our operations.

You want to know the future. Well, I do not see the United States or Israel in the region. Israel does not have the necessary means of survival in this region for more than a few decades, and those who live long enough will be witness to that.

15

VICTORY

May 26, 2000

After the collapse of US-led Syrian–Israeli negotiations in Geneva in March 2000, Israeli Prime Minister Ehud Barak strove to achieve an orderly withdrawal from south Lebanon that would finally comply with UN Security Council Resolution 425.[1] Hezbollah, however, continued to mount attacks within the "security zone," which had the convenient effect of both precipitating the SLA's disintegration and further pressuring the IDF further to leave as quickly as possible. On May 22, in a movement apparently uncoordinated by Hezbollah, masses of Lebanese civilians pushed southwards, with some attempting to locate long-imprisoned family members held in joint SLA–Israeli jails. The IDF, faced at one point with a crowd near the small southern village of Meiss al Jabal overflowing with emotion, fired, killing several Lebanese. Recognizing that a bloodbath might be imminent, Barak informed a surprised Washington that Israel would be out of Lebanon within 24 hours.

Thus, more than two decades after having first invaded Lebanon, Israel had been pushed out of an Arab country unconditionally and ostensibly by the force of Arab arms. From the perspective of Dennis Ross, the effect of all this on the remaining Palestinian–Israeli peace track, as well as the general situation in the region, was disastrous. "Suddenly there was a new model for dealing with Israel: the Hezbollah model. Don't make concessions. Don't negotiate. Use violence. And the Israelis will grow weary."[2]

For his part, Nasrallah's speech to a joyful audience of over 100,000 people, Muslims and Christians, at the key southern border town of Bint Jbeil, provided a clear indication of just how the party intended to keep on fighting in the future: by contesting the disputed Shebaa Farms area that Israel would continue to occupy in the south after liberation; by pressing for the release of the remaining Lebanese captives in Israeli jails; and by encouraging

1. For which see above, p. 68 n. 17.
2. Ross, *The Missing Peace*, p. 626.

and—as later became clear—directly assisting the Palestinians to carry out a range of violent operations, some against Israeli civilians. With Syrian President Hafez Assad's death only weeks away, the collapse of the Palestinian–Israeli Camp David talks shortly to follow, and a strong showing for the party at the summer parliamentary polls, Hezbollah would soon take up an even more secure position of supremacy in Lebanon and in the region—a position Nasrallah would famously contrast to that of Israel, which was, he claimed, "weaker than a spider's web."

In the name of God the Merciful, the Compassionate,

On the day of resistance and liberation, on the day of the great historic victory, we meet here in the heart of the area that has returned to the nation and made the homeland complete. On that fortieth day of Abi Abdullah,[3] [we] confirm anew that here blood triumphs over the sword, and has indeed triumphed over the sword and defeated it. Here too, blood has broken the chains that bind us, and has humiliated despots and arrogant men.

We meet here to celebrate the victory achieved by martyrdom and blood. When we speak of this victory, the liberation of our land, man's freedom, the dignity of our homeland, and the self-esteem of our nation, we are bound to mention all those who have contributed to it. First of all and last of all, we, the believers in God, declare to the whole world that this victory is a gift from God Almighty, who has led us to the path of resistance. He is the one who has led us to the righteous path, given us enduring courage and internal peace, and made us love martyrdom. He is the one who threw the stone and hit the target, destroyed enemy bunkers and fortified positions, killed the mighty, and fashioned this victory. We thank him, praise Him, ask for his forgiveness, seek His pardon, submit ourselves to Him, and pray that He may complete our victory by liberating all the land, our brothers, and this suffering and oppressed nation.

When we talk about God's creatures, we should first mention the martyrs, all of them: martyrs of the resistance in Hezbollah, Amal, and the Lebanese National Forces [i.e. the army]; martyrs of the Lebanese and Syrian Arab armies; and martyrs of the Palestinian resistance. We cannot but recognize that it is thanks, first and foremost and only after God Almighty, to the following

---

3 The third Shia Imam (see above, p. 52 n. 3).

martyrs that we owe our victory: the greatest among all the martyrs, Sayyed Abbas Mussawi; the Sheikh of all our martyrs, Sheikh Ragheb Harb; and our dear brother and resistance fighter who loved martyrdom, the *mujahid* Sheikh Ahmad Yahya, who died in the last few days. He was a pure and pious *mujahid* who insisted on being the first sheikh to carry out a martyrdom operation in the battle with the Israeli enemy. We have to admit to these martyrs—starting from Ahmad Kassir to Bilal Fahs and Ammar Hmoud—that their pure blood has made this victory possible, and admit it to the *mujahidin* in the resistance who sacrificed their lives and left their homes, families, universities, and factories and dedicated the prime of their lives and youth to warfare and jihad.

We also have to mention the martyrs' families, the prisoners still in jail, the wounded, and all their families; we have to mention those who brought them up and laid the foundations of this path of jihad and resistance. We have to mention the imam of all the *mujahidin* and martyrs, Sayyed Ruhollah Mussawi Khomeini (May God Sanctify his Soul); we have to mention the first founder of the resistance on Lebanese soil, His Eminence the absent imam, Sayyed Musa al-Sadr (may God return him to us safely);[4] we have to mention all the *ulema*[5] who made sacrifices and worked hard so that there would be, here in Lebanon, a pious, struggling, and resisting population ready for sacrifice. We have to mention the citizens of the frontier zone who suffered, bore their pain, and witnessed tragedy; we have to mention the villagers on the frontlines who withstood bombings on a daily basis, the peoples' stand on the side of the resistance, and the political forces, societies, personalities, political parties and clubs. We have to laud the official Lebanese position, especially under the presidency of President Emile Lahoud and the aegis of the present government of His Excellency Prime Minister Selim al-Hoss.[6] In addition to Lebanon, two states and two men have to be mentioned, and their roles acknowledged: the Islamic Republic of Iran, Assad's Syria; the leader Khameini, and the great Arab leader, President Hafez al-Assad.[7]

He who wants to be just and fair in diagnosing the truth has to acknowledge

4 For Khomeini and Sadr, see p. 26, n. 8 and p. 26, n. 6.

5 Muslim scholars engaged in Islamic studies.

6 General Emile Lahoud (1936–), the former commander-in-chief of the Lebanese army, was first elected president in 1998. He was later granted an additional three years in office as a result of a Syrian-engineered Constitutional amendment in 2004. Selim al-Hoss (1929–) served as prime minister three times: from 1976 to 1980; from 1987 to 1990; and then finally from 1998 to 2000.

7 For Khameini and Assad, see above, p. 54 n. 9; p. 34 n. 2 respectively.

the position taken by the leader Grand Ayatollah Sayyed Khameini who supported, endorsed, and prayed night and day for these martyrs to achieve victory, and to recognize the position of the Islamic Republic, which stood by Lebanon, Syria, and Palestine and lent them its support. On the one hand, pressures and threats were brought to bear on them, and on the other hand, rewards and promises were dangled in front of them to compel them to abandon this support; but they refused, because it was based on ideological, moral, and humanitarian principles. Assad's Syria, which protected, embraced, and guarded the resistance since its inception, and during all the difficult times, has endured a similar fate. Who can forget Syria in 1982, when it fought on Lebanese soil? Who can forget President Assad's role in the July 1993 war or his role in the April 1996 war? Who can forget his strength and steadfastness in Damascus, when the entire world met in Sharm al-Sheikh to condemn the resistance, describe it as a terrorist organization, and defended Israel?[8] Today, on this day of victory, on the day of resistance and liberation, I say thank you in all your names to every Lebanese, Arab, Muslim, and free human being who supported and stood by the resistance through his words, attitude, pen, money, prayers, endorsements, and smile.

The victory is, first, the liberation of a large part of our territory, a large number of our detainees in occupation jails, and the defeat of the enemy, thanks to jihad, resistance, steadfastness, and sacrifice. Today we enjoy freedom and security, and enemy warplanes dare not fly above your heads. I tell you, those who are afraid of dummy armaments, a toy, and a phony Katyusha platform in Kafr Kila,[9] are so cowardly that they do not dare come to you on a day like today. We are standing here on our own land thanks to our martyrs' blood, and to the people who needed no one's help, neither the United Nations' [help], which for 22 years failed to implement its own Resolution 425, the Security Council, the impure government [the United States of America], or [the help of] negotiations. Neither is it thanks to Barak's government, which withdrew from this land because it had no other choice but to do so. These are the sacrifices which, for the first time, have totally liberated an Arab land through resistance and the force of arms.

The second victory lies in the way the enemy was forced to withdraw.

8 For Sharm al-Sheikh and Assad's non-invitation, see Statement 9.
9 A small village south of Marjayoun next to the provisional Israel-Lebanon border.

You dictated the time, tactics, and manner of this retreat, and after it withdrew you proved that you are a people deserving of victory. The Israelis were planning to pull out several weeks from now, gradually hand over their positions to Lahd's militia,[10] and keep some of these positions, like al-Chaqeef and Dabcha, forts and a number of frontier posts, under their control. They thought that if the Security Council decided on what to do, and United Nations' forces arrived to take over from them, they would withdraw peacefully and honorably and release our prisoners in Khiam jail[11] as a gesture of good will on their part. But you rejected that scenario, and broke for the first time into Kuneitra, Deir Siryan, al-Kassir, and Taybeh and, in succession, towns were liberated, positions fell, and Lahd's militia collapsed one after the other.[12] In the span of a single night, the frontier zone was cut into two, and began to unravel. The enemy's inner cabinet met and found itself facing a choice between two options: either reoccupy its former positions, confront the enemy and incur further losses, or speed up its withdrawal. It chose the second, and left in a hurry, leaving behind for you all these tanks, troop carriers, positions, and guns—which is evidence that what took place in south Lebanon was a total Israeli defeat.

You dictated the manner and time of the enemy's withdrawal; you made the enemy drop its bomb in the midst of Lahd's militia, he who was hoping that this militia would dig deep in its positions and open fire. Then the United Nations envoy came to negotiate with the state, and in return for leaving their positions it was agreed that these criminal and treacherous enemy agents would benefit from an amnesty.[13] This issue is now over and done with; it ended in the most humiliating way for these agents whose pictures you have seen—pictures of their humiliation at the gate of occupied Palestine. You have also seen how the enemy has abandoned them.

After that, the whole world, including Israel, was certain that this region would not rejoice together at its victory and celebrate the liberation; they were equally certain that it would enter into a period of total darkness and endless civil strife. They thought that families from this village would exact

10 For the SLA, see above, p. 66 n. 13.

11 For Khiam, see above, p. 97 n. 24.

12 Nasrallah is here listing in succession a number of small villages that lay within the "security zone."

13 UN secretary-general Kofi Annan's special envoy for Lebanon was Terje Roed-Larsen. See p. 343, n. 9 below for details on Roed-Larsen.

vengeance on other families in the same or another village, or that one religious group would set upon another. The enemy thought that towns in this area would be destroyed like the town of Hanine,[14] that blood would be spilled, and massacres would take place. But you proved, as did the resistance in perfect harmony with the Lebanese state, that the people, state, resistance, and sects of Lebanon are deserving of the victory they are celebrating today. After Israel's departure, this region entered into a season of light, and emerged from an era of darkness that has lasted for 22 years—an era during which the citizens were oppressed and imprisoned by Lahd's militia, whose relatives and families still live among us here. Despite all the destruction of houses and oppression, was a single one of them killed? I said a few days ago that when the Nazi army collapsed in France, the civilized French resistance executed 10,000 French agents without trial. The resistance in Lebanon, and Lebanon itself, is more civilized than France and the whole world. Was anyone killed here? Was anyone beaten? Was one drop of blood spilled on this entire land? This is the ideal image that stunned the world; this is our second victory.

First: this achievement and this victory have to be protected, bolstered, and strengthened; this requires more effort and sacrifice, as well as a great deal of humility on everyone's part.

Second: we in this region have to prove that we deserve victory, and this is what we have done in the past few days. Do not allow anyone to interfere in your affairs in the coming days and weeks. I am not speaking about being apprehensive, but we live near an enemy that cannot abide all this happiness on your faces, for it is used to seeing them sad and in pain. It cannot abide the happiness in your eyes either, since it is used to seeing them weep. No one among you, neither Christian nor Muslim, should be fearful. I will not enumerate the villages and towns, but simply say: this is everybody's responsibility; each one among you should be responsible. This region needs fortifying after all the darkness it has lived through, and this responsibility should be shouldered by its Christian and Muslim religious leaders, and by its political forces, institutions, personalities, intellectuals, and families; they should heal the wounds of every town and every family in this region.

Third: the fate of these collaborators is a lesson to all the Lebanese. This

---

14 A town in south Lebanon heavily damaged by Israeli shelling in previous fighting.

is a new experience for us: you saw how they were humiliated and how they blamed their leader for betraying them. The agent Antoine Lahd said, "We were faithful to Israel for 25 years, but it betrayed and abandoned us in the span of a single night." This should be a lesson for every Christian and Muslim Lebanese: Israel does not care about anyone in Lebanon; it lies to the Christians and lies to the Muslims, while pretending to care about them. What Israel cares about in Lebanon and this whole region is its own interest, its own purpose and ambitions; in the eyes of these Zionists, we Christians and Muslims are mere servants and slaves to God's chosen people. To strengthen Lebanon's national security, it would be in the interest of all its religious groups to choose the national option and Arab option. To strengthen this particular region, these collaborators have to be brought to justice, held accountable, and most severely punished, to serve as an example for the future.

Fourth: I would like to make it clear on this day of victory that, as far as this area of the country is concerned, we in Hezbollah do not have any intention of replacing the state; we neither are a security force nor aspire to be one, neither are a security authority nor wish to be one. The state is in charge here; this region has returned to its control, and it alone can decide what to do: send security forces, reinforce police posts, or send other security apparatus. We do not bear any responsibility whatsoever for maintaining security in this region.[15]

Fifth: the responsibility for development and reconstruction: the amount of destruction in this region needs a state's attention. Of course, we in Hezbollah have given blood and sacrifice, and we will share the *mujahidin's* bread with the people of the area, but the responsibility falls on the state's shoulders. The state should proceed on the basis that this region's development is an emergency, and an extraordinary situation. The amount of development, reconstruction, and services required is bigger than any single institution's or ministry's ability; all ministries should therefore mobilize their potential and

---

15 Nasrallah leaves out any mention of the Lebanese army, whose presence in the south had long been contested by Hezbollah, and which did not meaningfully deploy in liberated south Lebanon until after the July–August 2006 war; that is, after Syria's May 2005 withdrawal from Lebanon, following the assassination of ex-Prime Minister Rafik Hariri the preceding February, and concurrently with the deployment of an "enhanced" UN force of more than 12,000 troops. Nasrallah's reference to the state being "in charge" generally would also not correspond to the reality on the ground in the coming months and years.

come here to assume their responsibilities. I mean specifically the liberated areas in the south and the western Bekaa or, more precisely, villages on the frontline that have, more than anywhere else, borne the brunt of the resistance by being on the receiving end of continuous shelling, aggression, and attacks. Furthermore, when we speak about development in this particular region, within the context of a wider development and reconstruction effort, we should not omit to mention the role that one particular area, namely Baalbek-al-Hermel,[16] has played as far as this resistance is concerned.

Baalbek, which saw the inception of the Islamic Resistance movement and embraced the *mujahidin* who came from the south and from Beirut, has endured continuous aerial bombardment; it has lost a great deal as far as its development and economy are concerned, and yielded up many martyrs from among its sons. It is difficult to find a village in the area of Baalbak-al-Hermel in particular, and the Bekaa in general, that has not given martyrs for the cause of liberating the south and the western Bekaa. Throughout these past years, this area has suffered because it placed liberation at the top of its priorities; and because it was convinced, as we were, that this lofty goal was worth all the patience and endurance. The native of Baalbak-al-Hermel who gave his son's blood to liberate the south has endured hunger and deprivation, and now the development of this region has to go hand-in-hand with the general regeneration effort in the area. We are talking here about an emergency committee for the two regions, if we really want to be true to the weak, the deprived, the suffering, and the poor among us who fought and made this victory possible.

Sixth: I would like to say to all the Lebanese people: you have to see this victory as a victory for all the Lebanese, not only for Hezbollah or for any other movement. This is not a victory for one sect and a defeat for another: he who believes or says that is wrong and ignorant. This is Lebanon's victory. This resistance was a force for the good of the country, and remains so; when this resistance was victorious it became humble, and when it gave up martyrs it became humble. I am telling you: you will find Hezbollah, and in particular the Islamic Resistance, more humble than ever before, because we feel in this victory the greatness, strength, and might of our God. How weak we humans are: if we only depend on ourselves we remain vanquished,

---

16 For Baalbek, see above, p. 77 n. 1.

but if we rely on God, He is the cherished and the Almighty One. I promise you that this victory will not be used by anyone to the detriment of this nation, or any part of His dear nation's population.

Seventh: Barak is today calling on Lebanon to consider the withdrawal a message of peace. This is treachery. He left having no other option—and now he wants us to consider the withdrawal as a token of peace, after having killed thousands of our civilians and no less than 1,276 martyrs from Hezbollah? If we add to them the thousands of martyrs from among our brethren in the Lebanese Islamic and national forces, what would be the final reckoning? In the wake of the death of tens of thousands of civilians in Lebanon, and the destruction of our country and economy; and while Barak still holds our prisoners in his jails, occupies territory dear to us— namely the Shebaa Farms[17]—welcomes the millionth Russian Jew and announces his readiness to welcome 1 million more immigrants in the next few years, he refuses to allow the Palestinian refugees in Lebanon to return their homeland and houses. What message of peace is this that Barak talks about before threatening Lebanon with untold miseries?

In light of his threats, menaces, and promises, I tell you: Sheikh Abdelkarim Obeid, Abou Ali al-Dirani, Samir Qintar,[18] and every prisoner in Israeli jails will soon, God willing, be back home among you. Barak and his government have no choice: I advise him to leave Shebaa Farms and put the issue to rest. The coming days will demonstrate that he has no other choice. We do not much care about international resolutions; all we know is that there is Lebanese territory under occupation that should be returned to Lebanon. The prisoners will come back, the land will be liberated, and the defeated

---

17 The Shebaa Farms is a 25km² strip of strategically positioned, water-rich territory astride the occupied Golan Heights which the UN, after the Israeli withdrawal, determined as being Syrian land subject to negotiations between Israel and Syria, as per UNSCR 350 of 1974—that is, not UNSCR 425, which covers Lebanon. After the declaration, a raft of evidence emerged, some produced by Israeli scholars, supporting the Lebanese government's and Hezbollah's claim that Shebaa was historically a part of southern Lebanon, and that Syria had in effect occupied it in the 1960s.

18 Three of the highest-profile Lebanese detainees in Israeli jails. Samir Qintar (1962–) holds the distinction of being the longest-held Lebanese prisoner. A member of the Palestine Liberation Front, he has been held since 1979 on charges of murder and terrorism. Sheik Obeid, a fiery Hezbollah cleric, was kidnapped by Israeli commandos in 1989. Al-Dirani (1952-), kidnapped in 1994, was the head of security for Amal during the 1980s, and was believed to have played a role in the capture and transfer of missing Israeli airman Ron Arad (for whom see above, p. 96 n. 21).

enemy will have no other choice. As for Israel's threats and menaces, they do not scare us anymore. They are the ones who sit today in fear along this frontier zone; they are the ones who feared the few women and children who stood at the iron barrier,[19] and the stones that were thrown at them. Here in Bint Jbeil you are now secure and happy, while in the settlements of occupied northern Palestine they sit in fear of their unknown future.

Gone are the days when we feared Israel's threats and menaces; they know full well that the days when their aircraft could violate our sky and their tanks our land are now long gone, and that any aggression on Lebanon will be met not with a complaint to the Security Council or with tears, but only with more resistance. Israel will pay dearly if it ever attacks Lebanon again.

Eighth: my fellow Lebanese, you deserve a great deal. You deserve liberation, the return of all the prisoners, the establishment of state institutions, this harmony between the resistance and the state, this sense of national responsibility, and this unity behind the nation. With our national unity we can confront all that is to come, and build for ourselves and for the next generations a nation called Lebanon—a new Lebanon whose strength emanates from its own strength, from its blood and its steadfastness. We can build a Lebanon whose strength is in its might, in its dignity and in its stubbornness in the face of hurricanes and storms; a new Lebanon for real communal living. No Muslim or Christian will ever again allow the Zionists to toy at will with us, with our next generations, or with our youth. The new Lebanon is the homeland of strength in the face of invaders, and of mercy in the way its citizens, groups, and sects deal with one another.

Ninth: we offer this victory to our oppressed people in Palestine and to the people of our Arab and Islamic nation; and from liberated Bint Jbeil I wish to address myself to the oppressed, suffering, and persecuted people of Palestine. Our dear people in Palestine: your fate is in your hands, you can regain your land with your own will, with the choice made by Izzeddin al-Qassam, and with the blood of Fathi al-Shiqaqi and Yahya Ayyash;[20] you

---

19. Most likely a reference to Fatima's Gate, a border crossing located near Kfar Kila.

20. Izzeddin al-Qassam (1882–1935), a Syrian immigrant to Palestine, was killed by the British in 1935 for his role in leading violent opposition to both their rule and continued Jewish immigration. Fathi al-Shiqaqi, secretary-general of the Islamic Jihad movement, was assassinated by Israel in 1995 in Malta. Yahya Ayyash (1966–96), Hamas's chief bomb-maker, was killed by an exploding cell phone in 1996, although Israel has neither confirmed nor denied responsibility.

can regain your land without your enemy bestowing on you a corner here and a village there. You can allow your families to return to their homes with pride and dignity, without having to plead with anyone; you can regain your land and legitimate rights even if the whole world abandons you; put all these obstacles and pretexts aside. O, people of Palestine, the road to Palestine and your road to freedom follows the path of resistance and *intifada*—a serious and genuine *intifada*, not an *intifada* within the context of Oslo nor an *intifada* at the service of the helpless negotiator in Stockholm, but an *intifada* and a resistance that accepts only the restitution of all the people's rights, as has happened in Lebanon. Lebanon refuses to allow even a small piece of its land to remain under occupation; we offer this lofty Lebanese example to our people in Palestine. You do not need tanks, strategic balance, rockets or cannons to liberate your land; all you need are the martyrs who shook and struck fear into this angry Zionist entity. You can regain your land, you oppressed, helpless, and besieged people of Palestine; you can force the invading Zionists to return whence they came, let the Falasha go back to Ethiopia and let the Russian Jews go back to Russia.[21] The choice is yours, and the example is clear before your eyes. A genuine and serious resistance can lead you to the dawn of freedom. Dear brethren and beloved people of Palestine, I tell you: the Israel that owns nuclear weapons and has the strongest air force in the region is weaker than a spider's web. O, People of Palestine: if you put yourselves in God's hands, He will give you victory and make you strong. People of Palestine: if God is on your side, no one will ever defeat you.

To our Arab and Muslim people, I say: O, Arab nation, dear Arab and Islamic nation, shame, defeat, and humiliation are a thing of the past. This victory paves the way for a new historical era, and closes the door on what is past. Put aside despair and arm yourselves with hope; put weakness aside and arm yourselves with energy and strength. Today, in the name of all the martyrs and the oppressed in Lebanon, I ask the Arab governments at least to cease their normalization with Israel, sever their ties with it, and impose their own positions and will on the enemy. I also ask the Arab people to stand by Palestine, and reject all kinds of normalization with the enemy. Greater Israel[22] has been defeated by the resistance; Greater Israel is being

---

21. For the Falasha, see above, p. 216 n. 5.
22. See above, p. 95 n. 20.

defeated by the resistance, and one of this victory's important manifestations is the continued resistance against normalization with Israel.

From Lebanon, the victorious Lebanon, the Lebanon of national Arab and Islamic dignity, and the honorable Lebanon; from the Lebanon of sacrifice, resistance, and martyrdom, I salute all the resistance fighters who defend this country, and would like to tell them, tell the Islamic Resistance, the Lebanese brigades for resistance against occupation, the Lebanese resistance fighters of Amal, the National Resistance Front, and the people of Lebanon: my fellow Lebanese, we live in the proximity of a conniving enemy whose character is marked by aggression and terrorism, and whose racist character compels it to scheme constantly against us. We should always remain on the alert and safeguard our resistance, our army, our state, and our national and domestic unity, so that we can fortify this victory and prove that Lebanon is the bastion that can neither be beaten by storms or hurricanes, nor shaken by the strongest earthquakes.

Congratulations to the Lebanese, the Arabs, the Muslims, and the Christians, and all the oppressed people in the world; congratulations to the spirit of Imam al-Khomeini, to Mousa al-Sadr, the leader al-Khameini, President al-Assad, every Lebanese, every martyr, and every honorable Arab. Blessed is this victory that has placed the entire nation at the threshold of an era of future victories, and placed Israel at the threshold of future defeats.

16

THE SECOND *INTIFADA*

October 5, 2000

Nasrallah's interview with the Kuwaiti daily newspaper Al-Rai Al-Aam *came less than a week after the start of what would fast become known as the Second* Intifada. *Expressing his wholehearted solidarity with the Palestinians, Nasrallah also provided a hint of what was to come five days later—the spectacular abduction of three Israeli soldiers (who had in fact died during the operation) in the disputed Shebaa Farms, after several months of relative calm along the border following Israel's withdrawal from south Lebanon. "Some Arab rulers," he says, "have placed before us two possible options: either war or normalization with and submission to the enemy. We are saying, on the other hand, that we have more than two options available to us; there are many others to choose from, besides war with the enemy." Ten days later, Nasrallah would further assert Hezbollah's use of carefully planned, asymmetrical operations, designed to apply a moderate and relatively calculable level of pressure on Israel, by the kidnapping of retired Israeli Colonel Elhanan Tannenbaum from the city of Dubai.[1]*

Both moves, however, came just before Barak and Arafat were set to hold a high-profile summit in Egypt with US President Bill Clinton, Egyptian President Hosni Mubarak and King Abdullah II of Jordan. Accordingly, the two abductions were cited by Hezbollah's opponents both in the region and in the US as yet a further example of the party's main—some argued patently non- or even anti-Lebanese—goal of consistently seeking to disrupt the soon-to-be-moribund Israeli–Palestinian peace process. The operations also came in the wake of the Lebanese Maronite Catholic Church's official call for the withdrawal of the tens of thousands of Syrian troops still effectively occupying Lebanon, and so may have been additionally designed as a domestic assertion of power by a party that had become Syria's most powerful military ally, and potential negotiating card, in Lebanon. Either way, the

1 Col. Elhanan Tannenbaum (1946–).

"bleeding wounds," as they would come to be described, of Lebanese prisoners in Israeli detention, the continued occupation (it was argued) of Shebaa Farms, and other Israeli violations of Lebanese sovereignty, were positioned at the forefront of Nasrallah's rhetoric—a reflection of the fact that an important segment of the Lebanese public continued to believe that violent operations against Israel were legitimate and, perhaps more than this, strategically necessary even though the UN had certified the Israeli withdrawal.

AL-RAI AL-AAM: *The confrontation in the occupied Palestinian territories has resulted in over 50 martyrs, and 1,000 injured, and looks more like a real war. What does it mean for you? Is it an attempt [by Israel] to tame the Palestinians by fire, and submit them to the conditions of the settlement, or a bloody requiem for this settlement?*

HN: What is taking place in occupied Palestine today is, to say the least, a real and large-scale *intifada*, and bloody confrontations are taking place with whatever means the dispossessed Palestinian people have at their disposal.[2] As to what the outcome would mean, and how each side factors in the consequences, there is of course a difference between the two sides. On the Israeli side, you could say that they are trying to tame the Palestinian people by fire, since they want Palestinians to submit to their dictates. The Palestinians are forbidden to protest, or even demonstrate, against Ariel Sharon's violation of their most sacred shrines, or the outcome of the Israeli–Palestinian negotiations, and Israel only knows how to oppress and tame.[3]

On the Palestinian side, they are trying, I believe, to take advantage of popular anger, past and present confrontations, and the challenge that the Palestinian people have thrown to the Israelis on the negotiating table. These Palestinian young men of 16, 17 and 18 years of age, who have gone onto the streets and who are probably not affiliated to any organization or party, or trained and directed by anyone, are the true expression of the Palestinian people's feelings. In my opinion, the Palestinians are currently at a very

2 The second, or Al-Aqsa *intifada* (September 29, 2000 to the present) has been significantly more violent than the first *intifada*. To date, it has resulted in the deaths of over 4,000 Palestinians and 1,000 Israelis. For further details see http://www.btselem.org/English/Statistics/Casualties.asp.

3 Then Likud opposition leader, Ariel Sharon, had entered the Al-Aqsa mosque compound of Jerusalem's Haram al-Sharif, on September 28, 2000—a visit generally seen as marking the beginning of the second *intifada*. Sharon became Israel's Prime Minister in March 2001 and served until his official incapacitation in April 2006 following a stroke.

sensitive stage as far as their future is concerned, due to two important developments: the first is the way the negotiations are proceeding, and particularly the fact that they have not even secured their minimum requirements. Prisoners are still in jail, the Palestinian state is not yet established, refugees are still living in exile, Jerusalem is lost or about to be, there is no light at the end of the tunnel—and, if anything, the recent talks at Camp David have reconfirmed these facts. The best that these negotiations can achieve is a Palestinian state that lacks sovereignty, has no army, borders Israel on all sides, [has] its economy under total Israeli control, lives on foreign assistance, and is made up of several strips of non-contiguous territory.[4] Jerusalem will be lost, and neither the West Bank nor the Gaza Strip will be totally under Palestinian control, which only means more desperation.

The second development is the flip-side of the first. The victory achieved by Lebanon has given the Palestinians hope that their resistance will eventually succeed in expelling the Zionists from of the Gaza Strip, so that it becomes completely ours, and allowing us to force Israel out of the West Bank and East Jerusalem—the minimum conditions on which all Palestinians agree. However, while some Palestinians say that Palestine extends from the Mediterranean Sea to the Jordan River, others believe that it consists only of the territories occupied in 1967. The Palestinian people have tried the *intifada* option in the past,[5] and found that they could impose their will on the world; today they are attempting to do just that.

In the final analysis, I believe that each party has its own calculations and objectives, and that regardless of whether or not Israel succeeds in curbing the *intifada*, the fact that it exists at all, coupled with the events of the past few days and current incidents on the ground, is very significant and important. It sends a very clear message to all concerned, and has the potential to affect the whole situation in Palestine.

AL-RAI AL-AAM: *The agreed ceasefire has not held, and American–Israeli–Palestinian contacts took place a few days ago in Paris. What can we expect from these contacts, and will we see a truce that allows an intermittent war to continue?*

---

4 Of course, these criticisms were some of the main points for negotiation between the Israelis and Palestinians at the Camp David Summit, held in the US on July 11–24, 2000, and were still points then being negotiated by both parties in an effort to reach a final status settlement.

5 For the first *intifada* see above, p. 95 n. 18.

HN: We have seen this kind of warfare before during the so-called *intifada* of the Holy Sanctuary Tunnel, when the Israelis tried to dig a tunnel under the Sanctuary and provoked an angry response by the Palestinians. The ensuing confrontations led to the martyrdom of many Palestinians, and the wounding of several others, before the situation was contained through security arrangements and the like.

No doubt the American administration will do its utmost, seeking the help of various international parties and of Arabs capable of exerting the required amount of pressure on the Palestinians, to put an end to the *intifada*. They believe that its consequences would be very dangerous for the Israeli–American settlement plan, which they hope to impose on the Palestinians.

On the other hand, the options available to Arafat are clear, and he obviously wants to improve his negotiating position. But we also have to watch his current state of mind, because this level of confrontation can have a negative impact on the negotiators, and on those who are willing to offer further concessions. I do not know how he will calculate, what the talks in Paris will amount to, or whether they will succeed in calming down the [Palestinian] street and containing the situation. What I do believe, however, is that things will be more complicated than before.

AL-RAI AL-AAM: *Can we say that the* intifada, *in its present state, started where the Lebanese victory left off?*

HN: I always thought that an *intifada* would break out right after the victory in south Lebanon, as both a reaction to it and a consequence of it, and that this victory will change the rules of the conflict. But very intense efforts were at the time underway to prevent the *intifada* from breaking out, as demonstrated by the American call to hold talks at Camp David. These talks went on for months behind closed doors, and witnessed relentless efforts to reach an agreement of sorts, as if they were telling the Palestinians, "Wait a while longer—the negotiations will produce some sort of result."

The hurry to hold the Camp David talks, out of the blue and without prior preparation, was due to Lebanon's victory and to the fear that a large-scale *intifada* would break out in Palestine. But the talks produced

247

no final agreement, and a number of issues remained unresolved—not because Arafat did not offer enough concessions, but because the Israelis have a bottom line beyond which they are not willing to go. They tried to improve Arafat's image as much as they could, and introduce him as the "steadfast hero" who defends the interests of the people of Palestine, but in vain. For it was later revealed, and confirmed a few days ago at the press conference held by Presidents Hosni Mubarak and Bashar al-Assad,[6] that Arafat had agreed to cede East Jerusalem's Jewish Quarter and al-Buraq Wall to Israel, and that the latter had rejected the offer because it wanted more.

This means that the person they were trying to portray as a hero had clearly ceded parts of East Jerusalem that were occupied in 1967, after already having ceded West Jerusalem at Oslo.[7] In spite of all this, there was no final agreement because Israel wanted certain things that even Arafat could not afford to give, or even contemplate giving; this is why the *intifada* broke out.

Sharon's visit to the Holy Sanctuary is responsible for igniting the fire that had been smoldering under the surface for several months; in this sense, the *intifada* is the result of the victory achieved in Lebanon, for it feeds on its spirit and draws inspiration from it. Even if the Paris talks had succeeded in calming the situation down, it would have been just a temporary truce before the ultimate explosion. This is exactly what had happened in the first *intifada*, which was not a series of ongoing daily incidents, but rather a swell of activities that continually ebbed and flowed.

AL-RAI AL-AAM: *President Mubarak's words gave the impression that the division of Jerusalem was acceptable. Does President Assad's silence indicate an implicit acceptance?*

HN: Egypt's position is not surprising for, as we all know, Arafat coordinates

---

6 Bashar al-Assad (1965–) had succeeded his father as president of Syria a week after the latter's death on June 10, 2000.

7 For the Oslo Accords see above, p. 100 n. 1. Permanent status issues such as Jerusalem were deliberately excluded from the Accords. Moreover, although Arafat eventually assented to the principle of "what is Arab is Palestinian and what is Jewish is Israeli," as far as the neighborhoods of Jerusalem were concerned, an overall agreement, including this point, was not forthcoming.

his position with Egypt's. As to the Syrians, I do not think there is any change in their position. Their position regarding Jerusalem, and Arafat's policies in general, is clear, and I do not think that Mubarak's words, in Assad's presence, indicate a new shift in Syria's position.

AL-RAI AL-AAM: *Calls for an Arab summit meeting to discuss developments in the occupied territories are multiplying. Do you believe that any such summit can extricate itself from the settlement framework, and what do you expect to come out of it?*

HN: Any Arab summit held now would inevitably be confined to the settlement's framework, and would only seek to improve the Arab negotiating position. At the same time, any Arab gathering, or coordination, is always beneficial.

AL-RAI AL-AAM: *Hezbollah has called on Arab countries that have relations with Israel to sever them. Do you think the current political climate would allow such a thing to happen?*

HN: This is a sort of confrontation. Some Arab rulers have placed before us two possible options: either war, or normalization with and submission to the enemy. We are saying, on the other hand, that we have more than two options available to us; there are many others to choose from, besides war with the enemy.

As we see on our television screens, Palestinians are today being killed in cold blood, and condemnation, pleas, appeals, and rejection by Arab countries are not enough. All these words have no value in the political world, especially with regard to an enemy that has become addicted to massacres that elicit nothing but Arab condemnation. Arab badmouthing has no value, either, as far as Israel is concerned; what is required right now is for the Arabs to bring pressure to bear on Israel. Those who do not want to go to war against it could at least freeze their relations and cease normalization. When Israel realizes that killing Palestinians would ruin its relations with the Arab countries and bring all their efforts at normalization to an end, it will have no choice but to reconsider its policies.

AL–RAI AL–AAM: *How will Hezbollah respond to the Palestinian intifada, and what will be the nature and extent of its assistance to it?*

HN: We are committed, in principle, to supporting this *intifada* and standing side by side with the Palestinian people; but we would rather not talk about the quality and quantity of our assistance to them. One of the best ways we can lend our support to the *intifada* is by not mentioning how we ought to conduct it.

We have a moral, humanitarian, religious, patriotic, and national duty towards this people, and believe that it is our collective duty to stand by its side; but each one of us should determine the nature and size of his assistance to the *intifada*, according to his abilities, circumstances, and position.

AL–RAI AL–AAM: *Do you think that the situation in south Lebanon will affect what is going on in the occupied Palestinian territories? Is the situation under control, especially in view of the ongoing tensions along the Blue Line[8] and the threats by Palestinian officials in Lebanon to "bring on a flood" to save Palestine?*

HN: I cannot claim that the situation in south Lebanon is completely under control, and no one in Lebanon can guard the Israeli entity's borders. The resistance and Lebanese army are the guardians of Lebanon, not Israel.

The situation in the south is open to various possibilities, depending on how the situation will pan out in the next few days and weeks. Until now nothing has happened, though the Israelis are violating Lebanon's sovereignty by flying their reconnaissance planes and helicopters along the Lebanese coast between Tyre and Naqoura. These violations are tantamount to an attack on Lebanon, and the Lebanese therefore have the right to mount a resistance and defend their country and their sovereignty.

No one can definitely predict how the situation will develop in the south over the next phase—especially if the situation in the Palestinian territories takes a new turn and the Israeli enemy overreaches in its violation of Lebanon's sovereignty, and resorts to provocative measures.

8 The UN-delineated Blue Line indicates the deployment of the IDF at the northern Israeli border prior to the first Israeli invasion of Lebanon on March 14, 1978. The Line, while not an official border between Lebanon and Israel, was subsequently acknowledged by the UN, in June 2000, as means of confirming the belated Israeli withdrawal.

AL-RAI AL-AAM: *How do you explain Israel's reference to the existence of a Hezbollah infrastructure in the occupied Palestinian territories, and to preparations underway to target Israeli interests around the world? Is it a sign of other things to come?*

HN: After liberation, I said to the Lebanese people, in particular, do not believe that our problems with Israel are over; Israel will try to wreak revenge on the Lebanese because they have defeated it, and will try to blame Lebanon and its people for everything that will happen. Some say that we should allay Israel's fears, but we tell them that nothing can allay Israel's fears, even if we send the army to the south and remove all the weapons of the resistance; it would still not be enough. The Lebanese have to become spies, inside Palestine, to protect Israel and its interests in the world against any military action; and if it fails to do that, Israel wants to be able to pin the blame on [the Lebanese].

What the Israelis are doing is a part not of their usual scare tactics, but of their preparations to wreak revenge on Lebanon the moment any military activity occurs. If one day an Arab or a Muslim, anywhere in the world, fires a shot at an Israeli embassy in reaction to what he sees happening on television or in the occupied territories, Hezbollah would be blamed—just as Ehud Barak and Shaul Mofaz have said. This is illogical and unacceptable.[9]

Israeli declarations are among our main indicators, as far as keeping Lebanon and the resistance on the alert is concerned—when the Israelis decide to attack Lebanon, they will not have a shortage of excuses and pretexts.

AL-RAI AL-AAM: *You said in an indirect response to the patriarchs' call for the withdrawal of Syrian forces from Lebanon*[10] *that Syria is the only guarantor of civil calm*

9 Nasrallah is most likely referring to Ehud Barak's frequent threats during his term as prime minister that any cross-border attacks following an Israeli withdrawal from south Lebanon (or, for that matter, any attacks on Israeli forces still within the "security zone") would be met with a massive response. Nasrallah's allusion to an overseas embassy attack also harks back to the June 1982 assassination attempt on Israel's ambassador to the United Kingdom, Shlomo Argov (1923–2003), probably by an Iraqi-backed Palestinian faction opposed to the PLO—an event that provided the ostensible justification for then Israeli Prime Minister Menachem Begin (1913–1992) to launch Israel's second invasion of Lebanon that same summer.

10 See above, p. 244. Cardinal Mar Nasrallah Boutros Sfeir (1920–) is patriarch of Lebanon's Maronite Christian community. Elected head of the Maronite Church in 1986, he served thereafter as a major power-broker in Lebanese confessional politics.

in the country. The Maronite patriarch, Cardinal Mar Nasrallah Sfeir, considered this a veiled threat that either the Syrians stay, or chaos would reign (...)

HN: I was neither making a veiled reference nor responding to anyone. Hezbollah is among those who care about Lebanon's future, given that it is a Lebanese party that represents a large cross-section of the population. When we speak about existential issues, we have to stop placating one another, and start calling a spade a spade when we talk about facts on the ground.

When some say that what happened in Lebanon was a war between foreign parties, and insist on that point, they mean that those who were fighting were the mere tools, agents, and soldiers of others, and this is unacceptable. We see things in an entirely different light—this is just our point of view, not an unshakable fact. We believe that what really took place were confrontations between various Lebanese parties, during which each of them took advantage of its brothers, friends, and enemies. What led to the war was the intersection of the interests of various political parties and sects in Lebanon with those of parties outside Lebanon. And although we believe that there exists a really serious problem in Lebanon—namely sectarianism—I did not call for the abolition of religious sectarianism, which is the result of sectarianism per se and its impact.

We said that this problem does indeed exist, so let us discuss it. I never went to war against political sectarianism, nor demanded its abolition; all I said was, let us get together and discuss the issue in view of either reaching a solution or learning how to live with it. We should therefore forget any notion of going to war against either political sectarianism or total secularism; these are the words of a wise and responsible official who wants to solve existing issues without erecting obstacles between the Lebanese people. I am sure that this issue is linked to the Syrian presence in Lebanon, and relevant documents are there to prove it. There were no Syrians in Lebanon before civil war broke out; they came into the country because of the civil war, and their presence here is therefore an outcome of intra-Lebanese issues.[11]

---

11 Although, in June 1976, President Suleiman Frangieh (1910–1992) had requested Syrian intervention in the one-year-old civil war as the result of mounting internal pressures, especially on the Maronites, Assad's assent to the request was arguably predicated less on intra-Lebanese issues than on Syria's regional interests—in particular with regard to Israel and the increasing radicalism of leftist and Palestinian groups in several countries, including Lebanon and Syria itself.

The Syrians, who are now here in Lebanon, were the main catalyst in bringing stability to the country; the political agreement was the second catalyst. Furthermore, a political agreement without a force to maintain security in the country is not conducive to stability; we have seen many agreements come and go, but they have all quickly failed, just like the Tripartite Agreement did.[13] The consolidation of civil calm needs the presence of a strong force that imposes security in the country under a general political umbrella, and this is what the Syrian troops have done in Lebanon. I neither made veiled threats nor exaggerated the situation; we simply need more time. We have wasted a lot of time in the past ten years—and are still wasting it—hurling accusations at each other, without ever sitting down face to face.

At present the Syrian forces are the guarantors of Lebanon's security; as for the Lebanese army, its past and present leaderships have exerted a lot of effort to build it along national lines, and keep it as such; but this also requires additional time, because the process is still incomplete.

Let me ask frankly, had the Syrian troops and the Lebanese national army not intervened to contain the incidents in al-Dinniye[14] and their sectarian ramifications, who would have guaranteed the survival of the state's institutions in the face of such a challenge? Officials who head these institutions were not to blame for this situation, but were to blame for the real problem we inherited—namely sectarianism.

In order to take advantage of the time that the Syrian military presence—which provides Lebanon with a security and political blanket—is affording us, I called for the initiation of a dialogue among the various parties in the country. In the past, we talked with the sound of explosions ringing in our ears, and therefore had to travel to Lausanne, Geneva or Damascus to be able to do that. Now these explosions have ceased, and the Lebanese people are demonstrating many very good intentions. They reject civil war, preferring to solve their problems through dialogue, [and] Lebanon has now a real state and real institutions, and has held national elections with fewer people boycotting them. There are thus many positive signs on which to capitalize

---

12 See above, p. 30 n. 17.

13 In January, a small band of radical Sunni Islamists based in the northern-Lebanese town of Dinniye declared an Islamist mini-state. It took a reported 13,000 Lebanese soldiers several days to defeat and scatter the partisans, some of whom fled to Palestinian refugee camps that continue to lie largely outside the authority of the Lebanese state.

and start a dialogue, with the aim of reaching an understanding on how best to build our country.

AL-RAI AL-AAM: *Some have raised the issue that the weaker party—namely the Christians—say that civil calm is doing very well, while the stronger party—the Muslims—say that civil calm is under threat, and that the Syrian presence is therefore still essential. What is your opinion about that, and how do you view calls for the Syrian army to leave Lebanon?*

HN: I never said anything about giving guarantees to the Muslims or Christians. I spoke, rather, about guarantees for a nation and its people, without exception, and about preventing everyone from going back to war. We are not afraid of going back to war per se; what we are afraid of is Israeli agents provoking an incident, here or there, by targeting Christians and Muslims, and playing on their religious and sectarian instincts, thus taking us back to the atmosphere that led us into war.

Now that Israel has withdrawn from the country, we Lebanese have to ponder the fact that there were foreign agents among the Muslims and the Christians in the country. The resistance and the state have reassured everyone on this account, but certain Christian groups raised havoc regarding what took place in south Lebanon, and made references to security enforced through militias, and various violations. Not a single drop of blood has been spilled.

If the Syrians withdraw from Lebanon and problems occur here or there, there will be voices raised. What I am telling you is that there are people working hard to push the Syrians out of Lebanon and stir up divisions among the Lebanese. One does not need large specialized organizations to do that; a small "security network" capable of provoking a number of incidents that appeal to hardcore sectarian fanaticism in the country would be sufficient. This would thrust Lebanon's unresolved problems once again to the fore, amid a total lack of security and stability in the country, and the only solution would then be the dispatch of international peacekeeping forces to the country. In other words, the objective is to restart the civil war in Lebanon, and turn the country into another Kosovo; the only solution would then be the presence of an international force and the imposition of tutelage over it. The strong Lebanon that had allied itself to Syria and defeated Israel would no longer exist.

I want to call even upon those who want Syrian troops to be withdrawn from Lebanon to ponder carefully the post-withdrawal phase. We should avoid going back to infighting at all costs; for although we did take part in it, we never allowed ourselves to be sucked in. What do they want with us, for us, and from us? We have to calculate very carefully, away from raw emotions and complaints; we cannot deal with complaints by continually raising the bar, for at some point this bar will no longer exist.

17

"THE AMERICANS HAVE SENT
US A POLITICAL BOMB"

November 16, 2001

The most significant challenge that Hezbollah's continuing armed presence faced after the Israeli withdrawal was posed unexpectedly, following the multiple attacks orchestrated by al-Qaeda on US soil on September 11, 2001. Hezbollah immediately halted its activities along the border, acknowledging publicly that the potential costs of any violent operations had been dramatically raised.

The move was obviously well considered: in a rhetorical turn that clearly had implications for the party, US President George W. Bush addressed America and the world on September 20, and declared, "Our war on terror begins with al-Qaeda, but it does not end there. It will not end until every terrorist group global reach has been found, stopped, and defeated."

Perhaps in an attempt to lighten the party's difficult predicament, Nasrallah suggests in this interview with the Kuwaiti daily newspaper Al-Rai Al-Aam *that, after September 11, the US offered the party a deal via intermediaries: total disarmament, an end to support of violent groups within Israel, and assistance in tracking down Sunni terrorists in exchange for a deal including US recognition, economic aid, and wider electoral and governmental power. As with news reports of a similar post-withdrawal package in 2000, US officials vehemently denied that any such deal had been offered. However, the prior contacts with Hezbollah by UN secretary-general Kofi Annan, the British ambassador to Lebanon, and a host of EU officials—where the prospects of disarmament were reportedly discussed—seemed to lay the foundations for such an offer.*

A clearer indication that such a package might in fact have been proposed was provided in mid-November 2001, only weeks after Hezbollah's first (albeit mostly symbolic) post-September 11 operations in Shebaa Farms on October 3 and October 22, and following the first tenuous attempts by the US to bring to bear the legal instruments of the new "War on Terror" against the party. Led by prominent Republican, the Honorable Darrell Issa, a large Congressional delegation visited Beirut and declared upon leaving: "We are taking back assurances that Hezbollah does in fact have a limited scope ... You must differentiate between any organization working here from other organizations that might have a global reach."[1] Although President Bush had by this time already called Hezbollah a terrorist group of "global reach," and had formally added the group to a list of organizations whose assets would be targeted, the Congressional statement, as well as reports that the delegation had sought a direct meeting with Hezbollah leaders through the influential Lebanese Deputy Prime Minister Issam Fares, signaled at the very least that the carrot-and-stick approach could be resolved in favor of a rapprochement if Hezbollah followed the script.

As with all prior US–Israeli deals couched in such maximalist terms, Hezbollah and Nasrallah were able to capitalize on the fact that, while the party abhorred al-Qaeda and condemned the September 11 operations, it found little reason to trust the US's motives or approach, claiming that all the US wanted was to take advantage of the current situation to destroy Lebanon's ability to resist Israel's overwhelming and, Nasrallah stressed, historically destructive power.

AL-RAI AL-AAM: *What do you think of the political bomb that the intermediaries carried with them from the United States?*

HN: After September 11, the United States thought that we would be scared to death, so they sent us intermediaries with the hope that after September 11 we would be willing to give up what we had previously refused to [give up]. These intermediaries made two US proposals: after praising us profusely for not being involved in what took place in New York and Washington, D.C., on September 11, they proposed the establishment of very special relations with us, whereby they would let bygones be bygones—especially the bombing of the Marine headquarters in Beirut, and other such incidents.

I interrupted the intermediaries to stress the fact that we had nothing as a party to do with these incidents—a fact we had reiterated several times before, and everybody knew what the situation was like in Lebanon at that time. But since the Americans had dispatched intermediaries to discuss these matters with Hezbollah, they naturally did not put our Party's name on either the first or the second terrorist list.

1 Nicholas Blanford, "US officials sought visit with Nasrallah," *Daily Star*, November 18, 2001, p. 1.

The intermediaries asked us for three things in return for letting bygones be bygones, and turning over a new leaf. They wanted Hezbollah to adopt a new policy that distinguished between Islam and terrorism; between what is religious and legitimate, on the one hand, and what is criminal and terrorist on the other. They wanted us to do this because they recognized that Hezbollah enjoyed a lot of credibility in the Arab world and among Muslim populations. They wanted our party to sever all its connections to the Palestinian cause and to the Arab–Israeli conflict; they told us, "Now that you have liberated your land, you should stop supporting the Palestinian *intifada*; sever your relations with the Hamas and Islamic Jihad movements, and disengage from your relationship with Syria." They assumed that because we are an Islamic movement, we maintain relations with other Islamic movements and have information about all of them. They therefore wanted to establish security cooperation with us, so that we could provide them with information about those whom they believed had carried out the September 11 attacks.

AL-RAI AL-AAM: *What was Hezbollah's response?*

HN: We do not accept the premise that anyone could teach us the difference between what is religious and legitimate and what is criminal and terrorist. As for their demand that we sever our connection to the Arab–Israeli conflict, I told the intermediaries that that this would mean the total elimination of Hezbollah's head and heart, a complete disregard for the martyrs' blood, and a betrayal of their families' tears, of our people and of their sacrifice. It would also mean giving up our religious and legal duty to come to the assistance of Palestine. Our response was equally clear in relation to Syria: our relationship with it is a strategic and solid one, and does not depend on transient local developments, because if Syria is weakened, Lebanon will become an easy target.

As for security cooperation, the Americans have tried, through their intermediaries, to place us in a state of confrontation with what they called "Sunni fundamentalism." They tried to provoke us along these lines, on the grounds that, in the future, Sunni fundamentalism will pose the gravest threat to Shiism. They reminded us of the large-scale massacre the Taliban committed against the Shia in Mazari Sharif a few years ago, and the murder of the

Iranian diplomats.[2] One should bear in mind that many Sunnis were also killed in that massacre, and that the Taliban's objective was to incite the Islamic Republic of Iran to retaliate, and thus provoke a worldwide Shia–Sunni confrontation. But Iran behaved reasonably, overcame its grief, and did not fall into the trap. Any talk about Sunni fundamentalism and its dangers, therefore, holds no water with us; our position in this regard was clear from the very first day the Americans attacked Afghanistan.

Of course, we rejected all these proposals because we believed them to be nothing but a political bomb meant to destroy Hezbollah, since they cannot of course destroy us by dropping a nuclear bomb on us. When we rejected these proposals, the United States placed Hezbollah once again on its third list of "terrorist" organizations. If anything, this makes it clear that the United States is not willing to tackle the regional situation except from the perspective of Israel's interests.

AL-RAI AL-AAM: *Are you satisfied with Lebanon's official and public rejection of the American terrorist list, which requires Hezbollah's financial assets to be frozen?*

HN: The Lebanese position is a very good and important one; so is Syria's steadfast position, which positively influences the official position of Lebanon. We should also be aware that the requirement that Hezbollah's assets be frozen is first and foremost aimed at eliciting an admission that the party is a terrorist organization. This was done not only as part of the campaign against so-called "terrorism," but also as an attempt to foment internal sedition in Lebanon of the kind that Lebanon has already had to overcome at both the official and public levels.

Furthermore, and in order that everybody is clear on this, we have no assets in the party's name, and everything we receive by way of contribution we spend immediately, because our needs exceed our income.

In my opinion, the issue is far more than simply one of freezing our assets; it is a bid to eliminate Hezbollah, starting with the freezing of its assets, then its activities, followed by the arrest of its *mujahidin*, the confiscation of its weapons, its elimination from political life, and finally, placing an embargo

---

2 In August 1998, the Taliban took the northern Afghan city of Mazari Sharif, and executed as many as 5,000 locals, including a number of Iranian diplomats stationed there.

on its movements. Seen through American eyes, all these efforts are meant to advance Israel's interests in the region. The call to freeze Hezbollah's assets is therefore nothing but an attempt to sow the sedition that the Lebanese people have already rejected. We should also thank God that the noteworthy official and public Lebanese positions have thwarted these attempts, and did not respond positively to them at all.

Similarly, the position of the Maronite patriarch, Mar Nasrallah Boutros Sfeir,[3] and of the Christian community in general, forms a substantial part of this patriotic and popular rejection of America's demands. It is worth mentioning that our main preoccupation at the time was the liberation of our land and the expulsion of the aggressors. In this context, I remember well how, when we liberated the greater part of the south and the western Bekaa Valley, the Council of Maronite Patriarchs issued a statement praising the performance of the resistance and the wisdom of its leaders.

(...) I was astonished at National Security Advisor Condoleezza Rice's statements, in which she expressed her surprise that Lebanon would officially defend Hezbollah, "which has killed innocent people." The irony is that her statement coincided with a massacre committed by American troops that same day in a suburb of Jalalabad, killing 300 innocent Afghanis.[4] We have never, ever targeted innocent civilians; and the United States itself has admitted through the April Understanding[5] that we have the right to carry out military operations against the Israelis as long as they occupy Lebanese territory.

We need to stress that our options and positions have not changed after September 11, and will not change in the future from what they were prior to September 11. We are no strangers to the American carrot-and-stick policy of wooing and threatening; we were able to stand fast in the past, and therefore are not worried about the future. After the liberation of the south, we refused one such American offer to woo us, and today we face another round of threats, which will not intimidate us either.

After the liberation of the south and the western Bekaa, we received a message from the Americans, through intermediaries, suggesting an exchange they may have thought we would find tempting. They had three requests

3 See above, p. 251 n. 10.
4 Nasrallah may be referring to the successive US air strikes on October 10, 2001 on the Sultanpur mosque in Jalalabad, which killed as many as 190 people.
5 For the April Understanding see above, Statement 9.

in return for four proposals. First, they wanted us to stop resistance operations in the occupied Shebaa Farms area; second, they wanted a commitment from us—even an oral one—that we would cease all aggressive cross-border activities against Israel; and third, they wanted us to stop supporting the Palestinian *intifada* and put an end to our relationship with Syria as far as the Golan Heights were concerned.[6]

In return, they proposed the following: first, giving the party, exclusively, enormous sums of money to spend on the territories from which the Israeli enemy had withdrawn, and equivalent sums to spend on deprived areas of the country, for which we had appealed for assistance in order to alleviate the suffering of their people; second, establishing new and excellent relations with the party, and lifting all constraints imposed on it; third, introducing Hezbollah with the utmost ease into Lebanon's political life, and applying pressure on Lebanese officials to include the party in the government, as soon as Washington lifted its veto on our participation; and fourth, releasing all of our detainees and prisoners from Israeli jails.

We of course rejected their proposals, because our acquiescence to America's demands would simply have meant abandoning our faith, our people, and our history.

AL-RAI AL-AAM: *What about the secret issue of detainees and prisoners in Israeli jails—in particular after Israel announced that the three soldiers that the party had captured were not alive?*[7]

HN: We decided from the outset not to talk about the state of the three Israeli soldiers; let the enemy say whatever it wants—that they are dead, alive, half-dead, or half-alive. What they say will not change matters one bit.

From the outset, we told the mediators who came to attempt a prisoner exchange that there are two methods through which such an exchange could be accomplished. Either we give the Israelis information regarding the state of the Israeli soldiers in return for a human price—i.e. the release of our

---

6 A reference to the alleged link between continuing Hezbollah operations and Syria's desire to regain the occupied Golan Heights from Israel.

7 See Statement 16.

prisoners followed by negotiations over an exchange based on conditions we have specified earlier; or [conduct] negotiations over a comprehensive deal—i.e. a complete exchange of prisoners without the prior release of information.

At first, Israel chose the second method, but after several rounds of negotiations through their mediators, they wanted to revert to the first method—trading information for the bodies of our fighters. We did not agree to this, because the price we were seeking in return for information was the release of our live prisoners. It is worth mentioning that, in the negotiations that preceded the 1998 prisoner exchange,[8] Israel wanted information in return for the bodies of our fighters, including that of my son Hadi. At the time I rejected the proposal, and said that it was an honor for us to have these bodies buried in Palestine.[9] Similarly, we are now asking for living prisoners in return for information; they only agreed to give us bodies.

Ben-Eliezer[10] lies to the families of the three Israeli soldiers we hold when he says that he made an offer to Hezbollah in return for information, when in reality Israel never offered to exchange live prisoners for information. Israel is now once again engaged in back-and-forth negotiations through the intermediaries, and we express our readiness to negotiate through either of the methods we have outlined, and according to our earlier specifications.

AL-RAI AL-AAM: *Finally, what does the future hold, particularly in light of the present difficulties?*

HN: We are not at all worried. We are holding fast to the options that our legitimate, religious, national, humane, and moral commitments impose on us, and do not think that the US will carry out military operations in this region. At any rate, they do not have valid pretexts for doing so, and we stand firm in our position, our path, and our convictions.

---

8 See p. 170, n. 1.
9 See above, Statement 10.
10 Labour's Benyamin Ben-Eliezer (1936–) was then serving as Israeli defense minister.

18

"HOW CAN YOU AFFORD THAT?"

February 16, 2002

In this speech, delivered on the tenth anniversary of the assassination of Abbas Mussawi in the former secretary-general's birthplace of Nabi Sheet in the Bekaa,[1] Nasrallah focuses not so much on the aims and activities of the resistance, but rather on local concerns over economic well-being. His remarks, excerpted in the Lebanese daily An-Nahar, thus focus squarely on the populist theme of corruption as a primary agent for the inequality and underdevelopment afflicting many parts of Lebanon.

Nasrallah's emphasis on this theme in the relatively impoverished Bekaa region was not just an expression of long-standing Hezbollah policy and rhetoric; one could argue that it also signified the party's growing recognition that it needed to renew efforts to emphasize and address socioeconomic concerns following the Israeli withdrawal—especially in an area where, several years before, the former secretary-general of Hezbollah, Sheikh Subhi Tufeili, had led an intra-Shia protest against Hezbollah and the Lebanese government's alleged lack of concern for the Bekaa, known as the "Revolution of the Famished."[2] According to one International Crisis Group report in late 2002, despite Hezbollah's growing network of social services and organizations, Tufeili's actions had served as a "wake-up call to the Party leadership, which has since devoted greater attention to social demands."[3]

(...) The problem with those waiting in the political wings is that they only think about themselves, and about securing their needs, thrones, and interests; they belittle and debase themselves, plead their own cause, and do not hesitate to abandon the nation to its fate. Sayyed al-Mussawi, for his part, was a real example and a real inspiration.

---

1 See above, Statement 3 on Mussawi's funeral.
2 For Tufeili, see above p. 51 n. 2.
3 International Crisis Group, *Old Games, New Rules*, November 18, 2002, p. 27.

(...) People are feeling the weight of economic hardship, especially in the underprivileged areas like Baalbek-al-Hermel. God knows that the country's debt exceeds $30 to $35 billion, and the problem is growing and accumulating at a frightful pace. Successive governments have tried to deal with the issue by imposing new taxes, limiting expenses, securing loans, and seeking financial assistance. The only way to solve this essential and intractable economic problem is by tackling the issue of administrative and financial corruption in a genuine and fundamental manner.

Do not focus only on the newly rich who took advantage of the war, but also on those who took advantage of the peace to line their pockets. Your money, my dear Lebanese people, is in banks and company shares abroad, and should be brought back home. I would like to ask, however, how do we do that? In the past they used to ask the newly rich, "How can you afford that?" You should now ask those who are no longer in the state administration "How can you afford that?", "How much money do you have?", and "Did you open special files for those who came after you?" I do not want to point the finger of blame at anyone, but there are poor people who secretly became rich as the result of corruption. How did they position themselves in a way that would enable them to steal money from various projects?

The state should confront this problem, and if it fails to deal with state corruption fairly and squarely, there will be no gains to reap. Although a number of prominent middlemen and thieves could potentially benefit from that, the main winners would be the Lebanese people and their future. If this does not happen, additional economic and social collapse will inevitably ensue, and, in the worst-case scenario, crime will spread to every household in the country. How long can we afford to keep this problem without a solution?

If the government tackles the issue of corruption, people will be willing to pay taxes; the government, however, should recover all stolen funds, as President Emile Lahoud has said in his inaugural speech.[4] If it is not up to the task, it should at least stop the theft.

---

4 For Emile Lahoud, see above, p. 234 n. 6. Although Lahoud had made an inaugural pledge to crack down on corruption, little was eventually achieved—to the disappointment of many Lebanese, who thought the well-regarded army commander might be one of the few people in the country up to the task.

(...) When Sharon came to power a year ago,[5] we told those who feared the consequences that, in spite of his belligerent stance, he would not be able to stop the *intifada*. Sure enough, he has been trying to do just that for 100 days now, but has failed to grow larger than the size of a toad. Here we are, one year later, and Israel is in the grips of an unprecedented level of anxiety, while the largest number of Israelis was killed under the watch of Ariel Sharon, who possesses warplanes and tanks, and can bomb and destroy at will. Neither Sharon nor anyone else can do anything whatsoever as long as the Palestinian people, who live under occupation, have the will to resist, confront, challenge, and embrace the culture of martyrdom.

Lebanon is being replayed all over again in Palestine, complete with similar horizons and a similar impasse. The only thing that can change this equation is the will of the resistance and the people of Palestine, in spite of the difficult local, regional, and international situation. The *intifada* is closer to victory today than ever before, because the Israelis have exhausted all their options; neither securing the protection of Zionism, declaring self-martyrdom a sin, assassinating leaders and children, or targeting the [Palestinian] infrastructure have done any good. The snowball will continue to grow bigger and bigger as long as someone is rolling it down the hill—and both the *intifada* and the Lebanese resistance are well able to do that.

The Israeli army is confronting a resistance force, not a regular army, tanks or military formations: we are waging guerrilla warfare because a typical army with its weapons is not able to pursue individuals and kill them. What we are saying here is that those who want to protect Lebanon should endorse the resistance's presence in the south, and those who want to sacrifice the army should send it to the south.

(...) Today, the resistance is in good shape, and doing better than ever before. When George Bush speaks about an "Eastern alliance," and the important countries that are part of it, then moves on to [speak about] our region, and brackets Hezbollah and Hamas together, it is actually a testament to the ability of these two groups to influence the situation in the region. The fact that America wants to engage in an open confrontation with the resistance is proof that this resistance is able to confront and confound the situation, and impose its own conditions. All its threats, accusations, and

5 See above, p. 245 n. 3.

scaremongering do not scare us—and should not scare you, either, for we have gone through all sorts of situations in our lives. We should put our trust in God, prove our presence on the battlefield, never retreat, and be able to defeat any enemy who invades and occupies our land, no matter who he is.

19

ON THE THIRTEENTH ANNIVERSARY OF AYATOLLAH KHOMEINI'S DEATH

June 4, 2002

Interestingly, though not surprisingly given Hezbollah's increasing Lebanonization, Nasrallah's speech at the commemoration of the thirteenth anniversary of Ayatollah Khomeini's death is couched in overwhelmingly nationalist terms, thus omitting any reference to the controversial doctrine of wilayat al-faqih,[1] *or much in the way of religious dogma. Speaking at the Iranian embassy in Beirut, Nasrallah points to Khomeini's revolution as having "suffered in the past the same way the resistance factions in Lebanon are now suffering and have suffered in the past. It is also," he adds, "similar to the suffering the* intifada *and resistance in Palestine are going through at the moment." Accordingly, Nasrallah seems to invoke Khomeini as more of a tactician to be admired and imitated, especially in regard to his steadfastness and intelligence, than an absolute leader to be followed in Lebanon in all matters of war and religion.*

Nasrallah thus strikes precisely the sort of rhetorical balance that the party as a whole would resort to time and again, and with ever-greater emphasis on Lebanese national interests—all the more so as other parties, especially those unfavorably disposed to both Tehran and Damascus, seemed to steadily gain power in Lebanon and in the region.

In the name of God the merciful, the compassionate,
May God's peace, mercy, and blessings be upon you all.

As we commemorate the Imam, we return to him seeking inspiration, learning, and guidance. On this day we call upon everyone to revisit the Imam's experience, teachings, thought, biography, path, and project, with the hope of finding that which can help us overcome many of the crises

---

1 See above, p. 26 n. 9.

that face revival, liberation, and awakening movements throughout the Arab and Islamic worlds. The Imam's movement was not a political movement severed from its roots; nor was it a jihadi revival movement disconnected from its ideological background. The Imam's movement, path, and revival rested rather on very solid theoretical, intellectual, scientific, and doctrinal bases. This allows us therefore to draw upon a vast sea of knowledge, and learn from this comprehensive and exhaustive school all that helps us confront every occasion, challenge, and conflict.

Dear sisters and brothers, many might believe that the problem between the Imam and the Shah in early 1960–61,[2] when the Imam's movement first saw the light, was an internal problem, and that the Imam disagreed with the Shah's regime in Iran at the time on issues related to freedom, agriculture, rights, and other such matters, as though the issue was purely domestic. In fact, when we go back to the Imam's words and speeches in the early days of his revival movement, we find that his problem with the Shah's regime emanated from issues involving the nation, and from the notion of the great struggle, rather than from internal Iranian issues. We therefore used to see, even in the way the Imam prioritized his topics, that he always spoke first about the Shah's regime as an instrument of repression and an agent of the United States of America. He described it as an absolute client regime of the United States, and instead advocated Iran's independence from the mother of all catastrophes and corruption, and the greatest Satan of all. This is something that Iranians and many in the world know well, because they were also aware that the real rulers of Iran [at that time] were the Americans, who placed over 60,000 American experts throughout the state's civil, military, security, and political administrations and institutions. The first cause of the conflict between the Imam and the Shah, therefore, was the fact that the regime was an American agent, a stranger to its own citizens and to the culture, history, and civilization of its people and nation.

---

2 Nasrallah may here be referring to Khomeini's vocal opposition to Shah Muhammad Reza Pahlavi's "White Revolution"—a program of reform officially announced in January 1963, which called, among other things, for land reform, the sale of state-owned infrastructure, and a national literacy campaign. Khomeini accused the Shah (1919–1980) of violating Iran's Constitution, and of submission to America and Israel. He was arrested on June 5 the same year, and, although released, was rearrested the following year and sent into exile.

The second topic on which the Imam insisted in his speeches and decla-rations concerned the position of the Shah's regime on the conflict with Israel. This regime was strategically allied with Israel, and formed a rear base from which it could target the Arab nation. The Imam stood up and demanded that relations with Israel be severed, that oil supplies to it be halted, and that any kind of relations between Iran and Israel be brought to an end, and condemned the Shah's regime for its position and for what it represented. This means that in the early 1960s, when the Shah's regime supported Israel with free oil supplies, Imam Khomeini was in the city of Qom decreeing that payment of the *Zakat* and *Khoms* to the Palestinian *mujahidin* at the time should be allowed, regardless of their ideological background and whether they were Islamist, nationalist, Marxists or anything else.[3] He decreed that *Zakat* and *Khoms* could be given to them because they were fighting the Zionists and defending the entire nation; this was one of the biggest contra-dictions at that time in Iran. The third issue was internal—namely the oppres-sion, despotism, tyranny and repression the Shah's regime represented.

Thus, after Imam Khomeini's early speeches in al-Faydiya School in 1960, and after the Shah's men broke into this school, killed students, and threw them over the balconies, causing the martyrdom of several among them and wounding many others—after all this terrorism, they approached the Imam and told him, "If you want to deliver speeches and issue statements we will have no problems with that, but there are three red lines that you are not allowed to cross; first America, second Israel, and third the person of the Shah. If you want to talk about the Iranian government, the ministers, parliamentarians, programs, and ministerial projects, we have no objection, but mentioning the American administration, Israel or the Shah personally in your speeches is a red line: crossing it is punishable by death."

At the following celebration in memory of the martyrs of the Faydiya School, the Imam addressed the people saying: "Men from the Shah's Savak[4] came to see me and told me this and that; I am telling you that America is the mother of all catastrophes, Israel is a cancerous gland, and the Shah is a tyrannical and corrupt ruler who should be punished for all the crimes he has committed against Iran and the nation." From the very beginning, the

---

3 For *Zakat* and *Khoms* see above, p. 136 n. 29.
4 The Savak was Iran's brutal internal security organization under the Shah.

central issues around which the Imam's revolution against the Shah revolved brought into focus the nation's position regarding the struggle against the great Satan, Israel, and against oppression and tyranny, which this regime represented. He chose the path of a mass popular movement, and placed immense trust in his people. This revolution lasted from 1963 to 1979: sixteen years of struggle, jihad, challenges, confrontation, and blood that culminated in victory.

Sisters and brothers, Imam Khomeini's revolution and movement suffered in the past the same way resistance factions in Lebanon are now suffering, and have suffered in the past. It is also similar to the suffering the *intifada* and resistance in Palestine are going through at the moment. Beginning in the early 1960s, the Imam faced the first widespread doubts over the aims of his popular *intifada*. These doubts, alas, were not restricted to the campaigns of the Shah or the arrogant powers of this world, but also involved some of the simple and good-hearted friends who were not aware of the ominous dimensions of what was going on. They doubted whether the aim was realistic: "Old man, how is it possible to oust America from Iran, Israel from Iran, and the Shah's deeply rooted regime from institutions, circles of power, security services, government authorities, the economy and the media, when you have no weapons with which to do it? This is unrealistic, crazy, a figment of the imagination and a mirage. You are seeking a perfect world." While the Imam was facing all these doubts, he insisted that his aim was indeed realistic, and he was at first the only one who said to the people, "Yes, thanks to our reliance on God, and with your help and steadfastness we shall loosen America's grip on Iran, expel the Zionists from Iran, bring down this regime and expel the Shah from our land." He used to give them the example of Ibrahim, Moses, and Issa.[5] Among his most famous and best known examples was the one that made him ask, "Didn't Moses go alone to meet the oppressive and tyrannical Pharaoh, the absolute ruler of Egypt and the region, without anything in the world to his name except his brothers and a stick? Moses was victorious at the end, and his God is with all those who follow in his path and walk in his footsteps." This is exactly what the resistance in Lebanon has gone through since 1982, when we announced our aim to expel the occupation from our land unconditionally and without

---

5 Respectively, the Muslim names given to the three Prophets: Abraham, Moses and Jesus.

restraints, guarantees, rewards or gifts. Many used to say that this was an unrealistic aim, pure imagination, a folly, and a mirage, when in fact it was the enemy who constantly retreated and the resistance that advanced and advanced; our aim at the end was achieved.

The same is being said today about the *intifada* in Palestine. They repeat the same words: "You are dreaming, you Palestinian *mujahidin*, you Palestinian people. Can Israel even be expelled from the territories it occupied in 1967? You will not be able to do that." Israel is strong, America stands behind it, and the whole world supports it; but with their experience, perseverance and diligence the Palestinians will also be able to prove that their aim is genuine and realistic in every sense of the word.

Second, he faced doubt as to the legality of the means he employed, for it was not a military war that the Imam was waging against the Shah; he waged it through the people by bringing them onto the streets to overthrow the Shah's regime. The Shah's response, on the other hand, was so violent and bloody that some people—learned men, religious leaders, and members of the religious, political, and cultural elites—wondered whether all this spilling of blood was justified. I remember during those years some prominent personalities asking who would be answerable to God on judgment day, and who would assume responsibility for all this blood. These doubts reached Imam Khomeini's ears, and he said with all confidence, "I will stand on judgment day and answer for all this blood; it was spilled in the right place and in the name of God; it was spilled in the name of justice and the values for which He had sent his prophets and messengers." Doubt as to the means employed has been voiced in both Iran and Lebanon, and is today one of the main tools in the confrontation with the *intifada* and the resistance in Palestine, every time someone casts doubt on the raison d'être of jihad or the legitimacy of martyrdom operations.

Third, the Imam had to face the regime of the Shah's policy of violent and bloody reaction against the rebelling Iranian people. We should recall these incidents not only because they are worth talking about, but also to learn and benefit from this contemporary experience (we are talking about something that happened 50 years ago, during the last century—indeed, the second half of the last century—not about something that happened in the Middle Ages). Here, dear brothers and sisters, I would like to address those who get depressed by the number of martyrs and start wailing, lamenting, beating their chests, and calling for collapse and submission. On the 15th of Khordad,[6] 1963, the Imam ordered the people to go onto the streets, and they did so. In the span of a single day, and in only one city, Tehran, the Shah's men killed 5,000 Iranian men, women, and children, and the Imam had to face up to [the consequences of] this bloody and violent reaction. Some voices were raised to tell the Imam: This is the result of your speeches, your statements, and your movement, and their disastrous consequences have been visited on our men, women, and children, whose blood has been spilled.

The Imam, however, had another way of facing up to this carnage, and these blood-soaked policies. The carnage, dear brothers and sisters, whether in Tehran on the 15th of Khordad, in Sabra and Chatila, in Qana, earlier on in Deir Yassin, or later on in Jenin,[7] carries within it the seeds of one reaction and its opposite at the same time. We can take these massacres and smear our faces and clothes with the blood of its victims, rue our fate, and use this blood to spread despair, depression, and fear in the people's hearts, and kill their hope. This massacre carries within it the possibility of this first outcome. At the same time, we can take this massacre, paint our beards, faces, and clothes with its blood, and turn it into anger, revolution, and determination, and a witness to the impasse in which the enemy finds itself. An army that shoots on unarmed and helpless people is in the final analysis a weak one, on the verge of collapse. We turn this massacre into a tool of mobilization, a strong incentive, and a spiritual, moral, and humane impetus to generate victory, hope, and trust, and strike fear into the enemy's heart. This is exactly what the Imam did in Iran on the 15th of Khordad, and never, ever forgot it. For 16 years this massacre was omnipresent in his

6 In the Persian calendar, the third month of the year, which usually starts on May 21 and finishes on June 21.

7 Nasrallah is referring to a number of massacres in recent Middle East history: the massacres in the South Beirut Palestinian refugee camps of Sabra and Chatila in September 1982, when Phalangist Lebanese militiamen, under the watch of the IDF, murdered hundreds of Palestinians and Lebanese; Israel's bombing of the UN compound at the South Lebanese town of Qana during Israel's April 1996 Grapes of Wrath campaign (for which see Statement 9); and, the farthest back, the Deir Yassin massacre in April 1948, when over 100 Palestinians were killed by Jewish forces. In April 2002, Israel launched Operation Defensive Shield against a number of towns in the West Bank, including Jenin's refugee camp, which was partially destroyed by bulldozers. For further details about Operation Defensive Shield, see below, p. 279 n. 9.

speeches, literature, and spirit. This is entirely different to what usually happens in the Arab world: we remember the massacre of Deir Yassin on its anniversary, we remember Sabra and Chatila on their anniversary, and the massacre at Qana is no different. Barely a few weeks after it happened, the massacre at Jenin was forgotten by the Arab media, by the Arab spirit, and in Arab literature. To confront the blood-soaked policies of Sharon successfully, these massacres have to be borne into every heart, mind, will, and sinew, and turned into willpower and determination to pursue the path and keep up the resistance. [They] should not become a pretext for dejection, depression, and the spreading of despair among the Palestinians and citizens of this nation.

Fourth, the Imam had to face his *intifada*'s isolation by the entire world. Indeed, America and the whole Western world at that time worked to isolate the Imam's movement, with the help of pro-American Arab regimes. This is why, between 1963 and 1979, the Iranian people stood alone on the confrontation lines; no one in the world held conferences about the move-ment, and no one demonstrated in its favor. Yes, there was some activity in this regard in Lebanon, and in particular the considerable effort exerted by His Eminence, the absent Imam and leader, Sayyed Mousa al-Sadr.[8] But the Imam stood largely alone, as did the Iranian people—either for nationalistic reasons, or on the pretext that they "are Iranians and we are Arabs", or because "we have nothing to do with him." At other times they used sectarian pretexts—namely that "This movement is Shia and therefore we Muslims are not concerned by it," and the like. Yes, they managed to isolate the Imam's movement in Iran, but he remained loyal to his principles, values, and religion, and when the Revolution was victorious he sought to bring Iran back into the national fold, because he knew very well the real reasons why his movement had been isolated for all those years.

This is what the resistance in Lebanon had to face, and also what the resistance and *intifada* in Palestine came up against—namely, its isolation, the siege [laid against it], and the abandonment of the Palestinian people. He who supports them by word is a terrorist; he who gives them money is a terrorist; and he who supplies them with weapons is a terrorist who should be punished, according to the law of the new American world order.

---

8 For Sadr, see above, p. 26 n. 6.

Fifth, in the last few years, the Imam had to face various settlement propositions, especially after he left Najaf for Paris. This is a very important aspect of the Imam's movement and experience. They approached him in Paris when they realized that the Shah's regime was about to collapse, and proposed to him a compromise solution, which is what usually happens with jihadi movements and popular *intifadas*. When the oppressors find themselves about to expire, they resort to compromise solutions, to pseudo-settlements humiliating in certain cases, and in others appearing to be superficially fair. So they came to him and proposed a settlement. One such settlement said that he could return to Iran and establish any regime of his choice; even if he wanted the people to hold a referendum, they would agree. But he should leave Mohammad Reza Pahlavi on the throne in the manner of Queen Elizabeth. The Shah would not interfere in the country's political and administrative affairs—he would, in fact, have no responsibilities at all, like Queen Elizabeth. He cared about an enthronement ceremony and other trappings of the monarchy, which is the symbol and authority of the country. But the Imam refused. Even some of his friends told him, "Master, this is an equitable solution. Does this symbolic position deserve that we keep up the demonstrations and offer more martyrs"? The Imam said to them, "Yes, we ask that this criminal be tried, not that he be rewarded and enthroned King of Iran once again, this time with our consent. Second, even from the point of view of the wisdom of such a move, leaving Mohammad Reza Pahlavi as the symbolic king of Iran is tantamount to keeping the American–Israeli hegemonic nail in Iran's back—a nail that could lengthen still, develop, and later on regain the upper hand." The Imam refused all these humiliating settlements, and insisted on having his own way. He persevered, and was very patient; he had to endure a lot of sacrifice, and had reached the end of the road.

The same thing happened with the resistance. Beginning in 1983, and even after 1985, they proposed to Lebanon that Israel withdraw as part of a peace agreement. The resistance's steadfastness, however, forced the Zionists to retreat from asking for a peace agreement to asking for security arrangements, security negotiations, and security guarantees. They said: "We do not agree to give any guarantees; let Lebanon, for example, give us guarantees that our borders will not be subject to attack, and that the resistance will stop at this point." At the end of the day, however, the resistance succeeded in achieving the objective that people said was unrealistic, and the enemy withdrew without settlements, guarantees, compromises, limits, or conditions. This backtracking, which we all witnessed together, is very important as far as our brothers in Palestine are concerned.

Imagine the point which the desperate situation in Palestine today has reached—though I do not wish to repeat what others have said before me. The slogan of an independent Palestinian state has always been raised high, but so far there is no independent Palestine—there is a self-administration or, let's say, a Palestinian authority that exercises self-rule. In spite of that, where is this independence? The Americans and the Zionists who committed atrocities, and those who protected them, are the ones imposing organizational structures and reforms, ordering the unification of the security services, and interfering in the election of officials. Since no political party could ever accept the same for itself, how can it then accept it, after all those decades of heavy sacrifice, for the framework that is to become the Palestinian people's state?

Dear brothers and sisters, we are not speaking about stubbornness in the face of the current state of affairs—we are simply advancing a vision, an idea, an experience, a path, and a theory that other people have tried before us, and which we in Lebanon have lived through. The enemy can be defeated through continued determination, steadfastness, and resistance. Today in Israel, the Israeli press, politicians, and military officials are talking about Operation Defensive Shield's failure, and no one is speaking anymore about its success.[9] Ben Eliezer and Mofaz were optimistic when they spoke about the resistance in Palestine being able to rebuild its jihadi infrastructure in four months. And look, a few days later the Palestinian *mujahidin* successfully executed a series of operations in the West Bank and in the 1948 territories, about which we have all heard.[10] This explains why Israel has shifted gears, and is

9 Operation Defensive Shield, which lasted from the end of March 2002 until mid-May the same year, was directed at a number of West Bank towns, most notably the refugee camp at Jenin and the city of Ramallah, where Arafat remained under effective siege. The operation was ostensibly prompted by a month of violence against Israelis in March, which left more than 135 Israeli civilians dead in attacks committed by Hamas, Islamic Jihad, and the Al-Aqsa Martyrs Brigade. According to a UN report of August 2002, Operation Defensive Shield claimed some 497 Palestinian lives, with a further 1,447 wounded (for the full report, see http://www.un.org/peace/jenin/). Human Rights Watch subsequently criticized the report as being a "watered-down account of the very serious violations in Jenin" (http://hrw.org/english/docs/002/08/02/isrlpa4185.htm).

10 "The 1948 territories" refers to the boundaries of Israel that existed up until the June 1967 war.

following today a new policy it calls Revolving Door, which means they enter and exit from Nablus, Tulkarm, Qalqilya or whatever city at will.[11] They continually enter to destroy homes, arrest the *mujahidin*, and terrorize the citizens. Here, let me say once again that he who caused Preventive Wall to fail, in spite of all the sadness, sacrifices, and pain, could also cause Revolving Door to fail, in spite of all the suffering. The response, dear brothers, to the massacres, the blood-soaked policies, and to the violence, is the same as the response to the 15th of Khordad, when 5,000 Iranians were killed in one hour, which was for the blessed Islamic *intifada* to go on until it achieved victory 16 years later. The response to the massacres of Sabra and Chatila was for the resistance to become active in Lebanon; the response to Qana was for the resistance to continue in Lebanon; and the response to Iron Fist in the south of Lebanon, before the 1985 withdrawal,[12] was for the resistance to take root, become more martyrdom-oriented, exert more effort, and become more generous and of a higher standard. Just as the response to Defensive Shield was an increase in the number of martyrdom operations that foiled the objectives of that actual wall, all responses have to be similar in fashion and style. This the Palestinian has it within his power to do. What else does the Palestinian have? Does he own the Security Council, international organizations, or international and regional relations that can tip the balance in his favor against Israel? This is the only asset the Palestinian people have—and those who give up on the resistance are killing all over again the martyrs of Jenin and in Nablus. If the Lebanese people had given up on the resistance, they too would have been complicit in the massacres of Qana and Sabra and Chatila.

This is the path we are pursuing, and the one we learned from the Imam. We should persevere in our jihad, our struggle, and our resistance; we should be present on the field, never submit, and spread hope and optimism in the people's hearts. We have to redirect the battle's path towards that place where they will be the ones who scream in pain; these murderers are the killers of prophets, of messengers, of the innocent, and the poor, and therefore

11 Three Palestinian cities located in the northern West Bank.

12 Israel's "Iron Fist" policy in south Lebanon obliterated numerous villages, and instituted a particularly harsh crackdown on any persons believed to sympathize with or be a part of militant activities in the area. It was initiated in concert with Israel's redeployment to the "security zone" in early 1985.

should be the ones to scream and retreat. This day will come, without a doubt. The school to which Imam Khomeini belonged has been reborn and anchored anew in a clear intellectual, doctrinal, political, and jihadi vision; it has witnessed all these experiences, sacrifices, and victories. Therefore, on this day of remembrance of the Imam whose sun has never set, we should commit ourselves to the path on which we have indeed offered many martyrs and sacrifices, but have found at the end of it only victory, self-esteem, and dignity for ourselves, our people, the motherland, our citizens, our nation, and for every oppressed and suffering human being.

We pledge ourselves to our Imam on his day of remembrance, that he will remain ever present in our minds, our hearts, and the blood in our veins, until all our great and lofty objectives are achieved.

And may God's peace, mercy, and blessings be upon you all.

20

"ARABS ARE NOT RED INDIANS"[1]

October 22, 2002

Nasrallah's speech to the Islamic Institution for Culture and Education in Beirut has for years provided a key piece of evidence for critics who charge that Hezbollah is anti-Jewish, rather than anti-Zionist, and that the party seeks the destruction of Jews worldwide. The particular line at issue, published by the English-language Lebanese newspaper The Daily Star, *read: "If they [the Jews] all gather in Israel, it will save us the trouble of going after them worldwide." That particular translation, however, provided by reporter Badih Chayban, was subsequently disavowed by the* Star's *managing editor; but more to the point, the line does not appear in the excerpted version actually printed in Arabic the following day by* An-Nahar—*whose transcription serves as the original for this translation. There is, though, a break at the point where Nasrallah could have made the remark, leaving open the possibility that he may in fact have delivered the comment subsequently translated by* The Star, *reported and then circulated. However, given* An-Nahar's *generally critical stance towards Hezbollah over the years, sometimes even despite Lebanese government (and Syrian) efforts at media censorship, such an omission would appear unlikely.*

Apart from this, Nasrallah strikes an especially defiant and indeed triumphant tone, following the general softening of rhetoric by Israel in regard to Lebanon's stated—and on October 16, fully realized—aim of diverting more water from the Wazzani river, a coveted source for the River Jordan, which, like the Hasbani river, also in the south, sprang from Lebanese lands. In September, Sharon had stated flatly that such a diversion would be a casus belli—*a reminder of Sharon's long list of threats made and actions taken against Lebanon.*

Nasrallah makes clear that, although Hezbollah's forces had not carried out any operations during the crisis, "any aggression against Lebanon will not be met by weakness, retreat or

---

1 "Red Indians" remains a common reference for Arabic speakers to Native Americans in the United States.

submission; responsibility is responsibility and a decision is a decision." Although a standard element in Nasrallah's rhetoric, his assertion held added significance, since Hezbollah had significantly stepped up its operations over the previous eight months,[2] including occasionally outside the disputed Shebaa Farms, and quite despite Iranian Foreign Minister Kamal Kharazi's public statement in April in Beirut that the party should act with greater restraint. Iran's reformist-leaning government, Nasrallah had suggested at the time, could offer its insight, but ultimately it could not affect party decisions when it came to basic issues of territorial sovereignty. This particular stance, which aimed to liberate territory that Hezbollah and some other Lebanese considered as occupied, would prove ever more controversial in the coming months and years, as the specter of large-scale Israeli occupation faded, and as Lebanon's need for international assistance grew ever greater.

We will speak today in a language of hope, open horizons, and prosperous futures, so that no one will fall victim to the psychological warfare that the American administration is waging against the world, and especially against Muslim and Islamic movements. No one should be fearful or scared, for nothing that Sharon says, or does, should ever scare anyone. Israel no doubt has a high level of experience in waging psychological warfare, but even in such wars they make deadly mistakes, and inadvertently render us a great service without our saying or doing anything to earn it.

For example, a few days ago, Sharon returned from the United States and declared, "Hezbollah has missiles that can travel 300km, and this means that not a single populated area in Israel is safe from Hezbollah's missiles." Sharon wanted to use this statement to his benefit, and to the detriment of Hezbollah, Lebanon, Syria, and Iran. All he managed to do, however, was to scare his own people to death. If the resistance used only Katyusha rockets, it could cause the displacement of 2 million Jews, and these would have to look for somewhere else to live, probably in the center of Israel. How would it be, then, if Hezbollah's missiles, as Sharon says, could reach every single populated area in Israel? If these were launched, where would all the Israelis go? Would they run to where the *intifada* is raging in Tel Aviv, Jerusalem, and the West Bank?

---

2 Hezbollah's Deputy secretary-general Naim Qassem would later write that "During the Israeli 'Defensive Shield' operation ... the Resistance escalated its activities in the Shebaa Farms, increasing the frequency to a daily basis ... sending a message of solidarity with the Palestinian people's uprising and pain." Qassem, *Hezbollah*, p. 136.

And he continues [as published]: The United States, which is coming to impose its direct control over the region, knows very well that even if it brought all its military forces to Iraq, or elsewhere in the region, it would not be able to stay for long. The American and Israeli administrations have to understand that Arab and Muslim populations, and the people of this area as a whole, are not the Red Indians, whom they can annihilate or isolate in the desert or on mountains. The people of this area are alive, and their ancestry goes back to the first human beings that walked on this land, which they call 'the Old World'.

The onset of widespread American–Israeli barbarism in our region also marks the end of the United States' hegemony over the world, because it will unleash an open and unbalanced confrontation against it. The people on the other side of this confrontation are the leaders, officers, and soldiers, not a state that can be threatened, or a regime that can be dismantled and its financial resources dried up.

As we said a few days ago, what took place, and is still happening in Wazzani, was a great victory. The fact that Lebanon could do what it did, and that Israel keeps quiet about it, is in itself a great accomplishment. Israel could make a sales pitch for its silence to the Americans, the United Nations, France, and the European Union, but the fact remains that the whole world knows that its silence, and its political sales pitch, is insincere. They all know that, if Israel had been able to respond one way or another, before or after the opening of the Summit, it would have done so. Now we hear people say once again that, since the Francophone Summit is over,[3] Sharon may respond by launching an operation. I believe that it is a gross oversimplification to assume that Sharon did not bomb Lebanese installations before or after the opening of the Francophone Summit because it was being held in Lebanon. What he took into account when making this decision prior to the Francophone Summit, he will take again into account after the Summit is over.

It is wrong for the Lebanese to assume that their great accomplishment was all thanks to the Francophone Summit. This accomplishment came as a result of their unity, their state, their resistance, their people, and their

3 The annual Francophone Summit, only days before Nasrallah's speech, brought French President Jacques Chirac to Beirut, as well as the leaders of 55 states around the world. In a well-reported appearance, Nasrallah attended the opening ceremonies.

solidarity with Syria—in addition to the Islamic Republic of Iran's support, which endorses all Lebanon's endeavors to regain its usurped territorial, water, and other rights. All these things existed before the Francophone Summit, and will be there when it ends. We will reiterate everything we have said previously: any aggression against Lebanon will not be met by weakness, retreat or submission; responsibility is responsibility, and a decision is a decision. Today, any weakness or lack of resolve in our words, our logic, or our performance does not mean that the other side will respect us, appreciate our circumstances, or cooperate with us; rather, it will lead to more arrogance, more tyranny, and more aggression against Lebanon and the region.

21

THE IMPENDING IRAQ WAR AND "MUSLIM–CHRISTIAN ALIGNMENT"

March 13, 2003

One week before the US-led coalition began its bombardment of Iraq, Nasrallah told tens of thousands of demonstrators in the Southern Suburb of Beirut that the US should "not expect the people of this region to meet you with flowers, rice, and perfume; the peoples of this part of the world will receive you, rather, with guns, blood, weapons, and martyrdom operations." In the years that followed, Nasrallah's prediction would be borne out, although, ironically, it would impact the most on the governing ability of the US-empowered Shia majority in Iraq. Even so, just as the long and brutal Baathist domination of the Iraqi Shia appeared on the verge of elimination, Nasrallah harkened back to an earlier failed and supposedly humanitarian effort by the US in Lebanon: "When the Marines were in Beirut," he reminded his audience, "and their warships were roaming the Mediterranean, we were shouting 'Death to America!' in the Southern Suburb. Today, as this area fills with American soldiers and warships, our slogan remains unchanged."

(…) We in Lebanon should be proud of the national unity that our citizens from all sects, political leanings, parties, and regions have demonstrated once again. Both Muslims and Christians have expressed together their opposition to the American–Zionist aggression against our nation, America's war on the region, and on the Arab and Islamic worlds, and the clear and unequivocal objectives behind it. We should also mention Lebanon's official position in this regard, and especially that of the president of the republic, General Emile Lahoud.[1] This is a particularly opportune time to entrench this national unity, not waste the golden opportunity it provides, and take advantage of this historical and most vitally important meeting of minds among the

---

1 For Lahoud see above, p. 234 n. 6.

Lebanese people, to overcome the many difficulties that tear our internal cohesion apart and threaten it from time to time.

Today in Lebanon, not only are we in need of such national unity, we should also support the president of the republic, who has demonstrated over the past years a valiant sense of patriotism and nationalism, especially with regard to the resistance and the confrontation with Israel.[2] We are in dire need of men like him, and for such meetings of minds among the Lebanese people.

When the Lebanese people come together in such an impressive manner to defend the nation and their Arab brothers in the region, they are above all defending Lebanon, because it is an American–Zionist target, and is right at the center of their ambitions in the region. In the coming days and weeks, since war in the region—and particularly in Iraq—seems inevitable, no one in Lebanon should either feel completely at ease, or spread fear and panic among the people. People in Lebanon should not be unconcerned by the dangers threatening the region, and we shall not deceive them by denying them the truth. Lebanon lives in proximity to a savage country, led by the very ugly, terrorist government of Sharon—the same government that committed the Sabra and Chatila massacres and invaded Lebanon in 1982.[3] No one should therefore rest easy or feel reassured by small promises here or there. We should remain on the alert, with all that this entails from the point of view of readiness for various eventualities, and stay politically, publicly, psychologically, morally, and militarily aware of developments. The *mujahidin* and resistance fighters should work hand-in-hand on various levels and in different sectors, in cooperation with both the Lebanese national army and the Syrian Arab army deployed on Lebanese territory.[4] The American war on Iraq and the region will not weaken our resolve; let Sharon not imagine for a minute that the sight on television of his warplanes and missiles, which he could drop on any Arab country any time he chooses, can scare or deter us from confronting another of his attacks.

---

2 In contrast to Prime Minister Hariri, who had publicly criticized Hezbollah on a number of occasions over the previous two years—in particular when operations in the south had put his long-standing efforts to organize an international debt bailout in jeopardy—President Lahoud had vigorously and consistently defended the resistance's actions.

3 Sharon had been Israeli defense minister during the Sabra and Chatila massacres. See p. 204, n. 10.

4 In 2003 Syria was still believed to have over 14,000 troops stationed across Lebanon, in addition to thousands of intelligence agents and other officials.

On the national level, the country's religious and political leaders should take the initiative and do whatever is necessary to reinforce the cohesion of the Lebanese domestic front; this places a considerable responsibility on their shoulders. When we call for the deferment of certain Lebanese internal issues, we mean issues regarding internal differences, disputes, rivalries, apportioning of positions, and the race to gain advantages. But there are other domestic issues that should never be deferred, and I mean by this the low standard of living, poverty, and neglect from which several Lebanese regions suffer. Thank God that we in Lebanon have adopted a very good official political position, and do not have a big or acute problem in relations between people and the regime, for whatever reason. I wish to tell both the state and the government, however, that it is at such times that you should be closer to the dispossessed, the needy, the poor, and the residents of disadvantaged and less fortunate areas of the country.

Let me address the issue of occupied Palestine, and say that the main banner under which we are holding this great demonstration today, here in the Southern Suburb of Beirut, and in other regions of the country, is that of solidarity with the resisting, struggling, and revolutionary Palestinian people. These thousands of Palestinian flags are but a symbolic expression of our solidarity with them. However, allow [me] to tell our Palestinian brothers the following: be sure that you have succeeded in achieving great and marvelous things in record time. Some will tell you that your *intifada* is hopeless, and that it will not produce results; these words are nothing but deception, lies, hypocrisy, and treason to the blood of the martyrs, and to the orphans' and widows' tears in occupied Palestine. This Palestinian *intifada* has in fact—and for the first time in 50 years—succeeded in shaking the Zionist entity to the core, and threatening its very existence and survival. These are not mere slogans, and those who follow the political, psychological, and economic repercussions of the *intifada* on the Zionist entity know very well that what I am saying is the truth, and only the truth.

Let us now move on to Syria. In this bad, difficult, and tragic period for our Arab nation, it is our duty on this Ashoura Day, the day of courage and steadfastness, to stand in awe and respect for Assad's Syria, and its leadership, army, and people. In difficult days such as these, no Arab can disregard the words of a young Arab leader, especially in this particularly dangerous and significant time, of the stature of President Bashar al-Assad.[5] This young leader has his finger on the pulse of the Arab street and reflects its conscience, spirit, and feelings of anger and dejection. Nobody can simply or easily disregard him or his words, especially since he is president of a country being threatened by the United States, which tells him that his country's turn will come in the second or third round. His is also a country at which the US Congress is brandishing the Syria Accountability Act,[6] and threatening to implement it at any moment, and a country living in proximity to the Israeli entity, which may attack at any time.

In the Arab world today we need men like him—men who know how to lead. Such men will no doubt find themselves and their positions held close in the Arab people's hearts, because they are sick and tired of living in a state of constant humiliation, dejection, and submission to the will of the American ambassador, or this or that American officer.

From here in Beirut, we address ourselves to Damascus and tell Syria and its courageous Arab leader: You are not alone; the whole nation is with you; every honorable Arab is behind you; the whole of Lebanon supports you, and this resistance has fought, and is still fighting with you.

We declare our opposition to the American war on Iraq, and to all the deceptive, lying, and hypocritical American objectives and slogans about saving nations, instilling democracy, and granting people their freedom. From this place, we declare our condemnation of this diabolical, arrogant, and Zionist administration, and say: Do not expect the people of this region to meet you with flowers, rice, and perfume;[7] peoples of this part of the world will receive you, rather, with guns, blood, weapons, and martyrdom operations. This is the reception the people are preparing for the American invaders, for we have never been afraid of the United States. When the

5 At this point Bashar al-Assad was 37 years old. As the second son, Bashar was not originally groomed as his father Hafez's successor, only coming to prominence after the death of his elder brother, Basil, in a car accident in 1994.

6 Nasrallah is referring to the Syria Accountability and Lebanese Sovereignty Act (SALSA), which was passed by the US Congress in early 2003, but which would remain unimplemented by President Bush until May 2004, when he signed the law into effect. The measure was designed essentially to cut all trading ties between Syria and the US, and thus to further isolate and pressure the Assad regime internationally.

7 Possibly a reference to predictions variously expressed by supporters of an invasion of Iraq (and most famously by Iraqi exile Ahmad Chalabi and Iraqi–American academic Kanan Makiya) that US-led forces would be widely welcomed in their assault on Saddam Hussein's regime.

Marines were in Beirut, and their warships were roaming the Mediterranean, we were shouting "Death to America!" in the Southern Suburb. Today, as this area fills with American soldiers and warships, our message remains unchanged.

Muslims should also stand in a show of respect and appreciation for the position adopted by various Christian churches throughout the world—namely, the Eastern churches and countless Western churches, including the Vatican and Patriarchs in Syria, Lebanon, and all over the region. Muslims should appreciate such positions, in particular because they remove Bush's religious excuse for the war, which he says he is waging because he swore to accomplish what the New Testament says.[8] Yet these churches tell him that his war is immoral and illegal, and has nothing to do with the New Testament. This is a great and historic position, whose importance, at this stage, we need to understand and deal with appropriately. My advice to the Muslims, preachers, and members of the media is to avoid, in this political and media war, any terms that could offend or insult Christians opposed to the war. If the term "Crusade" insults them, we should then look for another one. Muslims should at all costs avoid using any word that offends Christians opposed to the war.

The Jews have long hoped for a war that pits a Jewish–Christian alliance against the Muslim nation. In this context I would like to say: Let us look to form a Muslim–Christian alliance to confront all those who attack Moses, Jesus, and Mohammad. Why don't we form a political alliance of this kind? Those positive positions, we see today, whether in the East or the West, are positions taken by Christian countries, churches, and prominent individuals and elites, and this only encourages the formation of such an alliance.

Why do we not seek a meaningful, public, and official Muslim–Christian alliance such as this, in the face of an American–Zionist scheme, which only seeks to spread ruin, destruction, war, humiliation, and corruption throughout the world?

---

8 In his 2002 book *Bush at War*, *Washington Post* reporter Bob Woodward described President Bush as "casting his vision and that of the country in the grand vision of God's master plan"—a point greatly reinforced for Nasrallah, and many Muslims, by Bush's speech the day after the September 11 attacks, when he declared that the United States was about to embark on a "crusade" against terrorism. See Bob Woodward, *Bush at War* (NY: Simon & Schuster, 2002) p.67. Although the White House soon retracted the statement, Bush's 2004 campaign for re-election later issued a letter that praised the president for "leading a global crusade against terrorism."

22

INTERVIEW WITH *60 MINUTES*

April 20, 2003

Nasrallah's appearance on the most widely watched television news program in America, 60 Minutes, *seemed to mark a nadir in his interaction with the US media and the Western media in general. Chopped down to a few sound bytes, juxtaposed against arguably exaggerated comments by Democratic Senator Bob Graham of Florida, who was then angling for a run at the presidency, and woven into an overall commentary strongly suggesting that Hezbollah would inevitably directly attack the US just as al-Qaeda had done, the presentation undoubtedly played an important role in ensuring that Nasrallah would never again grant an interview to a US television network. Indeed, with the exception of a small handful of interviews with the* Washington Post *and the* New Yorker *over the next three years, Nasrallah himself generally eschewed all US media, print or otherwise, even as Hezbollah faced a substantial challenge to its interests in February 2005, following the assassination of ex-Lebanese premier Rafik Hariri.*

Although 60 Minutes *reporter Ed Bradley's presentation is useful in providing an indication of how the US media was shaping public discourse on the region in the heady, and arguably complacent early days of the Iraq invasion, Nasrallah's own prediction of how the conflict might play out in the future seems perhaps more prescient in retrospect. "Lots of groups will surface," he says, "not necessarily al-Qaeda, and they'll be impossible to bring to justice."*

BRADLEY: *Now that the US has gotten rid of Saddam Hussein, one of the Bush administration's next targets may well be Hezbollah, the Lebanese-based Islamic organization which has very close ties to the governments of Syria and Iran. US intelligence is particularly concerned that Hezbollah, a sworn enemy of the US and Israel, may attack Americans here or in the Middle East in the aftermath of the US invasion of Iraq. That's what Deputy Secretary of State Richard Armitage had in mind a few months ago when he pinned this label on Hezbollah.*

Deputy Secretary Richard Armitage: Hezbollah may be the A-team of terrorists, and maybe al-Qaeda is actually the B-team. And they're on the list, and their time will come. There is not a question about it. And we're going to go after these problems just like a high school wrestler goes after a match. We're going to take them down one at a time.

BRADLEY: *What he's talking about started two decades ago as a ragtag militia group fighting the Israeli occupation of southern Lebanon. But there's no longer anything ragtag about Hezbollah. The Islamic government of Iran reportedly subsidizes Hezbollah to the tune of $100 million a year, providing its several thousand well-trained fighters with sophisticated weapons systems. Iran also sends advisers and, according to US intelligence, issues its marching orders. Senator Bob Graham, the Florida Democrat who chaired the Senate Intelligence Committee in the last Congress and is now running for president, says the Bush administration should be more concerned with Hezbollah than they've been with Saddam Hussein.*

Senator Bob Graham (Democrat, Florida): If the question is, Does Saddam Hussein or Hezbollah represent the greater threat to the people of the United States? In my opinion, there's no question that Hezbollah is that greater threat.

BRADLEY: *Because, he says, Hezbollah has a global network of radical Islamic supporters with enough operatives in the US to pose a terrorist threat here.*

Graham: It has a significant presence of its trained operatives inside the United States waiting for the call to action.

BRADLEY: *I know that you can't talk specifically about classified information, but if we were to know that classified information, would we be more concerned, would we be more afraid of Hezbollah than we are today?*

Graham: Well, I'm more concerned and more afraid than if I did not know what the scale of their presence was in the United States.

BRADLEY: *You say that without any hesitation.*

Graham: They are a violent terrorist group. And they have demonstrated throughout their now 25-year history a hatred of the United States and a willingness to kill our people.

BRADLEY: *Senator Graham is referring to the 1983 truck bombing of the Marine barracks in Lebanon, resulting in the death of 241 US Marines. Hezbollah supporters say that attack was a response to shelling by US warships of Islamic factions in the Lebanese Civil War. The US called it terrorism. But Hezbollah's leader, Sheikh Hassan Nasrallah, who we met in Beirut, insists that today his group poses no threat to the US. Unlike the leadership of al-Qaeda, he isn't hiding from anyone. You may never have heard of Nasrallah before, but he is a hugely popular figure not just in the region, but also among Arabs living in the West.*

BRADLEY: *You know that the top deputy to the Secretary of State Colin Powell has referred to Hezbollah as "the A-team of terrorism," in other words, better at terrorism than al-Qaeda.*

HN: Secretary Powell can say what he wants. I believe the Americans are just saying what the Israelis want them to say. I consider this to be an Israeli accusation coming out of an American mouth, and nothing more.

BRADLEY: *(Voiceover) When he became its leader ten years ago, Nasrallah turned Hezbollah into a formidable fighting force. Few people know more about him than journalist Nick Blanford, who has covered Lebanon for eight years and is now writing a book about Hezbollah and Sheikh Nasrallah.*

Blanford: People that know him, I talked to some Hezbollah fighters that speak of him almost as they would a wife or a mother, that they think of him before they go to sleep at night, that he's always in their thoughts. So he has this tremendous sort of power over the rank and file.

BRADLEY: *Enough power to recruit and train skilled commandos who specialized in attacking the Israeli forces which occupied southern Lebanon for 22 years. Their most effective weapon, remote-controlled roadside bombs, which were detonated when Israeli patrols passed by, as in this attack in southern Lebanon. All told, Israel lost more than 900 soldiers in Lebanon. In May 2000, the Israeli army withdrew.*

BRADLEY: *What did Israel's withdrawal do for Hezbollah in the eyes of the Arab world?*

Blanford: Well, it was an enormous boost for Hezbollah. I mean, this was a small Arab organization that had defeated the mightiest military force the Middle East has ever seen.

BRADLEY: *With the Israelis out of Lebanon, Nasrallah encouraged and assisted the Palestinian uprising against Israel. He has acknowledged sending secret agents carrying weapons to the West Bank, where he is considered a hero. Some kids in the Gaza Strip even dress up like him, down to the beard and the glasses. At this event, a boy playing Nasrallah is flanked by one child playing a security guard and another dressed as a suicide bomber. And in Lebanon, where Hezbollah runs a network of schools and hospitals and participates in local elections, Nasrallah, a Muslim, is a hero even to the country's Christian President Emile Lahoud.*

President Lahoud: For us, Lebanese, and I can tell you, a majority of Lebanese, Hezbollah is a national resistance movement. If it weren't for them, we couldn't have liberated our land. And because of that, we have big esteem for the Hezbollah movement.

BRADLEY: *President Lahoud has such high esteem for Hezbollah, he's ceded control of the border with Israel to them—a border where Hezbollah and Israeli soldiers now confront each other just a few yards apart.*

BRADLEY: *This side controlled by Hezbollah; over there is Israel. Hezbollah has already fired rockets across the border, and US officials believe that in the past two years they've been stockpiling rockets in this area, hidden in caves and underground bunkers, higher-quality Iranian rockets that could reach Haifa, about 50 miles away.*

BRADLEY: *Openly calling for terrorism against Israel, Nasrallah, in this speech, is urging suicide operations. 'In Palestine,' he's saying, 'these operations are the only way to root out the Zionists.' That's the kind of material Hezbollah broadcasts daily on its own television station, Al-Manar, which reaches a worldwide audience by satellite. Because of Washington's support for Israel, Hezbollah is conducting a ferocious propaganda offensive against the United States. This message broadcast on Al-Manar portrays US foreign policy as satanic. The image of the Statue of Liberty, a skull for her face, wearing a gown dripping with the blood of other nations. But even though he's one of the most powerful anti-American voices in the Middle East, he has no use for Saddam Hussein. In fact, he blames the US for Saddam's rise.*

HN: The US provided political and military support to the Iraqi regime for decades. They created this mess. I don't believe Saddam alone should be held accountable. We should also go after those who supported him, like the American government.

BRADLEY: *Sheikh Nasrallah has described war on Saddam as a satanic American–Zionist plan to dominate the Arab world. What is satanic about removing Saddam from power?*

HN: The United States isn't seeking democracy in Iraq, it's after the oil in Iraq, and that isn't exactly a humanitarian pursuit. The US wants to impose its political will on Iraq and wants to impose Israel's domination in the region. Certainly, these objectives are not moral objectives in my opinion. In fact, we say they are satanic objectives.

BRADLEY: *And yet, Nasrallah has spoken out against terrorist attacks on the US, including the attack of September 11.*

HN: We reject those methods and believe they contradict Islam and the teachings of the Quran, which do not permit this barbarity.

BRADLEY: *But Senator Graham doesn't buy it.*

Graham: There are a number of lessons that we should learn from September 11. One of those lessons is these terrorist groups tend to do what they say they are going to do. If they define the United States as being satanic, and that therefore they want to kill us, they will find ways to carry out that objective.

BRADLEY: *And are you convinced that they possess weapons of mass destruction?*

Graham: I'm not certain whether they possess them. But I am confident that they could possess them through their close affiliation with Iran, which has a larger warehouse of chemical and biological weapons, and is closer to gaining nuclear capability than Iraq.

BRADLEY: *So if Iran wants them to have weapons of mass destruction, they'll have them?*

Graham: They will have them, and they'll have them in large quantities.

BRADLEY: *Iran isn't the only country that supports Hezbollah. Syria allows them to train fighters in remote camps in Syria, and in territory under their control in Lebanon.*

Graham: In recent years, they have been infiltrating into this core in the United States people who have gone through their training camps and have the skills of terrorist activity.

BRADLEY: *According to the FBI, Hezbollah has never conducted a terrorist attack in the United States. The FBI says that its members here are raising money for activities overseas, nothing more than that.*

Graham: There has to be a first for every organization. The first for al-Qaeda was September 11, 2001. When will be the first attack against an American in America by Hezbollah?

BRADLEY: *We asked Lebanon's President Lahoud, a political ally of Hezbollah, if Americans have anything to fear from them.*

Lahoud: America? For sure not.

BRADLEY: *But the United States is the strongest backer of Israel. It's the same kind of thing you see with al-Qaeda, attacking the United States to get at Israel.*

Lahoud: Well, believe me, they don't have anything to attack the US or any US citizen for sure. But Israel is our enemy, that's something else. It has nothing to do with the US.

BRADLEY: *But that's not what Nasrallah said last month, just days before the war began. 'We are confident,' he said, 'the Iraqi people cannot accept the humiliation of a US occupation government, which,' he added, 'would really be a Zionist occupation government.' Then he warned the Americans they'd meet with rifles, blood, and suicide operations.*

HN: American policies in the region encourage this kind of retaliation whether we agree with it or not. I am expressing the reality. I believe the continuation of American policy will make enemies of all Arabs and Muslims, meaning hundreds of millions of Arabs and 1.4 billion Muslims around the world. Lots of groups will surface, not necessarily al-Qaeda, and they'll be impossible to bring to justice.

BRADLEY: *Just this week, Powell threatened Syria with tough new sanctions if it continues to support organizations the US classifies as terrorist.*

23

AFTER OCCUPATION

April 22, 2003

Speaking at a ceremony marking the anniversary of the revered Imam Hussein's death,[1] Nasrallah lays out his case for why the US's apparent triumph in Iraq, two weeks after the fall of Baghdad, in fact signaled "the beginning of the end of the American age in Iraq and the region." Exhorting the faithful to "closely observe what the Americans do, [and] not what they say," especially in regard to the emboldened voices in Washington then calling for another regime change in Damascus, Nasrallah asserts that the fall of Saddam Hussein was to be expected, since his was an oppressive regime faced by a superior military power. "What can really protect a regime," he adds, "are its own people and its own citizens if they had been treated well by it; if it oppresses them, none of its rallying speeches will do it any good."

Ignoring any discussion of whether Syria itself was guilty of being an oppressive regime, and therefore potentially susceptible to another US-led military effort to "spread democracy" in the Middle East, Nasrallah "admits" that "the American occupation is more astute than the tyrannical regime, for it will soon tell the Muslims, 'You can practice your religion freely and without any obstacles.' This is why some of us should not fall for that, and say, 'It is now better than before.'" All Muslims and Arabs, he adds, "are now facing real occupation and real hegemony that tells us, 'You can do whatever you want on condition that you do not claim ownership of your oil and your national wealth.'"

Although several of Nasrallah's predictions about Iraq, as well as US efforts generally in the region, would later materialize to varying degrees, his initial confidence that sectarian conflict between Shiites and Sunnis would be avoided proved sadly in error. Indeed, the increasing bloodshed in Iraq between the two main branches of Islam would serve as a focal point for Nasrallah's bitter anger towards the US, who, it was soon claimed, intentionally fomented sectarian conflict to its advantage.

---

1 For Hussein see above, p. 52 n. 3.

In the name of God the Merciful, the Compassionate,

(...) Tomorrow there will be another scenario which the Muslims, and the Arab and Islamic worlds, can examine closely and [of which they can] read the headlines and content. They will be able to see the future through Muslim eyes, and not through the eyes of an America that only seeks our defeat, collapse, and weakness to place us in front of a fait accompli of surrender.

Tomorrow will be similar to what happened in Lebanon on the first of Ashoura after the Israeli invasion of 1982, when many in Lebanon and throughout the world said after the Zionists' invasion of Lebanon, "Lebanon has now entered the Israeli age and will never emerge from it." A few months later, and again on "Ashoura" Day, the beginning of the end of the Israeli age was officially announced from Nabatiye.[2]

Tomorrow, those who can read should read and search for the truth in the eyes of the millions gathered in Karbala.[3] This truth will say that the fortieth anniversary of Imam al-Hussein's death (God rest his soul) will mark the beginning of the end of the American age in Iraq and the region—a fact that the next few years will confirm.

(...) We have successfully avoided two potential dangers:

First, Bush's Zionist administration was planning to turn the American war on Iraq into a Christian–Muslim war, in order to subsume all areas, energies, countries, and Christian institutions into a war that he said carried objectives from the Bible! This danger has been avoided thanks to the positions adopted by the Vatican, the patriarchs, and various churches, as well as by Islamic religious authorities and nationalist governments, movements, and political parties.[4]

2 Nasrallah is referring to the events of October 16, 1983, when, during the Ashoura festival in the southern city of Nabatiye, an Israeli military convoy provoked a violent reaction by insisting on traveling through the middle of a crowd of 50,000 worshippers. Two Lebanese Shiites were killed and 15 wounded by the IDF, in what came to be seen as a formative moment both for Hezbollah's ascendancy in Lebanon and for the decline of Israeli–Shia cooperation.

3 For Karbala see above, p. 52 n. 3.

4 The Vatican, as well as numerous religious leaders of many faiths, had spoken out strongly against the impending war in Iraq, with Pope John Paul II saying that war "is always a defeat for humanity." He had qualified this elsewhere, however, by saying that "the political leaders in Baghdad have an urgent duty to cooperate fully with the international community, to eliminate any motive for armed intervention." Reverend Wilton D. Gregory, "Statement on War with Iraq," (United States Conference of Catholic Bishops, March 19, 2003), p.1.

Second, the fomenting of sectarian sedition among Muslims—between Sunni and Shia. The American administration tried to portray its invasion of Iraq as a war for the liberation of Iraq and its people, especially the Iraqi Shia. The US took maximum advantage of voices raised through the media to present a picture to the world saying that the Shiites in Iraq and the world support this war in order to get rid of Saddam Hussein's regime. They took advantage of this angle in order to create a climate of hate among the Muslims, and sow the seeds of sectarian sedition between Shiites and Sunnis. This danger has also been avoided thanks to the positions adopted by major Shiite religious authorities, the main Islamic Shiite movements, and by the Iraqi people themselves, especially in the south of the country. On the other hand, we can also say that the various honest and truthful voices of Sunni Islamic scholars, Sunni movements, and popular and nationalist parties throughout the nation, have helped avoid this potential danger.

We are currently facing a number of catastrophic outcomes. There is the occupation of Iraq, American and Israeli arrogance, depression among many in this nation, the potential for more tension among Arab countries, and divisions among the people regarding what has taken place and will take place. We are also facing a new wave of American and Israeli threats against the nation and against countries of this region, in particular against Syria, Iran, Lebanon, and resistance movements in Palestine and Lebanon. This is the new reality we are facing today.

Given this situation, we should bear in mind a number of essential points:

First, in view of what is happening now, the first thing we should be careful about in Lebanon, Iraq, and Palestine, and throughout the nation, is not to fall prey to American slogans and claims. We should closely observe what the Americans do, not what they say. Those who speak about liberation, freedom, democracy, reconstruction, Iraqis ruling themselves, and Iraqi oil for the Iraqis, talk beautiful words; but it is rather to their actions that we should be paying attention. All that they do tells us that not a single word they say or claim they make is true.

When we see what is happening, we realize that, although the occupation and the war have indeed put an end to one particular Iraqi nightmare, instead of the liberation of their country Iraqis are now waking up to another nightmare, in the form of the American occupation.

George Bush says that regimes and governments should learn a lesson from what has happened; and we say, yes, we should all learn a lesson—so should the regimes in power in the Arab and Islamic countries. The lesson to be learned is that the army and security services can protect any oppressive regime, but that the army and security services of any oppressive regime will not be able to protect it if confronted by a stronger military force. What can really protect a regime are its own people and its own citizens, if they are well treated by it; if it oppresses them, none of its rallying speeches will do it any good. This is the lesson we need to learn from what is now taking place in Iraq. A country ruled by a tyrannical and oppressive regime has no future if confronted by an invading force stronger than the one it relies on for its protection.

We are confronting a new American scheme, a plan of occupation of unknown duration. The Americans are looking to establish permanent military bases—this means that we are facing not only occupation, but a further consolidation of the US presence. The political future of the regime in Iraq is also unclear. On what basis will it be established? All these issues will be clarified, but they should be closely watched, because they are laying the foundations for the future, for new political maps of the region, and for political regimes; this is therefore not only an Iraqi issue.

On the other hand, the Iraqi people have rid themselves of one nightmare, but are now facing another. We have to admit that the American occupation is more astute than Saddam's regime, for it will tell Muslims: "You can practice your religion freely and without any obstacles." This is why some of us should not fall for this, and think that things are now better than before. Now we face real occupation and real hegemony that tells us: "You can do whatever you want on condition that you do not claim ownership of your oil and your national wealth." The Iraqi people today are facing a great challenge; today, we too should respect this people's feelings and choices. There is consensus in Iraq behind the rejection of the occupation and the refusal to cooperate with the occupation forces. Not a single religious authority in Iraq, especially in holy Najaf, is ready to provide the occupation with cover or cooperate with it.[5] This people will undoubtedly confront

---

5 By November 2003, the US State Department's leading Arabist, Hume Horan, had met three of the four Grand Ayatollahs in Iraq. But he never met the main religious reference in Najaf, Grand Ayatollah Ali Sistani, although one meeting was reportedly scheduled, and then canceled after helicopter trouble. Following an assassination attempt on Grand Ayatollah Muhammad Sayyed al-Hakim in August 2003, Sistani publicly refused to meet directly with the Americans.

the occupation, but the means, style, time, and place should be left up to them. The popular options facing the Iraqi people are evident to the whole world.

The question that begs itself here is: Can we count on the Iraqi people to liberate their soil? We can say—not based on emotional reasons or out of friendship, but based on our knowledge and experience—yes, this is a people we can count on. We add our voice to all religious authorities in Iraq, and all Islamic and nationalist parties in the Arab and Islamic worlds, in calling for unity among Iraqis of all ethnicities and sects, and in stressing that the fear of sedition between Sunnis and Shiites, propagated in the media, is nothing but a bunch of lies and tricks.

(...) Today, Syria is subjected to enormous pressure, and threatened with sanctions and an economic embargo.[6] From experience, and based on our knowledge of Syria's leadership and people, we believe that this fortress has become used to these pressures and has the necessary courage, commitment, principles, and wisdom to deal with many of them, and overcome this phase for the sake of Palestine, Syria, and Lebanon. We should be prepared to come to Syria's defense at any time and place, and be ready for battle, because this is everybody's battle, and this position here is everyone's position. We view the threats against Syria as threats against Lebanon, Palestine, and the elements of strength and hope on which we pin those hopes.

As for the various adjectives America uses to describe Lebanon, and its claim that Syrian forces in Lebanon are occupation forces, I say that this is none of America's business. This is the nature of the treachery and exaggeration of those who occupy and pilfer Iraq.

6 See above, p. 285, n. 6.

24

PRISONER EXCHANGE

January 29, 2004

In what was widely described in the regional and international media as a public relations coup (and mostly derided within Israel as a massive capitulation), Hezbollah and the Israeli cabinet announced on January 24, 2004, via a German mediator, that a deal had been reached regarding a mutual prisoner exchange. In the first phase of the exchange, Israel released 400 Palestinians in exchange for retired Israeli Colonel Elhanan Tannenbaum[1] and the bodies of the three IDF captured in Hezbollah's October 2000 operation. Thirty-five Lebanese and other Arabs (but notably only 11 Hezbollah partisans) were then flown to Germany and on to Beirut, along with the bodies of 59 Hezbollah fighters and information concerning the fate of 24 others. They were met at the airport by a full state delegation, an honor guard, hundreds of thousands of Lebanese, and Nasrallah himself.

The dramatic spectacle featured the return of Sheikh Abdelkarem Obeid, a Hezbollah member, and ex-head of Amal security Mustafa al-Dirani, captured by Israel in 1989 and 1994 respectively. Noticeably absent, as Nasrallah emphasizes in this speech in the Beirut suburb of Hay al-Abyad, were three remaining (and much disputed) Lebanese detainees in Israeli jails, including Samir Qintar, who headed a Palestinian unit that infiltrated the town of Nahariya in 1979, and who was allegedly responsible for the deaths of Israeli Danny Hanan, his two daughters, Einat, four, and Yael, two, as well as policeman Eliahu Shahar.

According to subsequent published reports, it may well have been that Israeli premier Ariel Sharon, at the last minute, held back the remaining three prisoners openly demanded by Hezbollah (not to mention the maps of Israeli-planted landmines in Lebanon, which were reportedly a part of the deal) in order to maintain future negotiating cards. Indeed, Sharon had allegedly undertaken precisely the same maneuver in 2003, when a similar deal had

---

1. See Statement 16.

almost been sealed. Accordingly, Nasrallah points to the "bleeding wounds" that Israel, he says, insisted on keeping open: "These fools do not learn from their past mistakes; when they withdrew from Lebanon, they stayed in the Shebaa Farms and kept our brothers in custody. Had they let them go when they left Lebanon, there would not be a 'prisoner issue' now between Lebanon and the enemy. They opened the door for us and were fools enough to keep Samir Qintar."

Despite Nasrallah's proclamation that Hezbollah remains "Israel's worst enemy", he nevertheless asserts that "regardless of the reasons why the Zionists care about their prisoners, their dead, and the bodies of their dead, this is a matter worthy of our respect ... I stand here today in respect of this enemy because of the way he cares about his prisoners and the bodies of his dead soldiers, and because he works for them day and night and declares, unabashed, his readiness to pay what is sometimes exorbitant price to recover them."

For some Israelis, the total price paid—which included the 400 Palestinian prisoners, five Syrians, three Moroccans, three Sudanese, one Libyan, and one German—was indeed exorbitant; a dangerous lesson, it was argued, that would only embolden Hezbollah to pursue additional capturing operations in the future.

In the name of God the Merciful, the Compassionate,

May prayer and peace be upon the most honorable of creatures, the dearest of messengers, our Master and Prophet Mohammad, and on His good and pure family and companions, and on all God's prophets and messengers since Adam until the day of judgment.

May God's peace, mercy, and blessings be upon you all.

At moments like these our feelings are confused: we feel happiness and joy, sadness and yearning. Today, we are not the only people celebrating the return of our loved ones, for in the other world the holders of the trust, the prophets, and those who have passed on are also celebrating their loved ones' return. We remember them here, and send our congratulations to the spirit of the great Imam Ruhollah al-Mussawi al-Khomeini (may God sanctify his soul); we congratulate the spirits of all the martyrs of this conflict and this resistance, especially those of our brothers in the Islamic Resistance. I wish to congratulate the spirit of the chief of all our martyrs, our leader the beloved Sayyed Abbas Mussawi, and the spirit of the sheikh of all our martyrs, our scholar and beloved friend His Eminence Sheikh Ragheb Harb.[2] I address myself to all our dear ones who have departed this world, for be sure that they share with us tonight our great joy.

Yet there is indeed also pain and sadness, for our joy will not be complete as long as some of our dear ones are still in jail. From the very beginning until now, and through the long hours of negotiations, they were with us; and now, though we are happy, there is still sadness in our heart. We have all become used to these mixed emotions on many occasions in this nation—joy and sadness, joy and pain—and are now at a point where we can transcend these tearing emotions to be able to make the right decisions, pursue the right path, and continue our work. We are a nation that will not be torn down by sadness, and our sadness does not lead to desperation and defeat. We are also a nation that could not be torn down, will not be torn apart, by joy and victory, for our joy does not come from pride, arrogance, and selfishness. We are a nation of faith—one that has intellect, culture, and equilibrium, and is therefore capable of facing up to these emotions and challenges.

On the night of the Prince of the Faithful's [Hussein's] martyrdom in Ramadan, at the breakfast hosted by the Council for the Support of the Islamic Resistance, we said that, just as our land had been returned to us with honor and dignity, and without owing anyone a favor, our prisoners will return to us with honor and dignity, and without owing favors to anyone. Here they are back among us, having returned with honor and dignity, and without anyone doing us any favors. Tonight, however, there are certain relevant issues that ought to be addressed.

First, this achievement and [this] victory, of which we are all proud, are due to our nation, culture, civilization, religion, and our faith-based and human values. We are a nation that believes in the dignity and status of the human being, and that God has created heaven and earth, and life and death, for the sake of this human being. God has also sent him 124 of his best prophets, and made his holy books available to him. As far as we are concerned, therefore, this human being has integrity while he is alive, and has integrity after death. Our Quran says, "He who gives life to someone, is like giving life to all."[3]

---

2 For Mussawi and Harb, see above, Statement 3 and p. 53 n. 8 respectively.
3 Surah, al-Maaida, Verse 32.

We have not forgotten or ignored our brethren still in jail; nor shall we do so in the future. Human beings are our responsibility; so how is it, then, when this human being is the best, noblest, and most honest, self-giving and genuine that ever was? Our responsibilities towards him become double. This is why, when people ask about Hezbollah's reasons for focusing on the prisoner issue to such an extent, I tell them: "This is what our culture and religion, our Prophet and his family, noble ancestors among his companions, and those who came after Him, tell us to do. If we do not shoulder this responsibility, then we do not belong to this nation but to another, and would be strangers to it." We are not a foreign movement, and therefore this exchange of prisoners falls within this very context. Let me to tell you something about the enemy we face: there is a vicious war between him and us, and we speak openly about his savagery and barbarism; but even Islam requires us to acknowledge an enemy's positive traits when he has them. Therefore, regardless of the reasons why the Zionists care about their prisoners, their dead, and the bodies of their dead, this is a matter worthy of our respect. We are Israel's worst enemy, but I stand here today in respect of this enemy because of the way he cares about his prisoners and the bodies of his dead soldiers, and because he works for them day and night and declares, unabashed, his readiness to pay what is sometimes an exorbitant price to recover them.

Such are our values—though it is regrettable that, when prisoner exchanges do take place, we have only one, two or three prisoners to exchange from our side, while the Israelis have large numbers. This is due to a weakness not in our value system, but in the existing balance of power on the ground. Israel is a strong and mighty state that enjoys the support of the biggest hegemons in the world, and can arrest thousands of Lebanese and incarcerate thousands of Palestinians in prisons whenever it chooses. We, on the other hand, cannot do this on a regular basis and in such large numbers; but the reason [for this] has to do with an imbalance of power, rather than a lack of respect for our values.

Secondly, we have to correct a mistake, which we have all committed, including the media. When we speak about a prisoner exchange, the right wording for what has taken place is an exchange of prisoners in return for hostages. It is an exchange of [Israeli] prisoners kidnapped from occupied Lebanese territory in return for hostages taken from their homes. This is the right equation. While it is true that in some cases we did effect exchanges involving prisoners, in general we have exchanged prisoners for hostages. It is therefore the right of these hostages to demand anything they see fit from the international community, and if this entails any responsibility, the state, our brethren, and our dear people should shoulder it.

Thirdly, it goes without saying that all this would not have been possible had it not been for the resistance and for the *mujahidin*'s success in taking prisoner Israeli soldiers—both alive and dead—and using them in subsequent negotiations. These days, there are people who say that such exchanges are proof that peaceful methods can succeed and be productive. I say to these people, however, that the method that brought in three soldiers (an armed operation) and a reserve officer (a security operation) is the one successful and productive option. Peaceful methods that rely on weakness, submission, and kissing the threshold of the American embassy at Awkar,[4] will not bring results.

They talk in the Arab world about options and choices. Let us be objective: there is no argument about the fact that resistance certainly and undoubtedly brings results, and helps us achieve our objectives. On the other hand, the validity of other options remains debatable. We are pursuing a sure path because we are people who like certainty; as such, we choose the guaranteed path of resistance, and reject the way of possibilities, doubts, and probabilities, lest we sow confusion in our people, our nation, and what we hold most sacred. The feat that the Islamic Resistance has accomplished today, through the hard work of its *mujahidin*, is not a victory for a single group, faction, party, or state; we want it to be a victory for an entire culture and an entire path. This choice, this culture, and this path are those of the resistance on a field in which the occupiers oppose an honorable people that rejects, fights, and resists this occupation. This victory is the triumph of this notion and this culture.

Fourthly, the international community has to inquire into who really started the cycle of kidnappings in Lebanon: Was it the Lebanese or the Israelis? Were we the ones who first kidnapped Israelis, or was it they who occupied

---

4 After the April 1983 suicide bombing of the US embassy in Beirut, that killed 49, the embassy relocated to Awkar, north of the capital. A second bombing there, in September 1984, killed eleven.

our land, destroyed our homes, killed our women, men, and children, and built prisons in Ansar Camps 1 and 2, and in Khiam and Atlit?[5] They should also look into who among our loved ones still languishes in these prisons. Our response was simply a reaction to all this. When Kofi Annan paid us a visit after the south was liberated,[6] I told him that we could wait a few weeks or months, but that he had to secure the release of our remaining brethren in order that liberation could in certain respects be complete. If he did not, the international community would have to bear the responsibility. But since he did nothing, our response was simply a legitimate reaction, and we shall continue to act in this way as long as the enemy continues to commits acts of aggression and kidnap our people.

Fifthly, to put political analysts at ease, let me say that this exchange was a purely humanitarian operation as far as we were concerned. We recovered our dear brethren and the bodies of our martyrs, and we gave the enemy, through the mediator, what we had in our hands. At no point during the negotiations did we speak about political issues with the German intermediary— an intermediary whose honesty I attest to and wish to acknowledge once again here, and thank him and the German government that stands behind him—nor did he speak to us about politics.[7] We did not place any political conditions on the exchange; neither would we have accepted our enemy doing so. This exchange had nothing to do with politics or field-related issues, and the proof is the targeting of the tractor.[8] The Israelis said that they were negotiating, and that they would let the incident pass. On the ground, we will confront whoever attacks our country, and he will pay the price; but this is another matter.

Briefly, I would like to address those who wonder about Hezbollah, with all my respect for internal issues regardless of their importance, and those who speculate as to whether Hezbollah's mission is now over, and whether

5 A reference to Israeli-controlled prisons in south Lebanon. For Khiam, see above, p. 97 n. 24.

6 UN Secretary General Kofi Annan held a meeting with Nasrallah on June 20, 2000, described by Qassem as "a victory for Hezbollah in the sense that recognition of the Party had come through the highest representation of the international states, indicating the stature and importance that the Party had achieved in the eyes of global powers." Qassem, *Hezbollah*, p. 142.

7 The lead German negotiator was Ernst Uhrlau, coordinator for Germany's intelligence community.

8 Most likely a reference to Hezbollah's missile strike on an IDF bulldozer that had crossed the Blue Line on January 19, 2004, in an effort to clear explosives—an operation that resulted in the death of one IDF soldier.

the party will transform itself into a political party. In a word, let me say that the Hezbollah that is gathered in large numbers here and in the streets, and the Hezbollah that is in people's hearts and homes, is exactly the same after the prisoner exchange as before it. If anything, it is even more determined, and its faith, awareness, and determination to pursue the path of resistance are stronger. The achievement we are celebrating only confirms the correctness of our path. Our land is still under occupation; there are still Lebanese prisoners in Israeli jails; the enemy continues to attack us by land, sea, and air; and Lebanon is still under threat, with or without reason. We feel sad for those who still talk about removing the enemy's reasons for its aggression—as if this enemy ever needed an excuse when it saw its interest [in attacking] Lebanon, Syria, or any other country. I say, therefore, that the resistance and Hezbollah will continue being a jihadi resistance movement, committed to the defense of its homeland and the nation, the holy sites, and people's rights; it has not changed, and will not do so.

Sixth, I would like to emphasize, within the Lebanese context, three issues with regard to the Israeli enemy. The first is Samir Qintar; the second is Yahya Skaf—the Lebanese detainee whose presence in the occupying entity the enemy denies; and the third is our brother Nassim Niser.[9] Nassim is a Lebanese citizen whose father is Lebanese, and whose Jewish mother converted to Islam after she got married. Nassim had obtained Israeli citizenship due to extraordinary circumstances—this issue should be pursued. The release of Samir and Niser should become a national issue, just like the release of our other brethren; the resistance and the state should work together in this direction. But some people take away the credit due to the state, for it has helped, protected, supported, and coordinated with us, and you have been given the relevant details as they occurred and in a timely fashion. Today, in the same way that the state, the resistance, most of the Lebanese people, and the political parties and forces have worked together during the negotiations to liberate the prisoners, so they should in the battle ahead, regardless of whether it will be political, military or jihadist in nature—

9 Niser was convicted of spying for Hezbollah in 2002 by an Israeli court, although it is believed that he was held several years prior to his conviction. Israel denies holding Skaf, but has acknowledged holding an "illegal alien" that Hezbollah, among others, believes is the Lebanese citizen Yahya Skaf. Hezbollah would later argue, during the 2006 Summer War, that Israel held a fourth Lebanese prisoner, fisherman Ali Faratan. For Qintar see above p. 97 n. 24.

something that should become clear in the next few weeks and months. If the enemy is denying the existence of Yahya Skaf, and Nassim has Israeli nationality, then Samir is Lebanese and does not hold Israeli nationality. Let me tell you, the Israelis were stupid and wrong, so much so that one of their analysts said that they were donkeys, and that Hezbollah was riding roughshod on their backs. I tell them that this is in fact true, and the proof is that they chose to keep Samir Qintar in custody. These fools do not learn from their past mistakes: when they withdrew from Lebanon, they continued to occupy the Shebaa Farms and kept our brothers in custody. Had they released them when they left Lebanon, there would not now be a "prisoner issue" between Lebanon and the enemy. They opened the door for us, but were fools enough to keep Samir Qintar; they should have released him, and he should now be sitting here with us, but their political analyst spoke the truth. Now they are making the same mistake again: they should have let Samir Qintar go, [but they] failed to, and they shall reap the consequences.

Allow me to talk further about Samir and other brethren in Israeli jails, and about our dear and honorable brothers, the prisoners of the Golan Heights, whom the enemy has treated unjustly in this exchange and whose Arab identity and commitment to their motherland, Syria, and to their Arab nation, is beyond doubt. Allow me to go back to the prisoners of 1948 Palestine, to all our Palestinian brothers sentenced to long prison terms, to those with difficult and intractable cases, to all the Arabs, and to our Jordanian brothers. We will wait with the latter to see what will happen between now and Eid al-Adha,[10] and hope that their government will seriously pursue their case and not let this opportunity pass. Let me also go back to the families of the four missing diplomats in Lebanon—which, by the way, should be an issue of national responsibility, since they were guests in Lebanon. The group that kidnapped them has handed them over to Israel, and the latter should bear the responsibility for preserving their lives and uncovering their fate. To all of the above, to Samir who is now Hezbollah's main concern, and to all our brothers who are in the same boat as Samir, I say that we will not abandon or forget any of them.

Some wonder about our available options; in fact, there are several. There

---

10 Eid al-Adha is a three-day Islamic festival, commemorating the Prophet Abraham's willingness to sacrifice his son for God. In 2004, it fell on February 2.

is Ron Arad: we are determined to exert every effort to uncover, and as soon as possible, what happened to this Israeli pilot.[11] We have completed our discussions on the issue, and will work on it for as long as it takes; but I do not want to link the prisoners' fate to that of Arad. The second option is finding an original solution, and by that I mean both sides, but in particular the German intermediary. The third is the resistance option. I promise you, in the name of the *mujahidin* of the Islamic Resistance, that next time [the *mujahidin*] will give back [to the leadership] living soldiers—not dead ones, as in the past.

According to what we believe in, to our culture and our faith, Samir and our brothers in prison deserve our sacrifice, which we are ready for (...) After liberation, I said in Jibi Sheet,[12] when it became clear that Annan would not be able to further the situation, that there were options available to us, and that we would act. And act we did: for here, thank God, are our dear ones sitting among us today. I also said that such action was a national responsibility; Lebanon, its state and people, should all bear this responsibility. It is not possible for me to enjoy freedom and spend the feast with my family when my brothers are still in jail; this notion is still valid, and I am reconfirming it again today.

Seventh, in the presence of these good people, the smiles of the prisoners' families, and the tears of those whose sons are still in prison, at this celebration in honor of the *mujahidin* and resistance fighters, we should remember the imam of all the *mujahidin* and resistance fighters, and the founder of this movement, His Eminence the absentee Imam Sayyed Musa al-Sadr, and his two companions, Sheikh Mohammad Yaacoub and master Abbas Badreddin.[13] This occasion has deep bonds with this leader and imam, and with those brethren; this occasion is all about resistance, prisoners, detainees, and hostages; it is an occasion of freedom. I would like to seize this opportunity to address myself, calmly and courteously, to Colonel Muammar al-Gaddafi, and tell him the following: you are today dealing with several pending issues. I do not want to evaluate your actions, but you have to accept responsibility for the disappearance in Libya of Imam Musa al-Sadr and his two companions.

11 See above, p. 96 n. 21.
12 See above, Statement 15. Speech in Jibi Sheet
13 Yaacoub and Badreddin were the two religious scholars who accompanied al-Sadr to Libya. Both also disappeared with him.

You should take the initiative to uncover their fate, and return them to their families, their nation, and their resistance. I would like to tell Colonel Gaddafi with the utmost calm: you should have courage and reveal the whole truth about the al-Sadr issue, which you know in detail, and put an end, once and for all, to this painful and sad episode, no matter what the consequences. I would also like to tell the Arab world, its people, and governments, that we shall not abandon or forget the issue of Arab, Lebanese, Palestinian, or any other prisoners in Israeli jails; we have not forgotten them in the past, we do not forget them now, and will not do so in the future.

We do not ask for a reward from the Arab world, and our resistance has never asked anyone for such a reward; we are performing our duty, and no one owes us anything. All we want is to be able to stand before God on judgment day and answer his questions about our actions. We do, however, ask for their support, their compassion towards the resistance, and their cooperation in returning the imam of that resistance, Musa al-Sadr, back to Lebanon. We are not making this request because he is a Shiite imam, but because he is the imam of the resistance, the imam who focused his efforts on how best to serve the Palestinian cause. When some misguided Palestinians fired on his car, he announced from his platform: I will protect the Palestinian resistance with my turban and from this platform. We, who stand in front of you, are his sons and his students, and have been schooled right here, and have followed in his footsteps and his path. And for those who thank us, I say, we do not seek gratitude or praise from the Arab world; all we want is your help on this one issue.

Eighth, if May 25 is the day and feast of liberation, we should declare [today] January 29 the day and feast of freedom. This is a feast for all of us, the feast of all the heroes of the resistance in Lebanon, Palestine, Syria, and throughout the Arab world. It is the feast of our brothers, members of Lebanese and Islamic national parties, who offered up many martyrs and took grave risks in the confrontation with the occupation before and after 1982. This is everyone's big feast.

I wish to congratulate His Eminence the Supreme Leader, Imam Ayatollah Sayyed Ali al-Khameini; His Excellency the steadfast leader in this unfortunate Arab day and age, Doctor Bashar al-Assad; the leadership, army, and people of Assad's Syria; Lebanon and His Excellency the President, General Emile Lahoud; and all state personalities who supported, helped, and stood by us.

I also wish to congratulate our brethren in the Palestinian movements and factions, and the people of our dear and honorable Arab nation. I wish to tell them all that this is not our first victory, and will not be our last.

Tomorrow we have an appointment with the martyrs who embody national unity for the mere fact of belonging to several parties and movements. They are also the embodiment of the common struggle, because they are both Lebanese and Palestinian. Tomorrow, we have an appointment with the cortège of martyrs from Naqoura to Beirut; on Saturday we will lay the martyrs to rest; on Sunday, Monday, and Tuesday we will celebrate the feast; and after that, we shall meet to honor the prisoners and the martyrs, and to clarify the path and the responsibilities ahead of us. We hope to have cause to celebrate again—this time with Samir Qintar, Nassim Niser and Yahya Skaf, here in Lebanon and in similar weddings throughout the Arab and Islamic worlds. May you celebrate many such occasions in good health. Happy anniversary, and may God's peace and blessings be upon you.

25

THEY ARE A GROUP THAT "LIVES IN THE MIDDLE AGES"

March 2, 2004

Following a string of assassinations in Iraq, as well as several particularly violent suicide bombings in Baghdad and the holy city of Karbala earlier the same day, Nasrallah tells a huge crowd of worshippers gathered in the Southern Suburb for Ashoura[1] that, while the CIA and Mossad may be behind the violence, it may also be that "a fanatic and extremist group that lives in the Middle Ages and has no brain, no heart, no religion, no morality and yet claims to be Muslim, is responsible for these incidents." In that case, Nasrallah warns, "then this would be the gravest danger of all, and a calamity with which the whole nation has to come to grips." His words would be painfully borne out in the coming years, as Sunni–Shia violence in Iraq would soon spiral out of control, leading to the deaths and displacement of tens of thousands of Iraqis of both confessions.

I wanted to seize the opportunity, and use the short time available, to address the issue of the Greater Middle East Initiative,[2] which all the Arabs have rejected during various recent meetings, each for his own reasons.

I would have liked to address some regional issues, domestic matters, and Palestine—I never forget Palestine—but unfortunately a significant and ominous incident, which I cannot ignore, has taken place in the meantime. We need to give this incident some attention, because it is bound to have considerable and dangerous repercussions for the Muslims, the nation, Muslim scholars, and loyal visitors, and place them in front of big and grave responsibilities.

1 See above p. 52 n. 3.
2 Nasrallah is referring to the Broader Middle East and North Africa (BMENA) initiative, which was in fact only announced at the G-8 summit in June 2004, after having been substantially derided, and then watered down, in both public and private during initial discussions with both European and Arab states. The centerpiece of the initiative was a US-led effort to promote democracy and broad-based reform in the Arab world.

I regret to have to inform you that, this morning, a series of bombings took place during the commemoration of Abi Abdullah al-Hussein, may God's blessings be upon him, in Karbala and the al-Kazimiya Holy Sanctuary in Baghdad,[3] resulting in the martyrdom of dozens of people and injuring hundreds more. These events place the entire nation in front of great and dangerous responsibilities, and above all pose a grave challenge to [Iraq's] people, leaders, and religious scholars.

We do not need to analyze these events exhaustively to arrive at the conclusion that, no matter who the perpetrators are or whose hand has committed these crimes, the main objective behind them is to sow sedition among the Muslims. They will now tell the Shiites, as some already have, that it was the Sunnis who did these things, because they reject you, do not recognize you, and do not want you to celebrate your feasts in freedom and peace. They will tell you that the Sunnis enjoy spilling your blood and killing your men, women, and children, and that neither your lives, your blood, your sanctities, what you hold most sacred, your religious rites, nor your personal affairs will ever be completely safe as far as they are concerned. They will keep telling you this, as they indeed already are, until your blood boils in your veins and cries of revenge are heard. At this point, emotions will overcome intellect, feelings will overcome awareness, and we will fall into the trap and step on the landmine that our enemies and the enemies of our nation have placed in our path.

There are those who insist on carrying out this plan to the bitter end, and who will not be satisfied with what they have already done in Najaf—namely the assassination, [after] Friday [prayers], of the great martyr Ayatollah Sayyed Mohammad Baqer al-Hakim,[4] and dozens of other worshippers near where the Prince of the Faithful lies.[5] Others insist on killing people indiscriminately in the streets of Baghdad, Alexandria, Hilla, Najaf, Karbala, Falluja, Kirkuk, and other Kurdish, Sunni, and Shiite areas. We have to

---

3 In coordinated bombing and suicide attacks on March 2, 2004, 181 Shiites celebrating the Ashoura festival in Baghdad and Karbala were killed. Fifty-eight people in all were killed in Baghdad at the al-Kazimiya shrine, one dedicated to the Seventh Imam, Imam Musa al-Kazim (b.746-d.799) For Karbala see above p. 52 n. 3.

4 Ayatollah Sayyed Mohammad Baqer al-Hakim (1939–2003), a prominent Shiite Iraqi religious leader, was son of Muhsin al-Hakim (see above, p. 110 n. 12). In exile in Iran, he was founder of the Supreme Council for the Islamic Revolution in Iraq (SCIRI), dedicated to the overthrow of Saddam Hussein. He was assassinated in August 2003 by a car bomb, in Najaf, Iraq.

5 A reference to the shrine and possible burial site of Imam Hussein.

remain calm and absorb the shock; their objective is clear for all to see: it is to sow pure sedition, of which the primary beneficiary in Iraq is the American administration, which still pursues its policy of imposing total control over Iraq's oil, potential, and resources. At the same time, it is true that that Iraq's borders are open, and that anyone can enter the country and do whatever he wants. I can tell you, however, that the most powerful among them, those that succeeded in smuggling cadres, generals, and money, and in establishing networks into Iraq, are the Israelis and the Israeli Mossad. Israel is thus the ultimate and primary beneficiary. Sedition among the Muslims poses a strategic danger to the Palestinian *intifada*, to the resistance in Lebanon, and for all areas of strength and rejection throughout this nation. Sedition among Muslims means the loss of everything (...)

We know that the resistance in Lebanon comprised several parties, and each has its own leadership, even under occupation, as does the resistance in Palestine. Some of these fighters are already dead and buried, and some are in jail, while others move constantly from house to house because they are under threat of assassination on any given day, whether they are the leaders of Hamas, Islamic Jihad, al-Aqsa Martyrs' Brigade, or any other group. Who are those heroes who explode themselves and kill indiscriminately in Iraq? Who are their leaders? Which groups does the movement comprise? How do they think, and what are their objectives? They should address this nation, and try to convince it that their plans and ideology are sound. Why are they hiding? This is a very important question, which needs to be addressed these days, and the nation should come up with an answer.

Does it make sense for what is currently taking place in Iraq to continue unabated? In the past few weeks Iraqi civilians have been the target of assassinations: 50 killed in Baghdad, 50 in Alexandria, 27 in Falluja, and a few days ago, tens were killed and hundreds wounded in Irbil. We need to know the answer. At the commemoration for Sayyed al-Hakim, I said, and will say again today, that if it turns out that the Israeli Mossad is behind all this, and is being supported by the CIA, the American intelligence agency, it will somewhat console us. If, on the other hand, a fanatic and extremist group that lives in the Middle Ages[6] and has no brain, no heart, no religion,

---

6 Nasrallah would repeatedly voice his rejection and condemnation of Sunni extremists, including but not limited to al-Qaeda, who embraced the principle of *takfir* in fighting Shiism— that is, declaring that the Shia were apostates, and therefore subject to punishment by death.

no morality, and yet claims to be Muslim, is responsible for these incidents, then this would be the gravest danger of all, and a calamity with which the whole nation has to come to grips.

With Shiites dying on the very same day that we commemorate Sayyed al-Hakim, all Sunnis should express their rejection and condemnation of these acts; equally, when Sunnis die in this way, Shiites must express their rejection and condemnation. This is because when Shiites are killed, someone will come and tell them "Your killers are Sunnis"; and when Sunnis are killed, someone will tell them "your killers are Shiites." So, my dear compatriots, my dear kinfolk in Iraq, you who have been so wronged and suffer terribly, we call upon you to show wisdom, and move beyond this crisis and these seditious acts. Do not allow the Zionists, the Americans, or those fanatic murderers to push this nation to the brink. I assure you that all fanatics have no religion other than killing and bloodletting, and are people that everyone, the Sunnis before the Shiites, rejects.

In Iraq today, there are both tribes and families who are half-Sunni and half- Shiite. Iraq has never known sectarian strife of the kind we are witnessing today, and if such mindsets are behind these bombings, we must confront them, and it is everybody's responsibility to do so. Such mindsets are not only a danger to the Sunnis, the Shiites, and the entire country, but are also bound to keep the American occupation in place. They will soon become the only guarantor of peace and security in the country, by gradually convincing the people that without the American troops there would be no security, peace of mind, or stability in Iraq.

If, on the other hand, it is revealed that those who carried out the bombings in al-Kazimiya are suicide bombers, this will distinguish them from the others; for who other than ideologues carry out suicide operations in this day and age? Will anyone convince me that the Baathists of Saddam Hussein carry out suicide operations? We saw how, when they came face to face with the Americans, at the height of the battle, they failed to do anything of the sort, and this is where the difference lies; but, of course, it points the finger at specific people. Let me say it clearly: these kind of people are unwanted and rejected by this nation.

313

26

LETTER TO THE ARAB AND ISLAMIC *UMMAS*

July 30, 2004

Nasrallah's letter to both the Arab and Islamic nations, published in a number of regional newspapers, was prompted by reports in Israel that Jewish extremists were planning on demolishing the sacred al-Aqsa Mosque, Islam's third-holiest site, in Jerusalem. Nasrallah's apparent concern, whatever its basis in fact, leads him to reach out directly to all Arabs, "or simply people from other religions who respect the holy sites of other faiths," in an effort to prevent what would undoubtedly be a catastrophic and climactic event in the region.

Nasrallah's emphasis on the keystone position of Jerusalem, especially for Muslims, his attempts to bridge sectarian divisions, and his exhortation to states in the region "at the very least" to lodge substantive complaints, points, of course, to his strong pan-Arab and pan-Islamic perspective. At the same time, however, one can discern a certain note of desperation, and indeed exasperation—"At the very least," he reiterates, "the enemy should expect an intifada.*" This aspect of lurking concern over regional attitudes, especially among key Arab states, would only become more pronounced later on, when support from other historically anti-Israeli stalwarts like Saudi Arabia would be less than forthcoming during the 2006 July War.*

It came to our attention in the past, and we read many analyses in newspapers and books, regarding the possibility that a number of Zionists intend to destroy al-Aqsa Mosque in Jerusalem. We might have said, at the time, that these were simply the opinions of journalists; now, however, after hearing one of Ariel Sharon's government ministers openly say that a number of Zionist extremists are planning to destroy the blessed and holy al-Aqsa Mosque, we are facing in my opinion a very sensitive and dangerous situation. We have to respond to this new development in a very different manner than we have done in the past, irrespective of whether we are Muslims, Arabs, or simply people from other religions who respect the holy sites of other faiths. This development is not the same as the old stories, or journalistic opinions, we used to hear regarding the possibility that someone might be planning to destroy the al-Aqsa Mosque. These are the words of a minister in Sharon's right-wing government—itself an extremist government, which ought therefore to know what goes on behind the scenes and what is being planned in Zionist extremist circles.

Since we are facing a new reality, a new danger, and a new threat, we call upon the Arab and Muslim worlds and their governments, states, parties, elites, relevant cadres, the Islamic National Congress, the Arab National Congress, the Arab Parties' Congress, Muslim scholars, lay institutions, Muslim religious authorities, and, last but not least, the people themselves, to take this issue very seriously, and adopt a historic stance that tells the enemy not to dare consider undertaking such a move. We should not wait until this monumental disaster actually takes place before wondering what our reaction should be. We are duty bound, at this particular point in time, to think, plan, and work so that no one in this enemy entity would dare do such a thing, think of doing it, or even threaten to.

I heard a Knesset member say that such a move could lead to the annihilation of Zionism, because there are only 6 million Zionists in occupied Palestine, surrounded by [1.4 billion] Muslims. Are we in the Islamic world and nation up to the level of what this Knesset member expects of us? So far, all we have done is say that there should be a reaction at the Arab national level, and that such a move constitutes a threat and a danger to Arabs and Muslims. The message we ought to be sending to the Zionists and the Israelis, however, is that such a step—that is to say, the destruction of al-Aqsa Mosque, God forbid—will mean the end of the Zionist entity; and this is the message this nation should send. We should also be careful not to divide the issue by saying that a particular Israeli group should bear the responsibility for such an eventual catastrophe, when in fact the entire Zionist entity should do so.

The Arab nation should make this enemy entity, its government and political parties—whether right-wing, left-wing, moderate, extremist, or any other phony appellation—understand that they jointly bear responsibility for any danger befalling the al-Aqsa Mosque; the Arab nation would not be able to absorb a catastrophe of such proportions.

This is the message all of us should be addressing; as to how, where, by which means, and with which language and style we do it, each of us has

[his] own way, language, and style of doing things. We should all stand up, say what we need to say, issue condemnations, warn, and threaten in order to prevent such a dangerous development from ever happening. The Israelis have to understand that changing the map of the Holy Sanctuary will entail a change in the map of the entire region, and that this is contingent upon the will of the region's peoples and governments, and the will of the Arab nation that trusts its faith, its awareness, and its attachment to its holy sites. The enemy should have no doubt whatsoever that this nation will not allow anyone to harm its holy sites, whether by destroying, violating, or soiling them—and they only have to remember how the al-Aqsa *intifada* erupted the very moment Sharon defiled the mosque. If this move on Sharon's part gave rise to such a large-scale *intifada*, what would the reaction be then to an eventual destruction of al-Aqsa Mosque?

At the very least, the enemy should expect an *intifada* throughout the entire Arab and Muslim nation, which would bring down the entity and leave no stone or trace behind to tell the tale: this is what we are actually calling for. We are facing a great and historic challenge, and should therefore not stand idly by, watch lazily while events unfold—and then, when the deed is done, feel sad, lament our fate, and beat our chests in anguish, yet still remain idle. As of today, we have to take a strong stand and send appropriate messages that will, at the very least, prevent these people from even daring to consider such an eventual move. The nation should shoulder this responsibility, and, God willing, it will be up to the challenge.

III

FEBRUARY 14, 2005 AND AFTER

27

"YOU WILL TODAY DECIDE THE FATE OF YOUR NATION AND COUNTRY"

March 8, 2005

In the months leading up to the February 14, 2005 assassination of Lebanon's ex-Premier Rafik Hariri, Hezbollah and its ally in Lebanon and the region, Syria, had found themselves under mounting political pressure—externally from the Americans and the French, and internally as a result of a growing (though still tentative) pre-parliamentary election alliance between Hariri's mostly Sunni bloc and various Christian and Druze opposition groups. UN Security Council Resolution 1559, adopted on September 2, 2004, was a key instrument of this pressure, expressing the Council's displeasure over Lebanese cabinet approval the day before of a three-year mandate extension for pro-Syrian President Emile Lahoud, and calling for a full withdrawal of all foreign (read Syrian) forces from Lebanon. In what became known as the US portion of the resolution, 1559 also called for the disarming of Hezbollah and other Palestinian groups in Lebanon—a stipulation that made the overall package politically untenable within the country, even for those in the opposition who, like Hariri, viewed Lahoud's obstructionism and excessive Syrian control as having reached intolerable levels.

When Hariri, a close confidant of French President Jacques Chirac and Saudi Crown Prince (soon to be King) Abdullah bin Abd al-Aziz Al Saud, and a symbol of Lebanon's apparent rebirth, was killed by a car bomb in downtown Beirut on Valentine's Day, the full weight of 1559 seemed to bear down on Lebanon, and especially Syria and Hezbollah. Although the locally coined "Independence Intifada" took several weeks to gather steam, when Nasrallah spoke to some 800,000 demonstrators in Beirut adjacent to Hariri's downtown gravesite at Martyrs' Square on March 8, the pro-Syrian government of Omar Karami[1] had already essentially fallen

---

1 Omar Karami (1934–) served a disastrous year-and-a-half as Lebanon's prime minister, from 1990 to 1992, and later succeeded Hariri, in October 2004, after the latter resigned following his falling out with Damascus over Lahoud's mandate extension. Karami himself resigned on February 28, 2005, following protests in the aftermath of Hariri's assassination on February 14, only to be reappointed on March 10 by President Lahoud (although he served only a few more weeks as a result of renewed protests).

with his resignation, while the state's security services had made it clear they would not crack down on the growing anti-government protests then sweeping parts of the country.

Still, it was entirely unclear at this point whether Syria would be compelled to quit Lebanon anytime soon. Also unclear was whether the parliamentary polls would go forward in May, and whether there could be any kind of agreement on an interim government. Nasrallah's speech accordingly attempts to strike precisely the kind of rhetorical balance that Hezbollah had long successfully managed amid political calamity and sustained uncertainty. Ever mindful of domestic considerations, Nasrallah avoids drawing a red line over Syria's withdrawal, despite the obvious and immediate ramifications that such a withdrawal would have on the party's strategic position, saying instead that "if the opposition agrees that the Syrian presence in or withdrawal from Lebanon should solely be based on the Taif Accords,[2] then we have no problem agreeing with them." To this he adds what had already become Hezbollah's primary stipulation: if a Syrian withdrawal means implementing 1559, and thus disarming the resistance, then Hezbollah will reject such an effort wholeheartedly.

On March 14, 2005, shortly after Nasrallah's impassioned address, more than 1 million demonstrators converged on Beirut around Hariri's gravesite to demand Syria's immediate and unconditional withdrawal. Lebanon, it now seemed clear after a particularly tumultuous week, was neither in the midst of an unambiguously popular "Cedar Revolution"[3] or, for that matter, a short-lived outpouring of anger following the death of one beloved leader.

In the name of God, the Merciful, the Compassionate,

(...) You, who have come here from all regions, sects, and groups in Lebanon, and have answered the call to assemble in this place, will today decide the fate of your nation and country. You, the multitudes gathered here, are today above all suspicion, and there is no place for talk about gaps, here or there, among you any more. Today, you will answer the world, which is watching you, and I will always be one of you. Let me ask our partners in this nation, and those who watch us from abroad: Are all these people gathered here in their hundreds of thousands mere puppets? Are they all agents of Syrian and Lebanese intelligence? It is shameful to speak about

2 For the Taif Accords, see above, p. 64 n. 10.

3 A term introduced by the US State Department, following Hariri's assassination, that attempted to link developments in Lebanon with the 2003 "Rose Revolution" in Georgia, the 2004/05 "Orange Revolution" in Ukraine, and the "Purple Revolution" in Iraq—the last so named after the ink marks on voters' index fingers, designed to prevent fraud during the 2005 Iraqi elections.

one's compatriots in such accusatory, divisive, and humiliating language.

I call upon you all to avoid using any language, words or terms that offend any human being in this country; we live in a free and democratic country where anybody can express his opinion, but only within the limits of good morals and manners. Obscene words have been used at various venues, and I wish to say to those around the world who heard these words on television, and to Syria's leadership and people, that we, the Lebanese people, are known for our good manners, loyalty, and courteous behavior; we apologize for every obscene word that was said.

Brothers and sisters, we are gathered here today to endorse the goals we made public at the press conference, chief among them the need to offer our thanks to Assad's Syria: the Syria of Hafez al-Assad, the Syria of Bashar al-Assad, and to the honorable and steadfast Syrian people. We would also like to offer our thanks to the resisting Syrian army, which stood at our side during all the years of defense and resistance.

We are gathered here today to remind the world, and our partners in this nation, that this square, in which we are gathered today, Martyrs' Square, where you are gathered, has been destroyed by Israel and by civil war, but was unified, protected, and secured by Syria and the blood of its officers and soldiers. Sharon destroyed Beirut, and Hafez al-Assad protected it.[4]

We, the Lebanese people, are not ingrates; if anyone among us ever demonstrated a lack of gratitude, he has then behaved against the morality of the Lebanese people. We wish to say to Syria exactly what its own president, Bashar al-Assad, has said: your presence in Lebanon is not material or military; you are present in our hearts and souls, and in our past, present, and future. No one can expel Syria from Lebanon, or from the Lebanese people's minds, hearts, and future.

Second, we are here to endorse all the decisions adopted by the Higher Syrian–Lebanese Council,[5] which held its meeting yesterday, and want to

4 Of course, Hafez al-Assad's "protection" of Beirut, initially (and most notably) during the first Syrian intervention in Lebanon in 1976 (ostensibly to prevent a Palestinian–Leftist–Druze defeat of the Maronites), was not a purely humanitarian gesture. Indeed, Assad had long coveted Lebanon, which in pre-colonial days had been a part of Greater Syria, and he was, more importantly, motivated to intervene in great part by his own regional interests. Which is to say nothing of the estimated human and economic costs of Syrian "protection" over the years, widely—and publicly—decried after Hariri's assassination.

5 The Council was created following the 1991 Treaty of Brotherhood and Cooperation between Syria and Lebanon. Its main function was to provide a democratic and balanced veneer for what was essentially a Syrian-dominated political process in Lebanon.

assert that the decision as to whether Syria stays in or withdraws from Lebanon should be made solely according to the Taif Accords. We who are gathered here have come to tell the world that we reject Resolution 1559. If anyone in the opposition agrees that the Syrian presence in, or withdrawal from, Lebanon should be based solely on the Taif Accords, then we have no problem agreeing with them.[6] But to those who insist on the implementation of Resolution 1559, we say that we sense in your insistence on this Resolution an intention to overturn the Taif Accords and their provisions. This is tantamount to a coup against national consensus in Lebanon, against the blood and testament of the martyred Prime Minister Rafik Hariri, and a coup against the foundations on which Lebanon was rebuilt after the destructive civil war. I wish to stress, once again, that Syria's military presence in Lebanon should be dependent only upon the Taif Accords, the decisions of the Syrian and Lebanese governments, and the interests of the two countries, and not on international pressures and dictates, or the need to reward Israel.

Third, we who are gathered here wish to reiterate our condemnation of the heinous crime that led to the martyrdom of Prime Minister Rafik Hariri, his companions, and other citizens. We offer our deepest condolences to his family and relatives, and stress that we all want to know the truth, because once it is known, this truth will safeguard both Lebanon and Syria, eliminate the main factor of sedition in the country, and put everyone's mind at ease.

Today, from this square, we call for the separation of the issue of Prime Minister al-Hariri's martyrdom from the vicious circle of political polarization and exploitation; this incident is a national issue that concerns us all. We believe that martyr al-Hariri's family and loved ones are no longer a separate family, group, or movement, but have with this sacrifice entered the hearts of all the Lebanese people—and we in particular know the value of blood

6 The France–US sponsored UN Security Council Resolution 1559 called upon Lebanon to establish sovereignty through the whole country. It also stipulated that all "foreign forces" (implicitly, but not limited to, Syria) should leave the country, and that all militias in the country—foreign and Lebanese—should disband, as a prelude to a "free and fair electoral process" (for the full text of UNSCR 1559, see http://www.un.org/Depts/dpa/qpalnew/resolutions_new_qpal.htm). Although the 1989 Taif Accord was arguably the result of a national consensus, and did call for a phased withdrawal of all Syrian forces, as well as an eventual complete evacuation by mutual agreement, Syria had long used Taif's other unimplemented, and highly contentious, stipulations—such as deconfessionalization—to argue that redeployment was only mandated after all of Taif had been implemented.

sacrifice. Let us therefore extricate this family, this blood, and this issue from this vicious circle, because we all want to know the truth beyond the shadow of a doubt.

Fourth, I believe that the only way for us to overcome the political and internal predicaments that face us today is through the implementation of the following logical and reasoned steps: 1. As of tomorrow, we should embark with a sense of heightened responsibility on a series of parliamentary consultations, first to nominate and then to appoint one of the country's prominent personalities at the head of a new government. We should ask this new prime minister, in the name of all Lebanese parties and forces, to form a government of national unity and accord. If the opposition refuses to accede to this, allow me then to tell you frankly that, given the circumstances, a neutral government would have no meaning whatsoever.

This country, which is passing through a very difficult period, is in crisis and needs at the helm an accountable government capable of attending to its political, security, economic, and daily requirements, as well as to supervise the next elections. We cannot afford a power vacuum; the country needs a responsible government able to follow up the issue of Prime Minister Rafik Hariri's martyrdom with resolve and honesty.

If the opposition refuses to join a government of national unity, then let us change direction and go to the negotiating table. How long should we remain mired in the Bristol Hotel, Ain al-Tineh, the Third Force, and political parties?[7] How long should we continue discussing this dialogue before it actually takes place? Why do we, and the representatives of all these movements in Lebanon, not sit together around a table? When will they sit down and talk?

Let me ask everyone, in the aftermath of President Assad's speech,[8] and with this massive gathering in mind, to be sensible, reconsider their tactics and strategies, and agree to sit around the negotiating table. If you join a government of national unity, then discussions can take place there; if you do not join, then let us all sit together around the table, and deal with all impending problems and issues.

7 A reference to the various meeting places of opposition and pro-government political parties and alliances.

8 Only three days before, Bashar al-Assad had said in a televised address that Syrian forces would withdraw to the Bekaa, and then to Syria, although he failed to provide a specific timetable.

One of the most important issues that we should discuss at this stage, and in light of the outcome of the Higher Syrian–Lebanese Council's meetings, is the serious intent with which we should implement the remaining provisions of the Taif Accords.[9] We should be careful not to drop or postpone any of its provisions; to this end, we have to form committees to look into each of these provisions and formulate mechanisms for their implementation.

Dear brothers and sisters, if we succeed in discussing and deliberating matters among ourselves, I assure you that Syria will endorse everything that we will agree upon, and will back our unanimous decisions. Syria has always wanted what is good for Lebanon, and still does. Dear brothers and sisters— let me say it again—we are here to reject Resolution 1559 and defend the resistance, the option of resistance, and the duty and weapons of the resistance. We are here to reject the settlement policy [of nationalizing Palestinians in Lebanon]—not for racist reasons, God forbid, for our Palestinian brothers, who are residents and refugees in Lebanon, are our kin and loved ones, and will always be in our hearts and minds. We reject the settlement policy because we favor the alternative; in other words, the return of the Palestinians to their own towns, homes, and fields. The settlement option is nothing but a service and a reward to Israel. We are all here to safeguard our state-building project, the establishment of civil calm, and to prevent chaos. I tell you, some have wagered on chaos and atypical behavior on our part, but let us appeal again for security, peace, and stability in Lebanon, which are our joint responsibility, our joint interest, and a red line that no one should cross.

Let me seize the opportunity to address a few quick words to our partners in this country: come and join us in a dialogue. To those inside and outside Lebanon, I say, Lebanon is a unique experience, it is not Somalia; and if you are thinking about intervening militarily, let me remind you that Lebanon is not the Ukraine or Georgia. Lebanon is Lebanon, a unique experience in the world. If some people imagine that they can put the state of Lebanon, its regime, security, stability, and strategic option in disarray, or thwart its relationships and positions through street demonstrations, banners, slogans, or the media, they are simply deluding themselves.

---

9 Especially, for Hezbollah, deconfessionalization of the Lebanese political system, and thus, as a consequence, electoral reform.

Lebanon is a country that can be built only through the cooperation of its citizens, and through their mutual agreement, dialogue, and a meeting of minds. No one in this country can impose his own preferences on the others, neither by words nor even weapons. If this country loses its ability to hold meetings, engage in dialogue, or conclude agreements, everyone in it will be lost.

Allow me to address a few words to France, and to President Jacques Chirac: you love Lebanon, and you defend it; over the past years you have paid several visits to it, and we know that you have a personal interest in the country. Therefore, Mr. President, if you really care about the freedom of the Lebanese people and about democracy in Lebanon, you should view the situation from the right perspective. Are these people assembled here not part of the Lebanese population whom you love? The Lebanese people, whom you say you love, are telling you that they want to safeguard our historic and special ties with Syria. They are also telling you that they are committed to the resistance option and to the return of the Palestinian refugees to their country, and that they reject Resolution 1559. Based on the rules of the democratic tradition, the people here urge you, through this peaceful show of force, to renounce your support for Resolution 1559, which is neither supported by the people of Lebanon nor endorsed by a majority of them. Is this not the spirit of genuine Western democracy?

If democracy is synonymous with majority opinion, then the majority here rejects Resolution 1559; in the same vein, if Lebanese democracy is synonymous with agreement among its citizens, then where is the agreement over Resolution 1559? I therefore call upon France, and upon President Jacques Chirac to reconsider [*their*] position out of love for Lebanon.

To the United States, to President Bush, Ms. Condoleezza Rice, and to the American field commander in Lebanon, Mr. [David] Satterfield,[10] I would like to say: your plans for Lebanon are suspect; your plans for Lebanon are wrong. Lebanon is immune to partitioning, immune to sedition, and immune to defeat. Let me also tell you: this Lebanon is immune to death; it will never change its name, history, identity, or garb; it will neither change its skin nor throw its heart for your soldiers' dogs to eat. Lebanon will always

10 David Satterfield was at this point US Principal Deputy Assistant Secretary for the Bureau of Near Eastern Affairs. He had also been Ambassador to Lebanon from September 1998 to June 2001.

be Lebanon, a homeland for its people, for Arabism, for the resistance, and for the entire nation.

I would like to ask all of you present here—and would like your answer to reach the ears of the Commander of US forces in the region, and of the man of Lebanese origin, John Abizaid:[11] Are you, Lebanese people, afraid of the United States of America's awesome military fleet? This same navy has come here before, and was defeated; and here it comes again and shall be defeated once more. Let me tell the Americans: do not interfere in our internal affairs; let us be. Tell your ambassador to take a rest at his embassy in Awkar,[12] and leave us Lebanese alone. We, the people of Lebanon, care more than anyone else about our homeland, and about protecting it, building our state, maintaining our unity, coexisting, and preserving civil calm. Keep away, and take your seditious hands off our country.

My next message is to Israel, to Sharon, Mofaz, and Shalom:[13] forget whatever hopes and dreams you harbor about Lebanon; you have no place here among us in Lebanon. In 1982 you were at the peak of your power, and we were just emerging from destruction; yet we fought and resisted you; we held fast, offered up many martyrs, and defeated you. Today, we Lebanese, thanks to our unity, willpower, army, and resistance, are stronger than ever before, while you, the Israelis, are being defeated by the bare fists of our Palestinian brothers and sisters. I swear to you, Zionists of Israel, that what you failed to achieve through war, by God, you will never be able to achieve through political means.

My last words are to you people, and to all those who support you in Lebanon and throughout the world. We have come to this place from all areas, sects, ethnic groups, and parties in the country, to restate our attitude, vision, and position. I would like you to repeat after me, as we usually do at the end of every speech I deliver to such a large demonstration. We, who reject partitioning, refuse to allow Lebanon to die, and want it to remain strong, united, and cohesive, say together at the tops of our lungs: Long live the one and united Lebanon!

---

11 Now retired, General John Abizaid was from 2003 to 2007 Commander of the United States Central Command (CENTCOM), which oversaw US military operations from Africa to Central Asia, including the Middle East.

12 For Awkar, see above, p. 303 n. 4.

13 The Likud politician Silvan Shalom (1958–) was Israel's Foreign Minister from 2003 until 2006.

To Syria—to which the will of God, history, geography, kinship, and the common fate has bound us—we reiterate today our gratitude and solidarity, and wish for it a life of dignity and pride, and a head held high. We want Syria to remain the den of lions[14] it always was, and want to proclaim: Long live al-Assad's Syria! The den of lions in Damascus will always be a den for all the lions in Lebanon!

To the enemy that occupies our land and imprisons our brothers—from Samir Qintar, Yahya Skaf, and Nassim Niser,[15] to the Syrian, Jordanian, and Palestinian detainees—to the enemy lurking across the border, we will say and keep on saying: you have no place among us; death to Israel!

Brothers and sisters, we now come to the end of today's meeting. Our movement does not end here, however, but rather starts from here. We do not plan to hold fixed or semi-mobile gatherings, or bring together prearranged groups of people to preoccupy the world with our stories every single day. What we want is to hold a popular gathering, every two or three days, in one of Lebanon's cities. I am not saying that people from the south should trek up to the north; these gatherings will take place in different areas and, in order to prevent overcrowding and avoid obstructing people's means of livelihood, each will only cater to a particular area's citizens. The next gathering will take place on Friday, in Tripoli,[16] the city of generosity; and the one after that will take place on Sunday, in Nabatieh, the city of martyrs.[17] The committee, set up for this purpose by the union of Lebanese parties and forces, will announce the dates of other upcoming gatherings.

Thank you again, dear faithful ones, you good people of sacrifice. May you live long! Long live Lebanon! Long live the resistance! Long live Syria! May God's peace and blessings be upon you.

14 The Arabic word for "lion" is *assad*.

15 See above for Qintar, Skaf and Niser (p. 240 n. 18).

16 Tripoli, Lebanon's second-largest city, lies in north Lebanon. The powerful Karami family as well as some pro-Syrian parties are based there.

17 Although Hezbollah and its allies organized a 200,000-person-strong rally in the southern city of Nabatieh the following week, the massive anti-government protest in Beirut on March 14 convinced the party that subsequent rallies would not be in its interests.

28

A MESSAGE TO FRANCE

April 13, 2005

Nasrallah's open letter to France, carried simultaneously by the Lebanese newspaper As-Safir *and France's* Le Figaro, *represented a rare, direct address to a Western audience—one designed primarily to discourage Lebanon's old colonial master from advocating the so-called US portion of Resolution 1559, the disarming of Hezbollah, and, secondarily, to explain Hezbollah's stance on the assassination of Hariri.*

Couched in exceedingly moderate terms, the message was undoubtedly prompted by Syria's announcement only weeks before that it would fully withdraw its army, in accordance with Resolution 1559, by the end of April. But it was also a frank acknowledgement that in the upcoming May–June parliamentary elections, anti-Syrian parties, led by Hariri's Future Movement, would most likely control the levers of power from Beirut, thus further tying the interests and policies of Lebanon to those of France and the West in general.

It is interesting to note that Nasrallah and Hezbollah did not address a similar letter to America, 1559's co-author; nor did Nasrallah provide much in the way of high-level access to US media during these critical months. Although Nasrallah had by this time apparently exorcised references in his speeches to "Death to America," Hezbollah continued to oppose America unremittingly, but obliquely—in sharp contrast to the Bush administration's strategy which, following the Lebanese elections, would often seem bent on a direct confrontation with the party, either through pressure on the fledgling pro-Western government of Beirut or through various regional maneuvers against its allies, foremost of which were Syria and Iran.

As I write this, my country is going through a very difficult and dangerous period, due to a mixture of domestic and international developments that require us Lebanese to be cohesive, and our friends to stand by us. At the top of this list of friends is France, the country with which we have many cultural and historic interests in common, and with which we share similar views regarding issues of civilization, current politics, and, naturally, the hope for a better world where justice and peace prevail.

In 1982, with unlimited American support, the Israeli armed forces invaded Lebanon under false pretences, with the aim of achieving various strategic and economic objectives. While the world watched, they occupied our capital, Beirut, and no one did anything to stop them save for a few limited diplomatic *demarches*, and some useless condemnations and expressions of sympathy. The Israelis killed and wounded thousands of Lebanese citizens, and caused considerable psychological, social, economic, and material damage, with which Lebanon and the Lebanese people are still trying to come to terms.

The Lebanese people rose up, individually and collectively, in defense of their country against this occupation and its fallout, in spite of the disparity between the two sides, both on the ground and politically. They fought this occupation for almost 20 years, during which there was a great deal of suffering and tears, and two brutal engagements in 1993 and 1996,[1] before they were able to achieve a brilliant victory, forcing the invading army to withdraw from our country save for one small area that is still under occupation, the Lebanese Shebaa Farms.

Hezbollah, which was the spearhead and main backbone of the Lebanese resistance against occupation, succeeded through the will and sacrifice of the Lebanese people and the help of its brothers in Syria and Iran, in achieving one of the most important feats in Lebanon's modern history. France played a prominent role in forging the "April Understanding"[2] that opened the door wide for the resistance to operate on the ground, and at the same time provided it with wide international recognition.

Ever since the year 2000, when most of the Lebanese occupied territories were liberated, Lebanon's airspace has been the object of very serious violations that are impossible to stop. And although the United Nations has expressed its concern on several occasions, many Israeli officials still issue threats against Lebanon's security, territorial waters, and infrastructure, which the Lebanese people spent a great deal of money rebuilding. Meanwhile, the resistance has assumed a purely defensive stance across the international

1 For which see above, Statements 7 and 9.
2 For the April Understanding see above, Statement 9.

329

border, and has operated within the confines of the Lebanese government's defense strategy, and in cooperation with the Lebanese army, to repel any potential Israeli attack.[3] If such an attack actually takes place, it will cause much harm to our country and people, and expose the entire Middle East region to very dangerous possibilities.

The weapons of the resistance are vital for the strategic defense of Lebanon, and therefore are not something that it can easily give up, regardless of the pressures and threats brought to bear on it. For to do so would place Lebanon and its people at the mercy of the same Israeli firepower under which they lived for decades, and would rob them of their freedom and sovereignty, and of their right to decide their own future and opportunities for development.

It is within this context that Resolution 1559 saw the light at the Security Council of the United Nations, as part of an overarching and comprehensive deal between the United States and France at the expense of our small country. This deal intersected with very convoluted domestic events in Lebanon that culminated in the extension of the president of the republic Emile Lahoud's mandate for three additional years.[4]

The first article of Resolution 1559, which I call the French part of the Resolution, demands the withdrawal of all foreign forces from Lebanon, which implicitly means the Syrian troops. The second article, which I call the American part, demands the dissolution and disarmament of all Lebanese militias—implicitly meaning the Lebanese resistance. Together, these two articles produced a settlement plan that intersected with the already tense Franco-American relations over the issues of Iraq, commercial interests, and European security. This settlement, which is openly biased towards Israel, to the detriment of Lebanon, France's old and constant friend, placed three major challenges all of a sudden before our country. These are: the Israeli

---

3 Cooperation with the Lebanese army did not, of course, mean submission to its ultimate authority—especially if that authority was under the sway of a largely anti-Syrian government; nor, for that matter, could several of Hezbollah's various operations through the years, including the capturing operations executed in October 2000, be construed as purely defensive in the strictest definition of the word.

4 Although, according to the Lebanese Constitution, the president was permitted to serve only one six-year term, Emile Lahoud was granted an additional three-year extension until 2007 by Lebanon's parliament. Critics of the extension argue it was illegal because heavy Syrian influence was brought to bear on the voting process.

enemy, which lurks across the border waiting for the resistance to be disarmed; the international community, led single-handedly by the United States in the pre-emptive, so-called "war on terror" that has led to the occupation of Afghanistan and Iraq; and internal instability, which, we must admit, has only contributed to an already agitated domestic situation. Regardless of our position towards this Resolution, the stark reality forces us to admit that these factors have together generated a great deal of upheaval in Lebanon and the region—upheaval that primarily benefits the United States, which seeks to impose its unilateral control by force over the entire Middle East and its resources, especially oil.

On February 14 this year, a horrific crime took the life of former Prime Minister Rafik Hariri—the most important and controversial figure in Lebanon's modern history, thanks to his relentless efforts to serve and rebuild his country. Our relationship with him fluctuated between disagreement and cooperation, on many levels and on various domestic issues, until a deep understanding settled between us for good, and later developed into a close friendship. This understanding revolved around fundamental issues relating to Lebanon and the future of its citizens, and we were in total agreement regarding the importance of preserving the resistance as it is now: men and their weapons ready to protect the country against any eventual Israeli attack, within the framework of the state's defense strategy. We were also of the same mind regarding the building of a modern and just state able to ensure its citizens' security and equality, provide them with equal employment opportunities, and guarantee them a prosperous future without sectarianism. We were both committed to the application of the Taif Agreement[5] as a basis for our mutual and common understanding regarding the country's future.

This monumental event stunned the Lebanese people; but instead of [our] standing together in the face of its repercussions, a dangerous schism occurred and led to a confrontation between the Lebanese people. The blood of Rafik Hariri, which had not yet had time to dry, became a political tool to mobilize public feelings in an unprecedented manner. Very serious accusations were leveled here and there without adequate proof, and the Lebanese authorities implicitly blamed Syria for standing behind this abominable crime. This

5 For which see above, p. 64 n. 10.

invited foreign intervention in Lebanon's internal affairs by those who saw the situation as a golden opportunity for the immediate implementation of Resolution 1559; this in turn placed the country's defensive security in jeopardy, and exposed its internal stability to the elements. This state of affairs compelled us and our allies to take to the streets in force, to demand that the whole and unadulterated truth regarding Hariri's assassination be revealed, and to send a dual message to our partners in Lebanon and throughout the world.

At the demonstration we held on March 8, 2005 in Riad al-Solh Square,[6] we renewed our commitment to the Taif Agreement—and called upon opposition groups to join us in a genuine dialogue regarding all unresolved issues, without exception, and to submit to the people's will through free and fair elections. We reiterated the importance of maintaining the resistance's weapons as long as Israel continues to pose a threat to Lebanon from across the border, and our readiness to discuss various existential issues that face our country, including that of the resistance. We naturally also expressed our total rejection of all foreign interventions that detract from Lebanon's genuine and complete sovereignty, freedom, and independence.

On the 30th of this month, the Arab Syrian army is due to complete its withdrawal from Lebanon, after being present in the country since 1976. In the interim, it succeeded in putting an end to the civil war, integrating the Lebanese army by reconstituting it out of elements from various forces in the country, and rebuilding the country's political institutions. Moreover, it is thanks to Syria's open and continuous support that the Lebanese were able to expel Israel from south Lebanon, and we cannot but be thankful for and appreciative of their help. However, the mistakes that were committed by both Lebanese and Syrian individuals in various positions of authority— to which the Syrian president openly and courageously alluded[7]—led to the deterioration of relations between the two countries. We have always sought good relations with Syria, mainly because it is in Lebanon's interest, since Syria remains our main and strategic ally in the absence of a solution in the

6 See above, Statement 27.

7 In Bashar al-Assad's March 5 speech to the Syrian parliament, broadcast live to jeering (and intermittently cheering) protesters in downtown Beirut, the president said not "all our [Syria's] acts in Lebanon were correct." Donna abu Nasr, "Threats Alienate Syrians from Lebanon," *Associated Press*, March 19, 2000, accessed online.

region. It is also Lebanon's only economic gateway to the Arab heartland and the world. This is why building this relationship on forward-looking and objective bases that ensure the interests of both countries and peoples is one of Lebanon's main priorities in the near future.

Now that the withdrawal of Syrian troops is about to take place, and the international community has decided to set up an international investigation into the assassination of the martyr Rafik Hariri—the two important demands of Lebanon's opposition—we have to find ways to extricate ourselves from the impasse in which we currently find ourselves. I therefore seize this opportunity to renew my call to all Lebanese political groups to come together and engage in a serious dialogue regarding all fundamental issues that concern the future well-being of the next generations of Lebanese citizens. These issues are: the vital importance of national unity; peaceful coexistence between Christians and Muslims; rejection of the notion of winners and losers; rejection of the use of arms and a return to civil war; commitment to freedom and democracy; adoption of a just and representative electoral system; [the] building [of] a modern state based on the rule of law; and the rejection of all foreign intervention in Lebanon's internal affairs.

France, for which we in Hezbollah have much regard, has played a major role in forging the April Understanding and in effecting one of the prisoner exchange operations involving detainees in Israeli jails. I therefore call upon France, which the Lebanese people consider as their friend and with which they share a commitment to the principles of mercy, peace, and democracy, to work diligently towards fostering national dialogue and domestic reconciliation in Lebanon, given that its role in the formulation of Resolution 1559 has angered many of its citizens. It hurt people, even though they understand the complex web of international interests, to see France falling victim to America's savage and aggressive hegemony, especially in this rapidly changing world.

We also should not forget that our country— for complex geographical, political, and cultural reasons—is a microcosm of almost all the major problems in the region, impacts them and is in turn impacted by them. The American occupation of Iraq has endangered regional instability, and has created threatening conditions for Iraq's neighbors—namely Iran, Turkey and Syria. The Palestinian people are in the midst of an honorable struggle to liberate their land and gain their full right to freedom and sovereignty.

In the meantime, Israel refuses to implement any of the international resolutions; it has occupied the Syrian Golan Heights since 1967, and actively continues to build its nuclear arsenal, in defiance of international resolutions. Lebanon will not be able to confront these looming challenges if its citizens are not united and fully aware that their small and beautiful country deserves to live, and that they have earned the right to live there in freedom and dignity.

29

"WE WILL CONSIDER ANY HAND THAT TRIES TO SEIZE OUR WEAPONS AS AN ISRAELI HAND"

May 25, 2005

Only days before the first post-Syrian Lebanese parliamentary elections were set to begin, Nasrallah spoke to a rally in the same southern town of Bint Jbeil where he had previously delivered his first Liberation Day speech five years earlier. The setting provided a dramatic backdrop for two claims which would grab international headlines: that Hezbollah's arsenal contained "more than 12,000 rockets," and that the party would "consider any hand that tries to seize our weapons as an Israeli hand and [we] will cut it off."

The second assertion was perhaps the most significant domestically, since it was widely assumed that the "Rafik Hariri Martyr List," led by Rafik Hariri's son Saad Hariri, would gain the premiership and control a governing majority coalition. Although Saad Hariri had rejected Resolution 1559's disarmament clause and, in a few key districts, had even aligned his list with that of Hezbollah's and Amal's Resistance and Development List, Nasrallah clearly viewed the upcoming anti-Syrian, pro-Western government with great suspicion, especially when it came to the party's primary concern: maintaining its arms and its ability to conduct operations against Israel.

Immediately after the elections, however, that suspicion was largely sublimated, as Hezbollah chose to further protect its domestic embeddedness by joining the cabinet for the first time in its history. When the new premier, Fouad Siniora,[1] took office in July, Hezbollah thus counted a total of 14 MPs (it held a total of 35 seats through its joint list), one minister—Mohammed Fniesh, minister of electricity and water—and two other cabinet members

---

1 Fouad Siniora (1943–), a key ally of Rafik Hariri and member of his Future Movement Party, had previously served as Finance minister during Hariri's second term as prime minister, from 2000 to 2004.

considered close to the party. All in all, it was an impressive showing for a movement that had originally rejected the terms of the Taif Accord, and whose core rationale had been so strongly challenged by events since the Israeli withdrawal of 2000.

Here we are again on the anniversary of our victory in the city of Bint Jbeil, the city of jurists, scholars, good people, authors, and poets, and the city of martyrs—the very same place we met five years ago to declare liberation and victory. We are here to celebrate, once again, one of God Almighty's days on which he generously granted the *mujahidin*, the patient and steadfast people of this country, the victory and dignity they deserve. He gave victory to his servant, defeated the enemy, kept his promise, and cherished this country, its people, resistance, martyrs, and jihadists.

We meet to celebrate the anniversary of this historic victory, a victory fraught with dangerous repercussions and great omens for the region, the motherland, and the nation. We insist on celebrating this anniversary and on exerting every effort to reaffirm our joy in recalling the meaning of resistance and victory; we do this not to sing the praises of the past, patriotic songs or recite poetry, but to learn from the recent past all that might help us face the future with confidence, awareness, determination, and hope. Our enemies want us to erase from our memory all the glorious days of our lives and be left only with memories of catastrophes, setbacks, and the pain of defeat; they want us to forget the days of glory, dignity, joy, and victory. What we wish for ourselves, however, is to relive every year that same anniversary, and with it the spirit, culture, and deeds of the resistance, and its awareness and faith in its God, its people, its *mujahidin*, its weapons, and the families of its martyrs.

In this celebration, in the span of only one hour and in your blessed company, we will recall together a host of values, morals, and visions, and remember a host of martyrs, those who were wounded; the prisoners, and those who have been liberated; the resistance, and those who stand steadfast on the frontlines. We should make our enemy, and the world, understand that we in Lebanon are a strong, proud, and able people, and that what we have achieved on May 25, 2000, is something we can achieve again every day, God willing.

Neither in our lexicon nor among our options is there for us, people of this resistance, dignity and victory, a place for retreat, weakness, and shame.

Are we not, after all, the followers of that same imam who was martyred with his sons and companions under the banner of "We know not what shame means?"[2]

It is normal for people to have different expectations and feelings regarding this anniversary and the memories it conjures up, depending on their connection to the event, to the incident itself, and to what led to it. For example, Eid al-Fitr is a feast for all the world's Muslims, but those who enjoy it most are those who are fasting. Eid al-Adha is a feast for all the Muslims in the world, yet those who enjoy it most are the pilgrims in Mecca [who have just completed the Hajj].[3] Those who commit more and suffer more enjoy the feast all the more; for them it holds a different meaning. The anniversary of the resistance and liberation is an official holiday, and a feast to be celebrated by all the Arabs, Muslims, and honorable people of this world. Yet it is only natural that those who enjoy it most are those who sacrificed, and the families of the martyrs. On May 25, the mothers, wives, fathers, sons, daughters, brothers, and sisters of martyrs remember their relatives, and feel the pain of separation deep in their hearts; yet their faces are flushed with joy and pride for what their loved ones have accomplished.

The people in areas under enemy fire, and those who withstood the pressure and pain and made the necessary sacrifices to safeguard the resistance, are those who are now most joyful. Outside Lebanon, the happiest are naturally those who supported and stood by the resistance and were, as a result, the focus of international pressures and American and Israeli threats. We should mention in particular here Assad's Syria, its people, army, and armed forces. Some people in Lebanon might take issue with Syria's deeds and methods, but we would be ingrates if we ignored the fact that Syria has stood by the resistance, whose victory we are celebrating today. With respect to all the Arab countries, Syria has withstood more than any of them. Undoubtedly, therefore, the leadership, army, and people of Syria share our joy today, because they are our partners in victory.

By the same token, the leadership and people of the Islamic Republic of Iran have also stood by the resistance, and endured a great deal of pressure as a result. Today, as I remember the honorable stand made by

2 See Statement 3.
3 Eid al-Fitr is the Muslim holiday that marks the end of the month of fasting during Ramadan. For Eid al-Adha see above, p. 306 n. 10.

these two countries, I would like to ask all the doubters in Lebanon: Was the resistance not truly a national Lebanese movement that benefited from Syria's and Iran's support for Lebanon's struggle to regain its freedom, dignity, self-esteem, and strength? Those who point an accusing finger at the resistance still say it is a Syrian or Iranian tool. Five years ago, I stood right here and told you that we have to be humble in victory; today, however, I wish to say that if anyone has the right to issue patriotic certificates, it is the resistance. Those who, throughout our Arab and Islamic worlds, took part in our resistance are now our partners in victory, and I look forward to the day when May 25, the anniversary of resistance and liberation, becomes a real national occasion and a celebration for the whole nation.

Brothers and sisters, let us move on to today's concerns and the challenges of the current phase, even though there is not enough time to review the entire history and accomplishments of the resistance. To sum up, the resistance has managed to regain the large majority of Lebanon's occupied territories, release the greatest number of prisoners from Israeli jails, and establish a balance of deterrence that ensures the security of Lebanon, its people, and infrastructure. It has done this by confronting aggression politically—in other words, by enabling Lebanon to withstand new Israeli and American pressure aiming at subjugating Lebanon and submitting it to their dictates. It is the resistance as a factor of power for Lebanon that will be targeted in the phase that will immediately follow the upcoming elections—whether by America, by the West as a whole, or by Israel—and we should be ready to face the onslaught.

Some speak about the resistance's weapons as being separate from the resistance itself; [but] weapons without the resistance have no value. The real value of the resistance and its religious and national duty is its humanity, the human being, and above all you, the people; the weapons come after all this. It is the right of Sharon, Shalom, and Israel to be proud of their success in placing the international community in a confrontation with those who have defeated it in Lebanon. Israel has been able to place the international community face to face with the resistance through Resolution 1559.[4] Look at this paradox, brothers and sisters: in 1978 the Israeli army

4 For UNSCR 1559 see Statement 27.

invaded parts of south Lebanon, and the Security Council of the United Nations issued Resolution 425.[5] Yet the international community did nothing to implement this resolution. It did not threaten Israel with placing the resolutions under Chapter Seven of the UN Charter, which allows the Security Council to launch military action against a given country, and it took no measures whatsoever against it. It adopted Resolution 425, then put it in the drawer; 22 years have since passed, and this resolution has yet to be implemented. Nothing whatsoever was done to implement it. Neither the international community, international willpower, nor Israel's moral principles and remorse finally forced Israel to leave Lebanon. It was you, the resistance, and the people's blood and sacrifice, that removed Israel from Lebanon. Then the international community attempts to convince us that Israel has implemented Resolution 425, and that the issue is now closed.[6]

On the other hand, six or seven months ago, the UN Security Council adopted Resolution 1559, and international pressure immediately began to mount against Syria and Lebanon to force them to implement its provisions in less than seven months. They pressured and threatened Syria under Chapter Seven of the UN Charter, threatened it with war and, with all my respect to domestic factors, placed it in front of a difficult choice, in the face of which it opted to withdraw.[7]

The most important provision of Resolution 1559 was implemented in less than seven months, but nothing has been done for 22 years to implement Resolution 425. Why is this? Because Resolution 425 targets Israel, and Resolution 1559 is to its advantage and serves its interests.

Now Lebanon has entered into the vicious circle of foreign interference in general, and American interference in particular, and I do not believe that anyone in Lebanon needs further proof as to the level, depth, and detailed nature of this interference by foreign embassies in our country.

---

5 UNSCR 425, issued in 1978, called for Israel's unconditional withdrawal from Lebanese territory. See above, p. 179, n. 1.

6 See above, p. 250. n. 8.

7 Arab states, especially Saudi Arabia, also played a key role in convincing Syria to withdraw from Lebanon. Saudi Crown Prince Abdullah, a close friend of Hariri, allegedly told Bashar Assad before the latter's March 5 speech to the Syrian parliament that Syria would have to quit Lebanon within weeks or risk upsetting Syrian–Saudi relations. Nicholas Blanford, *Killing Mr. Lebanon*, p. 158.

Whether they are loyalists or from the opposition, this is what most political leaders in Lebanon are currently talking about: they talk about interference in elections, fixing electoral lists, and imposing timeframes and priorities. We have entered into a cycle of foreign control and interference.

What are today the priorities and objectives of these foreigners—particularly the Americans—who seek to interfere in our country? This is what we need to know in order to be able to confront them. Today, the Americans want to speed up the elections, regardless of the election law's nature, and want to establish a new state authority in Lebanon. Why is that? Because once this authority is in place, they will make demands on it that serve the interests of Israel.

Yesterday, a senior official from the US State Department said [that] after the elections, Hezbollah must disarm. If it does not, it should be aware that once the elections are over, internal pressure against it will mount. This US official is threatening us with mounting domestic pressure; this means that the US wants to pit the Lebanese people against one another for the sake of Israel. But in what climate would we be facing this challenge to the resistance and its arms? Why this American insistence? And how should we confront it? The current climate does not allow for a settlement in Palestine or the region, regardless of our principled position on such a settlement.

Yesterday in Washington, Sharon restated his "No's" and said: Jerusalem will remain the eternal, eternal, eternal capital of Israel. What kind of settlement is this? He said that there will be no return to the 1967 borders, and no return of the Palestinian refugees to their homes and country. In what kind of climate do the Americans ask Lebanon to hand over the weapons of the resistance? In what climate do the Americans want Hezbollah's resistance to lay down its arms? In a climate that allows Sharon to stand before the entire world—and I hope the political and religious leadership in Lebanon will carefully peruse his words—and say: all the treaties and agreements we have signed with the Arab states are not worth the paper they are written on.

What Sharon really wants to say is that military power, nuclear weapons, and supremacy over all people and states in the region are what really protects Israel, not treaties and agreements. While Sharon is saying this, the US comes to us in Lebanon and says, you must disarm the resistance (...). We tell them in return: all your guarantees and pledges are not worth the paper they are written on. Sharon possesses 200 nuclear warheads and the largest air force in the Middle East, and Israel is one of the strongest military powers in the world; and yet it is not reassured by the treaties and agreements it signed, because it has not given up yet its ambitions in the region.

But the UN Security Council, the whole world, and the international community want us, who own a modest arsenal of defensive yet effective weapons, to disarm the resistance in Lebanon, and [they] threaten Syria, Iran, and Lebanon for that same purpose. This is the sort of climate they want.

Under such circumstances, our region is doomed to weakness and disintegration; but then, who will protect whom? Who cares about whom? And who will seek help from whom? The Arab peoples and states will end up in a situation where each is preoccupied, tending to his own situation, his own problems and his own war, created by the Americans under the banner of democracy and so on. This is the climate under which the Americans will proceed, immediately after the elections, to disarm the resistance.

The question that once again poses itself here is: Why this American insistence? Is it for the sake of Lebanon's Christians, Lebanon's Muslims, or Lebanon's stability and security? No—it is all for Israel's sake. Sharon goes [to Washington] and says that the Palestinian refugees will not return home; and Bush tells Lebanon: you must either settle the Palestinians in your country or deport them to a distant place other than occupied Palestine.

The Israelis admit—although some Lebanese do not—that the resistance has imposed a balance of fear and deterrence; this is a fact, and this balance protects Lebanon and protects all of us here. Some were uneasy about my coming to this place today, but I told them, you should really be concerned about a booby-trapped vehicle placed on the road leading to this place, and about the fact that my killer would be unknown. On the other hand, when I stand here in Bint Jbeil among our own people, our own men, women, and resistance fighters, I challenge Israel to dare commit such a folly. There is a resistance in Lebanon that pledged itself to its God and its people not to remain silent in the face of this enemy's crimes. At a time when the resistance is imposing this balance of deterrence, Bush puts pressure on Lebanon, on the National Assembly, and on the new government, to disarm the resistance; all this is for the benefit of Israel, not Lebanon.

341

Forgive me if I am taking too much of your time—but how do we confront this? First of all, as Lebanese, we do so by being fully aware of the situation. The most dangerous thing we face today, as Lebanese, is this foreign interference in all our political and domestic affairs. We should be aware of the existence of such interference—that it serves the interests of the foreigner himself, not the Lebanese people; and that the first stage of this unfortunate situation is the issue of the elections.

I would like to address those leaders who objected to holding the upcoming elections according to the law of 2000, some of whom—namely the so-called Quadripartite Alliance—placed the responsibility for adopting this law on the speaker of parliament,[8] and accused him of impeding the enactment of a new elections law. I want to tell them the truth, which they perhaps already know. If they want to cause an uproar, they should do so elsewhere. I am not ashamed to say that we in Hezbollah have asked, with insight and pride, that the elections be postponed for three months. Does anyone really think that we asked this because we were afraid of the results? No, not at all. Does anyone really think that an electoral law could harm us? I have said on previous occasions that, if we want to think along party lines, then my reaction would be: do whatever you want. You want the district to become an electoral constituency? We have no problem. You want five governorates to become constituencies? No problem. You want nine governorates, ten governorates to become constituencies, or the central regions? No problem. You want a majority or a proportional system, or Lebanon as

8 The 2000 election law was generally viewed as being particularly unfavorable to Lebanon's Christians, since it was based on 14 large, gerrymandered districts in which pro-Syrian confessional candidates were assured of victory, instead of small districts where confessional candidates were more likely to be chosen directly from their respective confessions. In the case of the Christian vote, this generally meant that pro-Syrian Christian candidates were elected on the backs of (more likely than not pro-Syrian) Muslim votes. It should be said, however, that the 2000 law was drawn up under the auspices of Syria's head of security in Lebanon, Ghazi Kanaan, as a means of shifting more electoral power away from President Lahoud and towards Hariri, with whom Kanaan had a good relationship. It is therefore not entirely surprising that, despite the complaints of Christian members of the former March 14 alliance, especially General Michel Aoun's Free Patriotic Movement (which had yet to formally align with Hezbollah), Samir Geagea's now legalized Lebanese Forces, and the mainly Christian *Qornet Shehwan*, the "Quadripartite Alliance" – composed of Saad Hariri (1970–) and his father's Future Movement (Sunni), Walid Jumblatt's Progressive Socialist Party (Druze), and Amal and Hezbollah (Shiite)—nevertheless decided to keep the 2000 law in place for the upcoming parliamentary contest, although Amal and Hezbollah repeatedly stressed their preference for delaying the elections until a new law could be put into place.

a single constituency? We have no problem with that, either. We will have no problem with any election law that you enact for Lebanon; Hezbollah will always land on its feet.

We did not ask for a three-month postponement of the elections because we are afraid of losing our popularity, or because we want to amend an election law to fit our needs. Our logic is as follows: we cannot enact an entire, new, and detailed law in a matter of hours or in a day, and also vote on it; this is an important law of existential proportions. The second reason why we asked for a postponement has to do with the atmosphere prevailing in the country in the aftermath of two major events—namely the martyrdom of Rafik Hariri and his companions, and the withdrawal of Syria from Lebanon. Because these two incidents occurred in the span of just a few months, no one has had enough time to prepare for the elections. However, we discussed the issue with other major political forces in the country, and found that the elections could not be postponed because Lebanon is under threat from the United States, France, Kofi Annan, Terje Roed-Larsen,[9] and others who tell us: if you do not hold elections on May 29, you should bear the consequences. This is the truth of the matter. Therefore, because Lebanon is under threat, some of us thought we should proceed with the 2000 law, since it is ready and waiting. This is the whole story.

Therefore, I say in all frankness to those who criticize the 2000 law—and we also believe that it is a bad law—Hezbollah as a party prefers that the law be based on districts as the [electoral] constituency, but we know that such a law is not the right one for the nation as a whole. We wanted a law based on the district system, but we are all under the umbrella of the Taif Agreement, which proposed a governorate-based system.[10]

In any case, the fact is that we are witnessing the beginning of an interference cycle, in spite of all the song and dance, anger and frustration, protests and objections. There is no conspiracy by the so-called Quadripartite Alliance,

9 The Norwegian diplomat and UN Special Representative for the implementation of UNSCR 1559, Terje Roed-Larsen (1947–) was also a key facilitator for the 1993 Oslo Accords.

10 Taif divided Lebanon into six governorates for the purposes of parliamentary elections— Beirut, South Lebanon, Nabatieh, Mount Lebanon, Bekaa, and North Lebanon. Under the 2000 law voters cast ballots within 26 smaller, gerrymandered electoral districts, often composed of several smaller districts known as *cazas*. Seats were allocated by *caza*, but since candidates won by a majority vote, a popular candidate in one *caza* might not be secured a place unless he or she fared well in the other *cazas* within the district.

but there is at this stage foreign interference, imposing its will on the Lebanese people; and this is only the start of it. What I want to emphasize is that we must first be aware that this foreign interference actually exists, and that— regardless of where it occurs in the region—it will not foster genuine democracy, state institutions, reforms, or development. Wherever this interference happens, it only fosters chaos and dictatorship, albeit in a new guise and under new banners.

I wish to tell those Lebanese who today gamble on American support: do not tire yourselves out; those among us in Lebanon who wagered on Israel's support were abandoned in the middle of the road. America uses its agents and friends, and then throws them to the dogs or into the garbage cans of history. Israel and America are made of the same stuff, and are linked by their mutual interests, which they place before our own. We do not need any more wrong experiments; our collective interests, as Lebanese, are stronger and more genuine than any interests an individual Lebanese community may have with Israel or with the United States. We must bank on our unity, our internal harmony, and our mutual support to be able to confront this challenge.

Second, as Lebanese, we must work on achieving our priorities, and preventing the Americans from imposing their agenda and priorities on us. Those who gathered in Riad al-Solh and Martyrs' Square[11] were unanimous that our priorities for the next phase are the serious implementation of the Taif Agreement; political, financial, and administrative reforms; combating corruption; tackling the mounting debt problem caused by exorbitant interest rates; and dealing with the stifling economic and living conditions the Lebanese people are experiencing. Most important of all, the responsibilities of the new government should include, among others, the re-establishment of unity among the Lebanese people, the healing of their wounds, a genuine reconciliation among various groups. Also high on the new government's agenda should be ordering, rectifying, and restoring equilibrium in Lebanon's relations with Syria. I would like to point out that forging a special relationship with Syria would be in Lebanon's national, security, economic, social, and political interests.

We should not allow certain extremists to transform Lebanon into a country hostile towards its only Arab neighbor, Syria. We Lebanese should quickly

11 For which see above, Statement 27.

start implementing these priorities; for once the new government is formed, the Americans will undoubtedly try to push Lebanon towards meeting Israel's demands. They will ask, Where are the Palestinians' weapons? What did you do with the refugee camps? What did you do with the resistance and with Resolution 1559? At this point, awareness and consensus will not be enough. Allow me to say that it is also not enough for us to have unanimity. For instance, concerning the resolution of the refugee issue, we are all unanimous in rejecting the settlement of the Palestinians in Lebanon; the Palestinians themselves even reject this notion. We do have awareness and consensus, but if we lose our willpower we might have to meet tomorrow and say: the international community is pressuring and forcing us to settle the Palestinian refugees in Lebanon; we have no choice but to accept; what else can we do? If we start down this road, the Americans will lead this country into ruin, as they have done in Iraq. We must be wary and alert, and have the presence of mind, knowledge, necessary plans, and willpower— namely, the willpower to confront. What we want to accomplish at this stage is to garner as much political protection and assurances as possible for the resistance's weapons and role. The government has issued a clear, though nominal, declaration about the resistance and its weapons.[12]

I would now like to talk about the elections. The electoral alliances we forge are primarily political alliances that are then transformed into electoral ones. In the south, for example, the alliance between Hezbollah and the Amal Movement is primarily a political alliance that aims at protecting the resistance, to which both parties belong, and which has a single imam— namely, Sayyed Musa al-Sadr;[13] and at protecting its weapons, role, and duties. However, although this political alliance includes other politically friendly groups in the south, whenever people discuss or criticize it, they

---

12 According to Hezbollah, the Quadripartite Alliance deal struck with Hariri and Druze leader Walid Jumblatt, and which Hezbollah would later argue delivered as many as ten seats in one district alone to the Hariri list, ensured that the new government would protect Hezbollah's resistance from outside pressures, in exchange for Shiite votes for its candidates. The understanding was enshrined in a subsequent cabinet policy statement, which read: "The government considers that Lebanon's resistance is a sincere and natural expression of the Lebanese people's right to defend its land and dignity in the face of Israeli aggression, threats, and ambitions as well as of its right to continue its actions to free Lebanese territory." Amal Saad-Ghorayeb, "In Their Own Words: Hizbollah's Strategy in the Current Confrontation," *Carnegie Policy Outlook* (Washington, D.C., 2007), pp. 2–3.

13 For Musa al-Sadr, see above, p. 26, n. 6.

refer to it simply as the alliance between Hezbollah and the Amal Movement. Yes, we can differ at the level of municipal elections over purely developmental issues; yet the Lebanese people will portray these as political issues, when they are not. Municipal elections revolve around developmental issues, while parliamentary elections are above all political, as is this alliance.[14]

When we go to Beirut, Hezbollah's candidate will be on the martyr Rafik Hariri's electoral list, because we have forged a political alliance with Hariri's Future Movement; this fits in the same pattern and follows the same idea.

Today, on this Resistance Day and in view of the impending threat to the resistance, I would like to tell you something I've never before told you. I have said in recent weeks that I used to meet on a weekly basis with the martyred prime minister to discuss various issues. What I will tell you today, Sheikh Saad al-Hariri, the martyr's family, and witnesses who are still alive already know very well. One week before his martyrdom, we were discussing the upcoming phase, its challenges, and Resolution 1559, when Rafik Hariri said to me, "After all the experiences I went through, I want to forge an alliance with you, because you are an essential political force in Lebanon, and I want [the alliance] to be based on clear political principles." So we went ahead and delineated these principles: the Taif Agreement, relations with Syria, the [Palestinian] resettlement issue, and a number of other topics. When we reached the issue of the resistance, I said to the martyr, "I want a clear statement from you regarding your position on the resistance, and the disarmament of the resistance, mentioned in Resolution 1559." He told me the following: "If you want, we can bring pen and paper and I will write it down for you and sign it." I told him, "Forgive me, please; I do not want you to do that; I will accept your word. Just say it and it will be enough."

He then said to me, word-for-word, "After a careful examination of the resistance's experience, performance, wisdom, equilibrium, and efficiency, I came to believe in it. I can also tell you that if I become prime minister again, I will not implement that paragraph in Resolution 1559.[15] I agree

14 Hezbollah had already shown its grassroots strength in the 1998 municipal elections, and thus had effectively asserted its power on the ground in the face of its rival, Amal. In the next municipal elections, in 2004, Hezbollah, largely unrestrained by Syria as in the successive parliamentary contests, thoroughly trounced Amal, winning 21 per cent of the municipal seats countrywide.

15 A reference to Paragraph 3 of UNSCR 1559, which "Calls for the disbanding and disarmament of all Lebanese and non-Lebanese militias."

with you that the resistance and its weapons must stay until a comprehensive settlement is reached in the region." What he actually said meant that the resistance must continue, not only until the Shebaa Farms are liberated or the prisoners released, but until there is a comprehensive settlement in the region.

The late Hariri then said, "The day that there is a settlement, I will sit down with you and tell you that the resistance and its weapons are no longer needed. If we agree, all will be fine; if we do not, I swear to God and by my son, Husam,[16] that I will not fight the resistance or allow Lebanon to become another Algeria. I will simply resign and leave the country."

Today, I tell all those who loved the martyr Rafik Hariri and are loyal to him that this was his position, his testament, and his pledge to us; and this pledge was reconfirmed in principle by Sheikh Saadeddin [Saad Hariri] when he told CNN that Hezbollah was not an armed militia but an armed resistance movement for Lebanon. This is the kind of beginning we seek.

Other alliances will be forged in other areas of Lebanon, including constituencies in Mount Lebanon and some other places. What concerns us most regarding these alliances is not our winning or losing a seat here or there, but rather the position of the political force with which we are allied. Regarding the resistance and its weapons, because this is the most serious challenge that it will be facing in the next phase: We should accept, brothers and sisters, that we must settle all domestic issues through mutual understanding, dialogue, and agreement. There is nothing shameful in talking about an internal settlement, or in the Lebanese sitting together to seek solutions and make compromises with one another.

There will be no fear for the future of Lebanon from domestic issues if we are all ready and willing to make concessions and settle our internal disagreements; the real danger lies in targeting the resistance. And what would that mean? It would mean that Lebanon will become fair game for Sharon, for if the resistance is disarmed, the country will become the target of aggression. We will not be able then to drink the waters of the al-Wazzani River, or make decisions regarding our own affairs. The Israelis would soon start interfering in our election laws and electoral lists, vetoing the appointment of the army's commander-in-chief and the head of this or that service. We

16 Husam Hariri was Rafik Hariri's third son. He was killed at age 18 in a car crash in 1991.

do not want to arrive at, or return to, the day when Lebanon becomes an easy target for the Zionists. We should therefore fortify ourselves through electoral alliances, which are in effect political alliances.

I want to be very clear and decisive, on this Resistance and Liberation Day, so that no one is deceived: I want to share with you what I have said in the closed sessions of the past few months. With regard to the resistance, we are ready for an internal dialogue among Lebanese over issues of concern to some people, such as the weapons of the resistance. What we want is to preserve the effectiveness of the resistance; the way we do this, however, is as open to debate as any other topic. You want to expand the scope of the resistance? We are ready to do that; but let no one put forward silly proposals that would thwart its effectiveness, such as mothballing its weapons and only dusting them off if there is an attack. This would be taking the people for a ride. The importance of the resistance does not come from the fact that it owns weapons stashed away in storerooms, but from its being right there now, where the artillery, rockets, and weapons are. The weapons we shall stack in storerooms, under international supervision, will be there so that Israel will come and bomb them a few days later.

Another proposal suggests that we keep individual light and medium weapons, like Kalashnikovs, M-16s, rocket-propelled grenades, but not long-range artillery and rockets, such as the Katyushas. The proposal says, surrender the heavy weapons and there will be no problem with your keeping light and medium ones. A foreign ambassador made this proposal, and it is scandalous, because it shows that their aim is not to dissolve the militias per se, but to maintain Israel's security, since heavy weapons terrorize Israel.

I would like—not in a boastful manner, but in the hope that some of them will actually believe in our abilities—to tell those who qualitatively and quantitatively underestimate our rockets that at least all of northern Palestine, including its settlements, fields, ports, factories, and farms, is within reach of, and under the feet of, your sons in the Islamic Resistance. They want to take this force away from Lebanon, but the power of Lebanon's rockets is not in their numbers. They say the real number of our rockets is 12,000; but I say, with the commanders' permission, that we have more than 12,000 rockets. The real value and power of these rockets comes from the fact that they are in our hands, and that the Zionists know neither their number nor where they are deployed. They are fighting a hidden and an unseen enemy that could surprise them on any given day with this large number of rockets. These missiles are hidden for defensive reasons.

We have said on more than one occasion that we do not want to drag the region into a war, and that it is not our policy to provoke a regional confrontation. We want to protect our country, not destroy it; and we want to keep our weapons specifically for that reason. I have said in this context that we are ready for any internal discussion, and for any guarantees and solutions that would safeguard the effectiveness and ability of the resistance to deter and protect, and that the relevant details are open for discussion. We want to respond to this positive, clear, rational, and calm attitude with a clear, decisive, and transparent position, so that people will know where they stand. There is talk of the need to open up this issue for discussion, and we accept this—but there is also talk of withdrawing the weapons of the resistance; any serious thought about disarming the resistance would be pure madness.

We are the most eager to have peace, stability, and national unity in Lebanon; we do not wish to attack anyone, and never have, and will also not allow anyone else to attack Lebanon. But if anyone—listen to me—if anyone tries to disarm the resistance, we will fight him the way the martyrs fought in Karbala,[17] because we know that any action of this kind would be an Israeli action, an Israeli decision, and a move to further Israel's interests. We will consider any hand that tries to seize our weapons as an Israeli hand, and will cut it off. Apart from that, we are open to suggestions, because this is a Lebanese issue: it has to do with Lebanon's fate, and therefore concerns us all. Let us therefore sit together and discuss things; we are as open as can be in this regard, because we care about what is best for Lebanon.

As to what concerns Israel's interests, the world knows us well; we people do not speak to, or want to have a dialogue with, Israel. Israel is the one that started the cycle of killings, massacres, and destruction, and the dispossessed and oppressed people on the receiving end think the following: "Those against whom war is made, they have been wronged, and verily, Allah is most powerful and will grant them victory."[18] This issue has been decisively settled.

17 See above, p. 52 n. 3.
18 Surah, Al-Hajj, Verse 39.

Brothers and sisters, the current phase requires us to take an active part in the upcoming parliamentary elections in all constituencies. There are some respectable friends and personalities who decided not to run in the elections because of their personal circumstances, and we respect and understand that. There are also certain parties who, for political and electoral reasons, called for a boycott of the elections, and we also understand and respect their reasons. However, when elections are held and there is no reason why we should not take part, then we must be present, and we must vote; because, as I said a short while ago, it is one of the ways we can strengthen our political situation. We must take into consideration, however, the fact that there are friends and supporters of the resistance whose names appear on other candidate's lists, or are running as independent candidates, because, for one reason or another, they could not be included on lists we support. It is important for us to preserve these people's friendship and affection, and to endure their criticism.

Brothers and sisters, I call upon you to vote for the entire lists on which our candidates are running, and for the lists that have our support, because we have committed ourselves to this electoral political alliance based on accurately diagnosed and well defined major interests. One of our brothers or sisters here or there might have a remark to make about the details, but because this is above all a political battle, I urge you again, based on these major political interests, to adhere to our lists as a whole. We must continually follow the situation as it unfolds in the country over the next few months, because this is a critical and sensitive phase.

Today our al-Aqsa Mosque is threatened with destruction, and our Holy Quran is being desecrated by the Americans in Guantánamo Bay.[19] America is intent on attacking the region in order to dismember it, and trigger civil and sectarian wars. America is determined to confront the resistance in Lebanon and Palestine, and we should be ready for that. Within this context, we might soon ask certain things of you that might, of course, involve your

19 A reference to the alleged flushing of a Quran down a toilet by a US interrogator at the US military prison in Guantánamo Bay, Cuba. The story, first reported by *Newsweek* magazine on May 9, 2005, was later retracted. Nevertheless, according to subsequently released declassified documents, detainees at Guantánamo Bay were recorded as having complained repeatedly to US FBI agents about disrespectful handling of the Quran by military personnel and, in one case in 2002, said they had flushed a Quran down a toilet. Neil A. Lewis, "Documents Say Detainees Cited Koran Abuse," *New York Times*, May 26, 2005, p. A1.

presence in town squares and on the street—though I do not know, as yet, how far things will go. I have known you now for 22 years as a hardworking, patient, believing, and truthful people; I also know you as a people armed with faith and blood, a people who will never abandon those town squares. Let the world hear us, and in particular the Israelis, in whose proximity we stand: al-Aqsa Mosque is under threat, and when the need to confront this threat arises, it will call upon every Muslim, Christian, patriot, and honorable Arab in this world to come to its rescue.

We must be ready to respond to al-Aqsa's call at any level, and by any means at our disposal; we should be able to raise our voices and say, "Here we are at your service, O al-Aqsa." Our Holy Quran has been desecrated, and on Friday there will be public sit-ins in various areas. All our brothers and sisters are invited to participate and raise their voices in the face of this American who is desecrating our Quran, and say, "We are at your service, O Holy Quran." The confrontation with which the Americans are threatening us—oh, how I wish that they will be the ones to come and take our weapons away from us, rather than inciting some of our own people in Lebanon to do their and Israel's bidding. Let the whole world hear you: "We are at your service, O resistance."

30

AL QUDS DAY

October 28, 2005

Originally instituted by Iran's Ayatollah Khomeini as an annual reminder of the significance attributed by Islamists to the hoped-for liberation of Jerusalem, the 2005 commemoration of Al Quds (Jerusalem) day was instead employed by Nasrallah to publicly counter a number of challenges that appeared to be gathering force against both the party and its allies in Lebanon and the region. Indeed, only one week prior to this address in the Southern Suburb of Beirut, the first report of UN Special Investigator Detlev Mehlis had been released, strongly implicating Lebanese and Syrian intelligence in the assassination of ex-premier Hariri. Alongside this, another UN overseer, Terj Roed-Larsen,[1] had released his periodic report on the implementation of Resolution 1559, finding serious gaps in the resolution's implementation, especially insofar as the disarmament of Hezbollah was concerned.

Nasrallah's long and detailed critique of both of these investigations stands as a remarkable exercise in populist oratory—especially when one considers that his audience consisted mostly of poor and middle-class Shiite partisans presumably little acquainted with the intricacies and machinations of international law and theories of global power. At one point, Nasrallah submits that the international effort in Lebanon "imposes its will, classifies people, passes judgment, differentiates, decides on the details, and follows up on the smallest Lebanese issues." Then he asks, "Is this what sovereignty means? Is this real independence? Is this freedom? Is this what the Lebanese seek and aspire to?" Answering his own question, Nasrallah claims that "total international tutelage is being imposed on Lebanon and ... Larsen is the new high commissioner who carries the 1559 sword and uses it to chase after the Lebanese, the Palestinian, and the Syrian authorities."

Signaling what would soon become a major fault line for future conflict between the March 8 and March 14 camps (a reference to the earlier, dueling mass demonstrations shortly after Hariri's assassination), Nasrallah also expresses a deepening sense of skepticism concerning the

1. See above, p. 343, n. 9.

effort to investigate and try suspects in the Hariri case. "As far as America is concerned," he explains, Syria and its allies in Lebanon "have already been convicted and must be punished without argument, despite the fact that the report says that the investigation is not yet over and requires months, maybe even years, to be completed." He adds later, in an argument that harks back to past manipulation of supposedly international efforts in the region: "We fear that [an international tribunal] may be used as a lethal weapon in the big powers' game to promote their own ends and interests at the expense of Lebanon and Syria, or to impose suspect deals at the expense of Lebanon, Syria, and the blood of the martyred prime minister."

In retrospect, Nasrallah's speech seems to mark the beginning of a clear series of breaches in mutual trust between the various indigenous forces then vying to shape Lebanon's post-Syrian future. Sadly, from this point forward, that breach would only grow more pronounced, despite periodic efforts to bring about some kind of national reconciliation able to save the country from what all sides—at least publicly—feared most: yet another civil war.

In the name of God, the Merciful, the Compassionate,

(...) This blessed month is favored by God; its best days and nights are the last ten, and best among them all is this Friday.[2] That is why Imam Khomeini, may God sanctify his soul, chose the greatest, holiest, and noblest of days to be the day of the great, noble, and holy city of Jerusalem. The genius of Imam Khomeini, who was so knowledgeable of his time, led him to make this deeply intellectual, ideological, political, emotional, and popular connection between the most precious Islamic religious occasion and the most sacred and important of causes.

Ramadan is the month of worship and fasting; accepted prayers are those that forbid evil and wrongdoing, and man's accepted reason for fasting is the kind of piety in his soul that prevents him from committing shameful and evil deeds (...)

Brothers and sisters; dear worshipping and fasting Muslim nation, during this month of Ramadan: What wrong or sin is worse than the nation of the billion Muslims remaining silent in the face of its holy sites' occupation, and the violation of its sacred shrines in Jerusalem and Palestine by terrorist and bloodthirsty gangs whose entity was founded on massacre, usurpation, repression, and terrorism? O, fasting and worshipping nation of the billion

2 See above, p. 337, n. 3.

Muslims: How can there be fasting, worshipping, and celebration of the Eid while the blood of your Palestinian kin in Jenin, Tulkarm,[3] and the Gaza Strip is being spilled every day, while they are being bombed every night, and while they are being killed in every town square?

Would not these days be a divine signal to the nation of the billion Muslims who witness the greatest corruption and wrongdoing, and yet do not raise a finger, pursue good, forbid vice, utter a single word, or take action?

Brothers and sisters, we celebrate Jerusalem Day this year while great and ominous challenges face us. Throughout the past 25 years of conflict with the Zionist entity in this region, and ever since the Camp David Accords sidelined the biggest Arab country, Egypt, from the battle,[4] the burden of this conflict has fallen directly on the shoulders of the Palestinian people, and on Lebanon and Syria. The Palestinian people in Lebanon and Syria have always enjoyed unequivocal support from Iran, following the victory of its Islamic Revolution, and from honorable people all over the Arab and Islamic worlds, and from the world at large. However, we waged—and are still waging—this struggle mostly in the midst of complete official Arab and international silence, or clear and unjust bias in favor of the enemy. Despite their harsh and difficult circumstances, the Palestinian people have managed to pursue their resistance, which culminated in the blessed al-Aqsa *intifada*, which so far has led to the liberation of the Gaza Strip.[5]

Lebanon, through its resistance, people, national forces, and unity—the unity of the state, army, and people—was able to accomplish a historic feat on May 25. Before that, it succeeded in foiling the American–Zionist scheme, abrogating the May 17 Agreement, and expelling the humiliated Zionists from our land in stages.[6] During the past 25 years, Syria—its

3 For Operation Defensive Shield, see above, p. 275 n. 9. Since April 2002, Jenin has been under the direct control of the IDF. This may also be a reference to the recent (October 23) Israeli military operation in the West Bank town of Tulkarm, resulting in the death of Luai Saadi, head of the Palestinian Islamic Jihad. The Israeli operation had broken a recent lull in the violence.

4 A reference to the US-brokered Camp David Accords of 1978, signed by Egyptian President Anwar Sadat and Israeli Prime Minister Menachem Begin, which effectively took the most powerful Arab military actor, Egypt, out of the so-called "circle of confrontation" between the Arab states and Israel.

5 As part of the "Disengagement Plan" advocated by Prime Minister Ariel Sharon and approved by the Israeli government, all Israeli residents and soldiers were evacuated from the Gaza Strip between August 15 and September 12, 2005.

6 See above, Statement 15 and p. 204, n. 11.

leadership, people, and army—has also managed to remain steadfast, refused to submit to American and Israeli conditions, and kept up its historic support for the resistance in Lebanon and Palestine, on the path towards victory and liberation.

After that, several incidents took place, including the September 11 attacks, the Afghanistan war, the invasion of Iraq, and other ominous developments in our region that placed it squarely on the fault lines of global turmoil. Then came United Nations Resolution 1559, followed by the assassination of the martyr Prime Minister Rafik Hariri and his colleagues—a most tragic incident by any humanitarian and national standard. We are thus traversing a difficult, harsh, and bitter phase, though we sense that all that is currently taking place is aimed at this geographic triangle, and at those who support and stand behind it.

As far as the Arab and Islamic nations are concerned, offering financial and moral support to the resistance in Lebanon and Palestine has become, according to anti-terror laws, a punishable crime, incitement to commit terrorism, or a manifestation of anti-Semitism. And now we find the Islamic Republic of Iran facing a great deal of pressure as a result of its firm ideological stand in this conflict.

As for the situation in occupied Palestine, the Palestinian Authority is subjected to enormous pressure by the United States, Israel, and the international community to disarm the resistance groups, repress them on account of their terrorist credentials, and prevent them from exercising their most basic civil rights—even their right to participate in the parliamentary elections. The Palestinian Authority is required to do that while the Zionist occupation is still ongoing; the Gaza Strip is still under threat, attacked and besieged; Jerusalem is still usurped; and Palestinian refugees are still displaced throughout the diaspora.

Dear brothers and sisters, I tell you frankly that the international community does not seek to further the interests of the Palestinians, Lebanese, Arabs, or this entire region; rather, it is doing its utmost to advance the interests of the United States and Israel. The international community is fomenting civil strife among the Palestinians so that Israel can rest in peace, be safe, and impose once and for all its hegemony and conditions on this oppressed people.

The international community is blessing Israel's aggression, savagery, and murder, and acquiescing to the displacement of people in occupied Palestine; or, at the very least, is remaining silent in this regard. It hastens to condemn any Palestinian who defends his people, and accuses him of terrorism.

As is the case in Palestine, the resistance in Lebanon, be it Lebanese or Palestinian, is also targeted. This time, however, it is being done through the international community, after Israel failed to defeat the Lebanese resistance and was compelled instead to retreat in the face of its brave men's heroism, and after failing to crush the Palestinians in their camps and expel them from Lebanon.

The Security Council issued Resolution 1559, and appointed Larsen as overseer, supervisor, and official in charge of it.[7] He was asked to submit a detailed six-monthly follow-up report regarding the implementation of this resolution. It behooves us here to ponder this a little, and make a few quick and relevant observations.

First, before we read Larsen's report in the international press, and before it even reached Kofi Annan and the Security Council, we proudly learned the gist of his report from the Israeli press. It later turned out that everything the Israeli press had said regarding the contents of Larsen's report was in fact correct.

Second, it is strange that when the Security Council adopted Resolution 1559 it found it necessary to appoint an overseer and supervisor, and put an official in charge of it. Why was that? It was because the Council had placed certain demands on Syria and Lebanon, and had asked this overseer to submit a follow-up report every six months. What is strange is that no overseer, observer or official was appointed for any Security Council resolution pertaining to Israel; no deadline was set for their implementation; there was no request for follow-up reports; and the Security Council has not asked Israel about them for decades. Likewise, and irrespective of our position vis-à-vis some of these international resolutions, no overseers were appointed to follow up on Resolutions 194, 242, 338 and 425.[8] Why was that? It was

---

7 See above, Statement 27.

8 These four highly contentious and much-debated UN Resolutions arguably lie at the core of Arab claims towards the state of Israel—although the legitimacy of some of the Resolutions was only publicly recognized later by various Arab states. Among several stipulations, UN General Assembly Resolution 194 (1948) resolved "that the refugees [of the recent Arab–Israeli War] wishing to return to their homes and live at peace with their neighbors should be permitted to do so at the earliest practicable date." UNSCR 242 (1967) came in the wake of the June 1967 Arab–Israeli War, and enshrined the broad principle of trading land for peace. UNSCR 338 (1973) called for an immediate ceasefire in the October 1973 Arab–Israeli War, and the implementation of UNSCR 425 (for which, see above, p. 68 n. 17).

because the Security Council is required to protect Israel, and because Israel needs to be strong; whereas Lebanon, Syria, and the Arabs must always pay the price, with the sword of the international community, the protector of Israel, suspended above their heads.

Third, it is clear from Larsen's report and its details that an international tutelage is being imposed over Lebanon—a tutelage whose existence we in Lebanon deny, though it is clearly there for all to see. He spoke about everything in his report, not just about the provisions of Resolution 1559; he spoke about the need to hold parliamentary elections, and passed judgment on them. What does this have to do with Resolution 1559? He spoke about Hezbollah's participation in the government; he spoke about the type of relations that should exist between Lebanon and Syria; he spoke about the type of relations that should exist between Lebanon and the Palestinians; he spoke about the appropriate election law, and said, in so many words, that he intends to establish a suitable legal and professional plan of action to ensure a fair and free election process in Lebanon.

What business does he have with the law of the upcoming elections? He spoke about political, economic, and financial reforms; he spoke about the appointment of directors, and about introducing changes at the employee level. What is even more ominous is that he spoke about changing the culture. Which culture does Larsen want the Lebanese to change? This is evidence that total international tutelage is being imposed on Lebanon, and that Larsen is the new high commissioner, who carries the 1559 sword and uses it to chase after the Lebanese, the Palestinian, and the Syrian authorities. In the meantime, we in Lebanon must stand to attention every six months to give Mr. Larsen the answers he seeks; and every six months our leaders, ministers, deputies, and parties must submit to an oral or written exam by Mr. Larsen, who will ask them, "How far along are you as far as the implementation of the international recommendations is concerned"?

Fourth, in a long report, in which Mr. Larsen graciously included only two lines about the Israelis—namely, their ongoing violation of Lebanese airspace—he wrote: "Israel says that it does this for security reasons." He therefore mentions Israel's pretext for its actions, but omits do so when he criticizes the resistance.

Brothers and sisters, this demonstrates the international community's fairness in meting out justice. This is the international community on which we rely to regain our rights, and the same community to which Larsen wants the Lebanese government to turn in order to regain the rights that Israel has usurped from us. Look at some aspects of this justice; Larsen does all that and at the same time ignores Israeli shelling, the terrorizing of farmers in Shebaa and Kfar Chouba, and the kidnapping of the Lebanese shepherds who were later handed back to Lebanon by UNIFIL after it threatened Israel.[9] He also ignores the Lebanese prisoners held in Israeli jails. Are Samir Qintar, Yahya Skaf, and Nasim Nisr,[10] whom Larsen looks down on, not human beings with full human rights? As for the Shebaa Farms, he does not even recognize that they are Lebanese.

Fifth, when the issue concerns the Lebanese, Palestinians, and Syrians, Larsen says things as they are; but when it concerns Israel, Larsen omits to mention the perpetrator; this is the international report's sense of justice. He says that the heavy exchange of fire between Hezbollah and Israel on June 29 resulted in the death of a UNIFIL soldier and the wounding of four others, in reference to the French officer.[11] Because it was Israel who had killed the French officer and wounded the four other UNIFIL soldiers, because Israel was the perpetrator, Larsen does not mention the killer's identity; he just says that they were killed or wounded in a clash between Hezbollah and Israel.

Sixth, Larsen says that, to begin with, the resistance has no rights to Shebaa Farms. He never recognized the legitimacy of the resistance, anyway. I declare from this platform that I never said that the Shebaa Farms were Lebanese; Hezbollah did not say that they were Lebanese either. It was the government of the late martyr Prime Minister Rafik Hariri, and those that preceded it and followed it, the current government, and the National Assembly, who said so. On the eve of Israel's withdrawal from Lebanon,

9 Riyadh Hashem, 40, and Hussein Zahra, 15, were Lebanese farmers detained by Israel on September 20, 2005, in the disputed Shebaa Farms area. Israel released the two to UNIFIL after it said it had determined neither was involved in Hezbollah intelligence-gathering operations.

10 See above, p. 240 n. 18. It should be further noted that the Israeli government has publicly acknowledged holding more than two dozen persons of Lebanese origin, all of whom are either Israeli or Palestinian citizens.

11 Larsen actually refers to the "death of one Israel Defense Force's soldier, the wounding of four others and the death of two Hezbollah fighters." No UNIFIL personnel were killed or wounded in the incident. "Second semi-annual report of the secretary-general to the Security Council on the implementation of resolution 1559 (2004)," October 26, 2005, p. 8.

we in the resistance announced that we are committed to the liberation of any territory that the Lebanese state considers Lebanese, with our blood, our guns, and our lives. We never waited for Mr. Larsen, or any other, to bestow legitimacy on us.

Seventh, brothers and sisters—this is my last comment regarding Larsen before we move to another important and serious issue—the most ominous part of Larsen's report is that which incites and sows the poisonous seeds of sedition between the Lebanese people and the Palestinians, the Lebanese people and the Syrians, among the Lebanese themselves, and between the resistance and the government. Why do I say this? I say it based on his claim that the Lebanese prime minister, or government, had given him certain assurances.

When Mr. Larsen speaks about this and puts it in his report, he places us in a face-to-face confrontation. He wants us to doubt one another as Lebanese, and seeks to foment sedition among us, because what Mr. Larsen says in his report is different from what we say to each other in our private meetings, and different from the ministerial statements issued by the governments of Prime Ministers Mikati and [Fouad] Siniora.[12]

For example—and so that you can be sure that the international community is not only unjust, but an intriguer as well—in Article 49 Larsen says: "The government of Lebanon has assured me that it remains committed to the implementation of all provisions of Resolution 1559, but that it requires time." It means that the Lebanese government has assured him of the fact, but that it simply needs more time. I would like here to ask Mr. Larsen, which Lebanese government gave him this assurance—Prime Minister Mikati's or Siniora's? There was nothing of the sort in the two ministerial statements, so which government gave this assurance and made this undertaking?[13]

With these words, Mr. Larsen wants to tell us in Hezbollah, and tell the Palestinians, that we have been made fun of and that our time has been wasted—we who agreed to hold an internal Lebanese dialogue, agreed to protect Lebanon and the weapons of the resistance, and to hold a Lebanese–Palestinian dialogue regarding Palestinian weapons outside the camps and,

---

12 Najib Mikati (1955–) served as interim prime minister from April to July 2005, after which time he handed over power to Fouad Siniora (1943–). See above, p. 335, n. 1 for Siniora.

13 See above, p. 345, n. 12.

the control of those weapons inside the camps. He incites us against the government, incites the Palestinians against the government, and betrays government officials by claiming that they told him one thing and told us another. The position adopted by the Council of Ministers yesterday, or what was reported concerning positions taken at the Council of Ministers, to a large extent stops such incitement and fomentation dead in their tracks.

When Mr. Larsen says that he was promised that an internal dialogue would be held regarding the final outcome of Resolution 1559, what good will participating in such a dialogue do for us in the resistance? Why should we hold a dialogue at all? And why should the Palestinians hold a dialogue if it will only lead to one conclusion—that of disarming them? Some may say to us, Why hold a dialogue at all if the result is to maintain the weapons of the resistance? We never put forward such a proposition; we simply say, let us hold a dialogue on how to protect Lebanon. Does the resistance have a specific role to play and a task to perform, or not? We will decide what to do with the weapons on this basis.

Mr. Larsen, however, says that he was assured about the full implementation of all provisions of Resolution 1559, but that the matter would be settled through internal dialogue. Mr. Larsen also says, "The Prime Minister has informed me that he will also, as a first step, seek to establish order and control over such armed Palestinian groups inside the camps," meaning the control of weapons inside the camps. If this is the first step, what will be the second? Larsen also raises the issue of the demarcation of the Lebanese–Syrian borders; this is what he wants, and he insists on this demand in spite of the current tension between Lebanon and Syria. Why does he do that?[14]

What does it mean when Larsen praises the deployment of Lebanese troops along the borders with Syria? What does it means when he praises the besieging of Palestinian positions outside the camps? Larsen and his masters' ultimate aim is the disarming of the resistance and the Palestinians in Lebanon—the camps' modest weapons that help protect the Palestinians in their camps and protect their honor after [their] having gone through so

14. Although Syria had stated publicly that the Shebaa Farms were in fact Lebanese, it had refused to clearly demarcate the border area in general—a point that greatly hampered any renewed UN examination of the issue, since the UN had earlier determined the area to be Syrian, but under Israeli occupation.

much pain and suffering. Even if we disregard the issue of the Shebaa Farms, the weapons of the resistance will still be justified by the ongoing Israeli threat to Lebanon. This is unacceptable to the United Nations.

Brothers and sisters, look at the yardstick that the international community uses. Hezbollah, Lebanon, and the Palestinians in Palestine are forbidden to have modest weapons to defend themselves, their country, and their homeland. This is deemed a violation of laws and sovereignty, and should therefore be eliminated, in spite of their having said that our land, country, security, and sovereignty are threatened. At the same time, they are tight-lipped about Israel's 200 nuclear warheads, under the pretext that it is under threat. If Israel is threatened, it is alright for it to have nuclear weapons in violation of all international laws and conventions; it is alright for it to join the International Atomic Energy Agency, and it is alright if does not sign the Nuclear non-Proliferation Treaty regarding weapons of mass destruction. Why? Because Israel is threatened. But the Palestinians, who are being slaughtered in Palestine every day, are not threatened; the Lebanese, whose land Israel has invaded and might invade again one of these days, are not threatened, and have no right to own weapons.

He who does not respect the will of the Lebanese people when they say that Hezbollah is a resistance movement and not a militia; he who deals with them arrogantly, and objects to their point of view regarding the Lebanese identity of Shebaa Farms and the legitimacy of the resistance; and he who considers the presence of Hezbollah's resistance a violation of international resolutions, is on Mr. Larsen's side and in favor of the international tutelage which is as clear as the sun, and cannot be denied. It imposes its will, classifies people, passes judgment, differentiates, decides on the details, and follows up on the smallest Lebanese issues. Is this what sovereignty means? Is this real independence? Is this freedom? Is this what the Lebanese seek and aspire to?

Let us now turn to another important, ominous, and sensitive issue—that of the assassination of the martyred Prime Minister Rafik Hariri, the Mehlis report, and positions for or against Syria. When I addressed you during the March 8 demonstration—which the Mehlis report said was attended by 1 million people, and therefore was not a demonstration by one party, one faction or one sect—I was speaking on behalf of all the forces that participated in that demonstration.

We said at the time that we all condemn this assassination, and call for a serious and genuine judicial investigation. We all want the truth to be revealed and the culprits to be punished, regardless of who they are; the Lebanese were unanimous behind these demands, and there was no disagreement among them there. I also said, out of respect for the truth, for the blood of the martyred prime minister, and for Lebanon, that we must not allow the crime or the investigation to be exploited for political purposes. Some misunderstood what I said, and thought that we wanted to protect or defend someone; all we wanted was the truth, because politicization would squander the truth, while a serious technical investigation would lead us to it.

To avoid politicizing the issue, we called for the formation of a Lebanese–Saudi joint investigation committee and, after that, for an Arab investigation committee within the framework of the Arab League. Instead, an international investigation committee was proposed. We expressed reservations, and said candidly that we feared politicization, squandering of the truth, and opening of the door for the United States and others to conclude deals or impose conditions that serve their own purpose, at the expense of martyred Prime Minister Rafik Hariri's blood. The committee was formed and started its work; we kept silent out of respect for the will of some Lebanese—not a small number of them—and the feelings and wishes of martyred Prime Minister Rafik Hariri's family. We all waited for Judge Mehlis's report on October 21.

Something akin to a state of emergency was declared in Lebanon, as if another earthquake was expected. We were told that the October 21 report would reveal the whole truth to the world, supported by concrete, irrefutable, and tangible evidence. In Lebanon, Syria, and the entire Arab and Islamic world, the people waited with bated breath. We were, however, surprised when the Israeli media started talking about the contents of Mr. Mehlis's report even before it reached Mr. Kofi Annan, the Lebanese government, or members of Security Council. Unfortunately, all the information disclosed by the Israeli media regarding the contents of the Mehlis report turned out to be correct. The big question, however, is: How is it possible that information about such a sensitive, important, and serious report and its contents reaches the Israelis before it does the United Nations and the Lebanese government?

362

We were then surprised to find out that there were two different versions of the report: one was leaked by the British mission, and contained names, and the other was officially announced by UN secretary-general Kofi Annan.[15] This caused some embarrassment for Mehlis the next day, when he fumbled his answers in front of the press, making him appear confused, imprecise, and lacking in credibility. Anyway, the report was published in the media; we all read it, scrutinized it, and bided our time.

The next day, October 22, our brother Sheikh Saad Hariri gave a televised address in which he said, "The results which the international investigation commission has arrived at will not be the object of internal or external bargaining, because the blood of the Lebanese and of Rafik Hariri and his colleagues, as of today, is not subject to bargaining, nor will it become the object of political bartering." He added, "We will not allow this blood to become the tool of political or non-political revenge in other arenas."

Brothers and sisters, I am not simply being courteous when I say that these are responsible, rational, and carefully chosen words. However, regardless of our evaluation of the report, let us look at what has taken place since October 21. How did the American administration and others, including Israel, deal with it, and how did they use the outcome of this still unfinished investigation for their own political purposes? Gentlemen, has the American, Israeli, and international political punishment not already started, in more than one arena, specifically on Syria, Lebanon, and the Palestinians? The American administration—from Bush to Rice, and others—raised hell, and said that the report proved that Syria was involved in the assassination, and that the Security Council must immediately hold Syria to account and impose sanctions on it.

Brothers and sisters, for the Americans the investigation has reached its conclusion; there is therefore neither need to wait until December 15, nor for the Lebanese government to reopen the investigation after December 15.[16] The Americans consider the investigation over and done with, and have already apportioned blame; they acted as both prosecutors and judges.

15 Nasrallah is referring to a leaked draft of the Mehlis Report, which was widely circulated by the Lebanese and international media, and which allowed Microsoft Word users to reveal changes made to the document—including changes that eliminated specific names.

16 The date by which a second report from UN Investigator Mehlis was expected to be submitted to the secretary-general.

They have already convicted Syria, those detained in Lebanon, and all the other suspects,[17] and all that the UN Security Council needs to do now is to pass sentences on them. Had it not been for a number of rational international and Arab positions—and I believe that the family of the martyred Prime Minister Rafik Hariri and many among the March 14 forces reject this interpretation and this political punishment—had it not been for all these positions, the United States would have gone to the Security Council to declare war on Syria and its friends and allies, because, according to it, there was irrefutable and iron-clad evidence that [Syria] had committed this heinous crime.

The Americans did all that although the Mehlis report concludes with the following three lines: "The Commission is of course of the view that all people, including those charged with serious crimes, should be considered innocent until proven guilty following a fair trial."

As far as America is concerned, they have already been convicted, and must be punished without argument, despite the fact that the report says that the investigation is not yet over and requires months, maybe even years, to be completed. The report also uses words like "supposedly," "assumes" or "does not assume," "it may be" and "probably," and avoids the use of final, decisive, and definitive language; it also does not offer tangible, clear or direct evidence to support some of its conclusions. In fact, all that the report was able to put forward were suspicions that could be used as a starting point in the investigation. Though these suspicions might stand or fall in a serious and genuine investigation, the US administration behaves as though the truth has already been revealed, the issue clarified, [as though] it is time to specify the punishment that should be meted out to Syria, and [as though] it should be implemented forthwith.

Brothers and sisters, today is Jerusalem Day, the day of the truth; in this month and on this day no free person, rational believer, or fasting and

17 According to a June 2006 UN Security Council report, "On 30 August [2005], three suspects were arrested: Brigadier General Jamil al-Sayyed, the head of the Lebanese general security; General Ali al-Hajj, the head of the former Lebanese internal security forces; and General Raymond Azar, former Lebanese military intelligence head. At the same time, Mustafa Hamdan, the head of the presidential guard handed himself in. A fifth former Lebanese security official, Ghassan Tufeili, was arrested in November after he was named in the Mehlis report. All five had close ties with Syria. To date, they are still detained in Lebanon." http://www.securitycouncilreport.org/site/c.glKWLeMTIsG/b.1714865/k.6929/June_2006BRLebanon_UNIIIC.htm.

praying Muslim could ask for justice to be delivered through unfair and erroneous means. A report that seeks justice is the result of a serious and professional investigation that avoids politicization and seeks the truth; an investigation that rejects bargaining, deal-making, and exploitation for political ends. Indeed, this is the road to justice. We all support the martyred prime minister's family in its search for the truth, and stand with it in its search for justice. However, we must all reject the drive that the United States and Israel are leading to punish politically the Syrian leadership, people, state, and nation. This is what both justice and the truth require us to do.

We are seeing today the Mehlis report being used as a pretext to chastise Syria for a crime in which it has not so far been implicated, and as a means of punishing it for the political and strategic choices it has made. We in Lebanon reject this international, mainly American, incitement of the Lebanese people against Syria; we reject the slogans that replace "Israel, the enemy of God" with "Syria, the enemy of God," regardless of any emotional considerations. We also reject Lebanon's enmity towards Syria, and reject turning the latter into an enemy of Lebanon, while the Zionists count the blessings that have descended upon them from heaven these days, and hold celebrations with the expectation of major changes in Lebanon. They hope that Lebanon will enter into an era of Israeli domination, and replace its existing land borders with Syria, its gateway to the Arab world, with its borders with Palestine, as major Israeli analysts and officials have said. We reject, in principle, passing judgments on anyone in Lebanon or Syria, or on the Palestinians, without evidence and without a fair trial.

Brothers and sisters, dear Lebanese people, on this Jerusalem Day we voice our very grave concern that this sensitive and serious issue might slip out of the hands of those who seek justice for the spilled blood of their loved ones. We fear that it may be used as a lethal weapon in the big powers' game to promote their own ends and interests at the expense of Lebanon and Syria, or to impose suspect deals at the expense of Lebanon, Syria, and the blood of the martyred prime minister.

We sense here—from more than one international stance and from more than one international report—a flagrant drive towards incitement that aims at spoiling inter-Lebanese relations, Lebanese–Palestinian relations, and Lebanese–Syrian relations. For instance, why should the Mehlis report mention certain political leaders and figures by name, and present partial accounts of their testimonies, while the names of other figures and witnesses are kept secret? Why? Was it their intention to corner some of the political figures who testified ostensibly in an investigation that pretends to be professional, secret, and serious, and then present their incomplete testimonies to the world and to the Lebanese people to foment trouble, hatred, and conflict? What was the reason for that? Why were the names of political figures and parties included without any logic in the report, even though they are not directly involved in the investigation?

The report says that it found recordings of telephone conversations, and that they reveal the extent of the Syrian Intelligence services' involvement in the affairs of Lebanon. But the question is: Why choose from all these tapes only one tape or conversation with "Mr. X," whom some media later volunteered to identify as a well-known and central Shiite figure within Lebanon's political circles?[18] Do we need new groups to foment trouble between the Sunni and the Shia in Lebanon? And when something related to Mr. X is mentioned in the text, and it is then finalized and distributed, the Sunnis will be told, "Look what the Shia Mr. X has said"? Haven't they found anything besides this one conversation, regardless of whether it is true or not, and regardless of whether Mr. X is who they said he is or not? Why this intentional move? Is it a coincidence? Is it an attempt to foment trouble between Shia and Sunni in Lebanon, or to add names to the list of targets?

Frankly speaking, and in the name of those I represent, I consider what was mentioned in the Mehlis report about Mr. X to be a great national insult, and an attempt at sectarian incitement par excellence.

Then, in a paragraph introduced into it separately, the Mehlis report moves on to the Palestinians, and speaks about the involvement of a certain Palestinian party in the assassination, and says that it lent the effort logistical support. A day or two later—perhaps hours later—Mr. Mehlis himself said in New York that this Palestinian party was not a suspect.

Yes, dear brothers and sisters, we support the continuation of the investigation, we support the demand for evidence [rather than] suppositions, hypotheses, and possibilities. But it is necessary to question and criticize this report, or any other investigation, in order first to arrive at the truth, and

18 Mr. X was widely thought to be Speaker Nabih Berri, head of the Amal Movement (for Berri, see above, p. 25 n. 4).

second to see justice done. It is unacceptable that any Lebanese who criticizes the Mehlis report becomes the target of intellectual, media, and political terrorism, as though Mehlis were a prophet and his report a sacred book. It is in the interest of revealing the truth about Prime Minister Hariri's assassination that we refute and criticize the report; we need to refute and criticize in order to arrive at the truth, so that no innocent person, regardless of who he is, is charged with crimes he has not committed. We neither accuse nor defend anyone; all we want is for this serious issue to take its natural legal course, without being exploited by the major players.

Brothers and sisters, Lebanon and Syria are facing a great and serious crisis, and an existential challenge, as a result of recent ominous developments; there are those who want to push matters towards the worst possible outcome. It is in the interest of us all in Lebanon and Syria to think, consult, and take initiatives together to prevent the United States and Israel from using the situation to their advantage—and at the same time, provide the right climate for a serious investigation that will reveal the entire truth. This will serve two purposes: to prevent the exploitation of this issue, and to allow us to cooperate in finding a suitable and genuine opportunity for a serious investigation that will lead us to the truth.

We call upon the Arab League to intervene forthwith, before it is too late—as [was the case] in Iraq—and launch a serious Arab initiative to address all pending issues in relation to the investigation, and [in relation] to bilateral ties between Syria and Lebanon. Major Arab states, such as Saudi Arabia and Egypt, should shoulder big responsibilities in this domain; they cannot stand idly by and abandon Lebanon and the region into the hands of the American masters. What would be the result of an eventual hegemony by the American overlord in our region? It would be anarchy, infighting, destruction, ruin, disputes, sedition, division, and the realization of Israel's interests. Lebanon cannot be left to the whim of the international community, which will exploit its troubles and tragedies to achieve aims that that have nothing to do with the country's interests.

Brothers and sisters, in conclusion, in all sincerity and courage, and with a sense of responsibility, we wish to stress the following. We reject any attempt at pitting the Lebanese people against each other; we are committed to national unity, cooperation, brotherhood, and the extended hand. We reject any attempt to incite the Lebanese against the Palestinians, and vice versa; we insist on dialogue, and denounce any measures that could cause them harm. We reject any attempt at inciting the Lebanese against the Syrians, and vice versa, because, whether we like it or not, we share a common fate in this region, and because the ultimate aim is to foment internal strife to benefit Israeli interests.

We call for the solution of our problems—as Lebanese, Palestinians, Syrians, and Arabs—through dialogue, cooperation, and constructive initiatives, and by avoiding the use of force or the undertaking of negative actions. We emphasize our demand for, and desire to see, the truth revealed. We also emphasize our demand for justice, and our unanimous resolve to see it done.

We stress, with utmost clarity, our solidarity with Syria's leadership and people against American–Zionist intentions, and their attempts to punish it politically. Syria is being punished because it stands by Lebanon and its resistance, because it refuses to conclude a separate peace agreement, and because it stood with the Palestinians. Our loyalty to it demands that we stand by its side and not leave it a prey to American and Zionist ill will.

We stress our commitment at all levels to our Palestinian brethren in Lebanon—be it security, humanitarian or political—and reiterate our resolve to help them return to their homeland. We stress our determination to free every inch of our occupied land and, on this Jerusalem Day, reiterate our determination to liberate every prisoner in Israeli jails. We renew our pledge to Samir Qintar, Yahya Skaf, Nasim Niser, and all the martyrs, the missing, the prisoners, and the detainees in the jails of the occupation; God willing, we shall honor our pledge to them.

We confirm our stand with the state, the army, and all honorable Lebanese forces in the defense and protection of our country against any aggression or threat. Finally, we underline our belief that Jerusalem will return, free, proud, chaste, and purged from Zionist impurities. Our nation has offered hundreds of thousands of martyrs for Jerusalem, and great men have died on the road leading to it: Izz-al-Din al-Qassam, Fathi al-Shiqaqi, [Sheikh] Ahmad Yassin, Abd-al-Aziz al-Rantisi, Abu-Ali Mustafa, Abu Jihad al-Wazir, Abbas al-Mussawi, and Ragheb Harb.[19] Brothers, Jerusalem will not be lost

19 For al-Qassam and al-Shiqaqi, see above, p. 241 n. 20. The paraplegic Sheikh Ahmed Yassin (1937–2004), the co-founder (with Rantisi) of Hamas, was assassinated by an Israeli helicopter gunship on March 22, 2004 in Gaza City. Rantisi (1947–2004), Hamas's political leader after Yassin's death, was also assassinated by Israel on April 24, 2004, in Gaza. Mustafa (1938–2001),

as long as our nation boasts leaders such as these martyrs, and as long as the nation has men, women, children, and generations like those who have resisted and are still resisting in Lebanon, Palestine, and all over our Arab world.

On Jerusalem Day, we renew our pledge to Jerusalem, to its people, and to the cause and Imam of Jerusalem; their city will forever remain in our souls, and will continue to be our cause, our battle, and our ultimate objective.

May the peace and blessings of God be upon you.

---

the secretary-general of the Popular Front for the Liberation of Palestine, was assassinated by Israel on August 27, 2001, in the West Bank city of Ramallah. Abu Jihad (1935–1988), a co-founder of the PLO, was assassinated by Israel on April 16, 1988, in Tunisia. For Mussawi and Harb, see above, Statement 3 and p. 53 n. 8.

31

"I ASSURE YOU ONCE AGAIN [SAMIR], THAT YOUR HOPES ARE SOUND AND IN THE RIGHT PLACE"

April 24, 2006

Nasrallah's speech at a Beirut rally in support of Lebanese, Palestinian, and Arab prisoners held by Israel provided a clear indication that Hezbollah intended to carry out further capture operations as a means of bargaining for the return of Samir Qintar, the longest-held Lebanese detainee in Israel, among other prisoners identified by the party. Indeed, only five months earlier, Hezbollah had attempted one of its boldest operations in the disputed Shebaa Farms— an operation that ended disastrously in the deaths of four Hezbollah fighters at the hands of an Israeli sniper.

Still, Nasrallah's "promise" was mostly overshadowed by his comments concerning the ongoing sessions of the "National Dialogue"—an extra-legislative round table of Lebanese political leaders, including Nasrallah himself, tasked by Speaker Nabih Berri with hammering out a national consensus on the status of Palestinian armed groups in Lebanon, the formation of a national defense plan (presumably addressing Hezbollah's weapons), and a host of territorial and sovereignty issues concerning both Syria and Israel.

The sessions also reportedly dealt with the status of President Emile Lahoud, whose 2004 Syrian-extended mandate was not set to expire until 2007. Hezbollah's new ally, General Michel Aoun, had long been vying for the top Maronite post, but ever since his alliance with the March 8 camp, formalized in a written agreement between his Free Patriotic Movement and Hezbollah on February 6,[1] the pro-Western majority led by Hariri, Druze leader Walid

1. Former Lebanese army commander and acting Prime Minister and President (1988–1990) Michel Aoun (1935–) had returned to Lebanon in May, following the Syrian withdrawal in April 2005, after almost 15 years of exile in France. Although he had fought the Syrians in his self-styled "War of Liberation" towards the end of the civil war, and though his secularist Free

Jumblatt, and leader of the right-wing Lebanese Forces Samir Geagea,[2] had publicly resisted any deal giving Aoun—and now, they argued by extension, Hezbollah—the presidency.

Only 11 weeks later, however, all of these disputes, as well as the National Dialogue itself, would be subsumed—buried, at least for the moment, under the weight of a punishing 34-day war with Israel, initiated, though not consummated, by Hezbollah's "Operation True Promise."

(...) Let me seize this opportunity to tell the dean of all the detainees, the great resistance fighter and old *mujahid* Samir Qintar,[3] the following. I read your letters, especially that last one, in which you said that you are pinning your hopes on the resistance and on me personally. I assure you once again, that your hopes are sound and in their right place, and that the coming days and the spilled blood will prove me right. We look for excuses, and tell ourselves that perhaps it is the will of God that you stay where you are a

Patriotic Movement had been an integral part of the original March 14 alliance, he declined to join the electoral coalition under Saad Hariri, eventually striking an agreement with Hezbollah in February 2006, known as the "Paper of Common Understanding Between Hezbollah and the Free Patriotic Movement." See http://www.tayyar.org/files/documents/fpm-hezbollah.pdf

Almost immediately, the Understanding provided Hezbollah with the valuable sectarian cover, not to mention votes, that it needed more effectively to counter the parliamentary majority's control of the legislative and street-level political processes. This effort had become especially pressing by February 2006, as Nasrallah had only recently extricated Hezbollah and its ally Amal from a two-month-long boycott of the government. In the wake of a riot by mostly Sunni extremists the previous day in downtown Beirut—an action prompted by cartoons depicting the Prophet Mohammed that were deemed offensive, and which led to the burning of the Danish consulate—the Understanding also provided a welcome example of new efforts to establish Muslim–Christian cooperation.

Nasrallah, for his part, would consistently stress the strength of his partnership with Aoun in the coming months, proclaiming at one point during the signing ceremony at Beirut's Mar Mikhail Church that "Between Aoun and I there is transparency. Be honest and tell me I disagree with you over this and that or I want to disarm you next year ... today we created a clear document and we both have enough courage and honesty to commit to it." ("It's Official: Aoun and Hezbollah Are Allies," *YaLiban,* February 7, 2006, accessed online.)

Notwithstanding this, for Hezbollah as a political party, the Understanding was more than just a clear document or even an immediate political play. The result of months of negotiations between two parties that had long been opposed in both religion and politics, the Understanding was essentially the first comprehensive update to the party's 1992 parliamentary platform and the 1985 Open Letter respectively—even though there had been periodic predictions of just such a comprehensive effort following the Israeli withdrawal in May 2000.

2 In July 2005, an act of parliament released Geagea (see above, p. 342 n. 8) from prison, where he had been incarcerated since 1994 for the murder of several Lebanese political figures. For the Lebanese Forces, see above, p. 31 n. 19.

3 See above, p. 240, n. 18.

bit longer, so that you would remain our cause, though it will not be for much longer now. This is an apt moment for us to tell you that you are still the main cause of the Arabs, of the resistance, and of the patriots in this country of sects, most unfortunately shut off from one another. Besides being the cause of the Arab–Lebanese national struggle, you will also be the cause for the Druze in this conflict.

In this context, I do not want to omit mentioning the issue that some have raised recently regarding Lebanese nationals who either went missing or have been arrested in Syria; and I think that Syria and its leadership have dealt positively with this issue. We have already taken a number of steps, and will definitely pursue this issue further, in spite of the current contrarian mood in Lebanon. This mood sees it as our right to demand that Syria establish diplomatic relations with us, that it give us written documents proving the Lebanese identity of the Shebaa Farms, and that it agree to the redrawing of our common borders. At the same time, we want to reserve the right to attack Syria day and night, curse its leadership, and call for war and conspiracies against it, and this makes no sense at all. Those who want this accuse Syria of being negative and uncooperative, and of not dealing with them correctly over these issues. In any case, regardless of whether the political atmosphere in Lebanon is positive or negative, we shall keep on working with our brothers in Syria, and in cooperation with other Lebanese groups, to separate this purely humanitarian issue—that of the detainees and missing Lebanese nationals— from other pending issues, so that we can arrive at a conclusion.[4]

As you already know, the remains of some of the missing and detainees in Syria whose names appear on those lists, were found at various burial sites.[5] In any case, if we want to arrive at a solution, this issue has to be dealt with on a purely humanitarian basis, away from political bargaining, heated discussions, setting traps for one another, or the scoring of political points.

Let me clarify, in a few quick words, certain points relevant to the national dialogue. In the past couple of weeks, we heard certain Lebanese politicians say that "there was unanimity around the dialogue table on this or that

4 Nasrallah had only recently met for the first time with family members and leaders of the civil society group Support of Lebanese in Detention and Exile (SOLIDE), whose main focus was gaining the release of Lebanese presumed held in Syrian prisons.

5 Likely a reference to the recent discovery of human remains in and around former Syrian military and intelligence facilities in Lebanon.

point," and started imagining meetings that never took place, announced them to the world, and sought its reaction to them. I will mention one such example: they said that there was unanimity regarding the need to redraw the borders with Syria. In fact, there was nothing of the sort. On the contrary, the issue that took the most time around the table was that of redrawing the borders. However, I wish to urge the Lebanese people and their political leaders not to keep making mistakes, or add more to the ones that have already been made. All the issues on which there was agreement at the national dialogue were officially announced by Speaker Nabih Berri, whom we all acknowledge as the national dialogue's official spokesperson. Read the texts of Speaker Berri's announcements; is there anything there regarding redrawing the borders?

I told my colleagues around the dialogue table, on more than one occasion, that we have a firm patriotic, ideological, and political position regarding the redrawing of the borders while there is still an occupation in place, regardless of whether satellites can draw borders or not. I said that repeatedly, and this is why we took the decision to change the term "redrawing" to "delineating" the Shebaa Farms area, which means a general specification of their location.[6] After liberation, we can redraw every valley, mountain, hilltop, and palm tree between the Syrians and us.

The first step, therefore, is to delineate the area of the Farms, since we have not yet agreed on redrawing borders, although they still repeat on a daily basis that "the Lebanese are unanimous on this, and Syria refuses to comply with this unanimity." I do not want to mention other examples to avoid any misunderstandings, but this is a clear example of something we heard a lot about in the past few days (...)

Regarding the search for the weapons of the resistance, if we want to arrive at a solution and avoid going around in circles, we should not discuss this issue based on the premise that we—or at least some of us—have made commitments and undertakings to international parties that we would like to keep. This will guarantee that we will never arrive at a solution, because sitting around the dialogue table with such a pre-commitment will lead us nowhere. Are we not talking today about freedom, sovereignty, and independence?

I can say without hesitation that we are among those who approach these

6 For the Shebaa Farms, see above, p. 240 n. 17.

issues, as God only knows, with a patriotic mindset, and that our only yardstick is Lebanon's best interest, as we see it; let us all approach issues with this spirit. When we resume our dialogue, we should be able to discuss the resistance's weapons with a patriotic mindset and spirit; this is why we stated that we were ready to discuss anything. We could easily have said, from the very first day, that we are not ready to talk about it, that these weapons are a sacrosanct issue, that Israel is the aggressor, that our weapons will remain where they are, and that we do not intend to discuss them; what we said, instead, was that we were ready for dialogue. With the signing of the understanding between Hezbollah and the Free Patriotic Movement, there is now a clear statement that, after the Shebaa Farms and the prisoner issues, we should attend to the issue of Lebanon's strategic national defense.

The big question here is, How do we protect Lebanon? The fact that opinion polls conducted in Lebanon indicate that the people consider Israel to be the enemy of course means that the majority believes that Israel still has designs on Lebanon, and therefore poses a threat to it. Given that the majority believes that Israel still poses a threat to Lebanon, the question is therefore, How do we protect this country?

A few days ago, a suicide bomber from the Islamic Jihad movement carried out an operation in Tel Aviv, and for many hours after that, as has often happened in the past, a number of Israeli officials and some Israeli media accused Hezbollah of being behind it.[7] They said that Hezbollah sent a group of people into occupied Palestine, specifically to the West Bank, and that these [people] went later on to Tel Aviv, which explains why the Israeli Intelligence Service did not discover them earlier. What they are saying, in other words, is that since it is impossible for a Palestinian to go over the [West Bank] wall and overcome all the measures that Israel has put in place, Hezbollah must be the perpetrator. We had nothing to do with this incident, and do not have the honor of claiming responsibility for it.

In 1982, the Israelis attacked and invaded Lebanon before they even knew who had shot their ambassador in London—who, by the way, survived the attack.[8] Lebanon is under threat regardless of whether the Shebaa Farms is an issue or not.

7 A reference to the April 17 suicide bombing by Islamic Jihad and Al-Aqsa Martyrs Brigade at Tel Aviv's old central bus station, which killed 11 Israelis and wounded 60 others.

8 See above, p. 251 n. 10.

How do we defend our country? Will going back to the Armistice Agreement of 1949 protect Lebanon and its people? Are international guarantees, given by Bush, Blair or anyone else, sufficient to protect Lebanon? Let us debate whether Lebanon's security can be guaranteed by military alliances and mutual defense pacts, just like the one Israel has with the United States, which undertook publicly to defend Israel. Every two or three days, George Bush makes a speech in which he renews this public undertaking. What and who will protect Lebanon? Its own military power? It would be great if this was possible, but what and who is this military power? Is it the army? How so? Is it the army and the resistance together? How so? If we agree that it is the army and the resistance, we should bear in mind that there are people who are afraid of the resistance. How do we eliminate their fears? The resistance is one-colored. How do we make it multicolored? If we approach the negotiations with this spirit, we will arrive at a solution, because we will all be working towards the same objective, which is how to best protect our country and people. At the end of the day, we are not discussing a philosophical treatise, but a subject in which we have a lot of human and hands-on experience, and a situation we have lived under together for many years. Let us take these experiences, study them well, and then use them to resolve the issue of Lebanon's strategic national defense.

The final point concerns the issue of the presidency of the republic. We debated this issue in the national dialogue, and part of what we said was leaked to the press. Is there a particular mechanism we can adopt to discuss this issue? Some people suggested conducting an opinion poll to find out what the Lebanese people really want; and if we do not trust our local polling organizations enough, we could commission five Western polling organizations to conduct a survey each, and then designate whoever gets the highest score in all five surveys. This suggestion, however, was rejected, despite being quite practical. They said, "Lebanon's sectarian make-up is well known; some people did not want the current speaker of parliament to be elected speaker again, but you Shia said that you wanted him in that post, and got your way. Why aren't we Christians allowed to elect the president of the republic?" We told them, "the Shiites have unanimously chosen Mr. Nabih Berri as speaker of the National Assembly, and we had no problem doing that; now you, as Christians of Lebanon, are welcome to meet and unanimously decide on your choice for president of the republic, and we will support that choice." They said that this was correct in theory, but where would that unanimity come from?

The third option is for us to discuss a list of various names. We told them: let us sit down together at that table and discuss names; they refused, and asked for more time to undertake backstage negotiations.

We had a stake in these negotiations, and therefore got involved in them; and when you heard about four and five hours of discussions, we were actually debating very sensitive issues. Our brother, Sheikh Saadeddin al-Hariri,[9] in his capacity as the leader of the largest bloc in parliament, held talks with me, with His Excellency Mr. Nabih Berri, and with others, and it is his full right to be the focus of these negotiations. We held bilateral and trilateral rounds of negotiations, though we will keep their gist to ourselves.

What I would like to clarify today is that Hezbollah has so far not nominated a candidate in any of those side negotiations, be they bilateral, tripartite, quadripartite, five-party, small or large. We did not do so because we are not the real majority in the National Assembly; we are not the ones who should suggest a name, but those to whom a name should be suggested for discussion, in our capacity as a parliamentary bloc.

We then started to hear in the media that we, as a party, had suggested this or that name; this is not true. We suggested no names, although some names were indeed suggested to us; and while we rejected some of them, we said that some others were negotiable. In the past two weeks, some of the February 14 personalities, and members of the media, addressed themselves to the Free Patriotic Movement saying, "See how Hezbollah and the Amal Movement refused to nominate General Aoun to the presidency of the republic?"[10] They concocted stories and gossip around this issue, with the aim of sowing discord between the party and the [Amal] Movement, on the one hand, and the Free Patriotic Movement on the other. At that time, a sort of clear realignment was underway around the dialogue table, and some people thought it vital for their interests to drive a wedge between

9 For Saad Hariri, see above, p. 355.

10 Subsequent to the Understanding between Hezbollah and the Free Patriotic Movement—the latter having been an integral part of the million-person, March 14, 2005, protest and, for a time, the March 14 alliance—opposition parties insisted on referring to the remaining March 14 parties as the February 14 forces, in a reference to the date of Rafik Hariri's assassination.

Hezbollah, Amal, and the Free Patriotic Movement, and thwart their cooperation efforts. I wish to reassert that Sheikh Saadeddin al-Hariri was not at all involved in these machinations and leaks, and that the channels of communication between us are open and respectful of each other's views.

The aim of airing these matters in the press rests on the assumption that I would approach you and ask, "Are you for or against nominating General Aoun for the presidency?" People who do such things do not really care about General Aoun or about us; they just cannot imagine for a moment that General Aoun could become president of the republic. What, then, is the real aim of these people? Their aim is that, if you said, "Yes, we would like to nominate General Aoun for the presidency of the republic", they will seize upon your words, as long as the issue is not yet serious enough and is still in the public and media domain. If you say yes, they will take down your words and your picture and send them around the world to the American Congress, the French National Assembly, the European Union, and the British, Australian, and Italian Parliaments, and say, "Look, General Aoun is Hezbollah's, the terrorist organization's candidate in Lebanon!" Therefore, we will give them an answer only once the issue becomes serious, because mere talk is fodder for the media, and mere banter.

They believe that if the party nominates General Aoun to the presidency, he will be discredited throughout the world, because that world sees Hezbollah as a terrorist organization. If, on the other hand, we say, "OK, we will not nominate General Aoun," they will turn around and tell the Free Patriotic Movement, "See—now go at each others' throats"!

I therefore call upon these politicians and media organizations to stop playing this devious game. When we see the Lebanese people sitting down together to reach an understanding, establish cooperation among themselves, and forge closer ties, we will help by telling them, "Well done!" We will sit with them, and not foment sedition among them.

Finally, I would like to say that, in any case, if the February 14 forces are sincere and convinced about nominating General Aoun to the presidency of the republic, let them say so at the dialogue table on April 28, and they will hear our answer [...]

32

INTERVIEW WITH NEW TV

August 27, 2006

Nasrallah's first interview after the UN-mandated ceasefire of August 14 that effectively ended the 34-day war with Israel was widely heralded as a frank admission that Hezbollah had made a terrible mistake in capturing two IDF soldiers and killing eight others on the morning of July 12, 2006. Overshadowed by this apparent (and later substantially qualified) mea culpa, *however, were a series of responses given by Nasrallah to questions posed by Maryam al Bassam, a reporter for the Lebanon-based New TV station, that seemed to signal some of the potent political difficulties that lay ahead for the country—difficulties greatly exacerbated by the deaths of over 1,000 Lebanese, as well as the estimated $7 to $15 billion worth of damage sustained during the war.[1]*

Among these points, Nasrallah, while accepting UN Resolution 1701's deployment of additional UNIFIL forces, as well as its call for Lebanese army control in south Lebanon, made clear that Hezbollah would remain armed in the south and elsewhere, though hidden from view: "No logic," he tells Bassam, "says Hezbollah can get out of the area south of the Litani River." In a clear indication to domestic forces that had been privately—and at

---

1 As it had after previous conflicts, Hezbollah would later claim that government estimations of the war damage were grossly overstated, perhaps, Nasrallah himself argued, as a means of frightening the population and lining certain government pockets at the same time. As far as casualties were concerned, by late December 2006, *Associated Press* reported that, "More than 1,000 Lebanese civilians and combatants died during the summer war between Israel's army and Hezbollah guerrillas, according to tallies by government agencies, humanitarian groups and *The Associated Press*. Israeli authorities put the death toll for the Jewish state at 120 military combat deaths and 39 civilians killed by Hezbollah rockets fired into northern Israel during the July 12–14 Aug conflict. Both sides have revised their figures of Lebanon's war dead. The latest Lebanese and *AP* counts include 250 Hezbollah fighters that the group's leaders now say died…" "Lebanon Sees More Than 1,000 War Deaths,"*Associated Press*, December 28, 2006, accessed online. Additionally the Lebanese and Israeli governments estimated that the July War displaced 974,184 Lebanese and 300,000–500,000 Israelis.

times publicly—calling for Hezbollah's disarmament during the war, Nasrallah also warned that the party "could have staged a military coup and taken control of the country" if it had wanted to, but that it essentially chose not to follow this path. To this he added another contentious point: that Hezbollah's alliance with General Michel Aoun's Free Patriotic Movement implicitly meant the party enjoyed substantial support in the Christian street since, as Nasrallah claimed, Aoun represented "75 percent of the Christians today." As the FPM was not a part of the Lebanese government, Nasrallah argued further that its absence meant the government was essentially unrepresentative.

In all these points, Nasrallah lays out the basic contours of a political struggle that would only grow more divisive and dangerous in the coming period. Indeed, three months later, Hezbollah' and Amal's cabinet ministers, in addition to one Christian minister, would resign their posts, ostensibly over the process governing the Hariri tribunal, but more than this over the division of political power—both internationally recognized and otherwise—in a country that seemed destined to remain on the fault line of Middle East policy and praxis well into the future.

NEW TV: *All of a sudden I found myself face-to-face with the master of all events. They told me the interview would take place now, and the rest would be left to Hezbollah, as usual. How can this take place if I have not yet written the sweetest of words to Al Sayyed [Nasrallah]? I have not sent him the mothers' letters, which were perfumed with the scent of their martyred sons. Also I have not yet written to him about the days we lived during the war, dreaming of meeting with him. I spent every minute of the 34 days preparing an introduction to al-Sayyed in the hope of meeting him during the war; but here I am face-to-face with him at a time that is described as one of fragile peace. Your Eminence, you are welcome on New TV. I will begin from where I ended. Are we at peace? What about the Israeli exaggeration and some international talk about a second round of war against Lebanon? The latest words on this subject were spoken by Terj Roed-Larsen.[2]*

HN: In the name of God, the merciful, the compassionate. First of all, and in the name of the resistance, I would like to thank you as well as the television management and all workers, journalists, and media men in this establishment for the great efforts you made during the war. You, just like other institutions—to be fair to all—were our voice and the voice of the

2 For Roed-Larsen, see above, p. 343 n. 9.

resistance men and steadfast people who want glory, dignity, and loftiness for this country. Of course, any words of thanks to you, and all those who acted in solidarity with the resistance in this war, fall short of what should be said, but they must be said. Thank you.

NEW TV: *We consider this a national duty.*

HN: God bless you. As for the current or next stage, I do not think there will be a second round, for several reasons which I could address. Larsen's words seek to sow fear. It is very regrettable that Mr. Larsen's role is evident.

NEW TV: *Who does this role serve?*

HN: It clearly serves the Israelis. This is regrettable. I do not know if the Israelis asked him to scare the Lebanese government and people. He sometimes expresses a personal opinion which he thinks may benefit the Israelis. My information, and not only my interpretation, says the purpose of his words was to scare the Lebanese. This is the way I understand things, because certain issues continued to be discussed during the time between the cessation of military activities and the so-called ceasefire, and there were new Israeli conditions. There is an attempt to impose these conditions. For example, deploying international forces on the Lebanese–Syrian border is an Israeli demand. Another example is that, instead of deploying in the south, UNIFIL is required to be stationed at the airport and ports. This is also an Israeli demand. There is a host of Israeli demands that were not achieved over the past stage. Currently, pressure is being exercised on the Lebanese government to get it to succumb to these demands.

Currently there is no war, but there is exaggerated talk about a new war or second round, so that the Lebanese will be frightened and say, "What will keep the specter of war away from us? Will UN troops on the border between Lebanon and Syria do this? That will be alright. Do they want to come to the airport and ports? They are welcome." This means submission is demanded. I view all that was said in this context. What makes me say Larsen might have coordinated this issue with the Israelis is that, on the second or third day, a Dutch minister came and conveyed a message. I read this in the press. I do not know if that was accurate or not. He conveyed a message from the Israelis and said there is no second round. Who shall we believe? I, of course, believe the Dutch minister, because events confirmed what he conveyed.

First, in the field, the Israelis are daily withdrawing and reducing the number of their soldiers and tanks. By the way, they are present at limited points. This presence is decreasing daily. If they have plans for a second round, they would reinforce their presence in these areas, not reduce it. Second, their evacuees are returning. They also had evacuees in this war. The people of Haifa and the north returned to their cities, towns, settlements, and factories. The head of the enemy government toured these areas. He reassured the people and said the central goal of his government now is rebuilding the north. The one who acts in this way does not plan to start a second round. Third, the internal political situation in the enemy's entity, including the military situation and the situation of the army and generals, makes me say the overall current Israeli situation and available facts confirm that we are not heading towards a second round.

NEW TV: *What about the daily Israeli provocations? There are landing operations and abductions of civilians from their homes. This is in addition to the usual air, sea, and ground violations. Are these meant to prompt you to reply? Why do you not reply? Who do you fear? There is a reason to reply, but why do you not reply?*

HN: Since the cessation of military activity—that is, since Monday—we have acted. We of course are not mercenaries, militias, or an armed organization isolated from the people. The people are our people and kinfolk. When the evacuees returned to their villages and towns, our priority became the restoration of the social situation and giving the people time to breathe and feel comfortable. There is also a resolution on the cessation of military activity. We believe that war as an open war ended on Monday. Between the end of war on Monday and the ceasefire—whose time has still not been determined, because certain conditions have been set for it—it was clear that the Israelis were proceeding along two lines. The first meant to provoke us so that we would be dragged into a confrontation. This would depict us as violating Resolution 1701. Of course, there is a big difference.

When the Israelis conducted the landing in Buday there was no international reaction, and since they were the ones who violated the resolution, there was no international reaction.[3] The Americans and many Western countries did not speak up. The UN reaction was very subdued. The whole world remained silent. In contrast, if a much smaller violation is committed by us in response to an attack, the whole international community will raise a hue and cry and say: These people seek war and do not want peace, calm, or stability for Lebanon. Consequently, this reaction might then open the door for a renewed discussion of Bush's attempt to issue a second resolution on the resistance weapons, and other similar things. We, for more than one reason, said, let us exercise self-restraint at this stage, and not be provoked. It was clear that the Israelis were trying to drag us into a certain confrontation.

The second track on which the Israelis worked was that the resolution— and this is one of our reservations about the resolution—gave them the right to act under the pretext of self-defense. Their idea is that when the war stops and the evacuees do not return, the displaced will remain outside their houses, and this will put pressure on the resistance to accept new conditions. At the same time, the Israelis will take their time to carry out some security operations. True, it was a landing operation, but its aim was related to security. They wanted to kidnap or kill a leading Hezbollah figure.

The first landing operation after Monday—that is, after the end of the war—was carried out in Buday, but it did not achieve its aim, which was killing or kidnapping the leading Hezbollah figure. The second point is that the landing operation commander, who was a high-ranking officer in the Israeli paratrooper and special forces, was killed.

NEW TV: *They said some resistance men were also martyred.*

HN: No, there were no martyrs. A young man was slightly wounded. The clash took place at close range, and our men took them by surprise. The

---

3 Nasrallah is referring to a raid by Israeli commandos deep into eastern Lebanon more than five days after the international ceasefire was accepted by all parties. The raid may have been designed to capture a top Hezbollah commander, although Israel claimed at the time that their actions were designed to interdict weapons allegedly being smuggled into Lebanon from Syria in violation of UNSCR 1701's ban on weapons transfers to non-governmental entities.

officer was therefore killed during the first moments of the clash, and not later. When this loss and this failure occurred, they stopped their landing operations. I have no knowledge of any landing operations after the Buday landing. What stopped the landings were the failures and the losses of the Israeli side, not the international denunciations, which were never issued. What stopped them were their failures and their losses. They failed to achieve their goal and lost.

The Israelis are still present around some towns. They try to enter a house at night, or cut the road between one village and another, or kidnap civilians. This has to do with our policy for the current stage. Actually, we want the government to assume its responsibility at this stage. Is it not the government that says it is the one which wants to protect the citizens? [...]

NEW TV: *What about the Shebaa Farms?*

HN: Shebaa Farms are another issue. This is one of the outstanding issues related to national rights. When we expressed reservations about Resolution 1701, we said this resolution did not give Lebanon its national rights or the minimum of its national demands. With the exception of the issue of Shebaa Farms, which is a special one, and in connection with the recent war, we will consider it our right to fight Israel in any position it occupies. As for when and how to fight it, this is up to the resistance command.

NEW TV: *How will Hezbollah perform in the presence of the Lebanese army and UNIFIL troops?*

HN: [...] I said during the war that we trust the army and its command. It is obvious that the main and primary task of an army that goes to the border area upon a cabinet decision is defending the homeland. We will facilitate the work of the army and extend all support and backing to it. We said this in the media and communicated it to the army command. We will refrain from doing anything that will embarrass the army. When the army is fully deployed on the border, it will be in charge of confronting any ground violation, but in response to a political decision. It will assume this respon-sibility. The resistance will support the army ...

NEW TV: *Kofi Annan yesterday defined the task of this [UNIFIL] force. He said its task is not to disarm Hezbollah.*

HN: This is because all the US pressure was in this direction. As you know, at first there was no talk about the UNIFIL or reinforcing it. There was much talk about a multinational force under Chapter Seven [of the United Nations Charter]. The task of the multinational force under Chapter Seven—a force we rejected and considered to be an occupation force—was not protecting Lebanon against any Israeli aggression, but striking at, disarming, and terminating the resistance. This means doing what Israel could not do. The task of UNIFIL today is not disarming the resistance. As long as this is not its task, and as long as its main task is backing the Lebanese army—and we approve of and support the role played by the Lebanese army—I do not think there will be any problem at all in the area south of the [Litani] river, and all areas where the army or UNIFIL are deployed.

NEW TV: *What if something happens in the south—like an Israeli provocation—that requires Hezbollah's intervention, although the army is there? Will the army also defend the country?*

HN: The army's duty, as defined by the Council of Ministers, is to defend the homeland, protect citizens, their properties, and means of living, and to preserve security. The people used to go and tour the entire south even before 12 July. Did anyone see a person wearing a military uniform or carrying a Kalashnikov or wireless radio? There was nothing of the sort. The young people in the south are the people of the south. I recall that, in the negotiations that took place here, some said the Israeli occupation army should withdraw behind the Blue Line,[4] and Hezbollah should withdraw north of the Litani River. I used to tell them that I understood that the Israeli army should withdraw behind the Blue Line, because it is first and foremost a regular army, as well as a foreign occupation force, and must leave our territories. I asked them to tell me how Hezbollah could withdraw from the area south of the river. The people of Ayta were resisting in Ayta, and the people of Bint Jbeil were resisting in Bint Jbeil. The same applies

4 See above, p. 250, n. 8.

to the people of al-Khiam, al-Tayyibah, Mays, and all towns that fought.[5] I do not want to continue naming towns, as I may remember some and forget others, and they will then blame me. All the young men who fought on the front, and even rear lines in the area south of the river, are the people of these areas. They were not recruited from other areas. Can I tell the people of Ayta: the Israelis could not force you out of your town, but I will do so because a political agreement has been reached? Can I ask the people of Ayta to live in Nabatieh? The people of Hezbollah are the people of the region. No logic says Hezbollah can get out of the area south of the Litani River.

By the way, there is a funny thing. I do not know if there will be a chance to talk about this in this discussion. I am one of the people who believed before the war that Israel had [positive] points that could be discussed, although it is an enemy. I once said I respect my enemy for such things as caring for its prisoners and dead. One of the things we suspected in the past was that the Israeli media was credible. For example, when we carried out operations before 2000, and even limited operations afterwards, the young men used to say, for example, that they had killed six Israeli soldiers [in an operation]; but the Israelis would say only two had been killed. We said our men might have miscalculated the number, as the Israelis usually admitted the number of their killed soldiers. In this war, I discovered that the Israeli is a big liar in all that he says, talks about, and claims, and tells a lot of lies. This is proved by the fact that [Amir] Peretz, [Ehud] Olmert, [Tzipi] Livni and all Israeli officials throughout the past period said and continue to say, "We will not allow Hezbollah to return to south Lebanon."[6] Has Hezbollah left south Lebanon in order to say you will not allow it to return? Hezbollah is present north and south of the river. True, you carried out landing operations and reached hilltops here and there, but Hezbollah was still in the border villages. We have not left south Lebanon or the areas south of the Litani River to wait for permission from anybody to return to the areas south of the river. We are present there. The army's duty is therefore to

---

5 A reference to "frontline" towns and villages in south Lebanon that were the sites of major battles during the Summer 2006 Israeli invasion. The town of Bint Jbeil was the location of fierce fighting between Hezbollah and the Israeli military. Dozens were killed and injured on both sides, and much of the town was reduced to rubble.

6 A reference to Israeli Defense Minister Amir Peretz (1952–), Israeli Premier Ehud Olmert (1945–), and Israeli Foreign Minister Tzipi Livni (1958–).

protect people. Very frankly speaking, we will not be responsible when the army assumes responsibility.

NEW TV: *It is said for some reason that the Lebanese army overlooks Hezbollah's practices.*

HN: Let us be clear. The Lebanese army's duty is not to disarm the resistance or gather information about the resistance's weapons.

NEW TV: *How will the army act if it sees armed Hezbollah fighters or military equipment, although Hezbollah is invisible in the south and even Israel cannot see it? There are fears.*

HN: No, there is no reason for any fear in this regard, whether the army is there or not; this, however, becomes certain in the presence of the army. I took measures before the army's deployment in the border area. These measures said that there should be no armed manifestations at all. One of the reasons for the success of our resistance, its popularity, and its acceptance by the people, is that it avoids armed manifestations, and does not show off in mobilization, fighting, preparedness, presence, or even the burial of martyrs. Have you seen a gun or a rifle at the funeral of any martyr? There has been nothing of the sort. This is our policy. This has become a commitment on our part towards the Lebanese army and government. There is a tacit agreement that we, south of the river, avoid armed manifestations. Suppose the army finds a person carrying a weapon on a road or in a town; the army's natural right and duty will be to confiscate the weapon and apply the law to him. We have accepted this, because this is in line with the policy we adopted before July 12. Now we have underscored this as a commitment. There is something on which we agreed, and let this be very clear. Some may go and talk. They can say whatever they want. We will not comment on every word that is said. Part of what is said does not take into consideration the morale of the resistance men, the people of the south, or the feelings of the resistance masses. But at this extraordinary and critical stage we are ignoring what is said in the same way as we are ignoring many other things. There is a very clear thing on which we agree. It is the Lebanese army, as Kofi Annan said about UNIFIL. I told some officials here to speak like Kofi

Annan. Kofi Annan says it is not the job of UNIFIL to disarm the resistance. What about the army? It is not the task of the Lebanese army to disarm the resistance or spy on its weapons or plans. Is it the task of the army to spy on us, raid us, and confiscate things? Never. This issue has been decisively settled, and it is over.

NEW TV: *What will be your position on the Shebaa Farms? Hezbollah considers these farms Lebanese territory that is occupied by Israel, and Hezbollah's resistance law applies to it.*

HN: Not only Hezbollah's law. In accordance with international law, and regardless of UN opinion about the Shebaa Farms, I said at the negotiating table—and before that, on the eve of the Israeli withdrawal from Lebanon—that it is the responsibility, duty, and right of the resistance to fight and liberate any land the Lebanese state or government considers to be occupied Lebanese land. Therefore, I told them at the dialogue table: if you really want to liberate the Shebaa Farms, let us see how we can cooperate together to do so. If you want to get rid of the Shebaa Farms issue in order to get rid of us and our weapons, you can follow another path other than asking the United Nations to recognize the farms as Lebanese, and other than continuing to hold the Syrians responsible for not giving us documents or signatures. The Lebanese government can meet and say that the Shebaa Farms are not Lebanese.

NEW TV: *But until it meets...*

HN: No, they cannot do such a thing. The government and the Chamber of Deputies said that this is Lebanese territory. Can they change their mind? This is not something that can be tampered with in this way. Let us talk about the official Lebanon, and not Hezbollah. Let us talk about the current Lebanese government. If someone from the March 14 or February 14 forces[7] comes up to say the Shebaa Farms are not Lebanese, he is free to say what he wants. The current Lebanese government, the Chamber of Deputies, and

7 A reference to key pro-government figures like Walid Jumblatt, who argued that the Shebaa issue was a joint Syrian–Iranian–Hezbollah "invention" to prolong and justify their tripartite influence in Lebanon.

the Lebanese presidency consider the Shebaa Farms Lebanese. This is then Lebanese land under occupation. If it remains occupied, the right of resistance will continue to exist. But how can the resistance exercise this right? This is up to the resistance. We must not present assurances in this regard, nor say we are heading towards a large problem. I want to be realistic in this regard. Even during the past period, if you recall, we did not carry out operations every week, every two weeks, or every month. We used to carry out an operation once every several months. We called them reminder operations. Now we will wait for some time, while reserving our natural right to exercise resistance if certain developments take place. But we can wait and tell others: please do what you can, especially since the UN secretary-general is also concerned. There is a clause in Resolution 1701 that opens a door for discussion, although it does not solve the problem. Also, the Lebanese government has great international friendships; let us see what they can do. But this does not mean the resistance is committed to the cessation of operations, or to relinquishing its right of resistance as long as even an inch of Lebanese land is under occupation.

NEW TV: *Some in Lebanon may ask if Hezbollah has not learned from this recent experience. Allow us to ask your Eminence a question that goes back to July 12. Would you have done what you did if you had known in advance what the Israeli reaction would be? There are 1 million Lebanese evacuees, huge destruction, economic losses, over 1,000 martyrs, and many wounded. It was a big disaster for Lebanon. Now you say you cannot surrender, and say operations will not completely stop. Do you not go back to that date to remember the scene, and know that any operation, particularly in the Shebaa Farms, may cost Lebanon what the last aggression cost it?*

HN: There are two points in what you say. The first is that, regardless of one's decision, no one whose land is occupied can give security assurances to the Israelis. He cannot tell them: be reassured, and continue to occupy the land, because we are not going to do anything. This is wrong. The least I can say about this is that it is wrong on the national level. Therefore, Hezbollah will neither now nor in the future be ready to make a commitment to anyone. This discussion also took place in the negotiations during the war. There was talk about respect for the Blue Line. We respect this line, but as a resistance I cannot make a commitment to the Israelis and Americans and say this issue is over. I will not make such commitments as long as there is land under occupation. As for the way we act, this is another issue. Therefore, the Shebaa Farms is an occupied land, and was so from 2000 to 2006. How did we act in this regard? This is a clear point. The second part of the question ...

NEW TV: *But how did Israel act? You have kidnapped soldiers before...*

HN: This leads to the second part of the question. Although the second part of the question is in itself a whole subject, it may not be much related to the next stage, but it can always be discussed. Whoever says that the cause of the war is the two prisoners is mistaken. Things might have been unclear during the first and second days of the war, but—as noted in Seymour Hersh's article[8] and the detailed statements by [Muhammed] Haykal, and as indicated by more than one respectable journalist in the world, more than one respectable newspaper in the United States, Britain, and Europe, and by some Lebanese political leaders who are following the developments— it became certain that the issue was not related to the two prisoners. As to whether the capture of the two was an excuse or not, I will talk about that later. The issue is that there was a war plan and a big military decision taken by the US and Israel. If they did not implement it on July 12, they would have implemented it in August, September or October.

NEW TV: *This means you fell into the trap.*

HN: No, we did not fall into the trap. The Israeli side is the one which fell into the trap, not us. I will tell you the difference.

8 Both the US investigative journalist Seymour Hersh and Egyptian journalist (and former editor-in-chief of the pro-government Egyptian daily *Al-Ahram)* Muhammad Haykal had recently contended that the 2006 Summer War between Israel and Lebanon had essentially been planned in advance, with Hersh writing in the *New Yorker* magazine that Israel had shared its plans for a massive attack on Lebanon and Hezbollah months earlier with Washington (Seymour Hersh, "Watching Lebanon," *New Yorker*, August 21, 2006). In March 2007 Olmert would reportedly tell an Israeli investigating commission that such planning had indeed been undertaken as a means of strategically exploiting a probable future Hezbollah capture along the border (see, for example, Conal Urquhart, "Israel planned for Lebanon war months in advance, PM says," *Guardian*, March 9, 2007, accessed online).

NEW TV: *We should not give the world an excuse to stand against us.*

HN: All the facts that were later collected confirmed that the military oper-ation—or rather, the large-scale war—was timed to be carried out at the end of September or early October. There are several reasons for this. Some of these reasons are related to tourism in Palestine; they are not concerned about tourism in Lebanon. They did not think of October to allow us to benefit from the tourism season in Lebanon. The tourist season in Israel is much more important than the tourist season in Lebanon. But they know that if they start such a war on the basis of general rather than accurate information about Hezbollah's missile capabilities, their tourist season will barely be hit. They will therefore benefit the tourist season.

Second, they needed to complete their arrangements and preparations. They were preparing for war at the end of September or early October. The Israelis were planning to start the war at that time, with or without an excuse. They had US approval in this regard, and some European states would be put in the picture—if they were not already in the picture. It might also obtain some Arab cover by that time, or in advance. I will stop here, and not say more than this. On that day, when Israel launches the war, it will win the world's blessings, as this war will be part of the war on terrorism. None will then ask the Israelis why they attacked Lebanon; they do not need an excuse. Even if they want an excuse on that day, they could simply carry out accurate assassinations like those carried out by the Rafeh network.[9] They can bring six or seven Katyushas and place them at night in a valley in the south, and then fire them at the northern settlements.

NEW TV: *But they can distinguish between Hezbollah's Katyushas and...*

HN: Since they are the ones doing this, they can use this as an excuse. See how we did not fall into the trap. When we moved to carry out the capture operation—and I will soon speak about our assessment, as I do not hesitate to say things frankly, the way they happened—something happened that we did not intend. We were preparing for a clean capture operation. The

9 The Rafeh network was named after Mahmoud Rafeh, (b. 1947–), a retired policeman from the Lebanese town of Hasbaya, who confessed in June 2006 to having headed an Israeli-backed spy and assassination ring since at least 1999.

operation was not decided on the spur of the moment. We prepared for it for five or six months, and we were waiting for a group [of Israeli soldiers]. We had set up our ambush, and were waiting. Civilian vehicles used to pass by our ambush, but we left them unharmed because we did not want civilians—although civilians might be military men dressed like civilians. We were waiting for a military vehicle. Two such vehicles came, and a clash erupted. We wanted to carry out a clean operation, but the field dictated otherwise, as a number of the enemy soldiers were killed or wounded. We took two prisoners. The Israelis in that area carried out a quick operation in the field. They sent a tank to chase our men. The tank rolled through a field and hit a big mine. It was not actually a mine—they call it *nasfiyah*, in which there were hundreds of kilograms of explosives. It was there, but had nothing to do with the war or operation. The tank was destroyed, and four soldiers were killed. The situation became difficult and intolerable for them, as they had eight killed, three or four wounded, and two prisoners. We cannot control the way things eventually develop.

NEW TV: *You are enlarging the issue militarily to show us that you did not fall into the trap, and that their losses were large. But your Eminence said—and now you repeat—that this was going to happen in all cases.*

HN: But I will continue to say exactly what happened.

NEW TV: *But this could have happened without giving them an excuse. Our position might have been safer in front of the international community, Kofi Annan, Rice, and the young people who were working.*

HN: Let us talk about the difference between the two pictures. On the first day, the Israelis were confused about their reaction. At night they contacted the Americans, and then they met and made a decision. The war began on the second day. This means they decided on July 12 to do then what they had wanted to do in October. But there is a big difference between doing it now and [later]. First, the October plan depended on the element of surprise. If the October plan was the one implemented, it would not be known whether we would continue to exist in order to be blamed, or blame others. The October plan was supposed to be implemented when the country was in a state of calm, and the situation was normal in the south, in the suburbs, in the Bekaa, and in all areas where Hezbollah is present. People would be living their normal lives. According to the plan, the Israelis would all of a sudden strongly attack the border area and carry out landing operations in the Litani River area. They would control the area south of the Litani River, and strike at the resistance and all its missile capability. While mounting a ground offensive, the Israeli planes would pound the Southern Suburb, all of the south, all of the Baalbek-al-Hermel area, and Hezbollah's centers, houses of Hezbollah leaders, officials, and members. They would thus destroy the command, communications, administration, and control networks. Their assessment was that Hezbollah would be completely finished within 48 hours, and that whoever stayed alive would be taken to a new Guantánamo. That was the idea, and that was what was planned, and exposed by more than one foreign journalist.

NEW TV: *Were foreigners the only ones who knew about this?*

HN: No, these were the ones who exposed it. I do not know who had knowledge of it.

NEW TV: *Were there any Lebanese elements with such knowledge?*

HN: Let us focus on the foreigners. The idea was: this is what we will do, and within 48 hours after occupying the area south of the river, we will have thus delivered a blow to the resistance by destroying the centers and the houses of the leaders and officials, and even the houses of the young members. We would have thus dismantled the party, and whoever remains alive—a person with some young men or some equipment—will be limited to individual action that cannot change the course of the war. This was the plan. What took place on July 12 cost the Israelis the element of surprise after the capturing, and after there were deaths and injuries. We took the necessary precautions; we evacuated the area, and we were on standby and at the ready. We were ready for the war when it started. The element of surprise was therefore lost.

Second, the timing that the Israelis set for the war was no longer valid, and the war started at a time that they did not want. The timing of the operation foiled the main plan that they had prepared. We waged a war today, and we would have waged a war in October, but the war in October would have had conditions that would have been much harsher and more difficult, because the Israelis would have been the ones to set the time, prepare for the war, and use the element of surprise; whereas in July, the field situation and our performance changed the whole affair. We thus carried out the confrontation, we remained steadfast, we fought, and we ended the war in the manner it ended.

There remains a part of your question that I want to clarify—namely, we are a group, not an individual. I am not the one who takes the decision to carry out the capturing operation. The group has a political leadership and a military command. There are no less than 15 individuals involved in such a decision. These 15 individuals, be they political or military elements, have long political and jihad experience, and have been the leaders of the resistance from 1982 until 2006. We have thorough knowledge of the Israelis, and of how they think about and deal with issues. Based on all past experience, we carried out operations that were much more important than the July 12 capturing operation, and these operations resulted in much bigger losses on the Israeli side, but did not lead to a war of this scale. Very clearly—and I want to say this to you and the viewers, because it has caused controversy— we did not have a 1 percent probability that the capturing operation would have led to a war on this scale. If someone asks: Why did you not have a 1 percent probability? We respond that the logic of the way things have been since 1982 and judging by Israelis' actions, based on the resistance's experience over the past decades, and our analysis of the Israelis, led us to believe that it was not possible at all, especially at this time, because they have a tourist season just as we do, and have their own conditions, just as we do. It would not have been possible for a reaction to a capturing operation to be on this scale. I am not referring to the Israelis alone, but to experience throughout history.

NEW TV: *Had this been a reaction, UN Resolution 1701 would have included a paragraph binding Hezbollah to release the two soldiers immediately, and this did not happen.*

HN: I am saying that throughout the history of war, no state has ever waged war on another state because two soldiers were captured, or three or four soldiers were killed. War was never waged for this reason. You ask me now: If there was even a 1 percent chance that the July 11 [as stated] capturing operation would have led to a war like the one that happened, would you have done it? I would say no, absolutely not, for humanitarian, moral, social, security, military, and political reasons. I would not agree to it, and neither would Hezbollah, the prisoners in Israeli prisons, nor the families of the prisoners. This is absolute. What happened is not an issue of a reaction to a capturing operation.

As far as my culture goes—and my culture may differ from that of others— I believe in God and his will, I believe that even this 1 percent chance did not occur to any of the 15 political and military individuals, despite our deep experience. I believe that there is divine will here, because if there was a 1 percent chance, we would not have carried out the capturing oper- ation; and if we had not carried out the capture, the war would not have happened in July, but would have happened in October.

NEW TV: *This is why I asked if you would keep in mind in any future operation the destruction, death, and displacement that Israel has wrought. It is as if Israel is teaching you a lesson and telling you to beware that this will be the price of anything else you do.*

HN: Do not view matters from one angle. Today, even when we talk about returning to a second round or something of the sort, when Lebanon—as a state, a people, and the resistance—wants to make any decision, it will take into consideration everything that has happened. We cannot ignore it, and say that we will behave and make decisions as if nothing has happened. I would not be a human if I behaved in such a manner. We are definitely like this, and so are the Israelis. We are always looking at what happened on our side, but we do not see what happened on the Israeli side. Israelis today—not just Olmert and Peres, but anyone who will come in a future Israeli government—will think twice and three times before waging a war with Lebanon, because what took place on the Israeli side is also historic, strategic, and big.

NEW TV: *But there is no balance between the level of terror and weapons they used.*

HN: You must look at things in relative terms. Ultimately, there is a popular resistance movement in Lebanon fighting the strongest army in the Middle East, and the fourth- or fifth-strongest army in the world—as far as I hear, but I am not sure of this information. There is a debate going on in our country [in which] there is talk of victory, defeat, balance, and the impact of the war on them and us. I say: You do not have to listen to what I say or to what those who love and support the resistance say; I am willing to accept what the Israeli has to say. Let us see what the Israeli generals, politicians, journalists, experts, analysts, and public are saying, in addition to what the reserve soldiers and officers are saying. They are evaluating this experience, and I will accept the conclusion that the Israelis offer.

NEW TV: *The Israelis are preoccupied with other scandals. We were surprised to see matters pertaining to other scandals taking precedence over the war.*[10] *I have two questions...*

HN: Allow me first to conclude this point. You and the Lebanese must be confident that what happened was already planned for. The fact that it happened in July has averted a situation that would have been a lot worse, had the war been launched in October [...]

NEW TV: *From a military perspective, could the resistance have withstood the attack any longer, especially after its sources of supply were dried up and weapons could not get to them? Could the siege imposed on you have allowed you to continue if Arabs, the Europeans, and international parties had not arrived at a new international Resolution in the Security Council?*

HN: We have assumed since the year 2000 that a day like this would come, but we did not know when. I would be exaggerating if I were to tell you

---

10 Al Bassam is referring to the spiraling series of Israeli political scandals that were then coming to light, including alleged corruption by Prime Minister Ehud Olmert during his tenure as Finance Minister in the previous government; former Justice Minister Haim Ramon's resignation on August 18, 2006, and trial over charges of sexually harassing an 18-year-old female soldier; the charging of Israeli President Moshe Katsav for sexual harassment and assault; and Chair of the Knesset's Foreign Security Committee Tzachi Hanegbi's indictment on corruption charges.

when this day would come. We did not know when this day would arrive, but we knew it would come, because Israel cannot remain silent over its 2000 defeat. The victory of Lebanon and the resistance had strategic repercussions on the entire Zionist entity, and it is the direct cause of the *intifada* in Palestine, and of the settlement process coming to a standstill. Our evaluation and understanding led us to believe that the day would come when Israel would launch a large-scale attack, and annihilate the resistance that had achieved a historic victory against them in 2000. What took place in 2000 was a great victory, and what took place [recently] is also a great victory. The difference between the two is that, in 2000, the resistance liberated the land, while this victory is even greater than the one in 2000. Why? Because in 2000 someone could have said that there was a resistance that waged guerrilla warfare and a war of attrition, and that the Israelis grew tired after 18 years of it, and left. The resistance can liberate land, but if Israel wants to occupy Lebanon, can the resistance deflect such an attack? This is the new model.

In all the theories that were posed when we discussed defensive strategies, and even during the first days of the war, some people in Lebanon were theorizing and saying, Yes, the resistance can liberate the land as it did in 2000, but it cannot prevent an invasion. I never made the commitment that we could prevent an invasion, but we managed to do so. The resistance withstood the attack, and it fought back. It did not wage a guerrilla war either. I want to clarify this point: it was not a regular army, but [it] was not a guerrilla [army] in the traditional sense, either. It was something in between. It fought special and elite forces. The resistance stood fast here.

We predicted that a war of this scale would happen ever since 2000, but we did not know when exactly, which is why we started preparing ourselves. We prepared ourselves, and assumed that if a war were imposed on us and Lebanon, it would last for months and would be a very harsh and destructive war. We expected that the war that took place would happen one day, but not specifically on July 12.

Based on this, we logically and naturally assumed that, when Israelis waged such a destructive war, they would cut off all supply lines, and isolate areas and towns, which is why we spent the years between 2000 and 2006 preparing ourselves for such a contingency. We made sure that the capabilities we needed for a long war were available to us, and they still are. Anyone who wants to disarm us should know this. We divided our capabilities in a way that would make cutting off the supply lines futile. All of our combat locations are self-sufficient. For 33 days, the Israeli air force bombed every bridge, road, and ferry. Moving from one town to another was impossible. Despite all this, the rockets were being launched from the valleys and from areas and borders at the frontline. They were launched from any point we wished. The young men were able to fight in any location. Our level of preparedness was very high, and was based on the assumption of a long-drawn-out battle.

What *Yediot Ahronot* published two days ago, to the effect that the ceasefire saved the Israeli army from a greater defeat and disaster, is true, because all the fighting was still being waged by the same young men who had been fighting at the frontlines from day one. When they moved their attack and carried out airdrops into the second frontline, they found that our capabilities there were sound, that our young men were present and safe, and that our command was present and sound as well. They found that the battle had yet to begin for the young men at the second and third lines of defense.

NEW TV: *Throughout 33 or 34 days of aggression, to what extent did Israel manage to shake Hezbollah's military structure? News reports speculated that, if the war had continued, it would have disarmed Hezbollah at the frontlines.*

HN: The weapons of Ayta al-Shab[11] lasted for 33 days.

NEW TV: *Can you give us an idea of your losses? The first line of defense emerged safe and sound. We saw the young men on television screens despite rumors of the injury and martyrdom of Hezbollah cadres. The first and second lines of defense are safe and sound. Can you give us an account of actual losses? Israel said it killed 400, and stated every day that it killed this number of people and destroyed this much. What is the true picture?*

HN: Hezbollah's leaders who are known to the public are all safe, thank

---

11 The "Battle of Ayta al-Shab" in the south Lebanese border village just 1km north of the provisional Israel–Lebanon border seemed to epitomize the inability of the IDF to penetrate and successfully hold even those areas closest to its territory. The IDF lost as many as 13 soldiers in fighting in and immediately around the village.

God. If the war had been waged in October, matters would not have been so. [The Israelis] were planning to kill people as they slept in their homes, along with their women and children, just as they did with some of our young men in the south on the first day. On the first or second day following the capture, Israel targeted houses whose owners' only fault—some were not involved at all—was belonging to Hezbollah or supporting it. They destroyed houses while their owners, their wives, and children were still inside. This was their modus operandi during the first days in the south, especially south of the Litani River. Our political, executive, organizational, and media structures are all in good condition, although Al-Manar TV and Al-Nur Radio[12] were exposed to more than one raid. Our security and military commanders are safe. Our jihadis, and our military and security leaders, are all safe and sound. I can tell you—for the sake of transparency, and to respond to those who say that this entire war could not possibly have left all of Hezbollah's cadres unharmed—that we have had martyrs in our ranks. I have not counted the martyrs, because their funerals are being held every few days in the different villages. Those who wish to count them can do so themselves. There is no problem. We are not hiding anyone. These martyrs have families and relatives, and most of them are married with children. I cannot hide the martyrs. Most of the martyrs were fighters who were manning the rocket-launchers, or fighting at the frontlines against tanks, and so on. As for our military cadres, a brother who is an operations officer in the Bint Jbeil region axis, was martyred, in addition to another brother.

NEW TV: *Was his death announced?*

HN: Of course, and he was given a funeral a few days ago.

NEW TV: *What about the undisclosed martyrs?*

HN: There is no such thing. There are three Hezbollah officials who were martyred. It might be hard to explain this to the public. We have several organizational levels—the first, second, third, and fourth levels. We have

12 The two primary Hezbollah-affiliated media outlets. Despite an Israeli air-strike on Al-Manar's headquarters in the Southern Suburb of Beirut at the outset of the war, the station continued to broadcast throughout the 34 days, virtually uninterrupted.

only four organizational levels, and the last level is represented by the *mujahidin*. No one in the first or second levels was martyred. Three from the third level were martyred, including an operations officer in the Bint Jbeil axis, as well as another brother who is involved in logistics, and a third brother who works at the same organizational level, and was involved in fighting the forces in the field. Three or four young men were town commanders; we have a town commander who fights along with the men in the village, and his martyrdom is a source of pride, not weakness, because it means we have town commanders who do not run away. The town commander and his young men stood fast and fought, and he was martyred. Four or five officials in charge of villages were martyred. These can be called officials serving within Hezbollah's jihadist formations.

NEW TV: *Was the number of rockets launched on Israel the same number made public? In other words, were around 3,000 rockets launched?*

HN: The Israelis said that 4,000 rockets were fired. The actual number of rockets is bigger. The biggest number of rockets did not fall on settlements, but on military barracks, bases, posts, soldiers' assembly locations, and artillery emplacements.

NEW TV: *Was 50 percent of your military capacity depleted?*

HN: No, much less. I gave a speech and said that we had over 12,000 rockets.[13] I am accurate, and I cannot lie, even from a religious point of view. Some say that this is a psychological warfare tactic. We do not lie in psychological war; I do wage psychological war, but I do not lie. When I say there are more than 12,000, this does not mean 13,000 rockets, even though 13,000 is more than 12,000; 20,000 is more than 12,000 and so is 50,000. You can raise the number as high as you want. If I say, for example, that I was born after the Second World War, I will be truthful—yet I was not born immediately after the Second World War, but many years later. It would not be sound for us to declare the exact number of rockets and our military capabilities. Nobody does this. Therefore, calculations based on

13 See Statement 29.

the 12,000 figure, and that a figure larger than 12,000 means 13,000, are miscalculations.

NEW TV: *Are they largely inaccurate or are they close?*

HN: They are troubling themselves now with the embargo they are imposing at sea and on the seaports and borders. This is all futile. When we prepared ourselves, we did so on the basis that we were going to face a destructive, harsh, and long war. What we used in the war was therefore only a small part of what we had prepared. This is all I can say. I cannot go into any more detail.

NEW TV: *Do you rely on local manufacturing without any help from...*

HN: This is a security issue, not a political one. We do not answer security-related questions.

NEW TV: *Would you answer a question relating to reconstruction, politics, and some fears expressed, such as the ones voiced in a recent meeting of the March 14 forces.[14] The spokesman for those forces, Dori Chamoun, expressed fears and sent you a clear and direct message, asking you if you will establish a Shia state in Lebanon. In the past, such talk would refer to an Islamic state, and the response it received at the time was that no Islamic state would be formed. But nowadays, such a state has been further labeled as a Shia state. Why do you think this happened?*

HN: I heard these statements. In the first instance, some people can say that these statements are not new, but old statements repeated; namely, questions asking if we want to establish an Islamic state in Lebanon. We used to reply in detail and in public, in secret and implicitly to all this. I noticed something new in the question. In the past—as you said—they used to say "Islamic state," but now there is talk of a "Shia Islamic state." This means that, in the past, this question was intended to intimidate the Christians; but now

---

14 What remained of the March 14 alliance had recently demanded that the government conduct an investigation into the causes of the war—a call which, it was understood, would mean an examination into Hezbollah's role in "provoking" the war.

it appears that their political performance is developing, and they seek to intimidate the Christians and the rest of the non-Shia Muslims.

My response to those who posed this question is the same response as in the past. We do not change our views every other day. We were clear from the first day this issue was placed on the table. We say that we do not impose our options or ideas on anyone. This is a principle for us. In addition, Lebanon is a country with its idiosyncrasies, and is diverse and multiethnic. I do not pay much attention to this terminology, but some people prefer "diverse" to "multiethnic." Regardless of the terminology, this country cannot take the form of an Islamic state, a Christian state, a Shia Islamic state, a Sunni Islamic State, a Maronite Christian state, or an Orthodox Christian state. In order for this country to be united and solid, and in order for us to be able to build a state in it that is capable of protecting the country, its society, and its people's rights, and that is capable of serving them and preserving their dignity, there must be consensus.

When the government crisis happened and we called for consensus, those who were calling for consensus at the time stopped doing so. In any event, when we say we want a consensus state in Lebanon, we mean a state that makes all the sects in Lebanon feel represented, protected, and served by the state, which preserves their dignity. This is our discourse and our mentality. When we ran in the municipal and parliamentary elections, and participated in the Lebanese government, it was based on this vision. These fears are baseless. I will tell you what the story is. The whole story is that this is the line of discourse that they adopt with us, because they adopt a different discourse with our friends and allies in accordance with their position. However, when they want to deal with us, and to attack us from this political team, what would they say? "You robbed the state." They cannot [say] that. They cannot accuse us of looting, of corruption, or of being partners in corruption. They cannot say anything. They cannot accuse us of practicing injustice, killing, starting a civil war, committing internal massacres, collaborating with the Israelis, changing our stripes, switching sides, or flip-flopping. They can't say that.

The only tune that they have been hounding us with for the past few years is that we want to establish an Islamic state—and now they have recently started referring to it as a Shia Islamic state, as a means of provoking the rest of the Muslims against the Shia and mobilizing Christians against

Muslims. This is a purely American tune. I know where they are receiving their directions from: from the US embassy and Ms. Condoleezza Rice.[15] All they have to say is that we either want to establish an Islamic state or are an Iranian–Syrian axis, arm, or tool. What else can they say against us?

NEW TV: *[Israel] twisted your arm with the civilians.*[16]

HN: No, they did not twist our arm, but they did hurt us, because we are not a mafia or an armed gang. The civilians who were killed are our people; they are not civilians in Mozambique—even though we have humanitarian sentiments towards them. The civilians being killed are our women, children, sons, brothers, and family members. Because the Israelis know that we have feelings, are human, and are genuine in our love for our people, they pressure us with this point. What took place must be an element of reassurance.

The positions taken by General Aoun[17] are sound here. When I say that there is a party with such capabilities, and if I have intentions and they want to hold me accountable for these intentions, then they should look back to the day the Syrian forces exited Lebanon. Hezbollah, with its huge military capabilities, and the rest of its allies, who were and still are targeted, could have staged a military coup and taken control of the country. Could we not? We were capable of that and still are. You might say that I am scaring the people here. The problem does not lie here. The problem is that this party, from the very first day, clearly declared that its weapons were pointed at this enemy [Israel]. My weapons are to defend the country, and all Lebanese. My weapons, my blood, my self, my children, and all my beloved are in the service of all the Lebanese, Arabs, Muslims, and the honorable, so that their heads will remain held high.

15 Rice (1954–) was appointed US Secretary of State in January 2005. She was a vocal supporter of Israel's "right to defend itself" during the July War.

16 In other words, by striking civilian-populated areas and infrastructure.

17 Defying some expectations, Aoun pursued a supportive, if sometimes cautious, approach towards Hezbollah after the July 12 operation, at one point penning an article in the *Wall Street Journal* strongly critical of Lebanese and international parties who, he argued, had flatly refused to address Hezbollah's arms, as well as other related issues, in the same manner as he had in the Free Patriotic Movement's February 2006 Understanding with the Party. See also above, p. 370 n. 1, on the "Paper of Common Understanding." (Michael Aoun, "History Will Judge Us All On Our Actions," *Wall Street Journal*, July 31, 2006, accessed online.)

We did not take any such action—be that before the Syrian withdrawal or after it, or before or after July 12, or even now. Have we ever threatened the Lebanese? Have we ever used these weapons to wage a battle inside Lebanon? Have we ever used our weapons as a source of strength in municipal or parliamentary elections, or to impose certain shares or conditions? Never...

NEW TV: *You are saying to them, do not fear Hezbollah, but you are carrying your weapons. How can one not be afraid?*

HN: I am carrying my weapons to defend the country...

NEW TV : *...whereas they are not armed, I don't know...*

HN: OK, I am carrying my weapons to defend the country which Israel wants to gobble up, and whose waters Israel wants to plunder, and Israel wants to solve its problem—the problem of [Palestinian] refugees' right of return—at the expense of the country, by permanently settling them in the country which Israel has ambitions to rule within the framework of the new Middle East. Today, Hezbollah, along with its friends and allies, is the first defender of genuine sovereignty, genuine independence, and genuine freedom—and I add to them national dignity, honor, and pride.

This is the function of the weapons. Of course, even when we discussed the matter, I never said we would hold on to the weapons forever. We have always said that there are a number of issues, so let us come and solve them. That is what we were saying at the dialogue table. Let us solve them. A solution can be found for those weapons.

Therefore, let no one make the people afraid of our weapons—and the proof is the performance and the experience. I, as a party, have an experience with the Lebanese which is 10 years, 20 years, or 25 years old—is it not time, is it not time? What must one do to reassure? There are some people, my dear sister, who will not be assured unless we hand over our weapons, relinquish our political line and political thought, and go out with them to some European capital[18] and sit down, publicly or secretly—and if we do it

18 A reference presumably to Oslo, Norway, the site of negotiations that eventually led to the Oslo Accords of 1993.

publicly, so much the better—with the Israelis and say to them: We have forgotten everything called national dignity, sovereignty, sanctities, displaced people, permanent settlement, Palestinian refugees, national rights, Arab rights...

NEW TV: *Incidentally, there are views of various Shia elites, such as Al-Sayyed Ali Al-Amin and Al-Sayyed Hani Fahs.*[19] *They are addressing to you direct messages, your Eminence. I do not know if you see and read them...*

HN: Of course.

NEW TV: *They have a view which they address to you personally. They have a view which is somewhat different from yours...*

HN: With regard to this matter, actually, even we cannot say there is a Shia consensus on it. The split over the issue of the resistance is not a division on a sectarian basis; it is not that the Shia are with the resistance option, and the non-Shia against the resistance option. No. There are Shia who are for the resistance, and there are those who are for other options. The same applies to the Sunni, Christians, and Druze. The division on this matter is a political and national division; it is not a sectarian or a religious division. That is why, if a Shiite comes up with a different view—just as someone from among the Sunni may have a different view—now, can I classify the Sunni [in general] as being against the resistance option? Not at all [...]

NEW TV: *The prime minister is reported to have said that you were content with the position of renting [housing units], and you asked for the assistance of the Lebanese state. Is such talk true?*

HN: In any case, this dossier has created some anxiety in the country. Allow me to say here what is in my heart. For our land to be occupied while the world is watching us, that's OK. When we carry arms because the state has not liberated our land for us—not Hezbollah's land or the Shia land or the land of such-and-such a village: no, Lebanese land—take the initiative, fight,

---

19 A reference to two leading Lebanese Shiite critics of Hezbollah. Sayyed al-Amin had, on several occasions, asserted that Hezbollah's actions in "provoking" the summer 2006 war did not represent the will of the Shia community in general.

and give our blood in order to liberate our land, we are condemned, and we are monopolizing, and I don't know what. If no one asks about the prisoners in the [Israeli] jails—not their state, not anyone—never mind, let them stay in prison. But if we ask about them, we are adventurers.

We come to the reconstruction. Before the reconstruction, before the war: the deprived areas. Where are the deprived areas today? In the past, it was the Shia areas that were deprived. Now it is not only the Shia areas. Alas, balanced development has resulted in most Lebanese areas being deprived: Akkar, the north, the Kisrawan mountains, the al-Metn areas, and other areas.[20] If we come to an area where there is no hospital, the state is indifferent to it; and we build a hospital there. In an area where there is no school, we build a school. In an area where the road is not paved, we pave the road. They say: Oh, you are having a state within the state. Well, make me understand. You are the state: you don't want to liberate the land; you don't want to free the prisoners; you don't want to protect us from being killed or assassinated, or protect us from landings; you don't want to cure us; you don't want to feed us; and you don't want to teach us. You only want taxes from me. What kind of state is that? That the people are silent about such a state is in itself a miracle. People should not remain silent about such a state.

NEW TV: *But Hezbollah cannot take over the role of the state?*

HN: I am not taking over the role of the state in anything. Let me tell you something...

NEW TV: *What you are doing is the work of a state...*

HN: Look, we are faced with two options: either we are required to die—die by being killed, or die of hunger, or die as a result of illness—or to be ignorant and hold jobs as shoe-shiners, at best; although ultimately this is not an obscene job, since all jobs are respectable, and so are those who work and perspire in order to earn an honest living. However, that is the level

---

20 Nasrallah is here referring to mixed Muslim–Christian and, in the case of north Lebanon, heavily Sunni areas, which, together, emphasize his point that deprivation in Lebanon is not restricted to the Shia.

we are allowed to reach. Either we are like this, or we are accused of being outside the state, and [of being] a state within the state. Such logic is rejected. Such logic no longer has any value whatsoever.

Today, I say clearly about reconstruction and other issues, and the state is listening: where we have built a hospital, if the state builds a hospital, we will close our hospital; where we have built a school, if the state builds a school, we will close our school. When I talked about the issue of the resistance—which is more serious than the hospital and the school—when I said to them at the dialogue table, and the other day I said to them in a televised message: build the strong, capable, and just state that protects the Lebanese, and then you will have the right to say that there is no need for the resistance and its weapons. We are not an alternative to the state, but where the state is absent we must be present—we must do so by humanitarian, moral, and patriotic criteria, and not by sectarian and partisan criteria. Humanitarian, moral, and patriotic [...]

NEW TV: *Your eminence, all the people are asking where are you getting the money from? If you are telling me it is contributions, I do not know how the answer will be taken—and I do not say not seriously, for all your words are serious and true, and your promise is truthful; but contributions do not build homes on such a scale. You have mentioned 15,000 housing units?*

HN: Yes.

NEW TV: *So, from where?*

NEW TV: What is important to the people is that the money is honest, clean, pure, and without political conditions—and I repeat: without political conditions...

NEW TV: *It is that which arouses fears.*

HN: There are no political conditions, as demonstrated...

NEW TV: *If we are getting assistance from Iran, for instance, how do I know if tomorrow Iran will put conditions on us? The conditions will not be placed only on*

Hezbollah, they will be placed on Lebanon.

HN: Now Iran is accused of financing and arming Hezbollah.

NEW TV: *It is accused; is that not true?*

HN: It is accused. Regardless of whether that accusation is right or wrong, it is argued that it is owed a favor, and therefore it can now impose conditions more than if it had rebuilt some homes in the Southern Suburb, south Lebanon, the Bekaa or the north. With regard to this matter, I would like to be very reassuring. I say: the money that is spent, and the existing resistance, and all the aspects of the strength that are now available, will not be subject to any conditions that are not connected with the national interest. That is categorical and definite. I and my brothers do not take money, arms, or support with conditions attached from anyone.

NEW TV: *We have not felt that your eminence...*

HN: Of course, in any case, Iran, with regard to what you asked about the bridges, the Iranian ambassador yesterday announced that they—now with regard to the bridges, most of the volunteering quarters are personal, in addition to the associations—the Iranians are committed to rebuilding the roads, all the roads that have been destroyed, rebuilding the schools, rebuilding places of worship—mosques and churches—and rebuilding the hospitals. They considered that to be the minimum level of assistance that they would take upon themselves. It is possible that an Iranian team will come here and coordinate with the state, the municipalities, and the various quarters, and begin to rebuild on this level. They have promised to do that. More than that, the ambassador also announced that the vice-president of the Islamic Republic of Iran is coming next week to meet with the Lebanese officials to see how Iran can give support in other fields.

NEW TV: *All that has been announced. Can you tell us about what is not announced? When Hezbollah produces a box of money and begins to pay in dollars, why in dollars?*

HN: Let others do the same. Look, there are others—now what do we want with others. Let it go. Let others do the same, and they are welcome...

NEW TV: *[Some Lebanese] want assurances, at least?*

HN: What assurances? Tell me. We'll solve it tonight. Look, the fact is that in Lebanon everyone wants reassurance. Everyone wants reassurance. Today in Lebanon, any political party, any movement, any sect, any quarter, any group that says it is targeted, I will say to it: We are targeted more than you are. Well, you say you are targeted by Hezbollah, and that is not true, and that you are targeted by Syria, OK, and by Iran—but where is Iran? Iran is far away. We are targeted by the United States, Israel, and all their allies in the world. What happened in July was not an Israeli war on Lebanon. It was a world war on Lebanon, a world war on the resistance. Well, you are worried; we are worried. Am I ashamed to say I am worried? You want assurances, and we want assurances. The solution is not that I go along with you as you want; nor is it that you go along with me as I want. That is why, when we went to the national dialogue, we stated a phrase: "A strong, capable, and just state." Ghassan Tueni added the word "resisting."[21] It was not I who added it. "The resisting and reassuring." Great? Then I talked at the dialogue table, and now I will repeat it. I said to them, If we want to build a capable, strong, just, resisting, and reassuring state, the way to it is a national unity government. I answer all those who send me messages and questions in the media these days. You want to implement the Taif Agreement?[22] Who implements the Taif Agreement? One of the most important conditions for implementing the Taif Agreement is a national unity government. Where is the national unity government? If all the governments that have been formed from the time of the Taif Agreement to the present are not national unity governments, then come and form a national unity government, so as to implement the Taif Agreement.

After such a harsh and destructive war, why do we not form a national unity government in Lebanon? If we want to reconstruct Lebanon, do we

21 The former editor of the Lebanese daily newspaper *An Nahar*, Ghassan Tueni (1926–) was also the father of March 14 leader, Gibran Tueni (1957–2005), who was assassinated by a car bomb in 2005.
22 For the Taif Accord, see above, p. 64 n. 10.

not need a national unity government? Well, let us form a national unity government. The answer is: No, no. Why not? It was said at the dialogue table: We have the highest regard for the Free Patriotic Movement. You are proposing a national unity government so as to bring Syria's allies into the government. Well, first of all, we are in the government. At the minimum level, we and Amal are Syria's allies. Are we ashamed of it? We are not ashamed. Syria's allies are present in the government. Yet I told them, don't bother about Syria's allies. We will talk to them, and they will listen to us, and we will say to them: Stay outside the government now. Let the FPM into the government. I am today surprised that voices have emerged saying that the Christians have been excluded, are neutralized, and have no share in decision-making. Who is responsible for that?

It is said that delegations come from around world and meet with Speaker of Parliament Nabih Berri, and Prime Minister Fouad Siniora—with the Sunni Muslim and the Shia Muslim; it is they who are running the country, and who are making the decisions; and it is they who are the face of the country. Was this matter not raised within the Christian community? Great. That is a great flaw, but who is responsible for it? Those who are responsible for it are those who have obstructed the presidency, those who are preventing delegations from going to President Lahoud when they visit Lebanon.[23] Some people are prevented from visiting President Lahoud. Those who bear responsibility are those who put aside those who represent 75 percent of the Christians, and who did not agree to have them in the government except on conditions that annul them. Today, let us form a national unity government.

NEW TV: *Are you going back to the dialogue with all that you are saying? Perhaps now the dialogue has another importance...*

HN: That is why I am surprised today—I will answer your question—that for 15 years they have been talking about Christian frustration: What has changed now? The Christians who had participated in previous governments, did they not represent at least 25 percent of the Christians? Were they really completely without representation? No, they had representation. Some of

---

23 Although the Siniora government exhorted foreign states not to meet with President Lahoud, two states—France and the US—were the primary forces behind the relative isolation of Lahoud.

them were elected, and had won a high percentage of votes in their electoral districts. They say that a majority of the Christians were excluded from and neutralized in the political equation. Now, what's the situation? Now the result of the elections is that there are quarters that represent 75 percent of the Christians. Now it will be said that their popularity has increased or decreased. Why has your popularity increased?

Well, let us take the election results. [The Free Patriotic Movement] represent 75 percent of the Christians, today they are outside the government. Why do we not hear talk about Christian frustration? In order to tackle the Christian frustration or activate Christian representation, the solution does not lie in [the fact] that we bring a Christian to the government or the presidency who does not represent the 75 percent of the excluded. We have to be fair. Today my message to the Lebanese—our talk today is all Lebanese—is that he who wants to implement the Taif Agreement, he who wants to solve internal problems, he who wants everyone in the country to be reassured, he who seriously wants to build a state and a project for a state—[who doesn't want] to have a dictatorship—who wants to build the project of a real state, let him form a national unity government...

NEW TV: *I thank you, your Eminence, and thank you for granting this exclusive interview to New TV. I apologize to all the colleagues who wanted to sit down with you...*

HN: Who wanted to be ahead of you?

NEW TV: *But by chance I was in the television building, and I came here. All that time—as I said in the introduction—I was dreaming to sit down with you and see you, and to be reassured about you. I reiterate my apology to all my colleagues who could not see you, and, God willing, we will be able to see you again in an expanded meeting. Thank you.*

HN: You are welcome.

FURTHER READING

Unfortunately, despite the party's evident impact on the politics and culture of the region, English-language histories and analyses specifically related to Hezbollah, and especially to Nasrallah himself, have been few and far between.

One recent publication that helps to fill in at least part of the gap—that is, Hezbollah's relationship with the various premierships of Rafik Hariri—has recently been put forth by the author of this volume's introduction, Nicholas Blanford. His *Killing Mr. Lebanon* provides an important addition, and update, to Judith Palmer Harik's 2004 book, *Hezbollah: The Changing Face of Terrorism*, which itself provided a much-needed framework for understanding how domestic Lebanese politics intersected with regional and international interests, especially following the events of September 11, 2001.

Amal Saad-Ghoreyeb's 2002 book, *Hezbollah: Politics and Religion*, and Ahmad Nizar Hamzeh's 2004 book, *In The Path of Hezbollah*, both provide excellent bases for understanding the party's internal structure, as well as the various twists and turns, contradictions, and pragmatic reconciliations that Hezbollah's ideological stance has undergone over the years. Augustus Richard Norton's 1987 book, *Amal and the Shia* (which also makes the full text of Hezbollah's 1985 "Open Letter" available), his recent publication *Hezbollah: An Introduction*, as well as his scholarly articles (most notably *Hizballah of Lebanon: Extremist Ideals vs. Mundane Politics* for the Council on Foreign Relations), also all provide a rare, on-the-ground perspective for understanding the party's birth, as well as its approach to contemporary challenges (Norton was a UN officer in the mid-1980s and a frequent visitor to Lebanon thereafter). One should add to this Martin Kramer's work from outside Lebanon on both Sayyed Fadlallah and Hezbollah itself—work that helped to lay the basis for the generally dominant view in Western circles that the party's

"Lebanonization" has mostly been a cover for unrelenting Islamic radicalism (see specifically, "The Oracle of Hezbollah, Sayyed Muhammad Fadlallah," in *Spokesmen for the Despised: Fundamentalist Leaders of the Middle East*, and "The Moral Logic of Hezbollah," in *Modern Origins of Terrorism: Psychologies, Ideologies, Theologies, States of Mind*). For an alternative view of Fadlallah, see Jamal Sakari's 2005 *Fadlallah: The Making of a Radical Shi'ite Leader*). Hala Jaber's 1997 *Hezbollah: Born With A Vengeance* and Magnus Ranstorp's *Hizb'allah in Lebanon*, also 1997, also both provide valuable book-length investigations into the party's early development and post-civil war challenges.

In contrast to all of the above, Sheikh Naim Qassem's 2005 book, *Hezbollah: The Story From Within*, stands as the only publication written and researched by the party itself—and by Hezbollah's second-in-command, no less. Qassem's book, although predictably criticized in the Israeli media as pure propaganda and deception, provides one of the few point-by-point accounts of Hezbollah's history and stances over a wide range of events and subjects (the full text of the party's 1992 parliamentary platform is included in its Appendix). It also provides, arguably, more of an epistemological basis for Hezbollah's policies and practices than perhaps even Nasrallah himself has offered—indeed, Qassem is reputed to be the party intellectual, immersed in both Western and Islamic philosophical texts. Qassem's book therefore stands as an indispensable volume for any researcher interested in truly testing the party's rhetoric.

Among Israeli analysts, the seminal work of Daniel Sobelman has probably contributed as much to English-language scholarship on the party as any other. His 2004 *New Rules of the Game* offers what is undoubtedly the most accurate, comprehensive, and generally objective work on the conflict between Hezbollah and Israel. Indeed, his analysis has even been taken up by party leaders, including Nasrallah himself, who at times has publicly referred to Sobelman's understanding of the complex situation that prevailed at the border following the 2000 Israeli withdrawal. Sobelmen, as well as other Israeli analysts and academics, most notably Eyal Zisser, have also contributed to various report-length assessments of the party through the Jaffee Center, which has repeatedly offered trenchant analyses of both Hezbollah's strategy and Israel's own approach to the conflict. The Center's Strategic Assessment of the 2006 Summer War (Vol. 9, No. 3, November

2006) is especially valuable in this regard, although it should be read alongside Alastair Crooke and Mark Penn's October 2006 analyses in the *Asia Times* (published online under the overall title "How Hezbollah Defeated Israel"), which provide a somewhat different view from both sides of the border (including from Washington).

The International Crisis Group's (ICG) periodic reports on the situation in Lebanon, and specifically of the Israel–Hezbollah conflict, provide some of the most incisive and thought-provoking work available to the interested reader—especially to the extent that Hezbollah is clearly historicized within a domestic and regional framework. Their 2003 "Rebel Without A Cause?" and 2002 "Old Games, New Rules" stand apart from other such analyses, if nothing else by virtue of their deep investigation and access on all sides of the conflict. The ICG's 2005 "Lebanon: Managing the Gathering Storm" is also notable in this regard, providing one of the few comprehensive reviews of the party's position after the Hariri assassination and the Syrian withdrawal of that same year (the former in-country director for ICG Lebanon, Reinoud Leenders, has contributed several articles and scholarly works in recent years, several co-authored with Mona Harb, including "Know Thy Enemy" for the *Third World Quarterly* which offers one of the few investigations into the epistemological consequences of naming Hezbollah a terrorist organization).

As far as US-based analyses of the party are concerned, the work has generally been limited—which is ironic since Washington has consistently labeled Hezbollah the most dangerous terrorist group facing the United States. Nevertheless, Sami Hajjar's 2002 report, "Hizballah: Terrorism, National Liberation, or Menace?" provides an insightful and balanced view of the party, especially in regard to its changing character over time and the limited military options available to US policymakers. Daniel Byman, Anthony Cordesman, and Gary Gambill's work over the years—mostly in journal articles and occasional white papers—also provide thoughtful analyses of Hezbollah, although all three are mainly interesting as reflections of US strategic thinking generally, rather than as illuminating investigations into the party itself (see especially Byman's 2003 "Should Hezbollah Be Next?" in *Foreign Affairs*, Cordesman's 2002 "Israel and Lebanon: The Risk of New Conflicts" for the Center for Strategic and International Studies, and Gambill's 2004 "Dossier: Hassan Nasrallah" for *Middle East Intelligence Bulletin*).

Finally, for those readers interested in English-language interviews with Nasrallah, the *Financial Times*, *Independent* (especially Robert Fisk's columns), and *Washington Post* (Robin Wright and David Ignatius) provide the best periodic engagements with Hezbollah's secretary-general. The Saudi-owned daily *Al Hayat* also has available on its website at least one in-depth interview with Nasrallah (though roughly translated), from January 18–19, 2006, that provides critical insight into Nasrallah's stance between the Hariri assassination and the July War. Seymour Hersh and Jeffrey Goldberg, for the *New Yorker*, were also both afforded interviews, and both provide excellent frameworks for understanding the party's role in the region after September 11, as well as after the evident collapse of the peace process. Hersh's latest piece, entitled "Redirection," is particularly noteworthy as the only interview granted by Nasrallah to a Western reporter after the July War.

That said, one hopes that this handful of journalists, academics, and analysts will not be the only ones afforded access to Nasrallah in the future; and that their organizations are not the only ones willing and able to commit resources to a further investigation of Nasrallah, Hezbollah, and indeed Lebanon as a whole.

Byman, Daniel "Should Hezbollah Be Next?" *Foreign Affairs*, November/December 2003.

Cordesman, Anthony H., "Israel and Lebanon: The Risk of New Conflicts," Center for Strategic and International Studies, Working Paper, 2002.

Ghorayeb, Amal-Saad, *Hizbu'llah: Politics and Religion* (London: Pluto Press, 2002).

Goldberg, Jeffrey, "In the Party of God," *New Yorker*, July 14, 2002.

Hajjar, Sami G., *Hizballah: Terrorism, National Liberation, or Menace?* (Washington: US army War College, August 2002).

Hamzeh, Ahmad Nizar, *In The Path of Hezbollah* (New York: Syracuse University Press, 2004).

Harb, Mona and Reinoud Leenders, "The Politics of Naming," *Third World Quarterly*, 26: 1 (2005).

———"Know Thy Enemy," *Third World Quarterly*, 26: 1 (2005).

Harik, Judith Palmer, *Hezbollah: The Changing Face of Terrorism* (London: IB Tauris, 2004).

International Crisis Group, "Rebel Without A Cause?," July 30, 2003.

————"Lebanon: Managing the Gathering Storm," December 5, 2005.

————"Old Games, New Rules," November 18, 2002.

Jaber, Hala, *Born With a Vengeance* (New York: Columbia University Press, 1997).

Kramer, Martin, "The Oracle of Hezbollah, Sayyid Muhammad Fadlallah," in Appleby (ed.), *Spokesmen for the Despised: Fundamentalist Leaders of the Middle East* (Chicago: University of Chicago Press, 1997), pp. 83–181.

Norton, Augustus Richard, *Amal and the Shia* (Austin: University of Texas Press, 1987).

————*Hizballah of Lebanon: Extremist Ideals vs. Mundane Politics* (New York: Council on Foreign Relations Press, February 2000).

Qassem, Naim, *Hezbollah: The Story From Within* (London: Saqi, 2005).

Ranstorp, Magnus, "Between a Rock and a Hard Place," St Andrews Working Paper, October 2000.

————*Hizb'allah in Lebanon* (London: Macmillan Press, 1997).

Sankari, Jamal, *Fadlallah: The Making of a Radical Shi'ite Leader* (London: Saqi, 2005).

Sobelman, Daniel, "Four Years After the Withdrawal," *Strategic Assessment* 7, August 2004.

————*New Rules of the Game* (Tel Aviv: Jaffe Center, January 2004).

Zisser, Eyal, "Hizballah and Israel: Strategic Threat on the Northern Border," *Israel Affairs*, 12 (1), January 2006, pp. 86–106.

INDEX

Printed in the United States
by Baker & Taylor Publisher Services